T0305236

ENGINEERING DECISION MAKING AND RISK MANAGEMENT

ENGINEERING DECISION MAKING AND RISK MANAGEMENT

JEFFREY W. HERRMANN
A. James Clark School of Engineering
University of Maryland
College Park, Maryland

Published by John Wiley & Sons, Inc., Hoboken, New Jersey
Published simultaneously in Canada

For general information on our other products and services or for technical support, please contact our Customer Care Department within the United States at (800) 762-2974, outside the United States at (317) 572-3993 or fax (317) 572-4002.

Wiley also publishes its books in a variety of electronic formats. Some content that appears in print may not be available in electronic formats. For more information about Wiley products, visit our web site at www.wiley.com.

Library of Congress Cataloging-in-Publication Data:

Herrmann, Jeffrey W.
 Engineering decision making and risk management / Jeffrey W. Herrmann.
  pages cm
 Includes bibliographical references and index.
 ISBN 978-1-118-91933-0 (hardback)
 1. Engineering–Decision making. 2. Decision making. 3. Risk management. I. Title.
 TA190.H467 2015
 620.0068′4–dc23

                                                                2014041070

Cover image: iStockphoto © MaximGostev

10 9 8 7 6 5 4 3 2 1

1   2015

To L.G.H. and C.R.H.

CONTENTS

PREFACE

This textbook covers important topics on decision making, presents tools for helping engineers make better decisions, and provides examples to illustrate the concepts and techniques. Students and engineers who study this material and apply these concepts and techniques should become better decision-makers.

Like the products and systems that engineers design, this textbook began as an idea for meeting a need and went through many iterations and revisions over time. In this case, the initial discussions about engineering decision making involved my colleague Linda Schmidt, an expert on design methodologies and design education. She and I discussed how engineers in product development organizations shared information and made decisions, and we decided to begin studying this activity as a system. Then, with our colleague Peter Sandborn, we were awarded a grant from the National Science Foundation to study how firms used information about environmental impacts in product development decision making. After studying multiple firms and publishing our results, the next step was to develop a course in which we could share our insights about decision making with others. We jointly developed a course outline, and in the Spring, 2004, semester I taught the course for the first time. Although a traditional decision analysis textbook was used, the course included topics beyond its scope, so I created course notes and expanded them every time I taught the course.

In the meantime, our research continued, and I developed three perspectives on decision making. This led me to reorganize the course (and the course notes) around these three perspectives, which provide a new way to consider engineering decision making. In addition, I included various topics on risk management, a type of decision-making process. These changes also emphasized the challenges of using a traditional decision analysis textbook that was organized in a completely different way. The organization of this course was not increasing mathematical difficulty but increasing conceptual complexity, and existing texts on decision analysis were inappropriate. The first draft of this textbook was my reorganized set of course notes, which I then divided and rearranged again to form distinct chapters.

This text discusses three perspectives on decision making: (1) the problem-solving perspective, (2) the decision-making process perspective, and (3) the decision-making system perspective. The text introduces these perspectives in Chapter 1 and covers them in sequence as the following paragraphs describe. Techniques for modeling and managing risk are included throughout the text where appropriate within this framework.

Chapters 2-6 consider the components and structure of decisions, which is the problem-solving perspective. Chapter 2 reviews some fundamental topics, including the context of a decision situation, fundamental objectives and means objectives, influence diagrams, rationality, choice strategies, dominance, "framing" a decision situation, risk acceptance criteria, and types of measurement scales. Understanding these important fundamental concepts can help one improve decision making.

After Chapter 2 are two chapters about decisions without uncertainty (Chapters 3 and 4) and then two chapters about decisions with uncertainty (Chapters 5 and 6).

Chapter 3 covers multicriteria decision making, which is a traditional topic in decision analysis and an important skill that is the foundation of decision making. This chapter covers multiple techniques: the Pugh matrix, a version of the analytic hierarchy process (AHP), multiattribute utility theory (MAUT), and conjoint analysis. It also discusses the usefulness of the "Value of a Statistical Life" and the differences between compensating and non-compensating solutions.

Chapter 4 reviews techniques for group decision making. This material follows multicriteria decision making (Chapter 3) because the decisions do not have uncertainty. The chapter covers two primary techniques: ranking (including the Kemeny-Young method) and scoring, including the majority judgment technique. It also discusses the implications of Arrow's Impossibility Theorem.

Chapter 5 introduces decisions with uncertainty (risky decisions) and includes traditional material on decision trees, risk aversion, and expected utility. It discusses different types of uncertainties and subjective probabilities. It also defines different types of robustness measures and presents uncertainty propagation techniques, including sensitivity analysis, the method of moments, and Monte Carlo simulation. (Other approaches for making decisions in the presence of uncertainty are discussed in Chapter 7.)

Chapter 6 then discusses game theory. This chapter is placed after Chapter 5 because the existence of another decision-maker introduces uncertainty, but this uncertainty is quite different from uncertainties that can be represented as random variables (which are discussed in Chapter 5). The chapter discusses two-player simultaneous, zero-sum games (and finding optimal mixed strategies), two-player, simultaneous, mixed-motive games, and two-player Stackelberg games. Game theory is also useful for considering risks due to intelligent adversaries.

Chapters 7-9 discuss the decision-making process perspective: how people make decisions through decision-making and risk management processes. Because different situations require different types of decision-making processes, Chapter 7 begins this part of the text by reviewing many types of useful decision-making processes, the important roles of heuristics and search in decision making, and the composite nature of decisions. It also discusses the secretary problem, a special case in which the decision-making process can be optimized. This chapter also describes product development as a type of decision-making process.

Chapter 8 discusses the value of information, a traditional topic. The decision to gather more information is usually a decision with uncertainty, but it is included in this part of the text because it is a decision about what to do in the decision-making process. This chapter describes how to calculate the expected value of perfect information and the expected value of imperfect information and discusses more generally how to use experimental information to improve decision making.

Chapter 9 explicitly covers the process of risk management, which includes the decision of which risk mitigation activity (or activities) should be performed. The risk mitigation decision is another decision with uncertainty, but this material is included in this part of the text because risk management is a type of decision-making process, and Chapter 9 describes different risk management processes and risk communication, an important part of any decision-making process. Because choosing an appropriate decision-making process reduces the risk of making a poor decision, Chapter 9 discusses poor decisions and how to learn from those that do occur. Finally, because some risk management processes emphasize continuously monitoring an activity and intervening when needed to reduce risk, these processes can be viewed as a control system. This means that the risk management function is also a decision-making system, which is the third perspective.

In the last part of the text, Chapters 10 and 11 describe the decision-making characteristics of organizations and how to improve those decision-making systems, which is relevant to the decision-making system perspective. This perspective considers the flow of information between different decision-makers who have different roles. It views an organization as a dynamic system that makes decisions using decision-making processes, but the quality of the decisions that emerge depends upon not only the decision-making processes but also the culture and the patterns of behavior.

Chapter 10 describes the characteristics and structure of decision-making systems, including different roles and mechanisms of organizational influence. It also describes product development organizations as decision-making systems.

Chapter 11 discusses improving decision-making systems. Because decision-making systems are complex and involve human actors, the usefulness of quantitative techniques is limited. Qualitative approaches can represent more interesting phenomena. The chapter begins with different techniques for modeling decision-making systems, including rich pictures, swimlanes, root definitions, and conceptual models. The chapter also presents an improvement strategy that exploits the insights that these types of models provide.

Thus, the text begins with the aspect of decision making that is, conceptually, the simplest: given a set of alternatives and a decision-maker's preferences, which one should be selected? The text then looks "behind the scenes," so to speak, to describe the processes used to generate and evaluate the alternatives. Finally, the text "steps back" to look at the organization that, to achieve its goals, performs these processes and makes these decisions.

In the first part of the text (Chapters 2-6), the critical skill is choosing the right alternative. In the second part (Chapters 7-9), the critical skill is executing the right decision-making process. In the third part (Chapters 10 and 11), the critical skill is improving the decision-making system.

The content and organization of this text reflect both a pragmatic attitude about improving decision making and the scholarly concern with studying, organizing, and formalizing this activity. This approach has been formed by studying how engineers and others decide, using the quantitative, analytical techniques that are available, and helping others become better decision-makers. This text follows the view that the mathematical models used in the study of decision making, no matter how sophisticated, are merely approximations of what the mysterious human mind does and what complex human organizations accomplish. Thus, they are valuable if they are useful to those who need to make decisions. The text, therefore, includes a variety of models that have been generally useful. In some cases the numbers that using such a model produces may be less valuable than the conversations and negotiations that are required to construct the model. At the same time, studies of how people decide in practice have revealed that formal techniques are used less often than informal, intuitive rules or heuristics. Understanding this is valuable, of course, but improving decision-making requires learning how and when to use formal techniques as well.

The text's diversity may concern any who are committed to a single approach to the study of decision making, but I hope that they will see how each approach is an important part of a valuable perspective on decision-making. The organization of the text (around the three perspectives) provides a synthesis that places different approaches and techniques in relationship to each other, which is an important scholarly and pedagogical task.

The contents of the text will reveal the influence of many scholars, including those who have developed traditional decision analysis and those who have studied how people decide in practice. The work of Herb Simon has influenced the material greatly. His insights into how engineers design, how people solve problems, and how organizations make decisions have influenced the choice of material and the discussions in this text. His proposals for a curriculum in design remain relevant today. His descriptions of administrative behavior provide valuable, applicable insights for engineers, who must work with others in organizations. This text directly addresses his observation that an organization is a decision-making system. Simon wrote that creating the right representation of a problem makes the solution clear; this text takes up that challenge by describing multiple ways to represent decision making. The three perspectives discussed in this text are representations of decision making, and those who seek to improve their decision-making skills and choose an appropriate perspective will find promising opportunities. This text is intended to help develop an "intellectually tough, analytic, partly formalizable, partly empirical, teachable doctrine" (in Simon's words).

Although this text focuses on engineers, decision making occurs everywhere and is especially relevant in other professions that require selecting a possible solution from many alternatives. This includes architecture, law, and medicine, among many others. Of course, this text, which also reflects the preferences of the author and is bounded, cannot include every known technique. In particular, human cognition, behavioral decision making, introductory probability and statistics, optimization, advanced game theory, risk assessment, and decision support system design are beyond the scope of this textbook. Excellent texts on these topics are already available.

The text is designed for advanced undergraduates, graduate students, and engineering professionals who are comfortable with logical reasoning, calculation, probability, mathematics, and optimization, but it does not require advanced theoretical mathematics. Although students may have little experience with "real-world" engineering decisions that have large stakes, they make many decisions, and investing the time to study and improve decision making early will yield benefits throughout their careers.

Every chapter includes learning objectives that state what the reader will be able to do after studying the chapter and exercises for practicing the relevant skills. Every chapter cites interesting and useful books and papers that provide more details about the concepts and examples that were presented, give formal proofs of important results, and describe other related material. A list of references cited is provided at the end of every chapter. The strengths and weaknesses of the techniques are presented to indicate when each is most appropriate. The examples include both historical and contemporary events. Many of the papers cited can be found in online journals and databases and accessed via the Internet; others can be obtained through a university library. Most of the books can be found in libraries and bookstores everywhere.

Because the organization of this textbook does not follow the outline of most decision analysis texts, it may be out of place as a primary text for a traditional decision analysis course. It could be used as a secondary or supplementary text in such a course.

Thus, to help an instructor who wishes to teach a course in which the students learn the skills that are covered in this text, it seemed appropriate to develop and provide instructional support material that includes not only worked solutions to the exercises in the textbook but also daily lesson plans for lectures, in-class activities, slides, and spreadsheets for a course that covers engineering decision making and risk management. These materials are available from the publisher.

While conducting the study of decision making that has led to this text, I have been greatly influenced, encouraged, and assisted by my colleagues, including Linda Schmidt, Joseph Donndelinger, and Erica Gralla, and my students, including Peyman Karimian and Dennis Leber. Some of the material discussed in this text previously appeared in various papers that I and my collaborators have written, but all of the chapters are original.

1

INTRODUCTION TO ENGINEERING DECISION MAKING

Learning Objectives:

After studying this chapter, the reader will be able to do the following:

1. Identify and describe two types of decisions that engineers make (Section 1.2).
2. Classify the decisions that engineers make (Section 1.2).
3. Describe how optimization is related to decision making (Section 1.3).
4. Describe how problem solving is related to decision making (Section 1.4).
5. Explain why decision making is part of risk management (Section 1.5).
6. Identify problems that can occur in decision making (Section 1.6).
7. Identify the benefits of improving decision making (Section 1.7).
8. Describe a decision from three perspectives (Section 1.8).

1.1 INTRODUCTION

Why should engineers study decision making? What is engineering decision making?

People have always made decisions, but analyzing decision-making processes and developing better decision-making methods are more recent activities. Our ability to

Engineering Decision Making and Risk Management, First Edition. Jeffrey W. Herrmann.
© 2015 John Wiley & Sons, Inc. Published 2015 by John Wiley & Sons, Inc.

analyze decisions has increased as mathematics, especially the theory of probability, has developed. In the 1700s, Daniel Bernoulli analyzed risky decisions and described how the relative values of alternatives depend on the preferences of the decision maker (Bernoulli, 1954). Ramsey (1964) developed a theory for decision making based on probability theory and utility. von Neumann and Morgenstern (1944) formalized the theory of expected utility and the analysis of multiplayer games, which is now known as game theory. Early works on game theory include Borel (1921), von Neumann (1928, 1959), and Hotelling (1929), who analyzed a game related to product differentiation. The works of Savage (1954), Raiffa (1968), Schlaifer (1969), Benjamin and Cornell (1970), and Keeney and Raiffa (1976) have been cited as influential early textbooks. Buchanan and O'Connell (2006) surveyed the history of decision making and the roles of intuition, risk, groups, and computing in decision making.

Now, what about engineering decision making? Scientists use their observations of natural phenomena to generate scientific knowledge, but engineers use their knowledge of the world to design products and systems that can perform needed functions while satisfying certain requirements.

To design a product or a system or to plan an activity, an engineer must make decisions. The engineer decides that a component will use a certain material, will have a certain shape, and will be made in a certain way. The engineer decides how the activity will be performed, who will do which tasks, and when they will be done. There are many possible choices, and the engineer must select one. This is the essence of decision making.

The process of making a decision, similar to cooking, transforms inputs into outputs. Cooking transforms ingredients such as pasta, ground beef, tomato sauce, spices, mozzarella, ricotta, and parmesan cheese into an appetizing dish such as lasagna. Decision making transforms information. The input information includes knowledge about physical phenomena, manufacturing processes, costs, customer requirements, regulations, and existing designs. Of course, there may be uncertainties about this information. The output is new information: a description of a design or a plan. That is, engineering decision making transforms existing information into new information.

Those engineers who improve their ability to make decisions should generate designs and plans that are more effective and more efficient. This will help the engineers and their organizations to be more productive, more successful, and more valuable. Because engineers are trained in mathematics, statistics, analysis, and modeling, they have the prerequisites to study and understand the techniques necessary to improve decision making. Because engineers have experience in designing, testing, and building objects and systems, they have the skills to apply these decision-making techniques to real-world problems.

Some of the techniques covered in this text can help a decision maker find the "best" alternative (the "right answer"). Studying decision making, however, should produce not only better answers but also new ways of thinking about decisions. Thinking more carefully about a decision will lead to better understanding even if no formal technique is applied. It can help one to choose an appropriate process and avoid decision-making errors. It can encourage one to consider how much information is really needed. It can lead one to see the potential problems with the available alternatives and find ways to reduce those risks.

Thinking about the merits of the alternatives, the criteria used to evaluate them, and the uncertainties involved can help engineers articulate and record the rationale for their decisions, which can help them justify their decisions to their peers and superiors and avoid errors during future redesigns. Recording design rationale can also support collaboration, design reuse, and training other engineers (Lee, 1997).

This text discusses three perspectives on decision making: (1) the problem-solving perspective, (2) the decision-making process perspective, and (3) the decision-making system perspective. These are discussed in detail in Section 1.8. The material included herein will cover important topics on decision making, present tools for helping engineers make better decisions, and provide examples to illustrate the concepts and techniques. The author hopes that students and engineers who study this material and apply these concepts and techniques will become better decision makers.

Studies of how decision makers make choices in practice have revealed that some decisions are made using simple heuristics (Gigerenzer *et al.*, 1999), and others are made without considering multiple alternatives (cf. Klein *et al.*, 2010). Improving decision making can go beyond the valuable insights that are gained by understanding these phenomena, however. The mathematical models used in the study of decision making are, like all models, approximations of what really happens. Still, they can be valuable if they are useful to those who need to make decisions. The text, therefore, includes a variety of models that have been generally useful.

In particular, this text describes multiattribute utility theory (MAUT), the analytic hierarchy process (AHP), models for representing risk preferences, and game theory models. As Luce and Raiffa (1957) noted, such models do not describe what all decision makers do, and they do not describe what decision makers should do in an absolute sense (in all cases). They do, however, attempt to say which alternative is the best way to achieve the decision maker's particular goals.

This section began with two questions and provided some answers. These answers, however, lead to additional questions that this text will address:

- What is the value of improving decision making?
- Which alternative is the best one?
- How should our group make a decision?
- How can one compare alternatives in the presence of uncertainty?
- How can we decide when we do not know what the other guy is going to do?
- Which decision-making process is the most appropriate?
- Should we gather more information before deciding?
- How can we reduce risk?
- How do organizations make decisions?
- How can we improve decision making in our organization?

1.2 DECISION MAKING IN ENGINEERING PRACTICE

In practice, engineers make many different types of decisions as they design products and systems. In general, the decisions that engineers make can be classified into two broad categories:

1. *What should the design be?* Design decisions determine the overall structure, shape, size, material, manufacturing process, and components of an object or a system. These generate information about the design itself and the requirements that it must satisfy. Design decisions may involve manufacturing processes and systems. Deciding that gear hobbing will be used to make the bull gear for a rear differential is a design decision, and deciding where to place the equipment (including the horizontal hobbing machines) in a machine shop is a design decision, but deciding which machinist should operate the hobbing machine and which gears should be machined tomorrow is not, however (it is a production management decision).

2. *What should be done?* Management decisions control the progress of a design process or other activity. They affect the resources, time, and technologies available to perform activities. They define which activities should happen, their sequence, and who should perform them. That is, they determine what will be done, when it will be done, and who will do it. Project management includes many decisions, such as planning, scheduling, task assignment, and purchasing.

Example 1.1 Kidder (1981) described the development of a minicomputer (the Eclipse MV/8000) by a team of engineers at Data General. Although the technology described is now obsolete, the book depicted many of the decisions that the engineers made during the computer's development. Management decisions and design decisions occurred at different levels in the organizational structure. Decisions by those who had more authority and responsibility affected more people, more of the process, and more of the product. The following actions were some of the management decisions (the names West, Wallach, Rasala, etc., refer to people on the development team):

- The vice president of engineering approved the project.
- West decided to hire inexperienced engineers who had just graduated.
- West decided to have two teams: one for designing the hardware and the other one for designing the microcode.
- West decided that Wallach should be the architect.
- Wallach decided to begin designing the architecture by organizing the memory.
- West reviewed the designs.

- Rasala created the debugging schedule.
- West approved using microdiagnostic programs.
- West approved building a simulator for testing microcode.
- Alsing picked Dave Peck and Meal Firth to write simulators.
- West decided who would work on which new projects.
- Rasala decided to work in the lab to increase morale.

The following actions are some of the design decisions:

- West decided that the new computer should be a 32-bit computer that can run older programs written for another computer.
- Wallach decided to worry about preventing accidental damage, not malicious theft.
- Wallach decided that the memory protection scheme should use the segment number as the security level.
- Wallach defined the instruction set.
- Engineers negotiated the design details.
- West decided that the computer would use PAL integrated circuits.
- The engineers wrote the microcode and the schematics.
- Holland organized the microcode.
- West and Rasala decided to keep the arithmetic logic unit on one board by limiting its functionality.
- West decided which cables and connectors the computer should use.
- West decided how the machine should be started.

1.3 DECISION MAKING AND OPTIMIZATION

Decision making involves generating and evaluating alternatives and selecting the most preferred one that satisfies given requirements. Optimization involves finding the best solution from a set of feasible solutions (cf. Kirsch, 1981; Papalambros and Wilde, 2000; Arora, 2004; Ravindran *et al.*, 2006). From a certain level of abstraction, therefore, decision making resembles optimization.

Certainly, in some cases, the decision-making process is to formulate and solve an optimization problem. Such cases are characterized by a relatively large amount of useful knowledge about the situation and a clear consensus on the objective function. For example, automotive firms have used optimization to find the best structural design of an automobile frame in order to make it as strong and light as possible (see Detwiler *et al.*, 1996, for an early example at General Motors) and have developed multidisciplinary optimization approaches to find the most profitable vehicle design during the early design phase (Fenyes *et al.*, 2002).

When the optimization requires using analysis software (like finite element analysis) to evaluate designs, the computational effort of solving the optimization problem may be the primary challenge. The study of optimization is usually considered as a topic of interest in applied mathematics and operations research and engineering design.

Viewing decision making as optimization can be inappropriate, however, in situations when there is insufficient information to formulate an optimization problem or there is no consensus on the objective function. This will be discussed in more detail in Chapter 7.

1.4 DECISION MAKING AND PROBLEM SOLVING

Although the concept of decision making (the process of selecting an alternative) is generally clear, the idea of problem solving is less straightforward. For our purposes, it will be important to note two different types of problems.

The first type of problem is a predefined, clearly stated question that must be answered through calculation or search. There is usually a "right" answer that can be judged strictly objectively. Word problems in mathematics, operations research, physics, and engineering science textbooks are generally this type of problem (e.g., "Given this set of ten jobs that need processing on a set of ten machines, which schedule minimizes the total time needed to complete all of the jobs?"). Navigation systems and online map Web sites solve this type of problem when they provide directions for the fastest route from a starting point to a destination. Thus, some of these problems are optimization problems, which were discussed in Section 1.3. This type of problem may involve predicting how the state of a natural or a man-made system will change over time or determining unknown aspects of the system state from those that are given (Hazelrigg, 1996).

The second type of problem is an "issue," an undesirable situation that a person or an organization wishes to change. Solving this type of problem can be a messy process. When a piece of manufacturing equipment stops working unexpectedly, an issue has appeared, and the factory has a problem to be solved. To solve this problem, the firm has to investigate the cause of the problem and do something to get the equipment working again.

For this type of problem, Powell and Baker (2004) defined the following six-stage problem-solving process:

1. Explore the mess: search for problems and opportunities, accept a challenge, and start systematic efforts to respond.
2. Search for information: gather data and impressions, observe the situation from many different viewpoints, and identify the most important information.
3. Identify a problem: generate different potential problem statements and choose a working problem statement.
4. Search for solutions: develop different alternatives and select one idea (or a few ideas) that seem most promising.

5. Evaluate solutions: formulate criteria for reviewing and evaluating ideas and select the most important criteria, then evaluate and revise the idea(s), and then select a solution.
6. Implement a solution: identify implementation steps and required resources and then implement the solution.

Other discussions of problem solving consider very similar steps. This description shows that decision making is a component of the problem-solving process. The general decision is something like "What should we do to solve this problem?" Decisions occur in many contexts besides solving problems, however, so it is clear that decision making is not the same as problem solving.

Steps 3–5 of the above problem-solving process explicitly mention decisions: choosing a working statement (in Step 3), selecting the most promising ideas (in Step 4), selecting the most important criteria (in Step 5), and selecting a solution (in Step 5). Each is an interesting decision, and together, they are a part of how an organization decides what to do. The concept of how making a decision requires making many decisions will be considered further in Chapter 7.

1.5 DECISION MAKING AND RISK MANAGEMENT

In general, the term "risk" denotes uncertainty about what will happen in the future. Risk management is the process of identifying risks, assessing them, and selecting and implementing risk mitigation activities.

Problem solving handles issues, but risk management considers potential problems (cf. Kepner and Tregoe, 1965), how to prevent them from happening, and how to minimize their impact. A manufacturing firm concerned about the possibility of missing customer due dates will consider, among other things, the likelihood that a crucial machine will fail and what can be done to prevent its failure (by performing more preventive maintenance) and minimize the time required to repair it if it should fail (by investing in some spare parts, for instance).

Contingency plans are useful for risk mitigation, but problems can occur when they are activated, so one has to consider those potential problems and mitigate those risks as well. For example, installing a spare part is a reasonable contingency plan if the machine fails; however, a potential problem is that the spare part may be unavailable if it is lost or damaged before it is needed. Thus, mitigating that risk becomes necessary.

Formal processes of risk management (discussed in Chapter 9) include a decision-making step: which risk mitigation activity (or activities) should the organization perform? Ideally, organizations would implement many risk mitigation activities. Unfortunately, time, money, and other resources make this impossible, so firms have to choose. Important aspects of risk management are also covered in Chapter 2 (risk acceptance criteria), Chapter 5 (decision making under uncertainty), Chapter 6 (game theory), Chapter 7 (the decision-making cycle and analytic-deliberative decision making), and Chapter 8 (the value of information).

1.6   PROBLEMS IN DECISION MAKING

Debacles such as the Ford–Firestone feud and the design of the Denver International Airport are "decisions with bad practice producing big losses that become public" (Nutt, 2003). Engineers should avoid debacles. As might be expected, not all poor decisions lead to debacles; they lead instead to wasted time, unnecessary costs, lost opportunities, a poor reputation, damaged relations, and other undesirable outcomes.

Decision makers make poor decisions for many reasons. The causes range from the actions and characteristics of individual persons to the policies and culture of organizations. Decision makers can select the wrong process or mismanage the process; generate too few alternatives, too many alternatives, or useless alternatives; select inappropriate or irrelevant objectives; evaluate alternatives using outdated or incomplete or incorrect information; select inferior alternatives; implement the chosen alternative poorly; and fail to learn from these types of mistakes. Section 9.8 reviews specific problems and discusses how to reduce the risk of a bad decision.

1.7   THE VALUE OF IMPROVING DECISION MAKING

Improving decision making (through the use of structured decision analysis, for instance) not only helps decision makers select better alternatives but also gives them more insight into the decision situation. The first step is to think about how one makes decisions. Stepping back to reflect on the process to be followed can generate insights into the opportunities to improve the decision-making process. The possible improvements include more relevant objectives, better alternatives, more appropriate measures for evaluating the alternatives, and more logical techniques for combining these values into a measure that better reflects the decision-maker's values and preferences. Better decision-making techniques can save time by focusing time and attention on constructive activities. Standard decision-making processes can increase consistency and transparency and facilitate further improvement.

Consider Rose, a decision maker, who wants to improve her decision making with some type of tool or some other change in the decision-making process (which we will call the "improvement"). In theory, for a particular decision, Rose could calculate the difference between the expected value of the alternative that she would choose if she uses the improvement and the expected value of the alternative that she would choose if she does not use it.

By evaluating the difference between the best alternative (which was chosen) and the other alternatives, a review of 37 projects at Eastman Kodak estimated that using decision analysis added between $5.24 and $10.02 million per project (Clemen and Kwit, 2001). Gensch (2001) estimated that a manufacturer of heating and cooling systems more than doubled the profitability of its new products after implementing a new decision process that required gathering better information about the alternatives and used a mathematical model for evaluating them. Parnell and Bresnick (2013) reported that Chevron executives have estimated that using decision analysis was worth billions of dollars every year and that the benefits dwarf the small marginal cost of doing decision analysis.

In addition to the economic benefits, decision analysis has improved decision making by improving communication among those making the decision, identifying risk factors earlier, and planning contingencies (Clemen and Kwit, 2001).

1.8 PERSPECTIVES ON DECISION MAKING

Aristotle introduced the concept of four causes to provide a way to explain reality, and other philosophers, notably Thomas Aquinas, adopted this approach as well. In this approach, an object has four causes (Feser, 2009):

- a *final cause* that is the object's purpose or goal or end;
- a *formal cause* that describes its form or shape;
- a *material cause* that describes the material from which it is made; and
- an *efficient cause* that explains what made it or how it was made.

The traditional design concerns (function, form, material, and manufacture) correspond exactly to these four causes. These causes can be viewed as answering three questions: Why? What? and How? In the same way, to understand a decision, it is useful to consider the following questions about it: *Why is the decision being made? What is the decision? How is the decision made?*

The answer to "Why?" describes the relation among the objectives considered when making the decision, the decision-maker's other objectives, the location of this decision within the organization's decision-making system, and the roles of others in the organization. This is the *decision-making system perspective*.

The answer to "What?" describes the set of alternatives being considered, the constraints that the alternatives had to satisfy, and the objectives used to evaluate and rank the alternatives. This is the *problem-solving perspective*.

The answer to "How?" describes the process of generating alternatives, collecting information about the alternatives, and evaluating the alternatives. This is the *decision-making process perspective*.

The introduction to this chapter mentioned that decision making is a process similar to cooking. Let us extend that metaphor as follows. Picture a busy restaurant kitchen in which numerous chefs and other employees use various tools and appliances at different workstations to prepare and cook different types of food. The ingredients move around the kitchen and are used to make individual items (such as entrees and sides), and these items are used to prepare complete plates that are delivered to the customers. If we look at one particular plate of food, we can consider its contents, which answers the question "What?" If we look at the steps needed to make the food on the plate, we can understand the process used to transform a set of ingredients into dinner, and this answers the question "How?" Finally, if we look at the entire kitchen, we see a system of people who are processing food and creating dinners for customers, and this answers the question "Why?" In this image, each plate that is completed corresponds to a decision that is made; the different workstations in the kitchen correspond to the steps in the decision-making process; and the chefs and their staff are the organization (the decision-making system).

Example 1.2   Consider Boeing's decision to move its corporate headquarters to Chicago ("Inside Boeing's Big Move," 2001). *Why did Boeing make that decision*? Boeing wanted a new location for its corporate headquarters as part of its strategy to develop a headquarters that was distinct from its existing businesses and to focus on growth opportunities around the world. This decision followed other decisions about the company's strategic growth plans and led to many decisions about how to implement the move. *What was the decision*? Boeing chose an office building for the location of its headquarters. The building had to be near a major airport in the United States, and the company wanted to minimize travel time throughout the country and internationally and to be near politicians and financial firms. *How was the decision made*? The senior vice president of Boeing and other executives first picked a short list of three cities. Real estate professionals provided information about available buildings. Then, the senior vice president, with a team of colleagues, visited and evaluated multiple sites in those cities. Finally, he presented the information to Boeing's chief executive officer, who selected a site in Chicago.

Each of these three questions reflects a different perspective on the decision. The organization of this text is structured around these three perspectives. The text will first consider the components and structure of decisions (Chapters 2–6), which is the problem-solving perspective. Then, the text will discuss the decision-making process perspective: how people make decisions through decision making and risk management processes (Chapters 7–9). Finally, the text will describe decisions from the decision-making system perspective by considering the decision-making behaviors and information flow within organizations and how to improve those decision-making systems (Chapters 10 and 11).

EXERCISES

1.1. What are the two types of decisions that engineers make?

1.2. Give two examples of each type of decision.

1.3. Walton (1997) described the process that a team of Ford engineers used to develop the Taurus. Classify each of the following decisions as a design decision or a management decision:
   (a) Selecting a place for the development team to work.
   (b) Selecting the shape of the headlamps.

(c) Selecting which sketch to use for a clay model.

(d) Deciding to use a longer wheelbase.

(e) Agreeing to fund tooling and plant renovation.

(f) Deciding to have another market research clinic with current Taurus owners.

(g) Deciding to spend $200,000 to make a clay model of a competitor's car for the market research clinic.

(h) Approving $700 million in additional investment.

(i) Selecting inset doors instead of hard-top doors or limousine-style doors.

(j) Deciding to manufacture a one-piece bodyside.

(k) Deciding that the door sills will be black.

1.4. Why is optimization relevant to decision making?

1.5. What is the role of decision making in risk management?

1.6. List two problems that can occur in decision making.

1.7. List two benefits that can result from improving decision making.

1.8. What are the three perspectives for understanding a decision?

1.9. Consider a decision that you have made recently. Describe it from all three perspectives.

1.10. During the development of the Apollo spacecraft, NASA engineers (who were unsure about the actual conditions on the moon) decided that the landing gear design should be appropriate for surfaces like those found in Arizona (Nelson and Men, 2009). Is this a design decision or a management decision?

1.11. Ben Moreell was a civil engineer who later became an admiral in the U.S. Navy. Consider Moreell's decision to recruit skilled constructions workers for the Navy's Construction Battalions (the Seabees) in World War II (Kennedy, 2013). Was this a design decision or a management decision?

1.12. Consider Boeing's selection of a new corporate headquarters in 2001 (cf. "Inside Boeing's Big Move"). For each of the following aspects of this decision, note if it is most relevant to (1) the problem-solving perspective, (2) the decision-making process perspective, or (3) the decision-making system perspective:

(a) The availability of educated workforce and presence of other major business headquarters.

(b) Office buildings that would be available in September of that year.

(c) The roles of the board of directors, the strategy council, and the senior vice president.

(d) Flying around in a helicopter to look at potential sites.

REFERENCES

Arora, Jasbir S., *Introduction to Optimum Design*, 2nd edition, Elsevier Academic Press, Amsterdam, 2004.

Benjamin, Jack R., and C. Allin Cornell, *Probability, Statistics, and Decision for Civil Engineers*, McGraw-Hill Book Company, New York, 1970.

Bernoulli, Daniel, "Exposition of a New Theory on the Measurement of Risk," *Econometrica*, Volume 22, Number 1, pages 23–36, 1954. doi: 10.2307/1909829.

Borel, Emile, "La théorie due jeu et les equation intégrals à noyau symétrique gauche," *Comptes Rendus de l'Académie des Sciences*, Volume 173, pages 1304–1308, 1921. Translated by L.J. Savage in *Econometrica*, Volume 21, pages 97–100.

Buchanan, Leigh, and Andrew O'Connell, "A Brief History of Decision Making," *Harvard Business Review*, Volume 84, Number 1, pages 32–41, 2006.

Clemen, Robert T., and Robert C. Kwit, "The Value of Decision Analysis at Eastman Kodak Company, 1990–1999," *Interfaces*, Volume 31, Number 5, pages 74–92, 2001.

Detwiler, Duane, Shantaram Ekhande, and Mark Kistner, "Computer Aided Structural Optimization of Automotive Body Structure," SAE Technical Paper 960523, 1996, doi: 10.4271/960523, online at http://papers.sae.org/960523/.

Fenyes, Peter, Joseph Donndelinger, and Jing-Fang Bourassa, "A New System for Multidisciplinary Analysis and Optimization of Vehicle Architectures," AIAA-2002-5509, 9th AIAA/ISSMO Symposium on Multidisciplinary Analysis and Optimization, Atlanta, Georgia, September 4–6, 2002.

Feser, Edward, *Aquinas*, Oneworld Publications, Oxford, 2009.

Gensch, Dennis, "A Marketing-Decision-Support Model for Evaluating and Selecting Concepts for New Products," *Interfaces*, Volume 31, Number 3, Part 2, pages S166–S183, 2001.

Gigerenzer, Gerd, Peter M. Todd, and the ABC Research Group, *Simple Heuristics That Make Us Smart*, Oxford University Press, New York, 1999.

Hazelrigg, George A., *System Engineering: An Approach to Information-based Design*, Prentice Hall, Upper Saddle River, New Jersey, 1996.

Hotelling, Harold, "Stability in Competition," *Economic Journal*, Volume 39, Number 153, pages 41–57, 1929.

"Inside Boeing's Big Move," *Harvard Business Review*, Volume 79, Number 9, pages 22–23, 2001.

Keeney, Ralph L., and Howard Raiffa, *Decisions with Multiple Objectives: Preference and Value Tradeoffs*, John Wiley & Sons, New York, 1976.

Kennedy, Paul, *Engineers of Victory*, Random House, New York, 2013.

Kepner, Charles H., and Benjamin B. Tregoe, *The Rational Manager: a Systematic Approach to Problem Solving and Decision Making*, McGraw-Hill, New York, 1965.

Kidder, Tracy, *The Soul of a New Machine*, Little, Brown, Boston, 1981.

Kirsch, Uri, *Optimum Structural Design*, McGraw-Hill Book Company, New York, 1981.

Klein, Gary, Roberta Calderwood, and Anne Clinton-Cirocco, "Rapid Decision Making on the Fire Ground: The Original Study Plus a Postscript," *Journal of Cognitive Engineering and Decision Making*, Volume 4, Number 3, pages 186–209, 2010.

Lee, Jintae, "Design Rationale Systems: Understanding the Issues," *IEEE Expert*, Volume 12, Number 3, pages 78–85, 1997.

Luce, Robert D., and Howard Raiffa, *Games and Decision*, Wiley, New York, 1957.

Nelson, Craig, and Rocket Men: *The Epic Story of the First Men on the Moon*, Viking, New York, 2009.

von Neumann, John, "Zur Theories der Gesellschaftsspiele," *Mathematische Annalen*, Volume 100, pages 295–320, 1928.

von Neumann, John, "On the Theory of Games of Strategy," translated by Sonya Bargmann, in *Contributions to the Theory of Games*, Volume IV, A.W. Tucker and R.D. Luce, editors, *Annals of Mathematics Studies*, Number 40, pages 13–42, Princeton University Press, Princeton, New Jersey, 1959.

von Neumann, John, and Oskar Morgenstern, *Theory of Games and Economic Behavior*, Princeton University Press, Princeton, New Jersey, 1944.

Nutt, Paul C., "Breaking out of the Failure Mode with Best Practice Decision-making Processes," *International Journal of Business*, Volume 8, Number 2, pages 169–201, 2003.

Papalambros, Panos Y., and Douglass J. Wilde, *Principles of Optimal Design*, 2nd edition, Cambridge University Press, Cambridge, 2000.

Parnell, Gregory S., and Terry A. Bresnick, "Introduction to Decision Analysis," in *Handbook of Decision Analysis*, G.S. Parnell, T.A. Bresnick, S.N. Tani, and E.R. Johnson, editors, John Wiley & Sons, Inc., Hoboken, New Jersey, 2013.

Powell, Stephen G., and Kenneth R. Baker, *The Art of Modeling with Spreadsheets*, John Wiley & Sons, Inc., Hoboken, New Jersey, 2004.

Raiffa, Howard, *Decision Analysis: Introductory Lectures on Choices Under Uncertainty*, Addison-Wesley Publishing Co., Reading, Massachusetts, 1968.

Ramsey, Frank P., "Truth and Probability," in *Studies in Subjective Probability*, H.E. Kyburg, Jr., and H.E. Smokler, editors, John Wiley & Sons, New York, 1964.

Ravindran, A., K.M. Ragsdell, and G.V. Reklaitis, *Engineering Optimization: Methods and Applications*, 2nd edition, John Wiley & Sons, Hoboken, New Jersey, 2006.

Savage, Leonard J., *The Foundations of Statistics*, Dover Publications, New York, 1954.

Schlaifer, Robert, *Analysis of Decisions Under Uncertainty*, McGraw-Hill, New York, 1969.

Walton, Mary, *Car: A Drama of the American Workplace*, W.W. Norton & Company, New York, 1997.

2

DECISION-MAKING FUNDAMENTALS

Learning Objectives:

After studying this chapter, the reader will be able to do the following:

1. Identify the context of a decision situation (Section 2.1).
2. Select an appropriate decision-making approach for a decision context (Section 2.1).
3. Distinguish fundamental objectives from means objectives (Section 2.2).
4. Create a fundamental objectives hierarchy (Section 2.2).
5. Create a means-objective network (Section 2.2).
6. Draw an influence diagram of a decision situation (Section 2.3).
7. Identify types of rationality (Section 2.4).
8. Identify dominated alternatives in a multiple-criteria decision (Section 2.5).
9. Identify choice strategies (Section 2.6).
10. Use Benjamin Franklin's method to choose between two alternatives (Section 2.7).
11. Describe the importance of "framing" a decision situation (Section 2.8).
12. Identify risk acceptance criteria (Section 2.9).

Engineering Decision Making and Risk Management, First Edition. Jeffrey W. Herrmann.
© 2015 John Wiley & Sons, Inc. Published 2015 by John Wiley & Sons, Inc.

13. Identify types of measurement scales (Section 2.10).
14. Identify appropriate operations for specific measurement scales (Section 2.10).

This chapter discusses some important fundamental concepts that, when understood, can help one improve decision making. Understanding the decision context (Section 2.1) helps the decision maker select an appropriate decision-making strategy and choose relevant objectives. Identifying the fundamental objectives and the means for achieving them (Section 2.2) helps a decision maker focus on what is important and generate effective alternatives. Mapping the relationships among the decisions, the uncertainty, and the objectives using an influence diagram (Section 2.3) can clarify the decision situation. Understanding the principle of "rationality" (Section 2.4) can help a decision maker avoid bad decisions. Decision makers can benefit from using dominance properties (Section 2.5) to identify superior alternatives (and avoid inferior ones) and from knowing that there are multiple choice strategies available to them (Section 2.6). Benjamin Franklin's method (Section 2.7) is a popular decision-making method for choosing between two alternatives and exploits the basic idea of a tradeoff. Understanding that a decision must be "framed" properly (Section 2.8) can help decision makers choose relevant objectives and avoid solving the wrong problem. Decision makers also need to know when to accept risk (Section 2.9). Because decision-making techniques rely upon quantitative measures, understanding the different types of measurement scales (Section 2.10) can help decision makers be consistent and avoid logical errors.

2.1 DECISION CHARACTERISTICS

The characteristics of a decision include its context, its frequency, and its components. Decision-making contexts can be classified as follows (Snowden and Boone, 2007):

- In a *simple* context, clear cause-and-effect relationships are evident to everyone, and there are repeating patterns and consistent events.
- In a *complicated* context, cause-and-effect relationships are knowable but not obvious, expert diagnosis is needed, and there are known unknowns.
- A *complex* context is unpredictable and dynamic and full of unknown unknowns and many competing ideas.
- A *chaotic* context has high turbulence, which requires making many decisions, but provides no time to think.
- *Disorder* is a difficult context to recognize because multiple ideas and stakeholders create a "cacophony" of many voices.

Decisions range from routine to exceptional. Routine decisions are usually made frequently and have a limited impact (in terms of time or scope or cost). Exceptional decisions are made infrequently. As might be expected, one person's routine decision may be another's exceptional decision. For example, a mutual fund manager regularly buys and sells large quantities of stock. Any one of these decisions might be an exceptional decision by someone making their first investment in stocks.

The components of a decision are (1) the alternatives that are being considered, (2) the attributes (criteria, objectives, or performance measures) that will be used to evaluate and compare the alternatives, (3) the constraints that the alternatives must satisfy to be considered, and (4) the uncertainty in the outcomes and consequences that follow from selecting an alternative. This uncertainty may be represented with probability distributions or as a range of values.

Decision makers also vary in many ways. They think and communicate and learn in different ways. Some are risk averse, whereas others are risk neutral. Some prefer alternatives that are good on every important attribute, whereas others prefer alternatives that are great on some attributes (and weak on others) because the positives compensate for the negatives. Each decision maker has his own preferences, values, and goals, and these affect the relative desirability of the alternatives. Understanding the decision maker is an important step for improving decision making.

2.2 OBJECTIVES IN DECISION MAKING

In general, a decision maker wants to select the alternative that performs "best" on various attributes (also known as performance measures). For example, when faced with the need for a component in the design of a computer, an engineer may want to select one that is inexpensive, runs well, and would not fail. An engineer designing a liquid rocket engine will want to select a hot fire test plan that is affordable, does not delay the engine development project, and provides a certain confidence in the engine's reliability.

In general, we will use the term "objective" for goals such as minimizing cost, maximizing reliability (expected time to failure), and minimizing test time. When discussing the objectives of a decision, it can be useful to understand why the objectives are relevant and important, to see how multiple objectives are related to each other, and to consider how certain more abstract objectives can be represented with more concrete objectives that are easier to measure. In some situations, a discussion about the objectives can eliminate misunderstandings and build consensus, which simplifies decision making.

A *fundamental objective* is one that is important for its own sake; it needs no justification (Clemen and Reilly, 2001). For a product development team working in a manufacturing corporation, "maximize profit" may be a fundamental objective. For a government agency responsible for motor vehicle safety, "maximize safety" may be a fundamental objective. Fundamental objectives are ends, not means. (The means describe the ways in which one could accomplish the ends.)

Fundamental objectives, similar to "motherhood and apple pie" vision statements, are generally accepted as valid but can be imprecise. More specific objectives help explain what the more general objective means. Note that the more specific objectives are still fundamental; that is, they are still important as ends, not means.

For example, the fundamental (but general) objective of "maximize safety" can be made more precise by elaborating it with the following fundamental objectives that are more specific: "minimize injuries" and "minimize loss of life." These describe various types of safety (not ways to maximize safety). In turn, these can be made more precise by distinguishing between different groups. Those concerned about motor vehicle safety could distinguish among drivers, passengers, bicyclists, and pedestrians. Those concerned about hospital safety could distinguish among patients, visitors, and employees.

A *fundamental objectives hierarchy* is a way to organize these fundamental objectives (Clemen and Reilly, 2001). The fundamental objectives below a fundamental objective are the answer to "What do you mean by that objective?" The fundamental objective above a set of fundamental objectives is the answer to "What is the more general (or comprehensive) fundamental objective?" Figure 2.1 provides an example of a fundamental objectives hierarchy. In this figure, the boxes labeled "drivers," "passengers," and "pedestrians" represent the more specific but still fundamental objectives of "minimize injuries" and "minimize loss of life." In this case, the fundamental objectives for different groups are relevant because there will be different means for achieving these objectives.

Identifying the decision-maker's values that are relevant to a decision can help one identify the fundamental objectives. The importance of caring for people and being a responsible citizen may generate the objective to maximize safety. The importance of pursuing excellence may generate the objectives of maximizing performance. Management decisions, because they involve other people, often require thinking carefully about one's values. Some of the relevant values include caring for people, respect for others, avoiding conflict, keeping promises, self-discipline, survival, fairness, honesty, and integrity (Guy, 1990).

Some fundamental objectives can be used directly as attributes in a decision. For instance, a decision-maker who seeks to minimize loss of life may evaluate alternatives based on the expected number of lives lost if that alternative was selected. This depends, of course, upon having a valid method to estimate the expected number of lives lost. If no such method exists, the decision maker may want to use another objective as a surrogate for the fundamental objective. This other objective is a means to achieve the fundamental objective and is thus a *means objective*; it is important only because it is a means to the end. It is not important by itself.

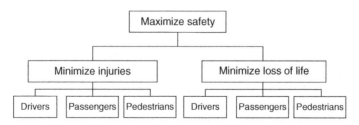

Figure 2.1   A fundamental objectives hierarchy for objectives related to safety.

The fundamental objective is the goal, also known as the ends. The *means objectives* are the ways in which one goes about trying to achieve the fundamental objective. The means objectives are surrogates for the fundamental objective.

For example, an aerospace engineer may wish to reduce the mass of a system that will be installed in an airplane. Why? Because that reduces the mass of the airplane, which reduces the fuel needed to fly the airplane on a certain mission, which reduces the cost of operating the airplane, which increases the profitability of the airline that owns and operates a fleet of these airplanes (and increases the desirability of the airplane). This example is a chain of means objectives, which is shown in Figure 2.2.

A mechanical engineer may wish to select a material that has good machinability when designing a part. The machinability of the material is correlated with tool wear, surface finish, cost, and quality (Dieter and Schmidt, 2012). Maximizing machinability is very important, but it is not a fundamental objective. It is a means objective because it reduces cost, improves part quality, and increases profitability.

Likewise, an industrial engineer who is creating a layout for a factory may wish to reduce the total distance that material moves throughout the factory. This is a means to reduce the cost of material handling, which is a means to reduce operating costs, which is a means to increasing profitability. Reducing the total distance is also a means to reducing the cycle time (the time required to complete a customer's order), which is a means to increase on-time deliveries, which is a means to increase sales and revenue, which is another means to increasing profitability.

It is sometimes convenient to draw a graph (a *means-objective network*) that shows the relationships between the means objectives and the fundamental objectives. The nodes in the graph are the various objectives, and each directed arc goes from a means objective to an objective that it achieves. If the nodes are arranged in such a way that all the arcs point generally toward the top, then moving down in the network from a node leads to the objectives that are the answer to "How could one achieve that?" Moving up from one objective leads to the objectives that are the answer to "Why is that important?"

For instance, for a highway safety agency, "maximize the number of vehicles with advanced safety features" and "maximize driving quality" are reasonable means objectives to "maximize safety" (there are many others). Neither is important to the agency on its own, but both are important ways to achieve the fundamental objective. The first may be possible to measure directly (if the agency can estimate the number of vehicles with advanced safety features), but the second may require surrogates that are means to maximize driver quality. For instance, "maximize the rigor of driving tests" (so that a driver can pass the test if and only if they are a very good driver), "maximize the number of drivers who take driver's education courses," and "minimize distracted driving" are three possible means objectives because they are ways to

Figure 2.2   A chain of means objectives.

maximize driving quality. These objectives are how one can maximize driver quality, and maximizing driver quality is why one would do these.

Thinking about means can lead to ideas for alternatives. For instance, considering how to minimize distracted driving might lead to the objectives "maximize use of hands free automobile controls," "maximize use of hands free cell phones," and "maximize enforcement of distracted driving laws." These lead clearly to technology and policy alternatives that focus on each of these three objectives. For example, requiring that drivers provide a gap of at least 3 feet (1 m) when passing bicyclists minimizes the likelihood of an accident, which maximizes bicyclist's safety. Increasing the gap is not a fundamental objective (protecting bicyclists is a fundamental objective), but this requirement is a policy that can be implemented.

Because the process of identifying means objectives can lead to ideas for alternatives, it is important to have a wide range of means objectives. It is also important to generate a set of attributes (performance measures) from the objectives, so that the decision maker will evaluate each alternative not only on the one objective that it apparently perfectly achieves but also on all other relevant objectives. The objectives should help one compare and choose between alternatives.

The following procedure can be used to organize the objectives that are relevant to a decision ("Structured decision making: introduction," 2012):

1. Brainstorm the "things that matter," survey a broad cross-section of interested people to identify the concerns that they would like to see addressed, and consider the concerns and questions of the key stakeholders.
2. State each objective as a quantity that matters and a direction in which the stakeholders would like it to move (usually, more vs. less, although no change is the goal in some cases).
3. Separate the objectives into means objectives and fundamental objectives (the ends).
4. Create a fundamental objectives hierarchy by grouping similar fundamental objectives, and draw a means-objective network to show why the means objectives are important.
5. Test the usefulness of the objectives, which should be complete, controllable, concise, measurable, and understandable (cf. Keeney, 1992; McDaniels, 2000).

Example 2.1 Consider the process of designing voting districts (wards) in the City of Edmonton (in Alberta, Canada), which was described by Bozkaya *et al.* (2011). The city policy documents list a set of criteria, some of which can be expressed as the following objectives: "maximize population equality among wards," "minimize the need for future revisions," and "minimize splitting community leagues between multiple wards." One of the criteria is the compactness of the shape of the district. City policy states that wards should be "relatively block-shaped with straight sides." That is, the districts should not be elongated, snakelike, or twisted shapes. This was important to avoid the appearance of gerrymandering and "to ensure that ward boundaries are drawn impartially." How can one increase "compactness"? Bozkaya *et al.* used two measures: (1) the total perimeters of district boundaries (where a smaller perimeter is better) and (2) the ratios of perimeters of districts to circumference of circles with the same areas. Thus, from this discussion, we can identify two of the fundamental objectives: "minimize the appearance of gerrymandering" and "ensure that ward boundaries are drawn impartially." The most relevant means objective is "maximize compactness of the voting districts" (this is a means for achieving both fundamental objectives). Because "compactness" is difficult to measure, two different means objectives are relevant: "minimize the total perimeters" and "minimize the ratios of the perimeters to equal area circles." These objectives can be organized in the means-objective network shown in Figure 2.3.

When choosing a means objective as a surrogate for a more fundamental objective, one should be careful because optimizing the wrong thing can lead to a poor solution. For instance, if one wants to minimize the time needed to machine cutouts in a flat metal part, one possible means objective is to maximize the material removal rate. An alternative means objective (suggested by Hazelrigg, 2012) is to minimize the material removed, which can be accomplished by cutting only the outline of the sections that need to be removed, which would cause them to fall out of the piece, as shown in the example in Figure 2.4.

It is convenient to view a product as a hierarchy of subsystems, subassemblies, and components. Since designing a product requires designing all these elements, a product development project involves a hierarchy of decisions. A decision at one level sets targets and constraints or provides information for decisions at another level. A typical example is aircraft design (see, for instance, Kalsi *et al.*, 2001). The conceptual design phase selects wing area, fuselage length, wingspan, take-off weight, and installed thrust, and the detailed design steps must respect these constraints. Setting these constraints makes component (or subsystem) design easier, although the constraints prevent system-level optimization (cf. Hazelrigg, 1996; and Keeney, 1992). The following are examples of explicit constraints that are means to more fundamental, implicit objectives (Hazelrigg, 1996):

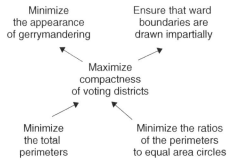

Figure 2.3 A network of means objectives relevant to designing voting districts (wards) in the City of Edmonton.

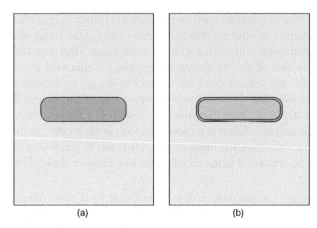

Figure 2.4 Two ways of machining a cutout: (a) the entire opening (the dark grey area) is machined and (b) only the outline of the opening is machined, and the interior part falls out. (Plan view of a flat part.)

- In a spacecraft trajectory design problem, the implicit objective is to maximize value of scientific data returned from spacecraft; the explicit constraint is that the spacecraft must not crash into the planet.
- In an aircraft autopilot design problem, the implicit objective is to achieve a safe and comfortable landing; the explicit constraint limits the deceleration of the airframe.
- In an image compression algorithm design problem, the implicit objective is to maximize image "quality"; the explicit constraint is that the probability of information loss must be near zero.

2.3 INFLUENCE DIAGRAMS

An influence diagram shows the relationships among the choices available to the decision maker, the sources of uncertainty (if any), and the objectives (Clemen and Reilly, 2001). A decision maker can use an influence diagram to identify, understand, and describe the various components of a decision. Understanding a decision can lead to making a better decision.

Influence diagrams have arcs and nodes. The nodes include decision nodes, chance nodes, intermediate consequences nodes, and payoff nodes. A decision node represents a choice that can be made. A chance node represents an event or quantity that is uncertain. An intermediate consequence node represents a measure or outcome. The payoff node represents the "bottom line" like total cost or profitability. The arcs can represent relevance or sequence relationships. Figure 2.5 shows these types of nodes for a generic decision.

Arcs into a chance node represent relevance, meaning that something affects that chance (the probabilities associated with that chance). (For instance, the weather

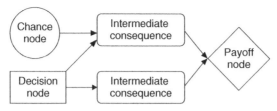

Figure 2.5   A generic influence diagram.

affects the chance of an accident, and the speed of the car affects the chance of an accident.) Relevance arcs can also go into consequences and payoffs, obviously, since the decisions and outcomes affect these.

Arcs into a decision node indicate sequence. That is, they show what is known when the decision must be made. The driver knows the weather before deciding how fast to drive.

In the basic risky decision, the decision maker must choose something safe or something risky without knowing what will happen in the future and which result will occur. The influence diagram for this type of decision typically has three nodes: a decision node, a chance node, and a payoff node. The decision must be made before the chance is resolved, so there is no arc from the chance node to the decision node. If the choice influences the likelihood of a future event, there is an arc from the decision node to the chance node. Both the decision and the uncertain future affect the payoff to the decision maker, so there are arcs from the decision node and the chance node to the payoff node.

Example 2.2   Consider a situation in which Rose must select a material to be used in a product, but she is not sure about the properties (performance) of some of the alternatives. Before selecting a material, she must decide how much testing to do (the test plan). The amount of testing and the unknown material properties influence the imperfect test results. The amount of testing determines the testing time and cost, which influences the schedule delay and development cost. After getting the test results, she must select a material, which influences the product quality and unit cost. The material properties also influence these metrics. The schedule delay, development cost, product quality, and unit cost all affect profitability. Because the testing is not perfect, there is still some uncertainty in the material properties, and that uncertainty makes the true product quality and unit cost uncertain. Figure 2.6 shows an influence diagram for her situation. This diagram shows the sequential nature of the decisions (first Rose decides how much testing, and then she selects a material after getting the test results) and the uncertainties (in the material properties and the test results).

Influence diagrams are usually not used for quantitative analysis; instead, they are used for understanding and communicating the key components of a decision. Representing every detail of every relationship or component is not as crucial as representing the most influential parts of a decision in a logical way.

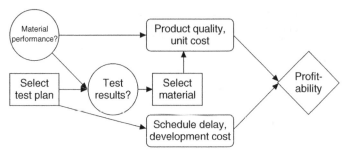

Figure 2.6   An influence diagram for a decision about conducting tests to gather information about material performance.

An influence diagram should be complete and accurate, and its usefulness depends upon clearly showing the key relationships between the important, relevant factors. Constructing an influence diagram, like creating other types of models, is an iterative process in which the diagram is updated as one identifies additional relevant factors and more appropriate ways to describe the relationships between the components of the diagram.

To begin creating an influence diagram, identify the important decisions, uncertainties, and consequences that are relevant to the decision. Then, consider the sequence in which decisions will occur and the uncertainties will be resolved. Add an arc from a chance node into a decision node if that uncertainty will be resolved and known before the decision is made. In a similar way, add an arc from one decision node into another decision node if the first decision will be made and the outcome known before the second decision is made. Add arcs into a chance node from the nodes for decisions and uncertainties that affect the distribution of outcomes. Both the choice of a route and the weather will affect the distribution of the time required to drive to work, for instance. Add arcs into a consequence node from the nodes for decisions, uncertainties, and consequences that determine that consequence. Add arcs into the payoff node from the nodes for the consequences that determine that payoff. For more details and examples, see, for instance, Clemen and Reilly (2001) or Chelst and Canbolat (2012).

2.4   RATIONALITY

Rationality is an important concept in the study of decision making. Most decision makers want to avoid being irrational. What types of things are irrational? Shooting from the hip (i.e., choosing the first thing that comes to mind when there is time to be more analytical), procrastinating (refusing to decide), and ducking (delegating the decision to someone else) may be viewed as irrational. Also considered irrational are decision makers who use invalid or incomplete information, those who do not consider the consequences of their actions, and those who allow emotion to override objective assessments (Simon, 1997). The Dutch Book Argument states that decision makers are rational if and only if their assessments of probabilities obey the laws of probability (Lyon, 2010). In particular, an irrational decision maker believes that the sum of the probability that an event occurs and the probability that the event does not occur is greater than 1.

In the most general sense, an action is rational because the one choosing it believes that the action will lead to a desired end. In the same way, a decision is rational because the decision maker is trying to achieve his goals. Stirling (2003) gave this inclusive definition of rationality: "A rational decision is one that conforms either to a set of general principles that govern preferences or to a set of rules that govern behavior." By applying these principles or rules, the decision maker selects an action that leads to acceptable consequences. Therefore, because different situations require different definitions of acceptability (and different goals and resource availability), which lead to different principles or rules, there are different types of rationality. Decision makers choose and use different types of rationality in different situations.

A particular decision-making method may be rational in some situations and irrational in others. At a football game, it is an accepted practice to flip a coin to decide who will kick off first. However, flipping a coin to choose a prime contractor for a new military tanker aircraft would be considered irrational. In the latter case, considering issues such as life-cycle costs, expected aircraft performance, and the supplier's reliability is a more reasonable approach.

Note that rationality is not the same thing as "making a good decision." The quality of a decision can be measured in different ways. The most common way is to look at what happened after the decision was made; if the outcome was desirable (or, even better, the best possible), the decision was a "good" one.

Looking only at the outcome can be misleading, however, because the future is uncertain, and "bad luck" can make any decision look bad. For example, consider the tanker aircraft contractor decision. One could very carefully consider the different contractors, the expected performance of the aircraft designs, the cost estimates provided, the strategic importance of the relationships, and other factors before selecting one. Suppose that, when production begins, the supplier is forced to shut down their final assembly facility due to damage from a severe tornado, which causes extensive delays in the production of the aircraft. The decision looks bad because of the outcome, but the decision process was appropriate and performed properly.

Multiple types of rationality have been identified. Stirling (2003) listed four types: substantive rationality, procedural rationality, bounded rationality, and intrinsic rationality. Gigerenzer et al. (1999) first distinguished between "demons" and bounded rationality. The models called "demons" are those that assume that human beings have unlimited power to find and evaluate alternatives (especially those that seem to have uncertain outcomes). This class they separate into two types: unbounded rationality and optimization under constraints. Unbounded rationality assumes that humans have unlimited time, knowledge, and computational capacity and do not consider the cost of searching. Optimization under constraints assumes that the decision maker considers the costs and benefits of searching for information but otherwise still has unlimited knowledge and computational capacity.

The following paragraphs describe these different types of rationality.

Substantive Rationality: *Nothing but the best will do.* A "substantively rational" decision maker makes choices according to the principle that one should select the alternative that is optimal in the total preference ordering (Stirling, 2003).

A key concept is the concept of ordering. A decision maker must have the ability to say that one option is better than another. Alternatively, we say that the decision maker prefers one option to another. Let $A \succeq B$ denote the fact that the decision maker prefers alternative A over alternative B or views them as equivalent. Then, certain properties must hold: *reflexivity* is the property that $A \succeq A$. The property of *antisymmetry* states that if $A \succeq B$ and $B \succeq A$, then $A = B$ (that is, the decision maker has no preference; they are equivalent). The property of *transitivity* states that if $A \succeq B$ and $B \succeq C$, then $A \succeq C$. The property of *linearity* states that, for any two alternatives A and B, either $A \succeq B$ or $B \succeq A$. (Of course, it may be that both hold.)

Substantive rationality is the paradigm that guides formal decision analysis. It deals with principles about preferences. First, for all the possible alternatives, the decision maker has a total ordering over them. Second, the decision maker should choose the alternative that is most preferred. That is, the decision maker *optimizes*. This total ordering can be represented as a *utility function U*, so that the decision maker prefers alternative A to alternative $B(A \succeq B)$ if and only if $U(A) \succeq U(B)$.

The selected alternative is a function of choosing this approach and the utility function. Most of the work involves collecting information and performing calculations to evaluate the utility function. (Of course, determining the utility function is not easy either.)

Although this rationality is conceptually ideal, there are two obstacles that prevent its widespread acceptance. A practical obstacle to this approach is that it requires a complete understanding of the situation and extensive computational effort. These may not exist in many settings. A conceptual obstacle is that it does not describe how people make many decisions in practice. Decision makers, especially in social settings, do not maximize their utility because that requires more time and effort.

Procedural Rationality: *By the book.* A "procedurally rational" decision maker makes choices by following specific rules or procedures (Stirling, 2003). In some cases, explicit company policies and government regulations require certain decision-making procedures and rules. In other cases, decision makers use knowledge about the behavior that is appropriate for given situations (called "scripts" by Gioia and Poole, 1984) to determine the best course of action.

For example, in a production scheduling environment, a policy that the factory should always manufacture the five most popular products every Monday is a decision-making procedure that avoids complex optimization routines. A bank can evaluate loan applicants by their credit rating and issue loans only to those who have sufficiently high scores (instead of making case-by-case decisions). Using the nearest neighbor algorithm (Figure 2.7) is a procedure to select a route for a traveling salesman problem (TSP). An automotive engineer who must read hundreds of accident reports would use a screening script to decide quickly which ones merit further investigation (Gioia, 1994).

The problem is that a rule may yield solutions with poor quality; usually there is no guarantee of optimality. For instance, using the nearest neighbor algorithm to solve

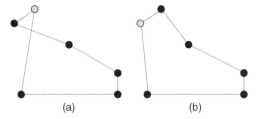

Figure 2.7 Using the nearest neighbor algorithm to generate solutions to a TSP with six points. In (a), the algorithm begins at the gray point, proceeds to the point slightly below it and then continues clockwise back to the first point. In (b), the algorithm begins at the gray point and proceeds clockwise back to the first point. The solution in (a) is 8% longer than the solution in (b).

a TSP can, in some cases, create solutions that are clearly not optimal (as shown in Figure 2.7) and, in others, create very bad solutions.

Bounded Rationality: *The best we could do in the time available.* Bounded rationality starts with the observation that information and computational power (computers or people) are limited in the real world, and this prevents complete optimization. Cognitive limitations that lead to errors in judgment and decision making are another limit on human decision making (Todd and Gigerenzer, 2003).

There are, however, two types of bounded rationality. In the first, the choice to stop searching (for information or alternatives) is viewed as part of a more comprehensive optimization problem. This returns the decision-maker to substantive rationality, where the time or computational limits are part of the decision, and the decision-maker needs to optimize the whole thing. (The calculation of the expected value of information, discussed in Chapter 8, can be seen as part of this approach.)

In the second, simple rules are used for stopping the search. These include the two overlapping categories of satisficing and fast-and-frugal heuristics. Satisficing is an important type of bounded rationality in which the decision maker has (or determines) minimum requirements on one or more attributes and searches for a solution until one that meets all the minimum requirements is found (Simon, 1981). The decision maker stops with the first satisfactory one. Fast-and-frugal heuristics (some of which may be satisficing) "employ a minimum of time, knowledge, and computation to make adaptive choices in real environments" and "limit their search of objects or information using easily-computable stopping rules, and they make their choices with easily-computable decision rules" (Gigerenzer *et al.*, 1999).

A simple algorithm for deciding how to treat heart attack patients is an example of a fast-and-frugal procedure (Gigerenzer *et al.*, 1999). Based on the answers to three yes-or-no questions, the algorithm classifies a patients as "high risk" or "low risk," and the strategy for treating the patient is based on this variable (a high-risk patient will receive a more aggressive and expensive treatment). The algorithm is fast (only three questions that require no computation) and frugal (it uses only some of the available information).

Intrinsic Rationality: *You get what you pay for.* This type of rationality looks at each alternative by itself. An intrinsically rational alternative is one that yields expected benefits that equal or exceed the expected losses (Stirling, 2003). Benjamin Franklin's approach, by comparing the pros and cons of doing something, follows this approach. If the alternative is a net gain, keep it, else discard it. Intrinsic rationality allows a decision maker to create a set of (intrinsically) rational solutions (instead of just one optimal or satisfactory solution). The overall quality of the solutions may vary, since some could have small benefits (with small costs) and some could have large gains (with large costs).

Intrinsic rationality could be used to select a small set of alternatives for an optimization approach or a set of alternatives among which a decision maker can pick and choose: Which new products should be developed? Which home improvement projects should we do?

The following scenario is another example: when selecting a vendor for a research and development project, a government agency will award a contract of a fixed amount to any vendor whose ideas meet certain performance criteria. The vendors are not compared with each other, only to the criteria. Because the cost of a contract is fixed, the intrinsic value of each vendor is determined by the quality of their ideas.

Ecological Rationality: *The right process at the right time.* The study of *ecological rationality* (Todd and Gigerenzer, 2007) seeks to determine when (i.e., in which situations) a given decision-making heuristic will be successful and when it will fail. For instance, to decide which of the two alternatives is greater on some criterion, the recognition heuristic chooses the one that is recognized if the other is not. This heuristic, which may ignore contradicting information about the recognized alternative, is ecologically rational if it makes the correct decision over half of the time. According to Todd and Gigerenzer, "environment structure—in the form of useful patterns of available information in the world—can be exploited by heuristics in the head to produce adaptive behavior. Heuristics—simple decision algorithms that can work well in appropriate environments—generate both routine behavior and important decisions."

Using simple rules is sometimes a response to complexity (Simon, 1955, 1978). In this case, the decision maker, faced with a problem that is too large or complex to solve optimally, falls back on a simple rule that makes sense based on what is understood. For instance, one can use the nearest neighbor rule to solve a large TSP. A fast-and-frugal heuristic similar to recognition can perform well in certain domains (Gigerenzer *et al.*, 1999). In general, choice strategies that do not use optimization may be more powerful in complex and messy problems.

The study of *heuristics-and-biases* has investigated, using the methods of psychology and economics, different decision-making shortcuts, such as availability, representativeness, and the simulation heuristic, and has documented these heuristics' inferior performance compared with optimal strategies (Tversky and Kahneman, 1974; Kahneman *et al.*, 1982). When using a simulation heuristic, a decision-maker visualizes or predicts what will happen and what new opportunities or problems might occur if a particular alternative is selected.

These simple heuristics can be viewed, however, as ways to save valuable time, so that a decision maker can react quickly, make more decisions per unit time, and gain an advantage on competitors (Klein, 2001; Todd, 2001). Humans use simple heuristics with little information and conduct searches that are appropriate for the environment; moreover, providing information in a way that is compatible with the heuristics that are being used leads to better decision making (Todd and Gigerenzer, 2003; Todd, 2007).

Because the mind is so mysterious and human behavior so complex, psychologists, economists, sociologists, political scientists, philosophers, and others continue to develop different ways to describe human behavior. Humans want a variety of goods, and they are resourceful and self-interested, but they are influenced by what others do and think, they love and help others, and they seek truth (Jensen and Meckling, 1994; Feser, 2009). Given this complexity, it is certainly hard to say absolutely that a given decision is irrational. It may be possible only to determine which type(s) of rationality it appears to fit.

2.5 DOMINANCE

According to Simon (1997), "A fundamental principle of administration, which follows almost immediately from the rational character of 'good' administration, is that among several alternatives involving the same expenditure the one should always be selected which leads to the greatest accomplishment of administrative objectives; and among several alternatives that lead to the same accomplishment the one should be selected which involves the least expenditure." This principle illustrates the concept of dominance. Among the alternatives involving the same expenditure, the one that accomplishes the most dominates the others. Likewise, among the alternatives that lead to the same accomplishment, the one that costs the least dominates the others.

In decision analysis, *dominance* is the situation in which one alternative is always better than another, where the words "always" and "better" depend upon the context. This section will consider the use of dominance in a multicriteria decision, in a decision under uncertainty, and in a two-player simultaneous game. These types of decisions are covered in more detail in the following chapters: Chapter 3 discusses multicriteria decisions, Chapter 5 discusses decisions under uncertainty, and Chapter 6 discusses game theory.

In general, given a set of alternatives, if one can determine alternative A is "always better" than alternative B, then alternative B is "dominated" and can be dropped from the analysis because it cannot be the best choice. Identifying and eliminating the dominated alternatives leave a set of "nondominated" alternatives from which the decision maker should choose the one that is most preferred. One benefit of finding the nondominated alternatives is that it requires little information about the decision-maker's preferences but can significantly simplify the analysis.

If there are M alternatives and n attributes, then finding the dominated alternatives requires $O(M^2 n)$ effort because, in the worst case, every pair of alternatives must be compared on every attribute. When $n = 2$, the set of nondominated alternatives can be visualized as a curve in the two-dimensional space (in which the two coordinates are the values on the two attributes). When $n > 2$, however, visualizing the set of nondominated alternatives is difficult, although some techniques using self-organizing maps have been proposed (Chen *et al.*, 2013).

Note that the set of nondominated alternatives is sometimes called the "Pareto front" or the "efficient frontier," and the nondominated alternatives are sometimes called the "Pareto optimal" or "efficient" alternatives.

Consider a multicriteria decision with n criteria such that the decision maker can determine, for any two unequal values of the same criterion, which one is preferred. That is, there is an ordering that we represent as follows: Let $x \succeq y$ denote the fact that the decision maker prefers value x to value y or is indifferent between them.

Let X and Y be two alternatives with values $(x_1, \dots, x_n)$ and $(y_1, \dots, y_n)$. Then, alternative X dominates alternative Y if and only if $x_i \succeq y_i$ for all $i = 1, \dots, n$ and there exists some criteria k such that $x_k \neq y_k$ and the decision maker prefers x_k to y_k (he is not indifferent between them).

In a decision with uncertainty, suppose that there are n possible states of nature that could occur after the decision maker selects an alternative. The probabilities of these states are not affected by the decision-maker's selection. Let $u(x, i)$ be the utility of alternative x if state i occurs. The decision maker prefers greater utility. Then, alternative X stochastically dominates alternative Y if $u(x, i) \succeq u(y, i)$ for all $i = 1, \dots, n$ and there exists some state k such that $u(x, k) > u(y, k)$. (This is a simplest type of stochastic dominance, but there are other conditions that lead to stochastic dominance.)

In a two-player simultaneous game, suppose that there are n possible alternatives for the second player, whose choice will be revealed after the decision maker (the first player) selects an alternative. Let $u(x, i)$ be the utility for the first player if he chooses alternative x and the second player chooses alternative i. The decision maker prefers greater utility. Then, alternative X dominates alternative Y if $u(x, i) \succeq u(y, i)$ for all $i = 1, \dots, n$ and there exists some alternative k such that $u(x, k) > u(y, k)$.

Example 2.3 Table 2.1 provides information about the strength, installation effort, and cost of various types of glass (Allen, 1997). Assume that Joe, the decision maker, prefers a stronger glass that is easier to install and has lower cost. In some settings, there may be other relevant attributes, including aesthetic concerns, the need to reflect light, or the need to reduce its transmission. For example, when choosing the glass to be used in his innovative lighthouse lens, Augustin Fresnel considered both flint glass, which was more dense but brilliant and clear and had a high refractive index, and crown glass, which was hard, light, and easy to mold but had a low refractive index (Levitt, 2013).

Consider, for example, the Standard SS and Standard DD types of glass. Both are easy to install, and both have a low cost. The strength of the Standard SS is poor, however, which is not as desirable as the strength of the Standard DD, which is fair. Thus, Standard DD dominates Standard SS. It is not worse on any attribute, and it is better on at least one. Likewise, glass block is an excellent strength alternative, but it is difficult to install and has a high cost, so tempered glass dominates that.

Among the 12 types of glass in Table 2.1, only two are not dominated: Standard DD and tempered. The Standard DD glass is the best low cost alternative, and the

TABLE 2.1   The Properties of Different Types of Glass (Allen, 1997).

Type	Strength	Installation Effort	Cost
Standard SS	Poor	Easy	Low
Standard DD	Fair	Easy	Low
Plate	Good	Easy	Medium
Tempered	Excellent	Easy	Medium
Safety	Excellent	Difficult	Medium
Wire	Excellent	Difficult	High
Insulating	Good	Difficult	High
Tinted	Good	Moderate	High
Frosted	Good	Moderate	High
Patterned	Fair	Easy	High
Mirror tiles	Poor	Easy	Medium
Glass block	Excellent	Difficult	High

tempered is the best excellent strength alternative. Both types are also easy to install. All the other types are dominated by at least one of these two. Joe can focus his attention on only these two types of glass.

2.6   CHOICE STRATEGIES

There are numerous strategies used to make a decision, especially when there are many alternatives and multiple criteria on which to compare them. The following list of choice strategies and the accompanying descriptions are from Hastie and Dawes (2001), see also Payne and Bettman (2001):

1. *Dominance:* Used to select an alternative or to discard one. To select one, find an alternative that is, on all important attributes, at least as good as every other alternative. To discard one, find an alternative that is worse than any other alternative on all of the attributes. This strategy eliminates inferior alternatives without eliciting the decision maker's specific preferences about the attributes. This strategy will not necessarily identify a single preferred alternative. Performing all the pairwise comparisons required can be time consuming if there are many alternatives.

2. *Additive Linear:* Used to find the best alternative. Assign every attribute a weight that reflects its importance. Calculate a total value for each alternative by determining its value on every attribute and finding the weighted sum of these values. Select the alternative with the greatest total value. This strategy identifies one "best" alternative but requires the weights for the attributes. Determining accurate weights that reflect the decision-maker's preferences can be time consuming. This comprehensive strategy assumes that a linear model of the decision-maker's preferences is appropriate, and this could be inaccurate.

3. *Additive Difference:* Pick two alternatives, estimate the difference between them on every attribute, and calculate the total net difference. Discard the loser and compare the winner to another alternative. Repeat until all alternatives have been compared, and then select the one that remains. This comprehensive strategy has the same advantages and disadvantages as the additive linear strategy.

4. *Satisficing:* For every attribute, determine a minimal acceptable (cutoff) value. Find the first alternative that is, on every attribute, at least as good as the cut-off value. This often occurs in engineering design when one does an iterative design process. One designs a component (or system) and then tests it. If the design meets all the requirements and constraints, the design is done. If not, then one redesigns it and tests the new design. And this continues until the meets all the requirements and constraints. This strategy requires less effort than the comprehensive strategies but will not necessarily identify the "optimal" alternative.

5. *Disjunctive:* For every attribute, determine a minimal acceptable (cutoff) value. Find the first alternative that is, on at least one attribute, at least as good as the cutoff value. One can use this strategy to find a diverse set of alternatives that are each very good on at least one attribute. Similar to satisficing, this strategy requires less effort than the comprehensive strategies but will not necessarily identify the "optimal" alternative.

6. *Lexicographic:* Identify the most important attribute and the alternatives that have the best value on that attribute. If there is only one, select it. Otherwise, keep these alternatives, discard the remainder, identify the next most important attribute, and find the alternatives that have the best value on that attribute. Repeat until only one alternative remains. This strategy identifies one "best" alternative but cannot consider tradeoffs between attributes.

7. *Elimination by Aspects:* Identify the most important attribute, determine a minimal acceptable (cutoff) value for that attribute, and discard all alternatives that have a lower value on that attribute. Select the next most important attribute, determine a cutoff value, discard the inferior alternatives, and repeat until only one alternative remains. This strategy identifies one "best" alternative but cannot consider tradeoffs between attributes. Because it keeps multiple alternatives at each step, it should require more effort than the lexicographic strategy.

8. *Recognition Heuristic:* Choose the first alternative that is recognized. This is a very simple strategy that requires little effort, but it will not necessarily identify the "optimal" alternative.

In general, these strategies provide a tradeoff between the comprehensiveness of the search and the mental effort involved. All can be considered rational in one way or another, which accounts for their popularity. As mentioned before, strategies that make sense in one domain may be poor choices in another.

Example 2.4 Consider the glass choice from Example 2.3. Applying the lexicographic choice strategy requires the decision maker to prioritize the attributes based on which are most important. In this situation, an attribute's "importance" reflects the decision-maker's preferences; one attribute is more important than another if the decision maker, given a choice between two alternatives, prefers the one that is better on the first attribute regardless of the values of the second attribute for the alternatives.

If Joe cares most about installation effort, he should sort the types of glass first by installation effort, which shows that six types are easy to install. If he cares more about cost than strength, he should sort these six types by cost, which shows that only two types (Standard DD and Standard SS) are low cost. Finally, considering strength, the only remaining attribute, shows that Standard DD is better, and Joe should choose that one.

Applying the additive linear choice strategy requires Joe to convert the properties to scores and to give weights to the different attributes. Chapter 3 will present multicriteria decision-making approaches that do this in a systematic way.

2.7 MAKING TRADEOFFS

When asked for advice, Benjamin Franklin did not pick an alternative for Joseph Prestly, his correspondent. Instead, in the following letter, he recommended a decision-making process ("Moral Algebra," 2012; Stirling, 2003).

London, Sept 19, 1772

Dear Sir,

In the affair of so much importance to you, wherein you ask my advice, I cannot, for want of sufficient premises, advise you what to determine, but if you please I will tell you how. When those difficult cases occur, they are difficult, chiefly because while we have them under consideration, all the reasons pro and con are not present to the mind at the same time; but sometimes one set present themselves, and at other times another, the first being out of sight. Hence the various purposes or inclinations that alternatively prevail, and the uncertainty that perplexes us. To get over this, my way is to divide half a sheet of paper by a line into two columns; writing over the one Pro, and over the other Con. Then, during three or four days consideration, I put down under the different heads short hints of the different motives, that at different times occur to me, for or against the measure. When I have thus got them all together in one view, I endeavor to estimate their respective weights; and where I find two, one on each side, that seem equal, I strike them both out. If I find a reason pro equal to some two reasons con, I strike out the three. If I judge some two reasons con, equal to three reasons pro, I strike out the five; and thus proceeding I find at length where the balance lies; and if, after a day or two of further consideration, nothing new that is of importance occurs on either side, I come to a determination accordingly. And, though the weight of the reasons cannot be taken with the precision of algebraic quantities, yet when each is thus considered, separately and comparatively, and the whole lies before me, I think I can judge better, and am less liable to make a rash step, and in fact I have found great advantage from this kind of equation, and what might be called moral or prudential algebra.

Wishing sincerely that you may determine for the best, I am ever, my dear friend, yours most affectionately.

B. Franklin

Although it is relevant for a binary choice (yes or no, go or no-go, A or B), this approach is an example of multicriteria decision making (Yoon and Hwang, 1995), and the method resembles the judgment processes that medical professionals use (Dawes and Corrigan, 1974; Shulman and Elstein, 1975).

This process relies upon the decision-maker's ability to determine the equality of dissimilar items on an implicit preference scale. Because the decision maker is comparing only two alternatives, only one simple relationship is needed, and comparing the items in the two columns is sufficient.

A force field diagram is a graphical version of this method. A vertical line down the middle of the diagram represents the alternative. Horizontal arrows pointing to the vertical line from the left represent reasons to choose the alternative, and horizontal arrows pointing to the vertical line from the right represent reasons to discard it. The length of each arrow indicates the "weight" of the corresponding reason. The force field diagram can show that the reasons to choose (or discard) the alternative dominate those on the other side. Straker (1995) discussed force field diagrams and provided examples and variations.

The method can be adapted for any decision between two alternatives. When a Ford engineer had the opportunity to leave for a position at Nissan, she created a chart on which she listed the benefits of staying on one side and the benefits of leaving on the other (Walton, 1997). The benefits of staying included Ford cars, health benefits, and the advantages of seniority. The benefits of the new job included more money, new opportunities, travel to Japan, a more diverse environment, learning new skills, health benefits, and Nissan cars. After comparing these, she chose to leave.

2.8 REFRAMING THE DECISION

The variety of choice strategies highlights the usefulness of choosing a different choice strategy (reframing the decision) when one strategy has led the decision maker into a difficult situation. This section briefly describes two examples where reframing the decision was valuable.

Example 2.5 This example was initially framed as a multiple criteria problem (cost vs. power and torque), but the experts reframed it as a satisficing problem (is the car powerful enough for her driving needs?). It is based on a letter written to Tom and Ray Magliozzi, better known as Click and Clack, who host the radio show "Car Talk" (Click & Clack, 2007). The writer, a woman named Kathleen, was trying to decide whether to buy a Ford Focus or a Nissan Versa. Both cars had four-cylinder engines and automatic transmissions. They had "similar" size, curb weight, quality, and warranty. The cost of the Focus was "slightly higher." She was worried about the horsepower and torque: the Focus had 140 hp and a maximal torque of 136; the Versa had 122 hp and a maximal torque of 127. She wrote, "I am just not sure if the difference is worth the slightly higher cost of the Focus. Can you tell me if it would make a positive difference in power and pickup during highway miles?"

Kathleen was struggling with a multiattribute decision-making problem and needed to make a tradeoff between cost and power (measured by horsepower and torque) because the other attributes mentioned were basically the same. (It is reasonable to assume that any attributes not mentioned were either equivalent or much less important.) Kathleen wanted to know if the better performance was worth the extra cost.

Click and Clack simplified the decision, however, by reframing the problem as a satisficing problem. In particular, they advised her to focus on whether the power was "adequate." They suggested that Kathleen test drive both cars in situations that reflect her normal driving patterns. They especially recommended trying to merge into high-speed traffic, with passengers in the car, if she would frequently need to do that. If she does not need to do that, or if both pass this test, she should not worry about the power anymore. If she needs to do that and both fail the test, she should consider a more powerful car. The remaining possibility was that she needs to do that and only one of the cars passes the test; then she should purchase that one. Therefore, the question was not whether the Focus's extra power is worth the extra cost; it was about how much power she needs and which of the cars provides that. Passing the highway merge test (if it is relevant) became a threshold that a satisfactory car must meet.

Example 2.6   In this example, adding another means objective leads to a better alternative. A textile cooperative in Ahmedabad, India, wanted to improve the reliability of their electricity supply because the local power supplier was unreliable ("Solar sewing," 2014). When the power was off, the women who worked there could not run their sewing machines, which limited their productivity and income. Their initial focus on the power supply led to a design for an expensive photovoltaic system to generate electricity. Considering the demand for electricity, however, led to a proposal to replace their overpowered, inefficient sewing machines with smaller ones that were still sufficiently powerful for their products and required less energy, which would require a smaller, less-expensive photovoltaic system. Moreover, the new machines had features that would improve production in other ways.

The initial set of objectives can be seen as "increase electrical supply" in order to "have enough power to run machines" in order to "avoid shutdowns" in order to "maximize productivity" in order to "maximize revenue." Unfortunately, this excluded the objective "reduce electrical demand," which is also a means to "have enough power to run machines." When this means objective was considered, it led to a feasible alternative (buying new machines and a smaller photovoltaic system).

2.9 RISK ACCEPTANCE

In a decision with uncertainty, a decision maker will consider the range of possible outcomes for every alternative. A risk-averse decision maker will avoid any alternative that has a very undesirable outcome (a "risk"). Among the factors that affect how a decision maker perceives risks are *dread risk* and *unknown risk* (Slovic, 1987). Items that are high on the dread risk factor are uncontrollable, dreadful, fatal, not easily reduced, and involuntary; they pose a high risk to future generations or could cause a global catastrophe. Items that are high on the unknown risk factor are unobservable, unknown, new, or mysterious; they may have a delayed effect. On the dread scale, caffeine and lawn mowers are very low, smoking and automobile accidents are in the middle, and radioactive waste and nerve gas are very high. On the unknown scale, automobile accidents and fireworks are very low, caffeine and smoking are in the middle, and DNA technology and cadmium are very high. Lay people are more likely to favor regulation of hazards that are dreadful or unknown. Known risks that are not dreadful can be avoided if they are too high.

For example, consider the risks associated with using compressed natural gas to power school buses. Compared with the well-known risk of using buses that run on gasoline, this risk may be viewed as relatively dreadful and unknown to a community, who may reject the idea for that reason. Although the risk can be assessed, an analysis that the expected number of fire fatalities per bus per year is 2.2×10^{-5} (Modarres, 2006) may be worth little unless the risk is shown to be less than that of using buses that run on gasoline.

A decision maker may decide to accept the risks associated with an alternative. For instance, anyone who drives or rides in a car accepts the associated risks. Decision makers use risk acceptance criteria (implicitly or explicitly) to evaluate the risks. If the risk meets the criteria (that is, if the risk is acceptably low), the alternative is considered "safe"; otherwise, it is "unsafe." In general, risk acceptance criteria provide requirements (or guidelines) on whether an alternative is acceptable or not; this can be used as a constraint or as a screening step in a decision-making process.

Risk acceptance criteria include relative risk acceptance criteria and absolute risk acceptance criteria (Modarres, 2006). An absolute risk acceptance criterion specifies the acceptable risk directly; a relative risk acceptance criterion specifies the acceptable risk as a function of other risks. For instance, the Nuclear Regulatory Commission has the following absolute risk acceptance criterion for nuclear reactors: "The overall mean frequency of a large release of radioactive materials to the environment from a reactor accident should be less than 1 in 1,000,000 per year of reactor operation." They also use the following relative risk acceptance criterion: "The risk, to the population in the area near a nuclear plant, of cancer fatalities resulting from nuclear power plant operation should not exceed one-tenth of one percent (0.1%) of the sum of cancer fatality risks resulting from all other causes."

In the Netherlands, where 55% of the country is flood prone, the Water Act includes absolute risk acceptance criteria for flood protection (Eijgenraam *et al.*, 2014). For instance, in some areas, the flood probability must be no greater than 1/1250 per year; in other areas, the flood probability must be no greater than 1/10,000 per year.

The Precautionary Principle is a guideline for when a risk should not be accepted (thus, it is a risk acceptance criterion). It is used in regulatory policy making and international treaties and agreements (Choo, 2009). According to Choo, the Precautionary Principle states that "when an activity raises threats of harm to human health or the environment, precautionary measures should be taken even if some cause and effect relationships are not fully established scientifically. In this context the proponent of the activity, rather than the public, should bear the burden of proof." Aven (2008) described it as follows: "The precautionary principle is the ethical principle that, if the consequences of an action (especially the use of technology) are subject to scientific uncertainty, then it is better not to carry out the action rather than risk the uncertain (possibly very negative) consequences."

The use of the value of a statistical life (discussed in Chapter 3) can be viewed as a risk acceptance criterion: the decision maker accepts the risk if the cost of reducing it is too large.

Gioia (1994) described the risk acceptance criteria that he adopted when working for Ford as a recall coordinator: "On moral grounds I knew I could recommend most of the vehicles on my safety tracking list for recall (and risk earning the label of a 'bleeding heart'). On practical grounds, I recognized that people implicitly accept risks in cars. We could not recall all cars with *potential* problems and stay in business. I learned to be responsive to those cases that suggested an imminent, dangerous problem."

2.10   MEASUREMENT SCALES

This text will follow, as much as possible, a well-established theory of measurement scales due to Stevens (1946). This theory classifies scales into four types: nominal, ordinal, interval, and ratio. Certain mathematical operations are valid for some (but not all) of these scales. For instance, consider the measurement of temperature using the Fahrenheit scale. Because of the way the scale was designed, it is certainly appropriate to consider the difference of two temperatures, say $10°C$ and $30°C$, and say that the second temperature is "warmer by $20°C$," but it is not valid to divide them and say that $30°C$ is "three times as warm." (One could, however, take the ratios of positive changes in temperatures.)

The first type of scale is the *nominal scale*, in which the items on the scale are essentially names. Using a nominal scale, one can determine whether two objects are equal (have the same value). One can determine the number of objects that have a particular value, and one can determine the mode (the value that occurs the most often in a set). The relative size of the numbers on a nominal scale has no meaning.

For example, the ZIP codes used to label towns in the United States with a unique number are a nominal scale.

The second type of scale is the *ordinal scale*, in which the values in the scale are essentially a sequence of grades like the standard letter grades (A, B, C, D, and F) or the names for grades on the Ordinary Wizarding Level exams in the Harry Potter series: O = Outstanding, E = Exceeds Expectations, A = Acceptable, P = Poor, D = Dreadful, and T = Troll. Using an ordinal scale, one can determine whether one object is greater (better) than, equal to, or less (worse) than another. Based on the speed of their sustained winds, the Saffir–Simpson Hurricane Scale (SSHS) classifies hurricanes into five categories, from 1 to 5. A category 1 hurricane is weaker than a category 2 hurricane, which is weaker than a category 3 hurricane, and so forth. In addition to the operations allowed on a nominal scale, one can determine the median (and middlemost) of a set of values and the percentiles. The Mercalli intensity scale for earthquakes and the Mankoski pain scale are also ordinal scales.

Summing and averaging a set of values on an ordinal scale (using numeric values) is an extremely common error. The numbers do not express any physical or logical quantity that can be added; they are merely a sequence of labels. It would be much more appropriate to summarize a set using the median and the range or with a histogram that shows the distribution of values.

The third type of scale is the *interval scale*. Determining the difference between two values on an interval scale is meaningful. Temperatures and clock times are measured using interval scales. An interval scale may have a zero, but it is merely relative. In addition to the operations allowed on nominal scales and ordinal scales, one can determine the mean (average) and standard deviation of a set of values on an interval scale.

The fourth type of scale is the *ratio scale*. Determining the ratio between two values on a ratio scale is meaningful. Most physical measurements and counts are ratio scales because there is an absolute zero. In addition to the operations allowed on nominal scales and ordinal scales and interval scales, one can divide values and determine the coefficient of variation of a set of values on a ratio scale.

Example 2.7   In 2012, the University of Maryland bus system (known as "Shuttle UM") used a number to identify each of 26 bus routes. The numbers, which ranged from 100 to 133, are a nominal scale. At any given time, each operating bus is on one route and has a single route number. One can determine how many buses on are a route and which route has the most operating buses (the mode of the population of operating buses). If one compares two buses, one can determine whether they are on the same route (or not), but one should not say that one bus is greater (or better) than the other based on the route numbers. It would also be meaningless to ask about the average route number or to find the ratio of two route numbers.

Suppose that Shuttle UM conducts a survey of the riders on every route. Among the questions is one in which the rider must assess the professionalism of the bus driver on a five point scale that has the following values: 5 = Excellent, 4 = Very Good, 3 = Good, 2 = Fair, and 1 = Poor. These values are an ordinal scale. Because it is possible to rank the responses (from Excellent to Poor), the Shuttle UM managers can determine each driver's minimum score on this item, maximum score, and median score from the responses of the riders. Calculating an average score is inappropriate because the differences between the values are not meaningful.

Suppose that Shuttle UM conducts a time study of the buses on one route. They measure the time at which the first bus in the morning returns to the beginning of its route every day for a month. These times are measured on an interval scale. They can determine the average return time (say, 7:51 a.m.) and the standard deviation of these times.

Finally, suppose that Shuttle UM keeps track of the number of accidents in which each bus driver has been involved. This number (a simple count) is a ratio scale, for there is an absolute zero. When comparing a driver's accident history, one can evaluate the ratio of accidents per day worked (measured on another ratio scale). If a driver had four accidents last year and two accidents the year before, one can say that the driver had twice as many accidents.

EXERCISES

2.1. Consider Boeing's selection of a new corporate headquarters in 2001 (cf. "Inside Boeing's Big Move," 2001). Which decision context best describes Boeing's selection of a new corporate headquarters?

2.2. For each of the following decision-making processes, in which decision context is it most appropriate?

  (a) Use a rule that clearly applies the same principles to every case.

  (b) Seek and analyze information from credible sources and experts and determine which alternative is best.

  (c) Look for patterns and generate new ideas before deciding what to do.

  (d) Make decisions quickly and reestablish order.

2.3. Describe the difference between a fundamental objective and a means objective.

2.4. In a *fundamental objectives hierarchy*, which of the following statements best describes the relationship between a fundamental objective (O) and the objectives (X, Y, Z) that are immediately below objective O in the hierarchy?

  (a) X, Y, and Z are fundamental objectives that are more general than objective O.

  (b) X, Y, and Z are fundamental objectives that are more specific than objective O.

(c) X, Y, and Z are means objectives that describe how to achieve objective O.

(d) X, Y, and Z are means objectives that describe why objective O is important.

2.5. In a *means objectives network*, which of the following statements best describes the relationship between an objective A and objective B if there is an arrow from A to B in the network?

(a) Objective A is a fundamental objective that is more general than objective B.

(b) Objective A is a fundamental objective that are more specific than objective B.

(c) Objective A is a means objective that describes how to achieve objective B.

(d) Objective A is a means objective that describes why objective B is important.

2.6. According to the IFRC Code of Conduct (IFRC, 2013), "The prime motivation of our response to disaster is to alleviate human suffering amongst those least able to withstand the stress caused by disaster." Based on this statement, what is the fundamental objective of disaster response?

2.7. The IFRC Code of Conduct goes on to state that "Thus, our provision of aid will reflect the degree of suffering it seeks to alleviate." Based on this statement, what is a means objective of disaster response?

2.8. Identify other means objectives in the IFRC Code of Conduct and how they relate to each other.

2.9. The following are some fundamental objectives for conducting ethical research (National Commission for the Protection of Human Subjects of Biomedical and Behavioral Research, 1979/2013). Organize these into a fundamental objectives hierarchy. Add other fundamental objectives if needed to complete your hierarchy.

- Acknowledge autonomy of subjects.
- Minimize expected physical harms to subjects.
- Maximize respect for persons.
- Minimize expected harms to subjects' families.
- Maximize efforts to secure well-being (beneficence).
- Maximize expected benefits to subjects.
- Minimize expected psychological harms to subjects.
- Maximize expected benefits to society.
- Protect those with diminished autonomy.

2.10. The following are some means objectives for conducting ethical research. Organize these into a mean objectives network. As needed, add fundamental objectives from the list of those mentioned in the previous question.

- Provide sufficient information to subjects.
- Allow informed consent.
- Avoid undue influence.
- Provide information to subjects in an appropriate manner.
- Describe risks and benefits to subjects.
- Avoid coercion.
- Minimize use of vulnerable populations.

2.11. The US Federal Motor Carrier Safety Administration planned in 2013 to issue rules that would limit the number of hours per week that truck drivers can work. The rules would reduce driver workweeks (fewer hours), restrict the number of nights that truckers can work, and require rest breaks during the day. The impacts could include keeping sleep-deprived drivers off the road, reducing crashes, preventing fatigue-related crashes, improving working conditions, reducing driver turnover, improving driver safety, saving lives, reducing injuries, and reducing fatigue-related health problems (Mitchell, 2013). What are the fundamental objectives for the government, trucking companies, and drivers? Draw a fundamental objectives hierarchy. What are the means objectives? Draw a means-objective network that shows the relationships between these objectives. (Feel free to add relevant objectives beyond those explicitly mentioned here.)

2.12. Sage (1977) listed the following factors as those that are relevant to selecting a site for a new power plant: economic factors, public approval, engineering feasibility considerations, environmental constraints, operating costs, construction costs, recreational potential, tax rates and policies, proximity to water supply, proximity to load centers, air pollution, water pollution, fuel costs, employee salaries, plant construction costs, and property acquisition costs. Formulate a set of means objectives that are related to these factors and organize as a means-objective network. (Feel free to add relevant objectives beyond those explicitly mentioned here if desired.)

2.13. This example is based on a case described by Gold (2013). Joe is considering installing solar panels on the roof of his home in Sun City, Arizona. If he goes forward, he will pay the installation firm but will save money on his electric bill. The amount he will save depends upon the amount of sun that Sun City will receive in the future, but he is not sure how many days of sun will occur. Draw an influence diagram that represents this decision situation. Include his decision, the uncertainty, and the outcome.

2.14. Consider Joe's situation again. Suppose that another uncertainty is present: Joe is not sure how much the electric utility will pay for the power that is generated by the solar panels. Draw a revised influence diagram that represents this decision situation. Include his decision, both sources of uncertainty, and the outcome.

2.15. Consider Joe's situation again. Suppose that another decision must be made: the installation firm offers a financing option in which Joe would pay them a fixed amount every month for 20 years, instead of a lump sum at the time of installation. Draw a revised influence diagram that represents this decision situation. Include both decisions, both sources of uncertainty, and the outcome.

2.16. Dyer *et al.* (1998) described the use of multiattribute utility theory to help the US government decide how to dispose of surplus weapons-grade plutonium. Thirteen alternatives were considered, and the analysts sought to identify the most desirable alternative. Which type of rationality does this approach reflect?

2.17. In 2013, the US Environmental Protection Agency (EPA) claimed that it had the authority to veto a permit for a copper mine in Alaska, but this claim was challenged by leaders in the mining industry and the US Senate, who asserted that this would violate the Clean Water Act, which states that the US Army Corps of Engineers has the authority to evaluate and issue such permits (McGroarty, 2013; Vitter and Wicker, 2013). In essence, the challengers were arguing that such a decision would be irrational. Which type of rationality would the EPA's action violate?

2.18. Explain why constructing and using a multiattribute utility function to make a decision is an example of substantive rationality.

2.19. Consider a multiple-criteria decision situation in which all the attributes (criteria) are equally important. Would using the additive linear choice strategy and using the additive difference choice strategy result in the same best alternative? Why or why not?

2.20. Consider the glass comparison example (Table 2.1). Suppose that the decision maker sets the following "acceptability" cutoff points: the strength must be at least good; the installation effort must be easy; and the cost must be no more than medium. Which type of glass could be selected using the satisficing choice strategy? Which type of glass could be selected using the disjunctive choice strategy?

2.21. Rose is hiring a new engineer for her product development team. She has a stack of resumes from the eligible candidates. She is most concerned about programming skills and teamwork skills. She compares the first two candidates by considering the difference in their programming skills and the difference in their teamwork skills and keeps the best one (the other resume is discarded). She then compares the one whom she kept and the third candidate in the same way and keeps the best again. She continues in this way until she has reviewed all the eligible candidates. Which type of choice strategy is this method?

2.22. This example is from Davidson and Fortin (2010), who compared three options for repairing flotation columns. There are five objectives (attributes): maximizing lining reliability (known is better than unknown), minimizing project costs, minimizing design complexity, minimizing installation complexity, and

TABLE 2.2 Three Plans for Repairing Flotation Columns (Davidson and Fortin, 2010).

Plan	Lining Reliability	Project Costs	Design Complexity	Installation Complexity	Maintenance Requirements
1	Unknown	High	High	High	Medium
2	Known	Medium	Low	Medium	Low
3	Unknown	Medium	Medium	Medium	Low

minimizing maintenance requirements. Table 2.2 lists the three plans and their performance on the five criteria. Does Plan 1 dominate Plan 2 or Plan 3? Does Plan 2 dominate Plan 1 or Plan 3? Does Plan 3 dominate Plan 1 or Plan 2? Which plan should be selected?

2.23. In 2009, the Department of Homeland Security (DHS) decided to locate a biological and agricultural research facility in Kansas. Six sites (in six different states) were considered, and the DHS wanted to minimize safety risk and security risk, to locate a site near an appropriate workforce and other research sites, to meet certain acquisition, construction, and operations requirements, and to locate a site in a community that would accept it. The ideal site would have low risks, be near workforce, be near research, have available acquisition, construction, and operations, and have community acceptance. Table 2.3 lists the six alternatives and their performance on the six criteria (US GAO, 2009). Do any of the sites dominate any others? Which sites, if any, are dominated?

2.24. Joe and Rose plan to send their daughter to an all-women's college. They are concerned with size (larger enrollment is better) and tuition and fees (lower is better). They are considering the colleges that are listed in Table 2.4, which includes the enrollment and tuition and fees for these colleges. Which alternatives are dominated? Which are nondominated?

TABLE 2.3 DHS's Site Rankings, Risk Ratings, and Evaluation Criteria (US GAO, 2009).

Site	Safety Risk	Security Risk	Near Workforce?	Near Research?	Available Acquisition, Construction, Operations?	Community Acceptance?
Kansas	Moderate	Acceptable	Partly	Yes	Yes	Yes
Texas	Moderate	Acceptable	Yes	Partly	Partly	Yes
Georgia	Moderate	Acceptable	Partly	Partly	Partly	Partly
Mississippi	Moderate	Acceptable	No	No	Yes	Yes
N. Carolina	Moderate	Acceptable	Yes	Yes	No	No
New York	Low	Acceptable	Partly	Partly	Partly	No

**TABLE 2.4   Enrollment and Tuition at Eight Women's
Colleges (Biemiller, 2013).**

College	Enrollment	Tuition and Fees
Agnes Scott	871	$43,133
Cedar Crest	1620	$40,357
Cottey	323	$23,100
Mary Baldwin	1783	$35,590
Notre Dame of Maryland	2929	$40,710
Pine Manor	343	$36,554
Spelman	2170	$37,974
Wilson	745	$39,850

2.25. Consider the example of the Ford engineer who had to decide whether to leave for a position at Nissan. The benefits of staying included Ford cars, health benefits, and the advantages of seniority. The benefits of the new job included more money, new opportunities, travel to Japan, a more diverse environment, and learning new skills, health benefits, and Nissan cars. Assume that the cars were equal to her and that the health benefits were equal to her. Assume that the more money and new skills (two benefits of the new job) had the same value as the advantages of seniority at Ford. Use Franklin's method to determine which is best for her. Which job should she take?

2.26. Consider again the decision situation in which Joe must decide whether to install solar panels on the roof of his house. Joe has framed this decision as a cost minimization problem: he wants to minimize the total costs. Joe's neighbors, offered the same alternatives, might view the decision differently. For instance, Rose may frame the decision as one of sustainability: which alternative is more sustainable? Louis may consider the aesthetics: are the solar panels sufficiently hidden that the appearance of his house is not significantly degraded? Why is the "frame" important in this case?

2.27. In the 10-year period from 1988 through 1997, commercial jet aircraft suffered 213 hull loss accidents (those in which the damage to the airplane is substantial) in 149.1 million departures, which was 1.43 hull loss accidents per one million departures. During the same period, 6566 persons onboard commercial jet aircraft were killed in accidents (Boeing Commercial Aircraft Group, 1998). What is the risk (fatalities per one million departures)? Is this risk acceptable?

2.28. US Food and Drug Administration (FDA) guidance recommends that manufacturers of coronary stents test "the durability of [their] stent to the equivalent of ten years of real-time use under pulsatile flow and physiologic loading that simulates blood pressure conditions in the human body" (FDA, 2010a). This 10-year guideline was chosen because FDA "believe[s] that ten years of durability data provides sufficient proof of safety of the device for most patients." Is this an absolute or relative risk acceptance criterion?

2.29. Under certain conditions, FDA rules allow a medical device manufacturer to market a medical device in the United States if the manufacturer can "demonstrate that the device to be marketed is at least as safe and effective, that is, substantially equivalent, to a legally marketed device" (FDA, 2010b). Is this an absolute or relative risk acceptance criterion?

2.30. For each of the following scales, identify whether it is a nominal scale, an ordinal scale, an interval scale, or a ratio scale:
   (a) The performance of an employee as "below expectations," "meets expectations," or "exceed expectations."
   (b) The number of hours that a truck driver works in a week.
   (c) The number of crashes by truck drivers in a month.
   (d) The numbers used to denote interstate highways in the United States: (I-10, I-70, I-75, I-95, I-275, etc.).
   (e) The time of day.
   (f) Julian dates.
   (g) The number of sunny days in Sun City, Arizona, in a given year.
   (h) The number of kilowatt hours consumed in a month by a household.
   (i) The numbers of the twelve Federal Reserve Districts.
   (j) A typical five-level Likert item: Strongly disagree, Disagree, Neither agree nor disagree, Agree, and Strongly agree.
   (k) The longitude of a location on Earth.
   (l) The Mohs scale of mineral hardness.

2.31. An undergraduate program evaluated student applicants in the following way: each member of the evaluation team rated each applicant as "excellent," "very good," "good," or "unqualified." These ratings were converted into numerical values (from 1 to 4), and the values for each applicant were summed together to generate the applicant's "total score." On which type of scale were the original ratings? On which type of scale is addition a valid operation?

2.32. Dieter and Schmidt (2012) presented the following 11-point scale for scoring the degree to which an alternative satisfies a criterion: 0 = totally useless solution, 1 = very inadequate solution; 2 = weak solution; 3 = poor solution; 4 = tolerable solution; 5 = satisfactory solution; 6 = good solution with a few drawbacks; 7 = good solution; 8 = very good solution; 9 = excellent (exceeds the requirement); 10 = ideal solution. Which type of scale is this?

2.33. Creating a House of Quality requires determining the relationships between customer requirements and engineering specifications (performance measures) and describing each relationship as strong, medium, weak, or absent. Often, the values 9, 3, 1, and 0 are used to represent these descriptions, and a weighted sum (using weights that describe the importance of the customer requirements) is calculated for each engineering specification to identify the most important ones (the ones with the largest weighted sums). Design changes that affect the most important engineering specifications should be evaluated carefully to ensure that important customer requirements are not being harmed. On which type of scale are the values of 9, 3, 1, and 0? Is the weighted sum a valid operation in this setting? Suggest a more appropriate way to identify the most important engineering specifications.

REFERENCES

Allen, B.W., editor, *New Complete Guide to Home Repair and Improvement*, Meredith Corporation, Des Moines, IA, 1997.

Aven, Terje, *Risk Analysis: Assessing Uncertainties beyond Expected Values and Probabilities*, John Wiley & Sons, Chichester, 2008.

Biemiller, Lawrence, "Armed With Data, A Women's College Tries a Transformation," *The Chronicle of Higher Education*, February 4, 2013. Online at https://chronicle.com/article/A-Womens-College-Tries-a/136969/, accessed 7 August 2013.

Boeing Commercial Aircraft Group, "Statistical Summary of Commercial Jet Airplane Accidents," Seattle, Washington, 1998.

Bozkaya, Burcin, Erhan Erkut, Dan Haight, and Gilbert Laporte, "Designing New Electoral Districts for the City of Edmonton," *Interfaces*, Volume 41, pages 534–547, 2011.

Chelst, Kenneth, and Yavuz Burak Canbolat, *Value-Added Decision Making for Managers*, CRC Press, Boca Raton, Florida, 2012.

Chen, Shahar, David Amid, Ofer M. Shir, Lior Limonad, David Boaz, Ateret Anaby-Tavor, and Tobias Schreck, "Self-organizing maps for multi-objective pareto frontiers," pages 153–160, IEEE Pacific Visualization Symposium 2013, Sydney, NSW, Australia, February 26 to March 1, 2013.

Choo, ChunWei, "Information Use and Early Warning Effectiveness: Perspectives and Prospects," *Journal of the American Society for Information Science and Technology*, Volume 60, Issue 5, pages 1071–1082, 2009.

Clemen, Robert T., and Terence Reilly, *Making Hard Decisions with Decision Tools*, Duxbury, Pacific Grove, California, 2001.

Click & Clack, "Power Crunching," *The Washington Post*, 2007.

Davidson, Thomas, and Joël Fortin, memorandum to Philippe St-Hilaire, April 12, 2010.

Dawes, R.M., and B. Corrigan, "Linear Models in Decision Making," *Psychological Bulletin*, Volume 81, pages 95–106, 1974.

Dieter, George E., and Linda C. Schmidt, *Engineering Design*, 5th edition, McGraw-Hill, Boston, 2012.

Dyer, James S., Thomas Edmunds, John C. Butler, and Jianmin Jia, "A Multiattribute Utility Analysis of Alternatives for the Disposition of Surplus Weapons-Grade Plutonium," *Operations Research*, Volume 46, Number 6, pages 749–762, 1998.

Eijgenraam, Carel, Jarl Kind, Carlijn Bak, Ruud Brekelmans, Dick den Hertog, Matthijs Duits, Kees Roos, Pieter Vermeer, Wim Juijken, "Economically Efficient Standards to Protect the Netherlands Against Flooding," *Interfaces*, Volume 44, Number 1, pages 7–21, 2014.

Feser, Edward, *Aquinas*, Oneworld Publications, Oxford, 2009.

Food & Drug Administration (FDA), "Non-Clinical Engineering Tests and Recommended Labeling for Intravascular Stents and Associated Delivery Systems," April 18, 2010a.

Food & Drug Administration (FDA), "Premarket Notification (510k)," http://www.fda. gov/MedicalDevices/DeviceRegulationandGuidance/HowtoMarketYourDevice/Premarket Submissions/PremarketNotification510k/default.htm, September 3, 2010b, accessed on July 16, 2013.

Gigerenzer, Gerd, Peter M. Todd, and the ABC Research Group, *Simple Heuristics That Make Us Smart*, Oxford University Press, New York, 1999.

Gioia, Dennis A., "Pinto fires and personal ethics: a script analysis of missed opportunities," in *The Ford Pinto Case: A Study in Applied Ethics, Business, and Technology*, Douglas Birsch and John H. Fielder, editors, State University of New York Press, Albany, New York, 1994.

Gioia, Dennis A., and Peter P. Poole, "Scripts in Organizational Behavior," *The Academy of Management Review*, Volume 9, Number 3, pages 449–459, 1984.

Gold, Russell, "Solar groups seek tea-party support," *The Wall Street Journal*, page A3, July 3, 2013.

Guy, Mary E., *Ethical Decision Making in Everyday Work Situations*, Quorum Books, New York, 1990.

Hastie, R., and R.M. Dawes, *Rational Choice in an Uncertain World*, Sage Publications, Thousand Oaks, California, 2001.

Hazelrigg, George A., *System Engineering: an Approach to Information-based Design*, Prentice Hall, Upper Saddle River, New Jersey, 1996.

Hazelrigg, George A., *Fundamentals of Decision Making for Engineering Design and Systems Engineering*, online at http://www.engineeringdecisionmaking.com/, 2012.

"Inside Boeing's Big Move," *Harvard Business Review*, Volume 79, Issue 9, pages 22–23, 2001.

International Federation of Red Cross and Red Crescent Societies (IFRC), "The Code of Conduct for The International Red Cross and Red Crescent Movement and NGOs in Disaster Relief," Online at http://www.ifrc.org/en/publications-and-reports/code-of-conduct/, accessed August 7, 2013.

Jensen, Michael C., and William H. Meckling, "The Nature of Man," *Journal of Applied Corporate Finance*, Volume 7, Number 2, pages 4–19, 1994.

Kahneman, Daniel, Paul Slovic, and Amos Tversky, *Judgment Under Uncertainty: Heuristics and Biases*, Cambridge University Press, New York, 1982.

Kalsi, Monu, Kurt Hacker, and Kemper Lewis, "A Comprehensive Robust Design Approach for Decision Trade-Offs in Complex System Design," *Journal of Mechanical Design*, Volume 123, pages 1–10, 2001.

Keeney, Ralph L., *Value-Focused Thinking: a Path to Creative Decision making*, Harvard University Press, Cambridge, Massachusetts, 1992.

Klein, Gary, "The Fiction of Optimization," in *Bounded Rationality: The Adaptive Toolbox*, G. Gigerenzer and R. Selten, editors, The MIT Press, Cambridge, Massachusetts, 2001.

Levitt, Theresa, *A Short, Bright Flash: Augustin Fresnel and the Birth of the Modern Lighthouse*, W.W. Norton & Company, New York, 2013.

Lyon, Aidan, "Philosophy of probability," in *Philosophies of the Sciences: A Guide*, Fritz Allhoff, editors, Wiley-Blackwell, Malden, Massachusetts, 2010.

McDaniels, Timothy L., "Creating and Using Objectives for Ecological Risk Assessment and Management," *Environmental Science & Policy*, Volume 3, Issue 6, Pages 299–304, 2000.

McGroarty, Daniel, "A potential copper bonanza runs afoul of the EPA," *The Wall Street Journal*, page A11, July 5, 2013.

Mitchell, Josh, "Truckers are losing sleep over 70-hour work limit," *The Wall Street Journal*, page B1, July 3, 2013.

Modarres, Mohammad, *Risk Analysis in Engineering: Techniques, Tools, and Trends*, CRC Press, Boca Raton, Florida, 2006.

"Moral Algebra," http://homepage3.nifty.com/hiway/dm/franklin.htm, accessed August 18, 2012.

National Commission for the Protection of Human Subjects of Biomedical and Behavioral Research, "Ethical Principles and Guidelines for the Protection of Human Subjects of Research," Online at http://www.hhs.gov/ohrp/humansubjects/guidance/belmont.html, April 18, 1979, accessed July 16, 2013.

Payne, John W., and James R. Bettman, "Preferential choice and adaptive strategy use," in *Bounded Rationality: The Adaptive Toolbox*, G. Gigerenzer and R. Selten, editors, The MIT Press, Cambridge, Massachusetts, 2001.

Sage, Andrew, *Methodology for Large-Scale Systems*, McGraw-Hill Book Company, New York, 1977.

Shulman, L.S., and A.S. Elstein, "Studies of Problem Solving, Judgment, and Decision Making: Implications for Educational Research," *Review of Research in Education*, Volume 3, pages 3–42, 1975.

Simon, Herbert A., "Behavioral Model of Rational Choice," *Quarterly Journal of Economics*, Volume 69, Number 1, pages 99–118, 1955.

Simon, Herbert A, "Rational decision-making in business organizations," in *Nobel Lectures, Economics* 1969–1980, A. Lindbeck, editor, World Scientific Publishing, Singapore, pages 343–371, 1978.

Simon, Herbert A., *The Sciences of the Artificial*, 2nd edition, The MIT Press, Cambridge, Massachusetts, 1981.

Simon, Herbert A., *Administrative Behavior*, 4th edition, The Free Press, New York, 1997.

Slovic, Paul, "Perception of Risk," *Science*, Volume 236, Number 4799, pages. 280–285, 1987.

Snowden, David J., and Mary E. Boone, "A Leader's Framework for Decision Making," *Harvard Business Review*, Volume 85, Issue 11, pages 69–76, 2007.

"Solar Sewing," *Mechanical Engineering*, page 14, January, 2014.

Stevens, S.S., "On the Theory of Scales of Measurement," *Science*, Volume 103, Number 2684, pages 677–680, 1946.

Stirling, Wynn C., *Satisficing Games and Decision Making*, Cambridge University Press, Cambridge, 2003.

Straker, David, *A Toolbook for Quality Improvement and Problem Solving*, Prentice Hall, London, 1995.

"Structured decision making: introduction," http://structureddecisionmaking.org/Objectives. htm, accessed August 14, 2012.

Todd, Peter M., "Fast and frugal heuristics for environmentally bounded minds," in *Bounded Rationality: The Adaptive Toolbox*, G. Gigerenzer and R. Selten, editors, The MIT Press, Cambridge, Massachusetts, 2001.

Todd, Peter M., "How Much Information Do We Need," *European Journal of Operational Research*, Volume 177, Number 3, pages 1317–1332, 2007.

Todd, Peter M., and Gerd Gigerenzer, "Bounding Rationality to the World," *Journal of Economic Psychology*, Volume 24, pages 143–165, 2003.

Todd, Peter M., and Gerd Gigerenzer, "Environments that Make us Smart: Ecological Rationality," *Current Directions in Psychological Science*, Volume 16, Number 3, pages 167–171, 2007.

Tversky, A., and D. Kahneman, "Judgment Under Uncertainty: Heuristics and Biases," *Science*, Volume 185, pages 1124–1131, 1974.

United States Government Accountability Office, "Observations on DHS's Analyses Concerning Whether FMD Research Can Be Done as Safely on the Mainland as on Plum Island," GAO-09-747, July 2009.

Vitter, David, and Roger Wicker, letter to the U.S. Environmental Protection Agency. Available online at http://www.epw.senate.gov/public/index.cfm?FuseAction=Press Room.PressReleases&ContentRecord_id=fd734426-f8c1-aa76-045c-d6f22f21117e, February 20, 2013, accessed July 12, 2013.

Walton, Mary, *Car: A Drama of the American Workplace*, W.W. Norton & Company, New York, 1997.

Yoon, K.P., and C. Hwang, *Multiple Attribute Decision Making, An Introduction*, Sage Publications, Thousand Oaks, California, 1995.

3

MULTICRITERIA DECISION MAKING

Learning Objectives:

After studying this chapter, the reader will be able to do the following:

1. Generate a Pugh matrix and use it to identify the best alternative (Section 3.1).
2. Use the AHP to identify the best alternative in an MCDM situation (Section 3.2).
3. Develop utility functions for attributes with justification (Section 3.3).
4. Construct a valid weighted linear additive utility function (Section 3.3).
5. Use MAUT to identify the best alternative in an MCDM situation (Section 3.3).
6. Analyze how the relative desirability of an alternative changes as the utility function changes (Section 3.3).
7. Use conjoint analysis to construct a preference function from data about the decision maker's choices (Section 3.4).
8. Explain how the "value of a statistical life" should be used in a decision-making situation (Section 3.5).

Engineering Decision Making and Risk Management, First Edition. Jeffrey W. Herrmann.
© 2015 John Wiley & Sons, Inc. Published 2015 by John Wiley & Sons, Inc.

9. Identify compensating and noncompensating solutions with justification (Section 3.6).

10. Develop a valid objective function that corresponds to a decision maker's preferences for compensation (Section 3.6).

When a decision maker is concerned about multiple criteria, it may be difficult to determine directly a ranking over the alternatives that have been identified. Consider, for instance, the glass selection example introduced in Chapter 2. Three criteria (which we also call "attributes") are important to Joe (the decision maker) in this context: the strength of the glass, the ease of installation, and the cost of the glass. Each type of glass can be evaluated on these three criteria. Some types of glass are stronger, some are easier to install, and some have a lower cost. Which one will Joe prefer? Of course, he would prefer a type of glass that is very strong, very easy to install, and costs very little. If he could find glass that has all three qualities, he would prefer it to any other type of glass. The situation presented in Chapter 2 is more common in practice, however: the types that cost the least are not strong, and the strongest types are expensive. Thus, it is not clear which is the best, and Joe has to make a tradeoff by considering his preferences.

Naturally, if the decision maker had another objective that was much more important, it would be useful to determine how changing the values of the attributes affects that objective and evaluate every alternative on that objective, which would simplify the problem. For example, instead of evaluating and comparing multiple alternatives for a new product (and selecting one) on the attributes of time-to-market, development cost, unit cost, and product performance, all of which affect the expected profitability of a new product, it would more relevant to estimate each alternative's expected profitability and select the most profitable one, because that is the manufacturing firm's most important financial objective. In a simpler case, the attributes may include the initial investment cost (which is spent now), the net revenue (or savings) in future years, and a future decommissioning cost. The techniques of engineering economics, based on the time value of money, allow one to convert all the expenditures and revenues in this cash flow into a net present value. The alternative with the greatest net present value has the best financial performance.

Unfortunately, there are cases in which the decision maker may not have a single most important objective or may be unable to express how the attributes that can be measured are related to the most important objective. Thus, the decision maker is left with a multicriteria decision.

In the context of designing a complicated product, multicriteria decisions occur with almost every component. For instance, when designing the Pinto, a subcompact car that was produced starting in 1971, Ford engineers were faced with a decision about the location of the fuel tank (Birsch, 1994). The two competitive alternatives were (1) placing the fuel tank above the rear axle of the car (the over-the-axle tank) and (2) placing the fuel tank underneath the trunk between the rear bumper and the rear axle (the behind-the-axle tank). The over-the-axle tank was less likely to rupture in a rear-end collision, but it required a circuitous filler pipe, which was more likely to disconnect in a collision. Moreover, it was closer to the passengers, it raised the car's center of gravity, it reduced trunk space, and it could not be used in the hatchback and station wagon versions of the car. The behind-the-axle tank was more likely to rupture in a rear-end collision, but it was not as close to the passengers. Furthermore, the behind-the-axle tank did not raise the car's center of gravity, it allowed more trunk space, and it could be used in the hatchback and station wagon versions of the car.

Based on the number of alternatives and the number of criteria, four cases of multicriteria decisions can occur, and we can identify the typical strategy for making each type of decision: (1) when the number of alternatives is small and the number of criteria is small, a decision maker may be able to compare the alternatives directly and make the tradeoffs implicitly without resorting to formal methods; (2) when the number of alternatives is small, but the number of criteria is large, a decision maker may use a method similar to Franklin's "prudential algebra" (Section 2.7) to weigh the advantages and disadvantages of the alternatives; (3) when the number of alternatives is large and the number of criteria is small, a decision maker may identify the nondominated alternatives (Section 2.5) and then make the tradeoffs implicitly without resorting to formal methods; and (4) when the number of alternatives is large and the number of criteria is large, a decision maker may use formal techniques (such as those discussed in this chapter) to identify the best alternative after comparing them on a common scale.

In this chapter, the examples will be relatively small to illustrate the approaches efficiently. As discussed in the previous paragraph, it may be possible to identify the best alternative in such situations without resorting to formal techniques. Still, these examples illustrate the most important aspect of these techniques, which is how they model the decision maker's preferences.

When the decision maker's fundamental objectives are hard to quantify, it may be useful to use surrogate metrics that are related to means objectives. It is important to choose these surrogate metrics carefully, however, because optimizing the metric that is used could lead to poor choices. For instance, one could evaluate a power tool's weight as a surrogate for its ease of use or use fuel economy (measured in miles per gallon or kilometers per liter) as a surrogate for the environmental impact of an automobile. A lightweight power tool may still be difficult to use, however, if the trigger mechanism is poorly designed or the handle is too small to grip comfortably. An automobile that gets more miles per gallon may still have a relatively large environmental impact if the advanced composites used to save weight (and improve fuel economy) require a manufacturing process that consumes a great deal of energy and emits excessive pollution.

The first four sections of this chapter cover formal multicriteria decision-making techniques: the Pugh matrix, the Analytic Hierarchy Process (AHP), multiattribute utility theory (MAUT), and conjoint analysis. No technique is ideal for every situation, and they all have limitations, as discussed in the sections below. Still, they can be useful.

Understanding how organizations make tradeoffs when human lives are at stake (Section 3.5) is an important topic, especially in policy making. Some decision makers have strong preference for (or against) compensating solutions, so being able to identify those solutions and model those preferences can improve decision making (Section 3.6).

Note that some authors use the term "multiple-criteria decision making," and others call this topic "multiattribute decision making." Despite the different terms, the key feature is that there are multiple criteria (attributes) for evaluating the alternatives. The central challenge is to specify a measure that is consistent with the decision maker's preferences about the individual criteria and the tradeoffs between the criteria. We assume that the alternatives are technologically feasible and are not illegal or unethical.

In general, we can formulate the problem as follows: Let n denote the number of alternatives; let m denote the number of criteria (attributes). For alternative i, let x_{ij} denote the value of attribute j (measured on the relevant scale).

A typical way to express a particular decision is as a table, with one row for each alternative and one column for each attribute, such as Tables 2.1–2.4 (more are given later in this chapter). Such a table presents the facts of the decision. It does not, however, express the decision maker's preferences. For each attribute, the decision maker may prefer larger values, smaller values, or values closer to a target. The "performance" of an alternative on an attribute is the relative desirability of its value on that attribute. For instance, the Standard SS and Standard DD types of glass perform well on the cost attribute because they are both low cost, which the decision maker prefers. In general, let $x_{hj} \succeq x_{ij}$ denote the fact that the decision maker prefers, for attribute j, value x_{hj} to value x_{ij} or is indifferent between them. As discussed in Chapter 2 (but with this slightly different notation), alternative h dominates alternative j if and only if $x_{hj} \succeq x_{ij}$ for every attribute $j = 1, \ldots, m$ and there exists some criteria k such that $x_{hk} \neq x_{jk}$ and the decision maker is not indifferent between them.

In addition to preferences about values for each attribute, the decision maker may prefer alternatives that have very good performance on the first attribute to those that are very good on the second attribute, or vice versa, or may prefer alternatives that have adequate performance on all the attributes to those that have very good performance on some attributes but poor performance on the others. This will be discussed more in Section 3.6.

3.1 PUGH CONCEPT SELECTION METHOD

The Pugh concept selection method is a useful way to compare alternatives when there are many attributes and little information about the performance of the alternatives on these attributes. Thus, it can be used in concept selection, where the alternatives are not completely specified (see, for instance, Dieter and Schmidt, 2012). Generating a Pugh matrix requires making only simple comparisons (worse, same, or better). Because it uses this simple scale, it ignores the strength of the decision maker's preferences about the differences. This might be acceptable when little information exists, but using this simple approach would be inappropriate when more specific information is accessible and sufficient time is available for more analysis. A Pugh matrix also ignores the importance of the attributes to the decision maker. Thus, it should be used only with attributes that are all approximately equally important to the decision maker. The decision matrix is way of organizing the strengths and weaknesses of the alternatives, which provides information to help the decision maker select one.

After the designers have generated multiple possible design concepts (the alternatives) and verified that they meet critical customer requirements, the Pugh concept selection method includes the following steps (given by Clausing, 1995):

1. Choose the criteria (attributes) by which the concepts will be evaluated.
2. Formulate the decision matrix (rows for the criteria, columns for the alternatives).
3. Clarify the design concepts (so that everyone understands them; this may also generate more good concepts).
4. Choose the datum concept from the set of alternatives. (Dieter and Schmidt recommend choosing one of the better alternatives as the datum.)
5. Compare the alternatives and the datum to complete the decision matrix. For each attribute, the decision maker compares an alternative and the datum and determines whether the alternative is better than, the same as, or worse than the datum. It is common to use the symbols "+," "=," and "−" to represent these results in the Pugh matrix, but some authors suggest +1, 0, and −1. That is, if alternative d is the datum and alternative i is the one being compared with the datum, then, for attribute j, "+" (or +1) is used if $x_{ij} \geq x_{dj}$, "−" (or −1) is used if $x_{ij} \leq x_{dj}$, and "=" (or 0) is used if both conditions are true.
6. Evaluate the ratings to see which alternatives did well. The relative value of an alternative can be estimated by the number of ways in which it is better than the datum (the number of "+" symbols) and the number of ways in which it is worse than the datum (the number of "−" symbols). An alternative with many more "+" symbols than "−" symbols can be viewed as superior to the datum. An alternative with few of either can be viewed as close to the datum. An alternative with many more "−" symbols than "+" symbols can be viewed as inferior to the datum. An alternative with many "+" symbols and "−" symbols is an interesting case, because it has not only many advantages but also many disadvantages (relative to the datum); thus, it could be seen as a compensating alternative (cf. Section 3.6). Examine the inferior alternatives and identify their good features, which could be to improve other alternatives, and their poor features, which could be improved using ideas from other alternatives.
7. Establish a new datum (the best alternative), eliminate the worst alternatives, include any new and improved alternatives, and repeat Step 5. This provides a different perspective and may identify more good features to improve the best alternative.
8. Examine the selected alternative for improvement opportunities.

TABLE 3.1   Pugh Matrix for Comparing Six Sites for a Biological and Agricultural Research Facility.

Site	New York	Kansas	Texas	Georgia	Mississippi	North Carolina
Safety risk	Datum	−	−	−	−	−
Security risk	Datum	=	=	=	=	=
Near workforce?	Datum	=	+	=	−	+
Near research?	Datum	+	=	=	−	+
Available acquisition, construction, operations?	Datum	+	=	=	+	−
Community acceptance?	Datum	+	+	+	+	=
Pluses	0	3	2	1	2	2
Minuses	0	1	1	1	3	2

Example 3.1   Consider the evaluation of the six sites for a biological and agricultural research facility (discussed in Exercise 2.23). The existing facility was in New York, so let New York be the datum. Table 3.1 shows a Pugh matrix based on the data in GAO (2009). These results imply that the Kansas and Texas sites are the superior alternatives because they have the most "+" symbols and only one "−" symbol.

Clearly, the Pugh concept selection method is limited: it uses a simple ordinal scale for each attribute and treats all the attributes the same. Still, it can be useful for eliminating inferior concepts and for identifying the good and bad features of the alternative concepts, which could be combined in some cases to generate even better alternative concepts. The process of constructing the Pugh matrix and discussing the results brings a team together to share information, generate new ideas, and build consensus. Bucciarelli (1994) described a conversation of this type by a team of engineers at a firm that designed automated color photoprinting equipment. The engineers wanted to use the Pugh method to select (from a set of 14 alternatives) a few possible concepts that would be studied in more detail. In particular, their discussions of the alternatives helped them identify the relevant criteria.

3.2   ANALYTIC HIERARCHY PROCESS

AHP is a popular approach for helping a decision maker analyze a multicriteria decision. For instance, Faulin *et al.* (2013) used AHP to select the most appropriate transportation route through a region based on economic, social, and environmental criteria. AHP is a systematic method for comparing alternatives on multiple attributes (Saaty, 1994). The three primary AHP functions are structuring complexity, measurement, and synthesis (Forman and Gass, 2001). AHP structures complexity through the use of a hierarchy, it measures judgments using a ratio scale, and it synthesizes these judgments using the hierarchy.

AHP uses an additive linear value function to model the decision maker's preferences. A decision maker uses AHP to estimate, for each attribute, the relative values of the alternatives (on that attribute) and to estimate the relative weights of the attributes.

To distinguish between the values of the attributes and the relative value used to evaluate the alternatives, we will use the term "score" to refer to these relative values. The scores are measured on a ratio scale. The scores are the relative worth (the usefulness or value to the decision maker). Because an alternative could be worthless to the decision maker, the scale has an absolute zero.

A key feature of AHP is the use of pairwise comparisons for estimating the scores and the weights. To perform a pairwise comparison, the decision maker directly compares two items and determines the ratio of their performance on a ratio scale. This simple comparison is repeated for every pair of items to yield a pairwise comparison matrix. The elements of this matrix are used to generate the relative scores (or weights) on a ratio scale. The redundancy of comparing every pair of items reduces the risk of inaccurate scores. This is similar in spirit to the practice of measuring and comparing the diagonals of a rectangular object or structure to ensure that the shape is true. In addition, relative judgments (the ratios) are generally more accurate than absolute judgments (Forman and Gass, 2001).

In particular, let S_i be the total score of alternative i. Let $s_j(x)$ be the score function for attribute j. This assigns a score based on the value of the attribute. Then,

$$S_i = \sum_{j=1}^{m} w_j s_j(x_{ij}).$$

For comparing the attributes, most texts on AHP state that one should compare the relative "importance" of the attributes. Here, however, we consider a modified approach designed specifically for multicriteria decision making (Dyer, 1990a, b, also proposed modifications to the AHP). The following paragraphs describe the steps of the procedure; an example follows to illustrate the process.

Step 1. For each attribute, form a pairwise comparison matrix with one row and one column for each distinct value of that attribute. Do not, however, include any values that the decision maker considers worthless. Each entry in the pairwise comparison matrix is the ratio of the worth of two values of that attribute. Let $x_{[h]j}$ be the hth distinct value of attribute j. Then, A_{hi}^j is the ratio of the worth of $x_{[h]j}$ to the worth of $x_{[i]j}$. Note that $A_{hi}^j = 1/A_{ih}^j$ and $A_{ii}^j = 1$ for all i.

More precisely, let S_0^j be the score of a hypothetical alternative, which has a worthless value for attribute j, let S_h^j be the score of a hypothetical alternative, which is the same as the first hypothetical alternative on every other attribute but has the value $x_{[h]j}$ for attribute j, and let S_i^j be the score of a hypothetical alternative, which is the same as the first hypothetical alternative on every other attribute but has the value $x_{[i]j}$ for attribute j. (Recall that the values $x_{[h]j}$ and $x_{[i]j}$ are not worthless.) Then,

$$A_{hi}^j = (S_h^j - S_0^j)/(S_i^j - S_0^j) = s_j(x_{[h]j})/s_j(x_{[i]j}).$$

Note that it is not necessary to determine the absolute worth of any value; the ratio is sufficient. (Traditional descriptions of the AHP recommend using odd numbers such as 1, 3, 5, 7, and 9 for the pairwise comparisons; here, however, we recommend using the positive number that best represents the decision maker's assessment of the ratio.) After completing A^j, the pairwise comparison matrix for attribute j, find the eigenvector of A^j that corresponds to an eigenvalue that is near n, the number of rows and columns. The eigenvalue λ_j will be a real root of the characteristic equation $\det(A^j - \lambda_j I) = 0$, where det is the determinant of a square matrix. The eigenvector v_j will satisfy $A^j v_j = \lambda_j v_j$. Normalize the eigenvector v_j so that the largest value in the vector equals 1. Then, the score $s_j(x_{[i]j})$ equals the ith value in the eigenvector v_j. If a value is worthless, its score equals 0.

Step 2. Create a set of hypothetical alternatives. Each hypothetical alternative has the best value for exactly one attribute (the value that corresponds to a score of 1 on that attribute) but is "worthless" on the other attributes. Thus, the number of hypothetical alternatives equals m, the number of attributes. Form a pairwise comparison matrix B with one row and one column for each hypothetical alternative. Each entry in the pairwise comparison matrix is the ratio of the worth of two hypothetical alternatives. That is, B_{hi} is the ratio of the worth of the hth hypothetical alternative to the worth of the ith hypothetical alternative. Due to the way that the hypothetical alternatives are defined, this ratio should equal w_h/w_i. (Note that traditional descriptions of the AHP recommend comparing the attributes directly based on their "importance," but considering the possible range of values on an attribute avoids problems that might occur if all the alternatives have approximately the same value on an attribute.) After completing B, find the eigenvector of B that corresponds to an eigenvalue that is near m, the number of hypothetical alternatives. The eigenvalue λ will be a real root of the characteristic equation $\det(B - \lambda I) = 0$, where det is the determinant of a square matrix. The eigenvector w will satisfy $Bw = \lambda w$. Normalize the eigenvector so that the sum of the values in the vector equals 1. Then, the attribute weight w_j is the jth value in the eigenvector.

Step 3. Combine the scores to calculate S_i for every alternative. $S_i = \sum_{j=1}^{m} w_j s_j(x_{ij})$. The alternative with the greatest total score is the most preferred alternative.

Given a pairwise comparison matrix A, one can use the elements of the eigenvector as estimates of the relative weights. Because the decision maker may be slightly inconsistent, the eigenvalue may be slightly greater than n. The difference between the eigenvalue and n increases as the pairwise comparisons become more inconsistent. Let n be the number of items being compared. The $n(n-1)/2$ pairwise comparisons are used to form a matrix A, where A_{ij} is the comparison of item i with item j. The ideal matrix A would be perfectly consistent; that is, the components of A would be the ratios of the scores $s^T = [s_1, \dots, s_n]$:

$$A_{ij} = \frac{s_i}{s_j}.$$

If this was the case, then one can easily verify that $As = ns$ and s would be an eigenvector of A corresponding to the eigenvalue n. The eigenvector is not the only way to derive the weights. If the matrix A is perfectly consistent, then taking the average of every row would also yield values proportional to the weights, and some texts recommend taking the average of every row instead of deriving the eigenvector.

One can also estimate the relative weights by taking the geometric mean of each row; if the matrix is perfectly consistent, the geometric mean will give the correct relative weights.

Although perfect consistency is not necessary, the results generated from a pairwise comparison matrix may be inappropriate if the entries of the pairwise comparison matrix are excessively inconsistent. To evaluate the consistency, Saaty (1994) proposed calculating the *consistency index* (CI) and the *consistency ratio* (CR). Given the eigenvalue λ, $CI = (\lambda - n)/(n - 1) = (\lambda - 1)/(n - 1) - 1$, and $CR = CI/RI(n)$, where $RI(n)$ is the *random index* for a matrix with n rows and columns. It is common to say that a pairwise comparison matrix is sufficiently consistent if its CR is not greater than 0.10.

Values for $RI(n)$ were calculated by Saaty by randomly generating pairwise comparison matrices and determining the corresponding CI. The calculated values are $RI(3) = 0.52$; $RI(4) = 0.89$; $RI(5) = 1.11$; $RI(6) = 1.25$; $RI(7) = 1.35$; $RI(8) = 1.4$; $RI(9) = 1.45$; and $RI(10) = 1.49$.

If a pairwise comparison matrix A has been analyzed by averaging the entries in each row, then one can estimate the eigenvalue λ. Let s be the vector of scores found by averaging the values in each row of the pairwise comparison matrix and normalizing by dividing by the greatest value (thus, the greatest value equals 1). After calculating the vector As and dividing each entry in the product As by the corresponding entry in s, the average of these ratios is an approximate eigenvalue λ. Normalizing the values in s will not change this approximate eigenvalue.

Example 3.2   Consider the selection of a two-phase cooling technology for a microprocessor cooling system. Rose (the decision maker) compared four different technologies on three attributes: temperature, power consumption, and volume required. The performance of these technologies is given in Table 3.2. Lower temperature, less power consumption, and smaller volume are preferred.

Tables 3.3–3.5 show the pairwise comparison matrices A^1, A^2, and A^3 for these three attributes. For instance, consider Table 3.5, the pairwise comparison matrix for volume, the third attribute. On this attribute, Rose determined that the worth of the volume when it equals 300 is three times the worth of the volume when it equals 600, five times the worth of the volume when it equals 700, and nine times the worth of the volume when it equals 1200. Thus, the first row of the pairwise comparison matrix is [1, 3, 5, 9]. The reciprocals of these values form the first column of the pairwise

TABLE 3.2   Four Cooling Technologies and Their Performance.

Technology	Temperature (°C)	Power (Watts)	Volume (mm^3)
Impinging jet	55	10	600
Pool boiling	65	1	1200
Air cooling	75	2	300
Flow boiling	55	10	700

TABLE 3.3   Pairwise Comparison of the Cooling Technologies' Temperatures.

Temperature (°C)	55	65	75
55	1	1.5	2
65	2/3	1	1.5
75	1/2	2/3	1

TABLE 3.4   Pairwise Comparison of the Cooling Technologies' Power.

Power (Watts)	1	2	10
1	1	1.2	9
2	5/6	1	8
10	1/9	1/8	1

TABLE 3.5   Pairwise Comparison of the Cooling Technologies' Volumes.

Volume (mm^3)	300	600	700	1200
300	1	3	5	9
600	1/3	1	2	9
700	1/5	1/2	1	7
1200	1/9	1/9	1/7	1

comparison matrix. Note that Rose also determined that the worth of the volume when it equals 600 is nine times the worth of the volume when it equals 1200. This matrix is therefore not perfectly consistent, and it has an eigenvalue that equals 4.21. The corresponding eigenvector (scaled so that the largest value equals 1) is [1, 0.44, 0.27, 0.06]. The CI of this matrix equals 0.07, and the CR equals 0.08, so the pairwise comparisons are sufficiently consistent.

Rose performed similar analyses for the other two attributes. For temperature, the eigenvector is [1, 0.69, 0.48]. The eigenvalue equals 3.00, and the CI and CR both equal 0.00 because this set of pairwise comparisons is very consistent. For power, the eigenvector is [1, 0.85, 0.11]. Again, the eigenvalue equals 3.00, and the CI and CR equal 0.00 because this set of pairwise comparisons is also very consistent.

To compare the attributes, Rose compared three hypothetical alternatives: A, B, and C. Hypothetical alternative A has superior performance (its score equals 1) on the temperature attribute, but it is worthless on the other two attributes (power and volume). Hypothetical alternative B has superior performance (its score equals 1) on the power attribute, but it is worthless on the other two attributes (temperature and volume). Hypothetical alternative C has superior performance (its score equals 1) on the volume attribute, but it is worthless on the other two attributes (temperature and power). Table 3.6 summarizes the scores of the hypothetical alternatives on the three attributes.

TABLE 3.6   Three Hypothetical Alternatives.

Hypothetical Alternative	Score for Temperature	Score for Power	Score for Volume
A	1	0	0
B	0	1	0
C	0	0	1

TABLE 3.7   Pairwise Comparison of Three Hypothetical Alternatives.

	A (Temperature)	B (Power)	C (Volume)
A (Temperature)	1	3	5
B (Power)	1/3	1	2
C (Volume)	1/5	1/2	1

As shown in Table 3.7, the pairwise comparison matrix B includes the decision maker's assessments of the relative worth of the three hypothetical alternatives. Rose stated that the worth of hypothetical alternative A is three times the worth of hypothetical alternative B, the worth of hypothetical alternative A is five times the worth of hypothetical alternative C, and the worth of hypothetical alternative B is twice the worth of hypothetical alternative C. The pairwise comparison matrix B is very consistent, and the eigenvalue equals 3.0037. The corresponding eigenvector (scaled so that its sum equals 1) is [0.65, 0.23, 0.12]. To check the consistency, note that CI = (3.0037 − 3)/2 = 0.0018. Because RI(3) = 0.52, the CR = 0.0036, which is much less than 0.10, so we have no reason to view these pairwise comparisons as unreasonably inconsistent. (Averaging the pairwise comparison values to find the weights yields the weights 0.64, 0.24, and 0.12, and the approximate eigenvalue equals 3.0049.)

Rose used these weights to combine the scores and determined the following total scores: The score for the impinging jet alternative $S_1 = 0.65(1) + 0.23(0.11) + 0.12(0.44) = 0.73$. The score for the pool boiling alternative $S_2 = 0.65(0.69) + 0.23(1) + 0.12(0.06) = 0.69$. The score for the air cooling alternative $S_3 = 0.65(0.48) + 0.23(0.85) + 0.12(1) = 0.63$. The score for the flow boiling alternative $S_4 = 0.65(1) + 0.23(0.11) + 0.12(0.27) = 0.71$. The score of the impinging jet is the best, and that alternative should be selected.

One criticism of AHP is that some versions of AHP (unlike traditional multiattribute utility approaches) determine the weights for the criteria without considering the alternatives. This can be resolved by making the decision maker consider the range of values that might occur for each criterion (when determining the relative impor tance of the criteria) and by scaling the scores on each criterion into a 0–1 scale (Dyer, 1990a, b), as the approach presented above does. This should eliminate the impact of adding or removing alternatives. Concerns about the validity of the assumptions that were used to justify the process and Saaty's definition of different types of ratio scales have been raised, and others have observed that the process can generate unexpected results (see, for instance, Schoner and Wedley, 1989; Warren, 2004). Harker and Vargas (1987) answered some objections to AHP, and later Forman and Gass (2001) and Gass (2005) reviewed the debate over the AHP but emphasized its usefulness.

3.3 MULTIATTRIBUTE UTILITY THEORY

For a general discussion of multiattribute utility functions, see Clemen and Reilly (2001). This discussion will use the term "utility functions." Note, however, that Dyer and Sarin (1979) used the term "measurable value functions" for problems with no uncertainty. They showed, however, that the value function and the utility function are the same under certain conditions. It is possible to use a value function to express the decision maker's preferences about tradeoffs between multiple attributes and a utility function to express the decision maker's preferences about risk (Nikolaidis *et al.*, 2011).

There are many works describing the application of MAUT. Edwards (1977) provided examples of using utility functions to make decisions about land use, research programs, and water quality. Dyer *et al.* (1998) and Butler *et al.* (2005) discussed the use of multiattribute utility to help officials in the United States and Russia decide how to dispose of surplus weapons-grade plutonium.

The most straightforward utility function is an additive utility function, which gives each alternative a utility on each attribute and then combines these utilities with a weighted sum to get an overall utility for that alternative. This function is valid if the corresponding tradeoff condition is satisfied (Keeney and Raiffa, 1993). Essentially, this condition states that the decision maker's preferences about changes in one attribute do not depend upon the values of the other attributes.

More complex utility functions have been used when the additive model is not an appropriate model of the decision maker's preferences. In particular, when the decision maker's preferences about the values of one attribute depend upon the value of another attribute, a multiplicative utility function may be a more appropriate model. Unfortunately, such functions have more parameters to estimate and usually require more effort to determine. For more information, see, for example, Keeney and Raiffa (1993).

An additive utility function can be expressed as follows. Let U_i be the aggregate utility of alternative i. Let $u_j(x)$ be the utility function for attribute j. This assigns a utility based on the value of the attribute. Let k_i be the weight of attribute j. Then,

$$U_i = \sum_{j=1}^{m} k_j u_j(x_{ij}).$$

The key to using this technique is to have good utility functions for each attribute and a good way to combine them. A natural starting place is to use natural metrics such as cost, profit, and wealth and performance attributes such as capacity, expected lifetime, and maximum speed.

Given a metric, the utility function must have anchors that give fixed points on the scale. If the utility function will be 0–1, where is the zero? What is a 1? Both should be specific and well-understood points. The attribute value of which the utility equals 0 can be a physical constant (similar to the freezing point of water), the current state, a worst-case scenario, or the value of a benchmark product. At the other end of the scale, the attribute value of which the utility equals 1 can be another physical constant (similar to the boiling point of water), the best case, or another benchmark (best practice). All the individual attribute utility functions should have the same direction and magnitude: 0 (worst) to 1 (best), for instance. Using a 0–1 scale for utility is not necessary, however. Changing the scale does not change the approach, just the values used; it is similar to changing the units from meter to kilometer or from degree Fahrenheit to degree Celsius.

When using a 0–1 scale, it is beneficial to have utility functions in which the utility of values near the worst and best plausible outcomes are close to 0 and 1. This makes distinguishing between outcomes easier. For instance, if the utility of absolute zero equals 0 and the utility of the temperature of the surface of the sun (say, 6000 K) equals 1, the utility of most outcomes on temperature will be very close to each other, which does not help the decision maker.

An exponential function is a common utility function to map values in the interval $[a, b]$ to the range $[0, 1]$. Let γ be the shape parameter for the utility function. Then, if the utility increases from 0 to 1 as x increases from a to b

$$u(x) = \frac{1 - e^{-\gamma(x-a)}}{1 - e^{-\gamma(b-a)}}.$$

As γ approaches 0, this function becomes nearly linear; $u(x) = (x - a)/(b - a)$ is the linear function. If γ is positive, then the increase in utility (the marginal utility) decreases as x increases. If γ is negative, then the increase in utility (the marginal utility) increases as x increases. Assessing the utility of a value of x somewhere between a and b will provide enough data to determine the value of γ. In particular, if the decision maker can assess the utility u' of the point $x' = (a + b)/2$, which is in the middle of the range, then one can immediately find the value of γ:

$$\gamma = \frac{2}{b - a} \ln\left(\frac{u'}{1 - u'}\right).$$

Example 3.3 Consider an increasing exponential utility function over the range $[100, 150]$. By definition, $u(100) = 0$, and $u(150) = 1$. If the decision maker determines that the utility of the value 125 equals 0.7, then $\gamma = 0.034$.

Combining individual attribute utility functions requires a way to give weights to the different utility functions, and there are many such techniques (see, e.g., Clemen and Reilly, 2001). The idea of swing weighting is to compare some hypothetical alternatives that make clear the decision maker's preferences about the attributes. Here we assume that, for each attribute, the utility of the best plausible value equals 1, and the utility of the worst plausible value equals 0.

1. Let m be the number of attributes. Define $m + 1$ hypothetical alternatives as follows. For $i = 1$ to m, the performance of hypothetical alternative i on all the attributes (except attribute i) is the worst plausible (the utility equals 0); on attribute i, its performance is the best plausible (the utility equals 1). Thus, each hypothetical alternative corresponds to exactly one attribute. The performance of hypothetical alternative 0 (the "benchmark") on all the attributes is the worst plausible.

2. Rank the $m + 1$ hypothetical alternatives from the most desirable to the least desirable. The least desirable will certainly be the benchmark (which performs poorly on every attribute).

3. Give the hypothetical alternatives ratings from 0 (for the least desirable) to 100 (for the most desirable of these hypothetical alternatives). These ratings should be consistent with the rankings. That is, if hypothetical alternative i is ranked ahead of hypothetical alternative j, the rating of hypothetical alternative i should be greater than that of hypothetical alternative j. As discussed below, a choice between hypothetical lotteries can be used to determine these ratings.

4. Sum the ratings, and divide each rating by this sum to determine the aggregate utility of the hypothetical alternatives. The weight k_i for attribute i equals the aggregate utility of hypothetical alternative i.

Because the hypothetical alternatives are carefully constructed so that the aggregate utility of hypothetical alternative i equals k_i, this method yields the relevant weights directly. This procedure finds the aggregate utilities of the hypothetical alternatives and uses this data to determine the attribute weights.

Kirkwood (1997) suggested that the decision maker consider the increases in value that changing each attribute yields. In particular, there are m increases in utility; each one is the increase in utility from the least desirable hypothetical alternative to one of the m hypothetical alternatives. Kirkwood advised the decision maker to identify the increase that has the least value and then determine the relative utility of every other increase as a multiple of the smallest increase (this is a type of pairwise comparison in which ratios are directly assessed, as they are in AHP). The weights for the attributes should be proportional to the utilities of the corresponding increases, so enforcing the constraint that the sum of the utilities of the increases equals 1 leads to a set of simple linear equations that can be solved to determine the weights.

It is important to note that an attribute's weight is not the overall or fundamental importance of that attribute; instead, it represents the importance of the change (or "swing") in that attribute from the worst value being considered to the best value being considered. If all the alternatives have nearly the same value for the most important attribute, then the change in that attribute will be relatively less important, and the attribute will have a relatively small weight.

"Pricing out" is an alternative technique for determining the weights on multiple criteria (Clemen and Reilly, 2001). The decision maker determines how much of one attribute he would give up to increase another attribute. For instance, if the decision maker wants to minimize cost and time, he should be asked, "How much would you be willing to spend to reduce the time to complete the project by 1 month?" This provides the information needed to create a multiattribute utility function over cost and time. Unfortunately, this technique can be difficult to use when considering changes in utility values.

Example 3.4 Consider again the decision discussed in Example 3.2: the selection of a two-phase cooling technology for a microprocessor cooling system. According to Louis (the decision maker in this case), the performance of the different technologies have the utilities shown in Table 3.8. (These were assessed directly; attribute utility functions were not generated in this case.)

Because there are $m = 3$ attributes, the swing weighting procedure created $m + 1 = 4$ hypothetical alternatives (listed in Table 3.9). Louis preferred lower temperature, less power consumption, and smaller volume. He ranked the hypothetical alternatives as follows: A(best), B, C, and D(worst). Then, he gave the hypothetical alternatives the following ratings: 100, 30, 20, and 0. Because the sum of these ratings was 150, the aggregate utilities of the hypothetical alternatives are 0.667, 0.2, 0.133, and 0. Thus, the weights for temperature, power, and volume are 0.667, 0.2, and 0.133, respectively, and the aggregate utility function is the following expression:

$$U_i = 0.667u_1(x_{i1}) + 0.2u_2(x_{i2}) + 0.133u_3(x_{i3}).$$

This utility function can be used to calculate the aggregate utility of the actual alternatives, which yields the following values: the total utility of the impinging jet $U_1 = 0.667 \times 1 + 0.2 \times 0 + 0.133 \times 0.7 = 0.760$, the total utility of pool boiling $U_2 = 0.667 \times 1 + 0.2 \times 1 + 0.133 \times 0 = 0.867$, the total utility of air cooling $U_3 = 0.667 \times 0.9 + 0.2 \times 0.9 + 0.133 \times 1 = 0.913$, and total utility of flow boiling $U_4 = 0.667 \times 1 + 0.2 \times 0 + 0.133 \times 0.6 = 0.747$. Thus, if these values represent his preferences accurately, Louis should choose the air cooling technology.

TABLE 3.8 Four Cooling Technologies and Their Utilities.

Technology	Temperature	Power	Volume
Impinging jet	1	0	0.7
Pool boiling	1	1	0
Air cooling	0.9	0.9	1
Flow boiling	1	0	0.6

TABLE 3.9 Four Hypothetical Cooling Technologies and Their Performance.

Alternative	Temperature	Power	Volume
A	55	10	1200
B	120	1	1200
C	120	10	300
D	120	10	1200

A choice between hypothetical lotteries can be used to determine a decision maker's utility for an attribute value or a hypothetical alternative. The basic idea is to setup a choice between two options. The first option is a sure thing: the decision maker will certainly get the alternative with the unknown utility. The second option is a lottery between two alternatives; one alternative has a utility that is known and high and the other has a known low utility. The probability of receiving the high utility alternative is varied until the decision maker is indifferent between the sure thing and the lottery. At this point, the utility of the sure thing must equal the expected utility of the lottery, which can be calculated.

Example 3.5 Consider again the decision discussed in Example 3.4: the selection of a two-phase cooling technology for a microprocessor cooling system. Under the assumptions that make an additive utility function appropriate, one can determine the utility of the values of one attribute independently of the utility of the values of the other attributes. Consider, for instance, the volume attribute. The value of 300 is the best volume, so $u_3(300) = 1$. The value of 1200 is the worst volume, so $u_3(1200) = 0$. Now, setup the following choice: the first option is a sure thing: Louis will certainly get a cooling technology with volume equals 600 (this has unknown utility). The second option is a lottery between two alternatives; one alternative is a cooling technology with volume equals 300 (the utility of which equals 1) and a cooling technology with volume equals 1200 (the utility of which equals 0). (The cooling technologies are alike in every other way.) Let p be the probability of getting the low-volume (high-utility) cooling technology. Then, the probability of getting the high-volume (low-utility) cooling technology equals $1 - p$.

When p is very close to 1, then Louis is highly likely to get the low-volume cooling technology, which he prefers to the cooling technology with volume equals 600, so he will choose the lottery. On the other hand, when p is very close to 0, then the decision maker is highly likely to get the high-volume cooling technology, but he prefers the cooling technology with volume equals 600, so he will reject the lottery and choose the sure thing. There is a value of p between 0 and 1 that makes the decision maker indifferent between the two choices. For any smaller value, he will prefer the sure thing, and for any larger value, he will prefer the lottery. At this point, the utility of the sure thing must equal the expected utility of the lottery. That is, $u_3(600) = p \times u_3(300) + (1 - p) \times u_3(1200) = p$.

This procedure can be repeated by replacing the cooling technology with volume equals 600 with a cooling technology with volume equals 700. This is less desirable, so the value of p at which Louis is indifferent between the two choices will be smaller.

When comparing the hypothetical alternatives created to determine the weights, a similar procedure can be used. In this example, let U_A, U_B, U_C, U_D be the utilities of the four hypothetical alternatives. Because D has the worst values on every attribute, $U_D = 0$. The other utilities are unknown, but, because they are equal to the weights, their sum should equal 1. That is, $U_A + U_B + U_C = 1$. Without loss of generality, assume that the decision maker prefers hypothetical alternative A to any of the other hypothetical alternatives; thus, $U_A > U_B$ and $U_A > U_C$.

Create a choice between hypothetical alternative B and a lottery over hypothetical alternatives A and D. Let p' be the probability at which the decision maker is indifferent between the two choices. Thus, $U_B = p' \times U_A + (1 - p') \times U_D = p' \times U_A$. In a similar way, create a choice between hypothetical alternative C and a lottery over hypothetical alternatives A and D. Let p'' be the probability at which the decision maker is indifferent between the two choices. Thus, $U_C = p'' \times U_A + (1 - p'') \times U_D = p'' \times U_A$. (If the decision involved more attributes and more hypothetical alternatives, additional choices would be required to determine additional relationships, but the approach remains the same.)

After substituting these expressions into the constraint on the sum, solving for U_A yields the following expressions that can be used to determine the utilities of the hypothetical alternatives, which are the weights for the attributes:

$$U_A + U_B + U_C = 1$$
$$U_A + p'U_A + p''U_A = 1$$
$$U_A = 1/(1 + p' + p'')$$
$$U_B = p'/(1 + p' + p'')$$
$$U_C = p''/(1 + p' + p'').$$

3.4   CONJOINT ANALYSIS

The AHP and MAUT approaches construct a function that represents the decision maker's preferences by identifying functions for each attribute and then combining these attribute-level functions to form the complete function over all the attributes.

Conjoint analysis, in contrast, is a decompositional approach that begins by creating a complete function that represents the decision maker's preferences (Green and Srinivasan, 1978). The term "conjoint" refers to the fact that the approach looks at the joint effect of the attributes. Conjoint analysis looks at the decision maker's preferences for complete choices (that specify values for all the attributes) and then analyzes these data to construct a complete function that includes functions for every attribute and the importance weights of these attributes.

In general, a conjoint analysis proceeds through the following steps (Green and Srinivasan, 1978):

1. Select a model that specifies the structure of the preference function.
2. Select a method for collecting data about the decision maker's preferences.
3. Construct a stimulus set (an appropriate set of choices).
4. Present the stimuli to the decision maker.
5. Construct a measurement scale to describe the decision maker's preferences.
6. Estimate the parameters of the preference function.

Conjoint analysis is an important technique in the area of marketing research, where it is used to identify heterogeneity within a market and to estimate the utility functions of the consumers in the market so that firms can predict the desirability and profitability of their products. The popularity of conjoint analysis has led to a wide variety of techniques that are focused on marketing applications.

Marriott International used a large conjoint analysis study during the development of its Courtyard by Marriott hotel chain (Green *et al.*, 2001). Marriott was targeting business travelers, and the study included 50 attributes in the areas of price, external décor, room décor, food service, lounge facilities, general services, leisure activities, and security features. Survey participants were shown pictures, three-dimensional models, and prototype rooms as cues for their responses. Marriott used the results to guide its design choices. The first Courtyard opened in 1983, and, by 2012, there were over 900 Courtyards in 37 countries (Marriott International, 2012).

Conjoint analysis is appropriate for constructing a preference function over the ranges of attributes where the decision maker will make tradeoffs (giving up a little on one attribute to get more of another). It would be inappropriate to construct a preference function over values that are completely unacceptable to the decision maker.

For details about the different techniques that have been used, see, for example, Green and Srinivasan (1978), Lenk *et al.* (1996), Allenby *et al.* (2005/2013), Grissom *et al.* (2006), Orme (2006), Abernethy *et al.* (2008), and Resende *et al.* (2012).

Conjoint analysis has been used to model the preferences of an individual decision maker. Example 3.6, which is adapted from one in Orme (2006), shows one way to do this.

Example 3.6   There is a generic "product" that has three important attributes: brand, color, and price. There are three distinct brands (A, B, and C) and two different colors (red and blue). Price can range between \$50 and \$150. The decision maker is given nine different hypothetical versions of this product. Each version is described by its brand, its color, and one of the three prices (\$50, \$100, and \$150). The decision maker considered the nine choices and gave each one a rating on a scale from 0 (least preferred) to 10 (most preferred). The conjoint analysis procedure treats this degree of preference as an interval scale, but this assumption is difficult to justify because there is no technique for measuring this degree of preference. It would be reasonable to determine the relative value of the hypothetical alternatives using the techniques discussed in Sections 3.2 and 3.3.

Dummy coding converts the discrete values of the attributes into separate binary variables. Each binary variable represents the presence of a "feature" (a specific brand, color, or price). To eliminate confounded variables, one binary variable for each attribute is dropped. This leaves five binary variables ($x_B, x_C, x_{blue}, x_{100}, x_{150}$) that represent the presence of B, C, blue, \$100, and \$150, respectively.

This analysis assumes that the preference function is a linear function over these binary variables. Thus, it has six parameters that must be estimated. Let Y be the preference for the alternative, b_0 be the constant (intercept), b_1, b_2, b_3, b_4, b_5 be the coefficients of the binary variables, and e be the error term:

$$Y = b_0 + b_1 x_B + b_2 x_C + b_3 x_{blue} + b_4 x_{100} + b_5 x_{150} + e.$$

Given the ratings shown in Table 3.10, one can use linear ordinary least squares regression to find the parameters. The results are the following coefficients:

$$b_0 = 5.11$$
$$b_1 = 2.33$$
$$b_2 = 3.00$$
$$b_3 = 1.17$$
$$b_4 = -2.00$$
$$b_5 = -3.67.$$

The coefficient of determination $R^2 = 0.96$, which indicates that the points fit the linear function well. The utility of each attribute value equals the coefficient of the corresponding binary variable, whereas the utility of any attribute value that was excluded equals 0. Thus, it appears that the decision maker prefers brand C (which has a utility of 3.00) to brands B (which has a utility of 2.33) and A (which has a utility of 0) and prefers the color blue (which has a utility of 1.17) to red (which has a utility of 0). Naturally, the decision maker prefers a $50 price (which has a utility of 0) to $100 and $150 (which have negative utilities).

The decision maker can use this function to evaluate and compare other alternatives. The utilities of the different brands and colors are specified, and the utility of a price can be determined by interpolating between the specified values.

Not all conjoint analysis techniques require rating alternatives on a scale. Choice-based conjoint analysis (also known as discrete choice analysis) can construct a preference function from data about the decision maker's choices without

TABLE 3.10   Hypothetical Alternatives Rated in a Conjoint Analysis.

Alternative	Brand	Color	Price	Rating
1	A	Red	$50	5
2	A	Blue	$100	5
3	A	Blue	$150	2
4	B	Blue	$50	9
5	B	Red	$100	5
6	B	Blue	$150	5
7	C	Blue	$50	9
8	C	Blue	$100	7
9	C	Red	$150	5

using a rating scale. The decision maker is given two (or more) alternatives at a time and asked to identify the preferred one. A set of responses over a sufficiently diverse set of pairs yields the data needed to construct a preference function. Although the technique is inefficient compared with other conjoint analysis techniques, it should be reasonable if there is only one decision maker to model. Logit, latent class, and hierarchical Bayes analysis techniques can be used to estimate the preference function (Orme, 2006).

3.5   VALUE OF A STATISTICAL LIFE

A particularly interesting (and somewhat controversial) issue in multicriteria decision making appears when one of the attributes is the number of lives saved (due to a new safety regulation or new safety features) and another is the expected cost. Clearly, most decision makers want to maximize the number of lives saved and minimize the expected cost. However, the safety regulations (features) that save the most lives often cost the most. In some cases, the decision alternatives are to (1) do nothing (which saves no one and costs nothing) or (2) adopt the safety regulation (which saves some lives but costs something). Should the safety regulation be adopted or not?

Note that this discussion is not relevant to decisions in which one particular person's life is directly at risk. Instead, it is relevant to decisions that could make small changes to the mortality risk of large numbers of people (National Center for Environmental Economics, 2013).

To approach this issue, it is useful to note that many people make decisions about whether or not to spend money to reduce the likelihood of dying. For instance, someone looking for a new car may consider spending more to buy a safer car. Homeowners purchase and install new smoke detectors in their houses. The typical person does not explicitly quantify the value of a life; they implicitly weigh the reduced risk versus the cost and make a decision.

Government agencies, however, cannot make these decisions implicitly. They must use explicit criteria. The advantages of using explicit criteria include increasing the transparency of the decision (i.e., people can better understand the rationale for the decision) and the consistency of the agency's decisions. Moreover, it can help them spend a limited amount of money on the activities that will have the most benefit.

Government agencies may do a cost–benefit analysis in these cases. For instance, the Environmental Protection Agency (EPA), like other government agencies, must decide whether the benefits of a new program or regulation are worth the cost. Consider a case in which the agency predicts that a regulation will cost $120 million but will save 100 lives. Is this benefit worth the cost?

One way to answer that question is to translate the expected reduction in mortality (the 100 lives saved) to a monetary value using the value of a statistical life (VSL). In 2004, the EPA adopted a value of about $7,200,000 for its VSL. (This value has changed over time and is adjusted for inflation.) Using this VSL, one can state that the benefit is equivalent to 100 times $7.2 million, which equals $720 million, which is greater than the cost. If the benefit were only 10 lives (equivalent to $72 million), then one would state that the benefit is not worth the cost.

There are many methods for determining an appropriate value for a VSL (Dockins *et al.*, 2004). The following excerpt describes the process: "Researchers try to figure out how much money it takes for people to accept slightly bigger risks, such as a more dangerous job. They also look at how much people will pay to make their daily risks smaller—such as buying a bicycle helmet or a safer car. 'How much are you willing to pay for a small reduction … in the probability that you will die?' asked Joe Aldy, a fellow at the Washington-based think tank Resources for the Future. The rest is more or less multiplication: If someone will accept a 1-in-10,000 chance of death for $500, then the value of life must be 10,000 times $500, or $5 million" (Fahrenthold, 2008).

3.6 COMPENSATION

Many decision methods use linear functions to evaluate the overall value (utility) of alternatives because such functions are easier to assess and use. Linear functions, however, may fail to capture the decision maker's preferences about compensation.

In general, in a multicriteria decision, each alternative has a degree of compensation. An alternative may be a compensating solution because great performance on one attribute compensates for poor performance on another. Another alternative may be a noncompensating solution because it has good performance on every attribute.

Example 3.7 Consider selecting a car from a car rental company. The first choice is a dependable subcompact that should deliver great mileage and sturdy construction for only $19 per day. The second choice is a full-size sedan that has plenty of room and many great features for $24 per day. And the third choice is a sports car with "futuristic styling" that "promises a fun ride" for $40 per day.

In this case, the subcompact and the sports car are compensating solutions. The low price of the subcompact compensates for its small size and poor horsepower, whereas the styling and performance of the sports car compensate for its high price. The sedan, which has a moderate price, space, and performance, is a noncompensating solution.

Example 3.8 A more subtle preference for compensating solutions appeared in the 2012 Olympic Games. In the women's gymnastics all-around finals, two women (Aly Raisman and Aliya Mustafina) tied for third place with the same total score (59.566). Raisman's scores on the vault, uneven bars, balance beam, and floor exercise were 15.900, 14.333, 14.200, and 15.133. Mustafina's scores were 15.233, 16.100, 13.633, and 14.600. The tie-breaker procedure dropped each gymnast's lowest score. Because Raisman's lowest score (14.200) was higher than Mustafina's lowest score (13.633), Raisman's new total (45.466) was lower than Mustafina's new total (45.933). Mustafina won the bronze medal (third place) because her high score on the uneven bars (16.100) compensated for her low score on the balance beam (13.633). By dropping the lowest score, the tie-breaker procedure rewarded the compensating solution.

Scott and Antonsson (2005) presented a way to consider aggregate utility and the degree of compensation. This discussion is for only two criteria, measured using 0–1 utility functions, where more utility is preferred, but the approach can be generalized to more criteria.

Given weights w_1 and w_2 (both non-negative with a positive sum) and a compensation parameter s, then the aggregate utility $P_s(u_1, u_2; w_1, w_2)$ of an alternative that has utility u_1 and u_2 is determined as follows:

$$P_s(u_1, u_2; w_1, w_2) = \left(\frac{w_1 u_1^s + w_2 u_2^s}{w_1 + w_2} \right)^{1/s}.$$

As the parameter $s \to -\infty$, this function becomes the minimum:

$$P_{-\infty}(u_1, u_2; w_1, w_2) = \min\{u_1, u_2\}.$$

As $s \to 0$, then this function approaches the geometric mean:

$$P_0(u_1, u_2; w_1, w_2) = (u_1^{w_1} u_2^{w_2})^{1/(w_1 + w_2)}.$$

With $w_1 = w_2 = 0.5$ and $s = 0$:

$$P_0(u_1, u_2; w_1, w_2) = \sqrt{u_1 u_2}.$$

If $s = 1$, the function is the weighted sum:

$$P_1(u_1, u_2; w_1, w_2) = \left(\frac{w_1 u_1 + w_2 u_2}{w_1 + w_2} \right).$$

As the parameter $s \to \infty$, this function approaches the maximum:

$$P_{+\infty}(u_1, u_2; w_1, w_2) = \max\{u_1, u_2\}.$$

Changing s changes the relative desirability of a noncompensating solution. A larger value of s means that the decision maker prefers more compensation: a compensating solution with great performance on one attribute compensates for poor performance on the other. This may be good when getting something "special" is very important because of its uniqueness or extreme qualities. A noncompensating solution is desirable if it has good performance on all the attributes, which may be good for groups.

Table 3.11 shows the aggregate utility for three solutions under three different values of s when $w_1 = 0.4$ and $w_2 = 0.6$. Note that the aggregate utility of the extreme points changes significantly as the compensation factor s changes. A low value of s causes the compensating solutions to be less desirable than the noncompensating

TABLE 3.11 The Aggregate Utility $P_s(u_1,u_2;w_1,w_2)$ for Three Solutions Under Three Different Values of s ($w_1 = 0.4$ and $w_2 = 0.6$).

(u_1,u_2)	$s=-1$	$s=1$	$s=2$
(0.94, 0.08)	0.126	0.424	0.598
(0.51, 0.41)	0.444	0.450	0.453
(0.01, 0.99)	0.024	0.598	0.767

one. At $s = 1$, the compensating solutions and the noncompensating one are about the same. A high value of s causes the compensating solutions to be more desirable than the noncompensating one.

Scott and Antonsson (2005) showed that, for a given set of nondominated alternatives and a specific alternative in that set, there is a specific combination of values for s, w_1, and w_2 that makes that alternative optimal. That is, it is possible to choose a ratio of weights and a degree of compensation to select any particular nondominated point.

To assess the aggregate utility function P, given the individual attribute utility functions, the following procedure can be used. First, the decision maker needs to consider four hypothetical alternatives:

Alternative A has $u_1 = 0$ and $u_2 = 0$.
Alternative B has $u_1 = 1$ and $u_2 = 0.1$.
Alternative C has $u_1 = 0.1$ and $u_2 = 1$.
Alternative D has $u_1 = 1$ and $u_2 = 1$.

Let $P(A) = 0$ and $P(D) = 1$. Assume, without loss of generality, that $w_1 + w_2 = 1$. Then, the decision maker must assess the utility of alternatives B and C; let $b = P(B)$ and $c = P(C)$. (Note that both b and c should be greater than 0.1 because the aggregate utility of an alternative with $u_1 = 0.1$ and $u_2 = 0.1$ must equal 0.1, and both alternatives B and C dominate such an alternative.) If $s = 0$, then bc should equal 0.1. If bc does not equal 0.1, then s is not 0. Then, from the definition of P, we know the following:

$$(w_1 1^s + w_2 0.1^s)^{1/s} = b.$$
$$(w_1 0.1^s + w_2 1^s)^{1/s} = c.$$

We can combine these equations to eliminate the weights (because their sum equals 1) and find that $1 + 0.1^s = b^s + c^s$. If there is a nonzero value of s that solves this equation, then we can find the weights as follows:

$$w_1 = (b^s - 0.1^s)/(1 - 0.1^s).$$
$$w_2 = (c^s - 0.1^s)/(1 - 0.1^s).$$

These values of s, w_1, and w_2 model the decision maker's preferences and can be used to determine the aggregate utility of the alternatives.

If no nonzero value of s solves the equation, then s must be 0. In that case,

$$P_0(u_1, u_2; w_1, w_2) = (u_1^{w_1} u_2^{w_2})^{1/(w_1 + w_2)}.$$

Because $w_1 + w_2 = 1$, we can determine the weights as follows:

$$w_1 = \ln c / \ln 0.1.$$
$$w_2 = \ln b / \ln 0.1.$$

Example 3.9 For instance, suppose $b = P(B) = 0.5$ and $c = P(C) = 0.8$. Because bc does not equal 0.1, s is not 0. Solving $1 + 0.1^s = b^s + c^s$ yields $s = 1.6$. Then, $w_1 = 0.31$ and $w_2 = 0.69$, and the aggregate utility function is $P_s(u_1, u_2) = (0.31u_1^{1.6} + 0.69u_2^{1.6})^{1/1.6}$.

3.7 THE IMPACT OF CHANGING WEIGHTS

The set of weights used to express the relative importance of different attributes is a critical component of a multicriteria decision-making method. It is natural to wonder how changes to these weights would influence the results of a method (the scores of the alternatives that are being considered). Exploring this question is a type of sensitivity analysis.

The simplest sensitivity analysis is to vary the weights by small amounts (while enforcing the constraint that the sum of the weights equals 1) and determine which alternatives have the highest score. If the same alternative always has the highest score, the decision maker's confidence in the alternative should increase because its superiority is robust.

One approach is to vary the weights over all possible combinations and, for each combination, determine the scores of the alternatives and identify the alternative with the highest score. The space of all combinations can be then divided into regions, where each region is the set of combinations in which one alternative has the highest score. Dyer *et al.* (1998) generated this type of *policy map* as part of their analysis of the alternatives for disposing of surplus weapons-grade plutonium.

If the number of attributes is large, an exhaustive search can be time consuming. In such cases, a Monte Carlo approach that randomly selects combinations of weights can give some insight into the conditions under which different alternatives have the highest score. To generate combinations of m weights according to a uniform distribution over the space of feasible weights, first randomly select $m - 1$ values according to a uniform distribution over the interval $[0, 1]$ and list these from smallest to largest. Then add the value 0 to the beginning of the list and the value 1 to the end of the list. The m differences between consecutive values in this list are a feasible combination of weights (they sum to 1 and are non-negative) from the uniform distribution (Devroye, 1986). Butler *et al.* (1997) demonstrated this approach for multiattribute decisions.

If the number of attributes is small and the number of competitive alternatives is small, it may be feasible to determine analytically the regions in which each alternative has the highest score. Let v_{ij} be the score (or utility) of alternative i on attribute j. Let V_i be the total score (or aggregate utility) of alternative i.

$$V_i = \sum_{j=1}^{m} w_j v_{ij}.$$

Then, alternative i has the highest score for weights $(w_1, \ldots, w_m)$ if the following is true for all other alternatives $h = 1, \ldots, n$ but $h \neq i$:

$$\sum_{j=1}^{m} w_j v_{ij} \geq \sum_{j=1}^{m} w_j v_{hj}.$$

Example 3.10   Consider the decision considered in Example 3.4: the selection of a two-phase cooling technology for a microprocessor cooling system. One can determine the range of weights for which the air cooling technology has the greatest aggregate utility as follows. Note also that $w_3 = 1 - w_1 - w_2$.

First, the aggregate utility of air cooling will be greater than or equal to the aggregate utility of impinging jet if and only if the following is true:

$$0.9w_1 + 0.9w_2 + w_3 \geq w_1 + 0.7w_3.$$

In addition, the aggregate utility of air cooling will be greater than or equal to the aggregate utility of pool boiling if and only if the following is true:

$$0.9w_1 + 0.9w_2 + w_3 \geq w_1 + w_2.$$

Finally, the aggregate utility of impinging jet will be greater than or equal to the aggregate utility of pool boiling if and only if the following is true:

$$w_1 + 0.7w_3 \geq w_1 + w_2.$$

After substituting to remove w_3 and rearranging terms, the above constraints are equivalent to the following:

$$-4w_1 + 6w_2 \geq -3$$
$$1.1w_1 + 1.1w_2 \leq 1$$
$$7w_1 + 17w_2 \leq 7.$$

The regions in which each alternative two-phase cooling technology has the greatest aggregate utility are shown in Figure 3.1. The boundaries are segments of the specific constraints given above and the general constraints that both weights

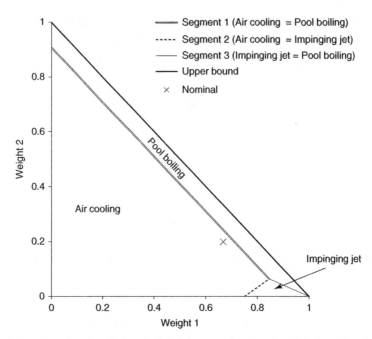

Figure 3.1 The regions in which each alternative two-phase cooling technology has the greatest aggregate utility. Weight 1 is w_1, the weight for the temperature attribute; weight 2 is w_2, the weight for the power attribute.

must be non-negative, and their sum must be less than or equal to 1. When $(w_1, w_2, w_3) = \left(\frac{93}{110}, \frac{7}{110}, \frac{10}{110} \right)$, then all three alternatives have the same aggregate utility. Note that the nominal weights, where air cooling has the greatest aggregate utility, are close to the boundary with the region where pool boiling has the greatest aggregate utility. If the first two weights (the weights for the temperature and power attributes) increased (and the weight for the volume attribute decreased), then pool boiling would have the greatest aggregate utility. The fact that the region in which air cooling has the greatest aggregate utility is the largest region does not imply that air cooling is the best alternative. The relative desirability of the alternatives depends upon the decision maker's preferences.

EXERCISES

3.1. In Fiscal Year 2011, the US Patent and Trademark Office (USPTO) began offering "prioritized examination," a procedure for expedited review of a patent application. An additional fee of $4800 is charged for prioritized examination; if the applicant is a small business, the additional fee is $2400. According to the USPTO, "The Office's goal for prioritized examination is to provide a final disposition within 12 months of prioritized status being granted" (USPTO, 2012).

Consider someone who plans to apply for a patent. Which criteria should be considered when deciding whether to pay for prioritized examination?

3.2. In 2010, the National Highway Traffic Safety Administration (NHTSA) proposed a rule to expand federal requirements for rear visibility in passenger cars, trucks, and other motor vehicles. This rule, when enforced, would effectively require manufacturers to equip every new car sold in the United States with a rear-mounted video camera and an in-vehicle visual display. The regulations are intended to decrease accidents in which vehicles back over people who are immediately behind the vehicle and not visible to the driver. On average, 228 people are killed in back-over accidents (Lowy, 2013), but the NHTSA estimated that the total cost to consumers would be $1.9–$2.7 billion per year and that the benefits include avoiding 95–112 fatalities and 7072–8374 injuries per year (DOT, 2013). Assume that $7,200,000 is an appropriate VSL. Is the benefit (saving 100 lives a year) worth the cost ($1.9–$2.7 billion a year)?

3.3. The US Federal Motor Carrier Safety Administration planned in 2013 to issue rules that would limit the number of hours per week that truck drivers can work; the agency estimates that the rules will cost the trucking industry $500 million per year and will save 19 lives per year (Mitchell, 2013). Assume that $7,200,000 is an appropriate VSL. Is the benefit (saving 19 lives a year) worth the cost ($500 million a year)?

3.4. Proposed EU legislation would prohibit "beaching" old EU-flag ships, which is done to dismantle them and recover scrap metal and other valuable components; instead, ships would be dismantled in dry docks or at piers. The industry employs about a million workers. India, Pakistan, and Bangladesh are the primary locations for this work. Beaching is a dangerous activity (40 deaths in these three countries in 2012) and can lead to spills of toxic wastes (including asbestos and other carcinogens) into the ocean (Paris and Mukherji, 2013). Workers accept the hazardous conditions in return for a steady income. Ship owners could change the flags on their ships to other countries to avoid the proposed ban. What objectives are relevant and should be considered by the EU when deciding whether to adopt this legislation?

3.5. (This is based on an example in Parnell and West, 2008.) Joe is analyzing three alternatives for a new rocket: the HW, the SC, and the PK. The three most important attributes are the speed, number of payloads, and range. The decision maker prefers more of each attribute. The raw data in Table 3.12 are available. Joe plans to use the AHP to analyze the alternatives in Table 3.12. After consulting the stakeholders, he determines that, for the payloads attribute, four payloads is worth three times as much as three payloads, four payloads is worth five times as much as two payloads, and three payloads is worth twice as much as two payloads. Create a pairwise comparison matrix for the payloads attribute and find a set of scores that correspond to these pairwise comparisons. (Scale the scores so that the largest score equals 1.)

TABLE 3.12   The Attributes of Three Rocket Alternatives (Parnell *et al.*, 2008).

Rocket	Speed (kph)	Number of Payloads	Range (km)
HW	66	4	14
SC	45	3	55
PK	30	2	36

TABLE 3.13   The Attributes of Four Hypothetical Rocket Alternatives (Parnell *et al.*, 2008).

Alternative	Speed (kph)	Number of Payloads	Range (km)	Rating
1	30	2	14	0
2	66	2	14	15
3	30	4	14	35
4	30	2	55	100

3.6. (Continued from Exercise 3.5.) After consulting the stakeholders, Joe determines that a rocket would be worthless if its speed were less than 15 kph, it carried no payloads, and its range were only 1 km. Specify the attribute values of the three hypothetical alternatives that should be compared to determine the weights for the attributes.

3.7. Consider the rocket selection example again. Rose is also analyzing the three alternatives listed in Table 3.12, but she decides to develop a multiattribute utility function. After additional consultation with the stakeholders, Rose determines the relative ratings of the four hypothetical alternatives shown in Table 3.13. Construct a linear multiattribute utility function that is consistent with this data.

3.8. (Continued from Exercise 3.7.) Rose needs to assess a utility function for the Range attribute. She wants the utility to be in the range of [0, 1]. After consulting the stakeholders, she determines that they would be indifferent between (a) a rocket with a range of 36 km and (b) randomly choosing between a rocket with a range of 14 km and a rocket with a range of 55 km if the probability of getting the longer-range rocket was 60%. What utility should she assign to the values 14, 36, and 55 km?

3.9. (Continued from Exercise 3.8.) If Rose uses an increasing exponential utility function over the range (14 and 55 km), what is the appropriate value of γ (assume that the utility of 34.5 km is approximately the same as the utility of 36 km)? Write out the complete utility function for range. Using this utility function, calculate the utility of 50 km.

3.10. (Continued from Exercise 3.9.) After more consultation with the stakeholders, Rose determines that the utility functions for speed and number of payloads are linear (and the utility of the worst value equals 0, and the utility of the best value equals 1). Based on this information and the answers to Exercises 3.7, 3.8, and 3.9, calculate the total utility of each alternative. Under what conditions (combinations of weights) does the optimal alternative remain optimal? (That is, if the weights did not satisfy these conditions, the best choice would be another alternative.)

3.11. Joe and Rose plan to send their daughter to an all-women's college. They are concerned with size (larger enrollment is better) and tuition and fees (lower is better). They are considering the following colleges and have the data listed in Table 3.14. Among the nondominated alternatives, which alternatives are compensating solutions? Among the nondominated alternatives, which alternatives are noncompensating solutions?

3.12. Louis, a program manager at a funding agency, is considering which of nine proposals should be funded. A review panel has evaluated each proposal's intellectual merit and broader impacts on a 0–1 scale, with 0 being poor (no intellectual merit or no broader impacts) and 1 being excellent (great intellectual merit or tremendous broader impacts). Table 3.15 lists the proposals and

TABLE 3.14   Enrollment and tuition at eight women's colleges (Biemiller, 2013).

College	Enrollment	Tuition and Fees
Agnes Scott	871	$43,133
Cedar Crest	1620	$40,357
Cottey	323	$23,100
Mary Baldwin	1783	$35,590
Notre Dame of Maryland	2929	$40,710
Pine Manor	343	$36,554
Spelman	2170	$37,974
Wilson	745	$39,850

TABLE 3.15   The Evaluation of Nine Proposals.

Name	Intellectual Merit	Broader Impacts
Barthle	0.2	0.6
Gude	0.3	0.5
Ullrich	0.3	0.4
McSweeney	0.35	0.25
Garrity	0.4	0.35
Renuart	0.4	0.45
Marek	0.45	0.25
Warner	0.45	0.55
Martin	0.5	0.5

TABLE 3.16 The Evaluation of Five Job Offers.

	Job A	Job B	Job C	Job D	Job E
Weekly salary	$2000	$2400	$1800	$1900	$2200
Schedule flexibility	Moderate	Low	High	Moderate	None
Skills developed	Computer	Manage people, computer	Operations	Organization	Time management, multitasking
Vacation days per year	14	12	10	15	12
Benefits	Health, dental, retirement	Health, dental	Health	Health, retirement	Health, dental
Enjoyment	Great	Good	Good	Great	Boring

and evaluations on each attribute. (The "Name" is the last name of the person submitting the proposal.) Louis would like to fund proposals that have high scores on both attributes. He plans to use a linear additive function to combine the two evaluations (IM and BI) into a total score S as follows: $S = w$ IM $+ (1 - w)$ BI. If $w = 0.6$, which proposal will have the highest score? For what range of w will the Warner proposal have the highest score? (*Hint:* it may help to graph the nondominated proposals to determine which proposals should be considered.)

3.13. This example is based on one in Mustajoki *et al.* (2005). Table 3.16 lists the attribute values for five jobs. Construct a Pugh matrix for these offers. Does any job offer appear to be the best? Use the AHP to identify the job offer that you would most prefer. Use a multiple attribute utility function to identify the job offer that you would most prefer.

3.14. This example is based on data given in Levitt (2013). In 1851, the United States Lighthouse Board conducted a study to estimate the costs of replacing the existing reflectors in American lighthouses with much brighter Fresnel lenses. The net cost of installing the lenses was estimated to be $410,000. The annual savings (compared with operating the reflectors) were estimated to be $112,000 due to lower expenses in oil, supplies, and transportation. Calculate the net present value of installing and operating the Fresnel lenses (assume a 10% discount rate and a 10-year time horizon). Would replacing the reflectors with Fresnel lenses be a reasonable choice?

REFERENCES

Abernethy, Jacob, Theodoros Evgeniou, Olivier Toubia, and Jean-Philippe Vert, "Eliciting Consumer Preferences Using Robust Adaptive Choice Questionnaires," *IEEE Transactions on Knowledge and Data Engineering*, Volume 20, Number 2, pages 145–155, 2008.

Allenby, Greg M., Peter E. Rossi, and Robert E. McCulloch, "Hierarchical Bayes Models: A Practitioners Guide," Available at SSRN: http://ssrn.com/abstract=655541, January, 2005, accessed January 9, 2013.

Biemiller, Lawrence, "Armed With Data, a Women's College Tries a Transformation," *The Chronicle of Higher Education*, Online at https://chronicle.com/article/A-Womens-College-Tries-a/136969/, February 4, 2013, accessed August 7, 2013.

Birsch, Douglas, "Introduction: the Pinto controversy," in *The Ford Pinto Case: A Study in Applied Ethics, Business, and Technology*, Douglas Birsch and John H. Fielder, editors, State University of New York Press, Albany, New York, 1994.

Bucciarelli, Louis L., *Designing Engineers*, The MIT Press, Cambridge, Massachusetts, 1994.

Butler, John C., Jianmin Jia, and James S. Dyer, "Simulation Techniques for the Sensitivity Analysis of Multi-Criteria Decision Models," *European Journal of Operational Research*, Volume 103, pages 531–545, 1997.

Butler, John C., Alexander N. Chebeskov, James S. Dyer, Thomas A. Edmunds, Jianmin Jia, and Vladimir I. Oussanov, "The United States and Russia Evaluate Plutonium Disposition Options with Multiattribute Utility Theory," *Interfaces*, Volume 35, Number 1, pages 88–101, 2005.

Clausing, Don, *Total Quality Management*, ASME Press, New York, 1995.

Clemen, Robert T., and Terence Reilly, *Making Hard Decisions with DecisionTools*, Duxbury, Pacific Grove, California, 2001.

Department of Transportation (DOT), "Federal Motor Vehicle Safety Standard, Rearview Mirrors; Federal Motor Vehicle Safety Standard, Low-Speed Vehicles Phase-in Reporting Requirements," Docket No. NHTSA-2010-0162, RIN 2127-AK43, http://www.nhtsa.gov/staticfiles/rulemaking/pdf/Rear_Visibility_NPRM_12032010.pdf, accessed November 27, 2013.

Devroye, Luc, *Non-Uniform Random Variate Generation*, Springer-Verlag, New York, 1986.

Dieter, George E., and Linda C. Schmidt, *Engineering Design*, 5th edition, McGraw-Hill, Boston, 2012.

Dockins, Chris, Kelly Maguire, Nathalie Simon, and Melonie Sullivan, "Value of Statistical Life Analysis and Environmental Policy: A White Paper," U.S. Environmental Protection Agency, National Center for Environmental Economics, April 21, 2004. Available online at http://yosemite.epa.gov/ee/epa/eermfile.nsf/vwAN/EE-0483-01.pdf/$File/EE-0483-01.pdf.

Dyer, James S., "Remarks on the Analytic Hierarchy Process," *Management Science*, Volume 36, Number 3, pages 249–258, 1990a.

Dyer, James S., "A Clarification of Remarks on the Analytic Hierarchy Process," *Management Science*, Volume 36, Number 3, pages 274–275, 1990b.

Dyer, James S., and Rakesh K. Sarin, "Measurable Multiattribute Value Functions," *Operations Research*, Volume 27, Number 4, pages 810–822, 1979.

Dyer, James S., Thomas Edmunds, John C. Butler, and Jianmin Jia, "A Multiattribute Utility Analysis of Alternatives for the Disposition of Surplus Weapons-Grade Plutonium," *Operations Research*, Volume 46, Number 6, pages 749–762, 1998.

Edwards, Ward, "How to Use Multiattribute Utility Measurement for Social Decision Making," *IEEE Transactions on Systems, Man and Cybernetics*, Volume 7, Number 5, pages 326–340, 1977.

Fahrenthold, David A., "Cosmic Markdown: EPA Says Life is Worth Less," *Washington Post*, July 19, 2008.

Faulin, Javier, Esteban de Paz, Fernando Lera-López, Ángel A. Juan, and Israel, Gil-Ramírez, "Practice Summaries: Distribution Companies Use the Analytic Hierarchy Process for Environmental Assessment of Transportation Routes Crossing the Pyrenees in Navarre, Spain," *Interfaces*, Volume 43, Number 3, pages 285–287, 2013.

Forman, Ernest H., and Saul I. Gass, "The Analytic Hierarchy Process: An Exposition," *Operations Research*, Volume 49, Number 4, pages 469–486, 2001.

Gass, Saul I., "Model World: The Great Debate-MAUT Versus AHP," *Interfaces*, Volume 35, Number 4, pages 308–312, 2005.

Government Accountability Office (GAO), "Observations on DHS's Analyses Concerning Whether FMD Research Can Be Done as Safely on the Mainland as on Plum Island," GAO-09-747, July, 2009.

Green, Paul E., and V. Srinivasan, "Conjoint Analysis in Consumer Research: Issues and Outlook." *Journal of Consumer Research*, Volume 5, pages 103–123, 1978.

Green, Paul E., A.M. Krieger, and Yoram J. Wind, "Thirty Years of Conjoint Analysis: Reflections and Prospects." *Interfaces*, Volume 31, Number 3, pages S56–S73, 2001.

Grissom, M., A. Belegundu, A. Rangaswamy, and G. Koopman, "Conjoint-Analysis Based Multiattribute Optimization: Application in Acoustical Design," *Structural and Multidisciplinary Optimization*, Volume 31, Number 1, pages 8–16, 2006.

Harker, Patrick T., and Luis G. Vargas, "The Theory of Ratio Scale Estimation: Saaty's Analytic Hierarchy Process," *Management Science*, Volume 33, Number 11, pages 1383–1403, 1987.

Marriott International, "2012 Travel Directory," http://www.marriott.com/Multimedia/PDF/Brand%20Directories/Courtyard_Downloadable_Directory.pdf, accessed October 31, 2012.

Keeney, Ralph L., and Howard Raiffa, *Decisions with Multiple Objectives – Preferences and Value Tradeoffs*, 2nd edition, Cambridge University Press, New York, 1993.

Kirkwood, Craig W., *Strategic Decision Making: Multiobjective Decision Analysis with Spreadsheets*, Duxbury Press, Belmont, California, 1997.

Lenk, Peter J., Wayne S. DeSarbo, P.E. Green, and M.R. Young, "Hierarchical Bayes Conjoint Analysis: Recovery of Partworth Heterogeneity from Reduced Experimental Designs," *Marketing Science*, Volume 15, Number 2, pages 173–191, 1996.

Levitt, Theresa, *A Short, Bright Flash: Augustin Fresnel and the Birth of the Modern Lighthouse*, W.W. Norton & Company, New York, 2013.

Lowy, Joan, "Rules on Rearview Cameras Delayed," *The Washington Post*, Page A15, June 24, 2013.

Mitchell, Josh, "Truckers are Losing Sleep Over 70-hour Work Limit," *The Wall Street Journal*, page B1, July 3, 2013.

Mustajoki, Jyri, Raimo P. Hämäläinen, and Ahti Salo, "Decision Support by Interval SMART/SWING--Incorporating Imprecision in the SMART and SWING Methods," *Decision Sciences*, Volume 36, Number 2, pages 317–339, 2005.

National Center for Environmental Economics, "Frequently Asked Questions on Mortality Risk Valuation," http://yosemite.epa.gov/ee/epa/eed.nsf/pages/MortalityRisk Valuation.html, 2013 accessed August 13, 2013.

Nikolaidis, Efstratios, Zissimos P. Mourelatos, and Vijitashwa Pandey, *Design Decisions under Uncertainty with Limited Information*, CRC Press, Boca Raton, Florida, 2011.

Orme, Bryan K., *Getting Started with Conjoint Analysis*, Research Publishers LLC, Madison, Wisconsin, 2006.

Paris, Costas, and Biman Mukherji, "A Scrap Over Beaching Old Ships," *The Wall Street Journal*, page B1, June 14, 2013.

Parnell, Gregory S., and Paul D. West, "Systems decision process overview," in *Decision Making in Systems Engineering and Management*, G.S. Parnell, P.J. Driscoll, and D.L. Henderson, editors, John Wiley & Sons, Inc., Hoboken, New Jersey, 2008.

Resende, Camilo B., C. Grace Heckmann, and Jeremy J. Michalek, "Robust Design for Profit Maximization With Aversion to Downside Risk From Parametric Uncertainty in Consumer Choice Models," *Journal of Mechanical Design*, Volume 134: 100901, 2012.

Saaty, Thomas L., "How to Make a Decision: The Analytic Hierarchy Process," *Interfaces*, Volume 24, Number 6, pages 19–43, 1994.

Schoner, B., and W. Wedley, "Ambiguous Criteria Weights in AHP: Consequences and Solutions," *Decision Sciences*, Volume 20, pages 462–474, 1989.

Scott, Michael J., and Erik K. Antonsson, "Compensation and Weights for Tradeoffs in Engineering Design: Beyond the Weighted Sum," *Journal of Mechanical Design*, Volume 127, pages 1045–1055, 2005.

U.S. Patent and Trademark Office, "USPTO's Prioritized Patent Examination Program," http://www.uspto.gov/patents/init_events/Track_One.jsp, December 20, 2012, accessed July 5, 2013.

Warren, Lewis, "Uncertainties in the Analytic Hierarchy Process," DSTO-TN-0597, Defence Science and Technology Organisation, Australia, December, 2004.

4

GROUP DECISION MAKING

Learning Objectives:

After studying this chapter, the reader will be able to do the following:

1. Use ranking as a group decision-making technique (Section 4.1).
2. Use the Kemeny–Young method as a group decision-making technique (Section 4.1).
3. Identify the strengths and weaknesses of ranking as a group decision-making technique (Section 4.1).
4. Use scoring as a group decision-making technique (Section 4.2).
5. Use majority judgment as a group decision-making technique (Section 4.2).
6. Identify the strengths and weaknesses of scoring as a group decision-making technique (Section 4.2).
7. Describe the implications of Arrow's impossibility theorem (Section 4.3).

Because engineers work in teams and committees and other situations in which the preferences of other persons influence a decision, they encounter group decision making. A *group decision* occurs when the individual decisions of the persons in a group

Engineering Decision Making and Risk Management, First Edition. Jeffrey W. Herrmann.
© 2015 John Wiley & Sons, Inc. Published 2015 by John Wiley & Sons, Inc.

are combined to make a collective decision. This assumes, as might be expected, that the members of the group individually agree to participate in the decision-making process and accept its results. The decision-making process to be used may be imposed by existing rules, precedents, or some other authority, or it may be chosen by the group.

In engineering firms, many decisions involve multiple people, but not all those decisions are group decisions. In some cases, when no other sources of data are available (or acquiring them is impractical), it may be reasonable to ask multiple persons to estimate a specific quantity like a sales forecast and then combine (aggregate) these individual judgments into an estimate for that quantity, which will be used to evaluate one or more alternatives. This process can reduce the error of the estimate (cf. Ashton and Ashton, 1985), but it is not a group decision.

In other cases, the members of the group provide different types of information. For instance, when a product development team needs to select a concept, they may ask the marketing analyst about what the customers want, ask the reliability engineer for durability test results, ask the manufacturing engineer for unit cost estimates, and then use this information as the input to a decision-making technique that identifies the best concept. Multiple people provided information, but this is not a group decision.

In some cases, after the members of the group provide their information or evaluations, the decision is actually made by the boss, the general, the CEO, or some other leader. Despite the input of many persons, this is not a group decision.

In other cases, the decision-making process includes different decisions that are made by different persons, but this sequence of decisions is not a group decision. (Chapter 7 discusses separations, and Chapter 10 discusses decision-making systems in more detail.)

This chapter discusses decisions in which a group of peers must select an alternative. The members of the group express their preferences for the alternatives, and these preferences are combined to select an alternative. The members have agreed to (or must comply with) the procedure for combining these preferences.

During the planning of the Mariner spacecraft missions to Jupiter and Saturn and their moons, the trajectories for the two spacecrafts were chosen by a group of scientists in 10 discipline-specific science teams who had different priorities (preferences) about the importance of different attributes for the trajectories and different levels of risk aversion (Dyer and Miles, 1976). Each team was treated as a single decision maker; the group was formed of the science teams. The project manager required that the teams achieve a consensus, so they had an incentive to participate in the decision-making process. He also required that the process should be "conceptually simple," which discouraged the decision analysts from constructing a multiattribute utility function for trajectory pairs. Thus, the problem was treated as a group decision-making situation.

A team of engineers developed a diverse set of 32 attractive candidate trajectory pairs that met physical and financial constraints. Each science team first ranked these candidates and then assigned a utility by determining a probability so that the team was indifferent between that candidate and a lottery involving their most-preferred and least-preferred candidates (this is one of the methods presented in Section 3.3). The decision analysts then used different rules (including ranking and scoring methods similar to those discussed in this chapter) to find a group ranking of the candidates. Due to the correlation of the rules and some similarities of the science teams' preferences, the evaluations of different candidates substantially agreed (for instance, all the rules ranked the same three candidates in the top three). A meeting of representatives from the 10 science teams reviewed the results of the rules and agreed to select one candidate as the preferred trajectory pair after it was modified to improve its performance on one attribute that was very important to one science team. In a postdecision survey, 9 of the 10 teams stated that the selected trajectory pair was good for them, and 8 of the 10 teams stated that the selection process was fair (the other two were neutral).

A design review can be a group decision, which is especially useful when the evaluation criteria include aesthetic and other subjective aspects. Because such aspects can be difficult to measure when evaluating building design proposals, some jurisdictions ignore them all together and evaluate the appropriateness of a building design using a limited set of objective measures related to zoning, building code, and similar regulations. Because concentrating the responsibility to assess the aesthetic aspects of a design in a single person could lead to arbitrary decision making (especially when the responsible person leaves and a new person, with a different view, arrives), a group design review is an effective process. For instance, the US Commission of Fine Arts (CFA) reviews design concepts for federal buildings and other projects in Washington, DC (CFA, 2013). It ensures that the concepts are visually, culturally, and historically appropriate and promotes high design and construction standards (Lewis, 2005). The CFA can approve, suggest improvements to, or reject a design. The commissioners have different views about the designs based on their experience and values, and the performance measures are subjective. Despite these complexities, however, because the CFA is a group of qualified persons who have no conflicts of interest and are committed to well-defined (though imprecise) goals, they are able to address aesthetic and subjective aspects in an effective way.

Some group decisions are much easier, however. Suppose, for example, that an organization needs to choose a gift that will be presented to visitors like those who give a technical talk to the engineering staff. A short list of four reasonable, cost-feasible objects has been compiled, and an ad hoc committee of five employees has been formed to pick exactly one of these. The alternatives are an ink pen, a coffee mug, a box of candy, and an USB external drive (all featuring the organization's name and logo). All members of the committee agree that the gift is intended to show the organization's appreciation for what the visitor has contributed. The ad hoc, subjective nature of the situation makes it unlikely that the group will spend time using a formal decision-making technique (such as those discussed in Chapter 3).

In a group decision, the individuals in the group have their preferences, and the problem is to combine their preferences in some "fair" way so that the group's decision reflects the individuals' preferences. Unfortunately, there is no procedure that is objectively fair in all cases. For instance, Arrow's impossibility theorem (Section 4.3) states that any process that converts individual rankings into a group ranking, especially by voting, has some shortcomings.

Effective group decision making relies upon the members of the group sharing a set of values and communicating to coordinate their cooperation (Simon, 1997). That is, after the members agree on the objectives that they are trying to achieve (e.g., collect valuable scientific data, maintain a beautiful city, or leave a visitor with a good impression), the question is one of means: what should be done to reach this objective and how?

Potential problems with group decision making include *groupthink* and *shared information bias*. When groupthink occurs, the members of the group fail to evaluate alternatives correctly. In particular, group norms that create illusions of unanimity and invulnerability bolster morale but cause the members to avoid criticizing their peers' ideas and to set aside their own concerns about the emerging consensus (Janis, 1971). Moreover, such a group fails to generate many alternatives, fails to consider the possibility of failure, ignores warnings and other negative information, and fails to reconsider and revise rejected ideas. In addition, some groups (especially those that value consensus more highly than criticism) have a shared information bias (Postmes *et al.*, 2001). That is, they value and use only information that is known to all members and ignore information known initially to individual members, even when it is shared with them, which causes them to evaluate alternatives incorrectly.

The following steps form a group decision-making process that avoids the problems identified by Frisch (2008):

1. The group should state, discuss, and acknowledge the key objectives and real constraints that are relevant to the decision situation.
2. The group should identify a diverse set of feasible alternatives, impartially evaluate the advantages and disadvantages of each alternative, and discuss their characteristics and ability to achieve the relevant objectives.
3. The members of the group should state their individual preferences (ranks or scores) for the alternatives that are being considered.
4. These ranks or scores should be combined (aggregated) and the alternatives should be ranked based on this aggregation. The best alternative should be selected.
5. If desired, search for more alternatives or more information, develop new alternatives that combine the best features of the existing ones, and return to Step 2. Otherwise, end.

This chapter will discuss different ways for the members to state their preferences and different ways to aggregate them.

4.1 RANKING

Ranking is a common group decision-making approach. In a ranking procedure, each member ranks the alternatives (from best to worst), and then some algorithm is used to combine the rankings. Ranking is desirable because it is relatively simple and requires less effort than other techniques. Unfortunately, it has many possible problems because the individual rankings convey little information. The ranks (unlike scores) do not describe the magnitude of the differences between alternatives.

Example 4.1 The 2002 Winter Olympics provided a memorable example of group decision making using ranking. The women's figure skating competition included two parts: the short program and the free skate (long program). In each part, nine judges ranked the skaters, and the ranks were combined by summing them. For instance, in the short program, Michelle Kwan was ranked first by five judges and second by four judges, whereas Irina Slutskaya was ranked first by four judges, second by two judges, and third by three judges. The sum of Kwan's ranks was 13, and the sum of Slutskaya's ranks was 17, so Kwan finished first in the short program, and Slutskaya finished second. Sasha Cohen finished third, and Sarah Hughes finished fourth. In the free skate, Hughes was first, Slutskaya second, Kwan third, and Cohen fourth. To determine the medals, these two rankings were combined by dividing the rank in the short program by two and adding it to the rank in the free skate. Thus, Hughes had $2 + 1 = 3$ points, Slutskaya had $1 + 2 = 3$ points, Kwan had $0.5 + 3 = 3.5$ points, and Cohen had $1.5 + 4 = 5.5$ points. Because Hughes was ranked ahead of Slutskaya in the (more important) free skate, Hughes won the gold medal, and Slutskaya received the silver medal, while Kwan, who won the (less important) short program, received the bronze medal. (Postscript: a scandal in the figure skating pairs competition occurred that year after a judge allegedly gave two Canadian skaters improperly low scores, and skating officials started using a new judging system two years later.)

The ranking methods start with the following information: each voter ($i = 1, \ldots, n$) gives a rank R_{ij} to each alternative ($j = 1, \ldots, N$). $R_{ij} = 1$ if voter i believes that alternative j is the best alternative, $R_{ij} = 2$ if voter i believes that alternative j is the second best alternative, $\ldots$, and $R_{ij} = N$ if voter i believes that alternative j is the worst alternative.

The *plurality vote* counts the number of times that each alternative was ranked first. More precisely, let $P_{ij} = 1$ if and only if $R_{ij} = 1$ and 0 otherwise. The alternatives are ranked by the sums: alternative j is ranked ahead of alternative k if $\sum_{i=1}^{n} P_{ij} > \sum_{i=1}^{n} P_{ik}$. Because it ignores the rest of each person's ranking, the plurality vote uses very little information (i.e., it is frugal). The best (highest-ranked) alternative is the one with the largest sum (the largest number of first place votes). Simple elections work this way. Each voter specifies only a first place choice, which is the only needed information.

The *Borda count* includes all the information in the rankings. Let $B_{ij} = N + 1 - R_{ij}$ be the number of points that alternative j gets from voter i. An alternative gets N points for being ranked #1, $N - 1$ points for being ranked #2, and so on, down to 1 point for being ranked #N. (The scale can be changed without any change in the result.) The Borda count of alternative j equals the sum of these points:

$$BC_j = \sum_{i=1}^{n} B_{ij} = n(N + 1) - \sum_{i=1}^{n} R_{ij}.$$

The alternatives are ranked by the Borda counts: alternative j is ranked ahead of alternative k if $BC_j > BC_k$. The best alternative is the one with the largest Borda count. The alternative with the largest Borda count also has the smallest average rank (the average of the R_{ij}) if no alternatives are given the same rank.

Among ranking procedures, the Borda count, which was designed to alleviate the problems with other types of voting schemes, has many desirable characteristics. The Borda count aggregates the results over all pairs (an alternative gets more points for being superior to more options). The Associated Press college football poll works this way: a team gets 25 points for a first place vote, 24 points for a second place vote, and this continues down to 1 point for a 25th place vote.

Using the Borda count to generate a complete ranking can yield inconsistent results, however. Consider an example with a group of 1000 people ranking three alternatives. Suppose 333 voters give the ranking [A, B, C] (from best to worst); 333 voters give the ranking [B, C, A]; 333 voters give the ranking [C, A, B]; and one voter gives the ranking [A, C, B]. The Borda count scores are $BC_A = 1001$ points for A, $BC_C = 1000$ points for C, and $BC_B = 999$ points for B. Thus, it is reasonable to declare A the winner (A also wins the plurality vote with 334 votes). A complete ranking of [A, C, B] may not be reasonable, however, because, if A were removed, then the fact that 666 voters ranked B ahead of C (and only 334 voters ranked C ahead of B) seems to contradict ranking C ahead of B. This example shows that the Borda count is not "rank compatible" (Balinski and Laraki, 2007). Moreover, using the Borda count may not choose, when it exists, the Condorcet alternative, which is the alternative that defeats every other alternative in pairwise simple majority voting (Condorcet, 1785; Young and Levenglick, 1978). The Borda count is useful for choosing a winner, but it is not appropriate for computing a complete ranking.

The *Kemeny–Young method* evaluates all possible rankings and evaluates each one by its "distance" from the voters' rankings (Young and Levenglick, 1978). The "least-distant" ranking is recommended as the group's aggregate ranking. Instead of evaluating the distance, implementations of this method often evaluate the similarity (the opposite of distance), in which case the best ranking is the one that is most similar. The similarity between two rankings is the number of times the rankings agree on the relative ordering of pairs of items. For instance, the ranking [pen, mug, candy, drive] and the ranking [pen, candy, drive, mug] have four similarities: both agree on ranking the pen ahead of the mug, the candy, and the drive, and both agree on ranking the candy ahead of the drive. The problem is to find the ranking that has the greatest total similarity, which is the sum of the similarities with the voters' rankings.

The Kemeny–Young rule can be expressed more precisely as follows. Let N be the number of items (alternatives) and n be the number of voters, all of whom rank-order the items. Let $E(a, b)$ be the number of voters who ranked item a ahead of item b (i.e., $R_{ia} < R_{ib}$). Note that $E(b, a) = n - E(a, b)$. It may be useful to view a voter's ranking as a matrix M_i that has a row and a column for every item (alternative). Every entry in this matrix is either 0 or 1, where $M_i(a, b) = 1$ if and only if voter i ranked item a ahead of item b. For two distinct items a and b, either $M_i(a, b) = 1$ or $M_i(b, a) = 1$, and $E(a, b) = \sum_{i=1}^{n} M_i(a, b)$.

Consider a group ranking τ, and let τ_i be the ith item in ranking τ (i.e., the item is ranked ahead of $n - i$ items). The total similarity of τ equals $\sum_{i=1}^{N-1} \sum_{j=i+1}^{N} E(\tau_i, \tau_j)$. This measures how often the group ranking τ agrees with the rankings by the voters. If all n voters have the same ranking, then $E(\tau_i, \tau_j) = n$ for all $i < j$, and the total similarity of that ranking equals $n(N - 1)N/2$. The Kemeny–Young rule chooses, from among the $N!$ possible rankings, a ranking that maximizes the total similarity. This is a *Condorcet method*, which means that, if there is an alternative a, such that $E(a, b) - E(b, a) > 0$ for all other alternatives b, then this alternative will be the highest ranked in any ranking that maximizes similarity (Young and Levenglick, 1978).

The computational effort of the Kemeny–Young method depends primarily upon the number of alternatives and is reasonable for a small number of alternatives (even if the number of voters is large). Motivated by the problem of scouting professional baseball players, Streib *et al.* (2012) developed a variation of the method for the situation in which the number of alternatives is large but the number of voters is small.

Example 4.2 To illustrate and compare these methods, consider the gift selection scenario. Suppose that each of the five committee members (each a voter) ranks the four alternatives from #1 (the best) to #4 (the worst). Table 4.1 shows the results.

The pen wins the plurality vote because it received three first place votes (i.e., $\sum_{i=1}^{5} P_{i,pen} = 3$). The Borda counts of the alternatives are the following: $BC_{pen} = 3 \times 4 + 2 \times 1 = 14$ (because the pen received three first place votes, which have a value of 4, and two fourth place votes, which have a value of 1); $BC_{mug} = 4 \times 3 + 1 \times 1 = 13$; $BC_{candy} = 4 + 3 + 3 \times 2 = 13$; and $BC_{drive} = 4 + 2 \times 2 + 2 \times 1 = 10$. Thus, the pen has the largest Borda count. It is not obvious, however, how to rank the four alternatives, although two rankings seem to be the most appropriate: [pen, mug, candy, drive] and [pen, candy, mug, drive].

To use the Kemeny–Young method to evaluate the similarity of these two rankings, first record that $E(pen, mug) = 3$ because three voters ranked the pen ahead of the mug. Likewise, $E(pen, candy) = 3$, $E(pen, drive) = 3$, and $E(mug, drive) = 3$. Three voters ranked the mug ahead of the candy, so $E(mug, candy) = 3$; the other two voters ranked the candy ahead of the mug, so $E(candy, mug) = 2$. Finally, because four voters ranked the candy ahead of the drive, $E(candy, drive) = 4$.

Consider the two rankings suggested by the Borda counts. The total similarity of the ranking $\tau_1 = $ [pen, mug, candy, drive] equals $E(pen, mug) + E(pen, candy) + E(pen, drive) + E(mug, candy) + E(mug, drive) + E(candy, drive) = 19$. The total

TABLE 4.1 Five Rankings of the Four Gift Alternatives.

Voter	#1	#2	#3	#4
Voter 1	Pen	Mug	Candy	Drive
Voter 2	Pen	Mug	Candy	Drive
Voter 3	Pen	Candy	Drive	Mug
Voter 4	Candy	Mug	Drive	Pen
Voter 5	Drive	Mug	Candy	Pen

similarity of the ranking $\tau_2 = $ [pen, candy, mug, drive] equals E(pen, candy) + E(pen, mug) + E(pen, drive) + E(candy, mug) + E(candy, drive) + E(mug, drive) = 18. Thus, τ_1, the first ranking, is more similar to the voters' rankings. (The reader can confirm that no other ranking has a greater similarity in this instance.)

4.2 SCORING AND MAJORITY JUDGMENT

Scoring is another common method for group decision making. Each member of the group (a "voter") gives each alternative a score (on a common scale), the scores are combined (aggregated) using a function (the social grading function) that calculates a single group score from the voters' scores, and the group selects the alternative with the highest group score. It is very common to use the sum of the scores or the average score as the aggregation function.

The benefit of scoring is that it captures the magnitudes of the differences between alternatives. Thus, an alternative that is scored just lower than another is not greatly punished. (However, the scores need to be anchored so that individuals are consistent between alternatives and from one to another.)

Example 4.3 Consider again the gift-selection decision from Example 4.2. Suppose that the five voters (the members of the committee) have each scored the four alternatives from 1 (very poor) to 10 (excellent). Table 4.2 lists the scores (which are consistent with their rankings in Table 4.1). If the sum of the scores is used as the aggregation function, the pen's total score equals 26, the mug's total score equals 27, the candy's total score equals 25, and the drive's total score equals 24.

The validity of adding the scores can be questioned, however, if the scores are merely values on an ordinal scale (such scales were discussed in Chapter 2). For example, if "10" is a symbol that means "excellent," "9" means "very good," and so forth, then what does "excellent" + "very good" mean? The scores need to be on an interval scale to be summed or averaged.

If each member of the group individually considers the alternatives and their characteristics and determines his utility for the alternatives, then the different utility values for an alternative can be combined (aggregated) using a weighted sum, and the alternative with the greatest weighted sum should be chosen (Keeney, 2013).

TABLE 4.2 The Scores of Five Voters on Four Alternatives.

Voter	Pen	Mug	Candy	Drive
Voter 1	10	9	8	7
Voter 2	5	4	3	2
Voter 3	7	1	3	2
Voter 4	3	8	9	7
Voter 5	1	5	2	6

This procedure is consistent with specific but reasonable assumptions about the members and the group, but it requires the group to decide collectively on weights for the members. Members can also strategically misrepresent their preferences to promote a specific alternative although complete transparency may mitigate this risk. In particular, a member may assign an unreasonably large utility to a favorite alternative or give an unreasonably small utility to a disliked alternative.

The *majority judgment method* avoids the problem of adding scores (Balinski and Laraki, 2007, 2010). The majority judgment method identifies the alternative with the largest majority grade as the most desirable alternative in the social choice context. The majority judgment method uses as a social grading function the middlemost interval, which provides protection against outcome manipulation by individual voters and is valid on any ordinal scale that is common to all the voters. This function is monotone (increasing one score for an alternative does not lower that alternative's ranking) and, if a majority of voters assigns an alternative the same score, assigns that alternative that score. Balinski and Laraki (2007) described other properties of the method and showed that no voter has an incentive to assign a grade other than the one that he believes is correct.

The method works as follows: each voter $(i = 1, \ldots, n)$ gives a score r_{ij} to each alternative $(j = 1, \ldots, N)$. The scores are on a common ordinal scale such that any two scores can be compared to determine whether one is greater than, equal to, or less than the other. A higher score is better.

Let $f^{maj}(r_{1j}, \ldots, r_{nj})$ be the *majority grade* of alternative j. This majority grade combines the n scores that the n voters gave to alternative j by finding the middlemost of these scores. In particular, if n is odd, the majority grade is the median score (there will be $(n-1)/2$ scores greater than or equal to the median score, and another $(n-1)/2$ scores less than or equal to the median score). If n is even, the majority grade is the lower-middlemost score (there will be $n/2$ scores greater than or equal to this score, and another $n/2 - 1$ scores less than or equal to this score). In either case, if the grade were strictly larger than the majority grade, then more than half of the voters would consider it too large; at the same time, if the grade were strictly less than the majority grade, then more than half of the voters would consider it too small.

More precisely, let $r_{[h]j}$ be the hth highest score given to alternative j. Then, if n is odd, $f^{maj}(r_{1j}, \ldots, r_{nj}) = r_{[(n+1)/2]j}$; if n is even, $f^{maj}(r_{1j}, \ldots, r_{nj}) = r_{[n/2+1]j}$.

Example 4.4 Table 4.3 shows the sorted scores of the four alternatives in the gift-selection decision described in Example 4.3. Because $n = 5$, the majority grade of each alternative is its third highest score. The majority grade of the pen equals 5. The majority grade of the mug equals 5. The majority grade of the candy equals 3. The majority grade of the drive equals 6. (Note that, if the drive's grade were 5, then three voters would consider this too low; if its grade were 7, then three voters would consider this too high.) The drive has the largest majority grade. Only two voters gave a grade lower than 6 to the drive, and only these two would consider the grade of 6 too high for the drive. For any other alternatives, however, three voters gave the other alternative a grade that is lower than 6 and would, therefore, consider the grade of 6 too high for that alternative.

TABLE 4.3   The Sorted Scores of Four Alternatives.

Pen	Mug	Candy	Drive
10	9	9	7
7	8	8	7
5	5	3	6
3	4	3	2
1	1	2	2

The majority judgment method ranks the alternatives by their majority grades; the resulting ranking is the *majority ranking*. One alternative will be ranked above another if the first alternative's majority grade is greater than second alternative's majority grade. (Note that the relative ranking is independent of the other alternatives.) If multiple alternatives have the same majority grade, then a score that equals the majority grade is removed from the set of scores for each alternative in the tie, and the alternatives are ranked based on the majority grades of the reduced sets of scores. This process is repeated as necessary. (Thus, this is a type of lexicographic ordering.) Only alternatives that have identical sets of scores will remain tied. Thus, it is unlikely that two alternatives will tie. A tie in this method, if it does occur, implies quite a lot about the scores of the tied alternatives, whereas the equality of two sums (or averages) implies little about the scores of the tied alternatives.

For instance, suppose $n = 4$. Alternative j will be ranked ahead of alternative k if one of the following conditions is true: (1) $r_{[3]j} > r_{[3]k}$; (2) $r_{[3]j} = r_{[3]k}$ and $r_{[2]j} > r_{[2]k}$; (3) $r_{[3]j} = r_{[3]k}$, $r_{[2]j} = r_{[2]k}$, and $r_{[4]j} > r_{[4]k}$; or (4) $r_{[3]j} = r_{[3]k}$, $r_{[2]j} = r_{[2]k}$, $r_{[4]j} = r_{[4]k}$, and $r_{[1]j} > r_{[1]k}$.

In Example 4.4, for instance, the majority judgment method will rank the drive first and the candy last. The pen and the mug have the same majority grade (5). After removing one score of "5," the majority grade of the remaining four scores for the pen equals 3. After removing one score of "5," the majority grade of the remaining four scores for the mug equals 4. Thus, this method will rank the mug ahead of the pen. The aggregate ranking is [drive, mug, pen, candy].

The majority judgment method never adds the scores. It requires merely an ordinal scale that all the voters use. If the ordinal scale contains only two values (for instance, "Good" and "Bad"), then the majority judgment method will rank the alternatives by the number of "Good" scores.

When there are a large number of voters, then it can be convenient, if every voter gave a score to every alternative, to first describe the scores given to alternative j as the triple (p_j, α_j, q_j), which Balinski and Laraki call a *majority gauge*, where p_j is the number of voters who gave alternative j a score better than its majority grade, α_j is the majority grade for alternative j, and q_j is the number of voters who gave alternative j a score worse than its majority grade. (The number of voters who gave alternative j a score equal to its majority grade equals $n - p_j - q_j$.) Given these triples, one can break ties quickly between two alternatives with the same majority grade. If $\alpha_j = \alpha_k$, then alternative j will be ranked ahead of alternative k if one of the following conditions is

Figure 4.1 The majority gauges for Example 4.5. The gray bars represent the votes that are better than the majority grade. The white bars represent the votes that are equal to the majority grade. The black bars represent the votes that are worse than the majority grade.

true: (1) $p_j > q_j$ and $p_k \leq q_k$; (2) $p_j > q_j$ and $p_k > q_k$ and $p_j > p_k$; or (3) $p_j \leq q_j$ and $p_k \leq q_k$ and $q_j < q_k$.

Example 4.5 Consider a case in which 100 voters scored three alternatives, and the majority gauges (triples) for alternatives 1, 2, and 3 are (44, "Good," 30), (39, "Good," 41), and (38, "Good," 46). Figure 4.1 visualizes and compares these majority gauges. Note that, for alternative 1, the grades that are better than "Good" are closer to the median than the grades that are worse than "Good," but the opposite is true for alternative 3. Although all three have the same majority grade, in the majority ranking, alternative 1 is ranked ahead of the other two because $p_1 > q_1$ but $p_2 \leq q_2$ and $p_3 \leq q_3$. Alternative 2 is ranked ahead of alternative 3 because $q_2 < q_3$.

The set of scores used should be a common language for those who provide the scores, and research on human's abilities to judge distinct values suggests that there is a natural limit on the number of distinct scores that should be used. Although skilled experts may be able to use scales with more values (over 20, say), in more common situations a scale with around seven values is more likely to be a common language in which voters can make absolute judgments (Balinski and Laraki, 2010).

4.3 ARROW'S IMPOSSIBILITY THEOREM

An important result in the area of group decision making is Arrow's general possibility theorem (Arrow, 1951), which is also known as Arrow's impossibility theorem. When we consider the group decision-making problem (with more than two choices), it is clear that it would be nice to have a "fair" procedure that combined the individuals' preferences about the alternatives (expressed as rankings) into a statement about the group's preferences about the alternatives while preserving the autonomy of each individual. Arrow very carefully defined what a "fair" procedure should do:

1. Each individual is free to order the alternatives in any way (this is known as the property of "unrestricted domain").
2. If a set of orders ranks alternative A before alternative B, and those who ranked B before A switch, then A is still before B (positive response).

3. If A is before B, then A is still before B if a third alternative C is ignored or added (independence of irrelevant alternatives).
4. There must be social orders with A before B and vice versa (not imposed).
5. It is not allowed to have one individual whose decisions dictate the social order (not dictatorial).

Arrow then showed that, in the general case, there exists no such procedure that satisfies all the criteria for a "fair" procedure. In particular, any social choice function that satisfies Axioms 1, 2, and 3 must be either imposed or dictatorial. That is, there is no social choice function that satisfies all five axioms.

This result raised some important questions about the rationality of social choices in the real world. Arrow introduced a special case in which one of the axioms is no longer valid and a fair procedure can be generated. In this special case, which is called "single peakedness," the alternatives can be ordered on some external one-dimensional ordinal scale (like size or position on the political spectrum), and each individual has a preferred value on this scale and orders the alternatives based on their "distance" from this preferred value. If two alternatives are both on the same side of the preferred value (either both are smaller, or both are larger), then the one that is farther away is less preferred. This is one way of limiting the freedom of individuals to order the alternatives.

Balinski and Laraki (2007) noted that Arrow's theorem shows that no collective decision exists when no common language exists. That is, Arrow's requirement that individuals need to state only their preferences as an ordering of the alternatives does not require a common language in which the individuals describe their evaluations of the alternatives on a scale that is understood by everyone.

Although multicriteria decision making in engineering settings has some similarities to group decision making, it is important to note that they are fundamentally different. In particular, the axioms of Arrow's theorem do not necessarily apply to multicriteria decision making. Therefore, this famous theorem should not be allowed to prevent one from using multicriteria decision-making methods or to make them appear irrational (Scott and Antonsson, 1999). However, it does indicate that methods be explicit and systematic, not arbitrary.

EXERCISES

4.1. Describe the tradeoff between using a ranking approach and using a scoring approach to select the best alternative using the preferences of the members of a group.

4.2. Consider again the rankings of the four gifts shown in Table 4.1. Suppose that the first voter changes his ranking to [pen, candy, mug, drive] (i.e., the ranks for the candy and the mug are switched). How does that affect the Borda count? Use the Kemeny–Young method to calculate the similarities of the possible rankings. Which ranking(s) would have the largest similarity value?

4.3. Write a computer program or program a spreadsheet to perform the Kemeny–Young method by evaluating the similarity of all possible rankings. The program input is a complete ranking for every voter. The output is the similarity of every possible ranking.

4.4. A faculty search committee with five members (whose initials are DD, AG, BH, JH, and MY) evaluated 10 applicants for a faculty position at Enormous State University. Each member gave each applicant a grade of "A" (highly qualified), "B" (qualified), or "C" (unqualified). Ten applicants (listed by codes) and the grades are shown in Table 4.4. Use the majority judgment method to rank these 10 applicants from best to worst.

4.5. Consider again the example in Problem 4. Suppose that two more members (KK and HB) join the committee and evaluate the 10 applicants. KK gives every applicant the grade of "A," but HB gives every applicant the grade of "C." How will the ranking generated using majority judgment change?

4.6. Consider a situation (based on one presented in Balinski and Laraki, 2010) in which 1000 voters scored four candidates on a scale from "excellent" to "to reject." The number of voters giving each score is given in Table 4.5. Verify that all four candidates have the same majority grade. Determine the majority gauges for these candidates and use this information to rank the four candidates.

TABLE 4.4   The Grades of the 10 Applicants from 5 Faculty Members.

Applicant	DD	AG	BH	JH	MY
SA1	A	B	A	B	B
DB2	B	B	B	B	B
AC3	C	C	B	C	C
MC4	B	B	B	B	A
JD5	A	A	B	A	A
SK6	A	B	C	A	A
MM7	A	B	B	A	A
AM8	C	B	A	A	C
LS9	C	C	C	C	C
GZA	B	B	B	B	C

TABLE 4.5   The Number of Voters Who Gave Each Score to Four Candidates.

	Bové	Laguiller	Besancenot	Buffet
Excellent	15	20	41	25
Very good	60	53	99	76
Good	114	102	163	125
Acceptable	160	166	160	206
Poor	257	259	226	264
To Reject	394	400	311	304

4.7. Consider the rankings and utility scores of the 10 science teams given in Table II of Dyer and Miles (1976). Find a group ranking of the trajectory pairs by summing the teams' ranks. Assume that all the teams have equal status, and find a group ranking of the trajectory pairs by sorting by the sums of the teams' utilities. Finally, consider the utility scores as a common language for the teams, and use the majority judgment method to generate the majority ranking of the trajectory pairs.

4.8. A consortium of three companies (A, B, and C) funds research at Enormous State University. A representative from each company evaluates every proposal on the following ordinal scale (from worst to best): poor, fair, good, very good, and excellent. This year, the company representatives gave the proposals from seven researchers the scores shown in Table 4.6. Use the majority judgment method to order these seven proposals from best to worst. Convert these scores into ranks (each representative ranks the proposals from #1 to #7; break ties arbitrarily). Combine the rankings using the Borda count and using the Kemeny–Young method.

4.9. An undergraduate program at Enormous State University evaluated student applicants in the following way: each member of the evaluation team rated each applicant as "excellent," "very good," "good," or "unqualified." These ratings were converted into numerical values (from 1 to 4), and the values for each applicant were summed together to generate the applicant's "total score." What is the problem with the method that the program used? Which method would be more appropriate?

4.10. In 2004, a committee of 10 athletic directors selected the 34 Division I men's basketball teams that should receive at-large bids for the NCAA tournament. To do this, the committee members had dozens of secret ballots in which they voted on the teams (Svrluga, 2004). After some eligible teams were nominated, the committee members voted: each member voted for their top eight teams (the ones most worthy of an at-large bid). Any team that received at least seven votes was moved to the "In" category. Each member then ranked the top eight teams not moved to the "In" category. These ranks were summed (one point for

TABLE 4.6   The Evaluations of the Seven Proposals.

Faculty Name	A	B	C
Barthle	Excellent	Good	Excellent
Gude	Very good	Very good	Fair
Ullrich	Good	Good	Poor
McSweeney	Excellent	Excellent	Very good
Garrity	Very good	Very good	Very good
Warner	Very good	Excellent	Very good
Martin	Fair	Poor	Very good

a #1 ranking, etc.), and the four teams with the smallest totals were moved to the "In" category. Similar votes occurred until 34 teams were "In," but at some points, the committee voted to remove teams from the "In" category. Suggest a group decision-making process that would require less effort to identify the 34 teams that should receive at-large bids.

REFERENCES

Arrow, Kenneth J., *Social Choice and Individual Values*, 1st edition, Wiley, New York, 1951.

Ashton, Alison H., and Robert H. Ashton, "Aggregating Subjective Forecasts: Some Empirical Results," *Management Science*, Volume 31, Number 12, pages 1499–1508, 1985.

Balinski, Michel, and Rida Laraki, "A Theory of Measuring, Electing, and Ranking," *Proceedings of the National Academy of Sciences*, Volume 104, Number 21, pages 8720–8725, 2007.

Balinski, Michel, and Rida Laraki, *Majority Judgment: Measuring, Ranking, and Electing*, MIT Press, Cambridge, Massachusetts, 2010.

de Condorcet, Marquis, Jean-Antoine-Nicolas de Caritat. *Essai sur l'Application de l'Analyse a la Probabilite des Decisions Rendues a la Pluralite des Voix*, l'Imprimerie Royale, Paris, 1785.

Dyer, James S., and Ralph F. Miles Jr., "An Actual Application of Collective Choice Theory to the Selection of Trajectories for the Mariner Jupiter/Saturn 1977 Project," *Operations Research*, Volume 24, Number 2, pages 220–244, 1976.

Frisch, Bob, "When Teams Can't Decide," *Harvard Business Review*, Volume 86, Number 11, pages 121–126, 2008.

Janis, Irving L., "Groupthink," *Psychology Today*, Volume 5, Number 6, pages 43–46, 1971.

Keeney, Ralph L., "Foundations for Group Decision Analysis," *Decision Analysis*, Volume 10, Number 2, pages 103–120, 2013.

Lewis, Roger K., "Widespread use of design reviews would be a fitting legacy for Atherton," *The Washington Post*, page F5, December 10, 2005.

Postmes, Tom, Russell Spears, and Sezgin Cihangir, "Quality of Decision Making and Group Norms," *Journal of Personality and Social Psychology*, Volume 80, Number 6, pages 918–930, 2001.

Scott, Michael J., and Erik K. Antonsson, "Arrow's Theorem and Engineering Design Decision-Making," *Research in Engineering Design*, Volume 11, Number 4, pages 218–228, 1999.

Simon, Herbert A., *Administrative Behavior*, 4th edition, The Free Press, New York, 1997.

Streib, Noah, Stephen J. Young, and Joel Sokol, "A Major League Baseball Team Uses Operations Research to Improve Draft Preparation," *Interfaces*, Volume 42, Number 2, pages 119–130, 2012.

Svrluga, Barry, "In the jury room, a job to do," *The Washington Post*, page E1, March 14, 2004.

U.S. Commission of Fine Arts (CFA), "Welcome to the U.S. Commission of Fine Arts," http://www.cfa.gov/, accessed on July 12, 2013.

Young, Hobart P., and Arthur Levenglick, "A Consistent Extension of Condorcet's Election Principle," *SIAM Journal of Applied Mathematics*, Volume 35, Number 2, pages 285–300, 1978.

5

DECISION MAKING UNDER UNCERTAINTY

Learning Objectives:

After studying this chapter, the reader will be able to do the following:

1. Identify aleatory and epistemic uncertainties and describe the difference (Section 5.1).
2. Assess a subjective probability (Section 5.2).
3. Determine whether an alternative stochastically dominates another (Section 5.4).
4. Create a decision tree for a decision with uncertainty (Section 5.5).
5. Evaluate a decision tree and find the optimal policy (Sections 5.6 and 5.7).
6. Generate a valid utility function to represent a risk-averse decision-maker (Section 5.8).
7. Define different types of robustness measures (Section 5.9).
8. Identify ways to estimate uncertainty in the outputs of a model given uncertainty in the inputs (Section 5.10).
9. Use sensitivity analysis to propagate uncertainty (Section 5.10).
10. Use the method of moments to estimate the uncertainty of a model output (Section 5.11).
11. Use Monte Carlo simulation to estimate the uncertainty of a model output (Section 5.12).

Engineering Decision Making and Risk Management, First Edition. Jeffrey W. Herrmann.
© 2015 John Wiley & Sons, Inc. Published 2015 by John Wiley & Sons, Inc.

Although life is full of uncertainties, it is unnecessary and impossible to consider all of them all of the time. The decision situations that were considered in the previous two chapters did not explicitly include any uncertainties. Although uncertainties were present, the evaluation of different attributes was done using expected values or most likely outcomes or somewhat vague or imprecise measurements.

When the uncertainties can have a significant impact on the outcome that results from choosing an alternative (and thus make the alternative more or less desirable relative to the others), it is prudent to consider them. We will first consider decisions in which the desirability of an alternative is affected by an event that has multiple possible outcomes, and the decision-maker can describe a probability distribution for these outcomes. Some authors refer to this situation as "decision making under risk" (Luce and Raiffa, 1957).

Note that this chapter deals with uncertainty due to random events (aleatory uncertainty) or uncertain knowledge (epistemic uncertainty). A very different case arises if the uncertainty is due to the as-yet-unknown action of another rational decision-maker. This type of uncertainty has been called "strategic uncertainty" (Golany *et al.*, 2009). In this situation, a decision-maker should consider game theory approaches to help identify the best alternative (Chapter 6 discusses this topic).

In the basic risky decision (Clemen and Reilly, 2001), the decision-maker must choose one of the two alternatives: the first is something safe, but the second is something risky (its outcome is uncertain). Suppose Joe must choose between two components for a system. Component A is a well-known component whose performance is certainly good but more expensive. Component B is an innovative, less-expensive component that has just appeared in the market. Its manufacturer claims that it performs much better than Component A, but Joe cannot independently verify this claim, so its performance is uncertain. There is a risk that Component B will not perform well at all, which will drive up costs. Joe faces a risky decision. Which should he choose?

During the planning of the Mariner spacecraft missions to Jupiter and Saturn and their moons, the trajectories for the two spacecrafts were chosen by consensus of a group of scientists in 10 discipline-specific science teams. Most of the teams preferred complementary missions that collected different types of data (and more overall), but one team was more risk averse and preferred redundant trajectories that both collected only the most important data (Dyer and Miles, 1976). In the context of a risky decision, the choice of redundant trajectories is the "safe" alternative, because it is highly likely that the most important data will be collected by at least one of the spacecrafts. The choice of complementary missions is the "risky" alternative because neither spacecraft will collect all of the most important data. If one spacecraft fails, only some of the most important data will be collected; if both succeed, however, additional valuable data will be collected.

Another common situation occurs when "the true state of nature" is unknown. The true state is not affected by the alternative, but the total cost of any alternative will depend on the true state, which is not known for certain until after the decision-maker chooses an alternative and implements it. For instance, consider the following example (from Benjamin and Cornell, 1970): as part of the process of creating a foundation for a building, Mary must decide whether to drive a 40-foot (12-m) steel pile or a 50-foot (15-m) steel pile into ground, where the depth of the bedrock is either 40 or 50 feet (12 or 15 m). The alternatives are the different piles. The possible states of nature are the different depths of the bedrock. Each alternative and state-of-nature combination has a different cost (including the cost of the pile and the pile driving).

- If she chooses the 40-foot pile and the bedrock is 40 feet deep, then there is no additional cost.
- If she chooses the 40-foot pile and the bedrock is 50 feet deep, then the additional costs include those for the idle equipment and crew and the cost of splicing and welding the pile to the correct length.
- If she chooses the 50-foot pile and the bedrock is 40 feet deep, then the additional cost is that for cutting off the pile to the correct length and scrapping the unnecessary piece.
- If she chooses the 50-foot pile and the bedrock is 50 feet deep, then there is no additional cost.

In general, risk management (discussed in Chapter 9) requires making risky decisions. Making risky decisions occurs in many areas besides engineering, of course. For a discussion of gambling and insurance, for example, see Kaplan and Kaplan (2006). Gathering more information can reduce uncertainty, but this costs time and money, so deciding to get more information is another challenge (cf. Chapter 8).

5.1   TYPES OF UNCERTAINTIES

Although uncertainty is acknowledged as an important factor in decision making, there are many different ways to describe and model uncertainty. The two key types of uncertainty can be described as *aleatory uncertainty* and *epistemic uncertainty*. Aleatory uncertainty refers to an uncertainty about a value or an outcome in which the variability is inherent due to randomness in the environment or the system and which cannot be reduced by obtaining further data. For instance, a natural phenomenon may be poorly understood and therefore unpredictable. Aleatory uncertainty is traditionally treated using classical probability theory. For instance, a manufacturing process may be inherently random due to the complex, dynamic interaction of the machinery and the materials involved, and we may describe its performance as random and model that randomness using a normal distribution. (This distribution would depend on the precision of the machine and the quality of the materials.)

Epistemic uncertainty refers to an uncertainty about a value or an outcome due to a lack of knowledge about the object or system; thus, data can be used to reduce the uncertainty. An engineer may lack knowledge about the true state of nature (for instance, what is the true depth of the bedrock?) or the future (for instance, will the component perform adequately?). Swiler *et al.* (2009) described a situation in which epistemic uncertainty about the properties of a rubber material filled with glass balloons existed. When a surrogate model is used to predict the performance of a product or system design, epistemic uncertainty may exist due to the limited number of observations to which the model was fitted. In these cases, one could gather data (via experiments or other means) to reduce the uncertainty about the unknown value. Even when one can observe an event or object, there may be uncertainty about it due to limitations in the observation process (which may be incomplete or lack detail) or a lack of knowledge about how to classify an object, which could be due to vague or imprecise terms (Groen and Mosleh, 2005). Epistemic uncertainty can be modeled using subjective probabilities, and these can be updated when new data become available.

In practice, uncertainties may contain elements of both types of uncertainty. For example, if the reliability of a product (which will be used under typical conditions) depends on the location where it was manufactured and assembled (because of differences in the processes used), then the lifetime of a particular unit is uncertain. There is epistemic uncertainty about the location, which affects the distribution of the lifetime, but this can be determined by a label, its serial number, or other data. There is aleatory uncertainty about the actual lifetime that cannot be reduced, only observed.

The likelihood of an uncertain event is expressed as a probability, and probabilities can be determined and manipulated using standard probability theory. However, there are multiple ways to view probabilities. The following operational definitions of probability were given by Cooke (2004):

- Classical interpretation (attributed to Laplace): a probability equals "the number of favorable cases divided by the number of equi-possible cases." This interpretation is the simplest and describes rolling dice, drawing names from a hat, and similar activities.

- Frequentist interpretation: a probability is the relative frequency of the event in a random sequence (von Mises, 1957). This interpretation underlies the use of test results and other experimental activities to estimate probabilities.

- Subjective interpretation: a probability is "the degree of belief of a rational subject," measured on a scale from 0 to 1. A probability statement expresses an "opinion regarding the likelihood" of an event occurring (Jordaan, 2005). One can measure the degree of belief by observing the decision-maker's choices. This interpretation is the most appropriate for the likelihood of one-time events (like whether the component will perform adequately). The odds set by gambling institutions (such as horse racing tracks) directly reflect these beliefs. For more about the subjective view, see de Finetti (1964).

Other interpretations of probability have been proposed, including the logical and propensity interpretations, and every interpretation has various versions that attempt to handle different difficulties (Lyon, 2010). In some cases, a decision-maker may reject using probabilistic methods on the grounds that the information available is not sufficient to create a distribution of any kind. If so, then the decision-maker can compare alternatives by considering the worst possible outcomes (cf. Section 5.9).

5.2   ASSESSING A SUBJECTIVE PROBABILITY

There are multiple ways to assess a subjective probability (see, e.g., Clemen and Reilly, 2001). The simplest is to ask the decision-maker for the probability. Unfortunately, people often have difficulty quantifying uncertainties. When assessing the probability distribution for an unfamiliar quantity, people can be overconfident and generate distributions that are too narrow (Alpert and Raiffa, 1982).

For assessing a continuous distribution, we can assess various cumulative probabilities for specific values that are in the range of the random variable. For instance, consider a situation in which the weather forecast calls for a freeze that could damage a farmer's crop. There is uncertainty about the damage that the freeze will cause. To assess the probability distribution, we could assess the probability that the damage will be less than \$20,000, \$25,000, and so forth. Some techniques, however, assess the values that correspond to the probabilities 5%, 25%, 50%, 75%, and 95% (or the probabilities 10%, 50%, and 90%).

Although the technique is simple for a single probability, rigorous protocols for acquiring expert probability assessments are needed to avoid problems that can occur due to bias or inconsistencies between different experts (see, e.g., Kirkwood, 1997; Merkhofer, 1987; Spetzler and Staël von Holstein, 1975).

A common indirect technique for assessing a single probability proceeds as follows:

1. Let E denote the event with the subjective probability. Let Prizes A and B be two outcomes that affect the decision-maker such that the decision-maker prefers Prize A to Prize B.
2. Let p be the current estimate of the subjective probability. Initially, set $p = 0.5$.
3. Ask the decision-maker to state a preference between the following two lotteries:

    In Lottery 1, the decision-maker receives Prize A if E occurs and Prize B if not.

    In Lottery 2, the decision-maker receives Prize A with probability p and Prize B with probability $1-p$, using a random number generator (such as a spinner or drawing a number from an urn or a bowl).
4. If the decision-maker is indifferent, then p is a reasonable estimate for the probability of event E. Stop.
5. If the decision-maker prefers Lottery 1, then p is too low; increase p and return to Step 3. If the decision-maker prefers Lottery 2, then p is too high; decrease p and return to Step 3.

The assessment method adjusts the probability p in the second lottery until the decision-maker is indifferent between the two lotteries. This value of p is the decision-maker's subjective probability that event E will occur.

Example 5.1   Consider a manufacturing firm that is developing a new product and consider building a factory to build it. The manufacturing yield of the new facility (if built) is a key uncertainty in deciding whether to build a factory or license the technology to another firm. To assess the probability of obtaining an excellent yield (a range that the company defines), Rose, the chief manufacturing engineer, was asked to choose between the following two lotteries: In Lottery 1, she will receive a new smartphone if the manufacturing yield is excellent, but she will receive a new mechanical pencil if not. (Clearly, she prefers the new smartphone to a new mechanical pencil.) Lottery 2 involves drawing a number from 1 to 100 out of a bowl; she will receive the smartphone if the number is less than 100 and the mechanical pencil otherwise.

Rose chose Lottery 2, in which the chance of receiving the smartphone is 99/100, which must be greater than the probability that the manufacturing yield will be excellent. (Otherwise, there would be very little uncertainty about it.)

This was simple, but then Lottery 2 was changed so that Rose will receive the smartphone if the number is less than or equal to 50 and the mechanical pencil otherwise. At this point, she again chose Lottery 2 because she believes that the probability that the manufacturing yield will be excellent is less than 50/100. Lottery 2 was changed again and again until the probability of receiving the smartphone was 10/100. At this point, she was indifferent between the two lotteries because she believed that both gave her the same probability of receiving the smartphone. When Lottery 2 was changed so that she will receive the smartphone if the number is less than or equal to 5, she preferred Lottery 1; this implies that the probability 5/100 is too small. Thus, the subjective probability that the manufacturing yield will be excellent equals 0.10. (To be more precise, it would be necessary to choose between Lottery 1 and other versions of Lottery 2 in which the probability of receiving the smartphone was 6/100, 7/100, and other values near 0.10.)

Another technique focuses on the maximum amount that the decision-maker would pay for a contract in which there is a reward of $S if the event E occurs and nothing otherwise (Jordaan, 2005). (The amount $S is usually significant but small to avoid risk aversion.) Let $P be the maximum amount that the decision-maker would pay. If the price for the contract were small (less than $P), then it would be preferred to doing nothing; if the price for the contract were large (greater than $P), then doing nothing would be preferred. Because the decision-maker is indifferent between paying $P for the contract and doing nothing, then the probability of the event E equals P/S.

Example 5.2   Consider again the problem (from Example 5.1) of assessing the probability of obtaining an excellent yield. In Lottery 3, Rose, the chief manufacturing engineer, will receive $100 if the manufacturing yield is excellent, but she will receive nothing if not. She is asked if she would pay $1 for a contract that guaranteed her the outcome of Lottery 3. She will say "yes." The price is increased from $1 until she says that she would not pay that much for the contract. (The search can be abbreviated by choosing the prices carefully to find the maximum acceptable price more quickly.) Suppose that she would pay $10 for the contract but not more. Then her subjective probability that the manufacturing yield will be excellent equals $10/$100 = 0.10.

A third approach, presented by Ramsey (1964), used a choice between a sure thing and a situation with uncertainty. Suppose that Joe will receive a reward of S if the event E occurs and a reward of T otherwise (where $S > T$). Joe has the opportunity to guarantee the reward of S if he pays for it. Clearly, if Joe is certain that event E will occur, then he would not pay much for the sure thing; in contrast, if Joe doubts that event E will occur, the guaranteed reward will be attractive. Let D be the maximum amount that Joe will pay. The two alternatives (keep the lottery and pay D for the sure thing, which yields a profit of $S - D) have the same expected monetary value. Let $P\{E\}$ be the subjective probability that event E will occur. Thus, $S - D = P\{E\} \times S + (1 - P\{E\}) \times T$, from which we can see that $P\{E\} = 1 - D/(S - T)$.

5.3 IMPRECISE PROBABILITIES

Generally, we think of probabilities as precisely known numbers, but various researchers have found this definition to be too limited when the information available is incomplete or conflicting. In the domain of risk analysis, Paté-Cornell (1996) discussed using a family of curves to represent epistemic uncertainty about the risks. Moreover, as Chapter 9 discusses, probability terms such as "likely" or "possible" are inherently imprecise. The three-color problem in Ellsberg (1961) involves imprecise probabilities. In this problem, a decision-maker must choose one of the two colors (red or black) before a ball is drawn from an urn. Suppose that Louis is the decision-maker. Louis will win a prize if the color of the ball matches his choice. Before he chooses a color, he is told that the urn has 30 red balls and 60 other balls; some (but not all) of the other balls are black, and the rest are yellow. A reasonable decision-maker might say that the probability of drawing a red ball is 1/3 (30/90). The probability of drawing a black ball is unknown, but Louis can say that it is between 1/90 (if only one ball is black) and 59/90 (if only one ball is yellow). If Louis wants to maximize the probability of winning the prize, which color should he choose?

In theories of *imprecise probabilities*, a probability can be an interval, not merely a precise number (Walley, 1991; Weichselberger, 2000; Dempster, 1967). The upper probability and lower probability are bounds on the subjective probability. For a random variable, the imprecise probability distribution can be drawn as a p-box (Aughenbaugh and Paredis, 2006; Ghosh and Olewnik, 2013). Imprecise probabilities can become precise probabilities when more evidence is collected.

Another way to deal with an unknown probability distribution is to discretize the distribution and assess a range of probabilities for each interval. The lower bound on this range is called the "belief" that the random variable will be in that interval. The upper bound on this range is called the "plausibility" that the random variable will be in that interval. Such an approach is an example of the use of evidence theory (Shafer, 1976). Swiler et al. (2009) used evidence theory to describe the uncertainty about the elastic modulus of a material.

Analyzing a decision with an imprecise probability is similar to doing a sensitivity analysis on the unknown probability. The use of bounds implies that there may be no best choice. One can then look at the worst case and select the alternative that has the best worst-case performance (here, worst case means the worst expected performance over the range of the imprecise probability, not the worst case over the possible outcomes).

Using imprecise probabilities can help an engineer avoid making incorrect decisions, but it can also significantly delay correct decisions (Aughenbaugh and Herrmann, 2009). This approach reflects the tradeoffs between the quantity and the quality of available information, which can be important when communicating uncertainty and managing information.

Aughenbaugh and Paredis (2006) presented a pressure vessel design example to show the value of using imprecise probabilities to model uncertainty when one has only a small set of sample data.

5.4   CUMULATIVE RISK PROFILE AND DOMINANCE

When the outcomes of the alternatives can be modeled as probability distributions over continuous variables (such as strength or time or cost), then one can directly compare the cumulative distribution functions to determine whether one alternative stochastically dominates another. (The distributions may be discrete or continuous.) Some authors and analysts use the term "cumulative risk profile" to refer to the cumulative distribution function of the outcomes of an alternative.

Stochastic dominance is an approach for identifying the best of two alternatives with uncertain outcomes without knowing the decision-maker's utility function (Hadar and Russell, 1969). This is very useful because one can reduce the number of alternatives that need to be further considered. If one alternative dominates all of the others, then it can be selected.

This section will briefly describe two types of stochastic dominance: first-degree stochastic dominance and second-degree stochastic dominance.

First-degree stochastic dominance is the following property: Let Y_i and Y_j represent the random outcomes of alternatives i and j. The decision-maker prefers a greater value and therefore wants to maximize the probability of a greater value, which is equivalent to wanting to minimize the probability of a smaller value. Thus, a random outcome that is less likely to be small is preferred. More precisely, Y_i *stochastically dominates* Y_j *in the first degree* if and only if $P[Y_i \leq y] \leq P[Y_j \leq y]$ for all possible outcomes y. That is, the value of the cumulative distribution function for Y_i never exceeds the cumulative distribution function for Y_j. If one graphed these two cumulative distribution functions, the one for Y_i, which dominates, would be below (and to the right of) the one for Y_j, which is dominated. If the decision-maker prefers a greater value, then alternative i should be preferred because the probability of a small value (an undesirable outcome) is smaller (and the probability of a greater value is greater) than it would be if alternative j were chosen. This holds for any utility function that monotonically increases (i.e., more is better).

Example 5.3   Consider Figure 5.1, which shows the cumulative distribution functions for the outcomes of three alternatives: a, b, and c, all of which are normally

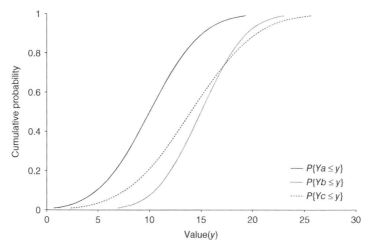

Figure 5.1   The cumulative distribution functions for the outcomes of three alternatives: a, b, and c, all of which are normally distributed random variables.

distributed random variables. Both b and c dominate a, but neither b nor c dominates the other one.

The same property holds for alternatives with discrete outcomes as well. For example, consider Figure 5.2, which shows the cumulative distribution functions for the outcomes of three alternatives: d, e, and f, all of which are random variables over discrete values. Both e and f dominate d, but neither e nor f dominates the other one.

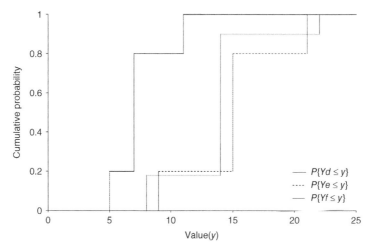

Figure 5.2   The cumulative distribution functions for the outcomes of three alternatives: d, e, and f, all of which are random variables over discrete values.

Second-degree stochastic dominance is the following property: if the support of Y_i and Y_j is contained within the closed interval $[a, b]$, Y_i *stochastically dominates* Y_j *in the second degree* if and only if, for all values of t in $[a, b]$,

$$\int_a^t P[Y_i \leq y]dy \leq \int_a^t P[Y_j \leq y]dy.$$

That is, the area under the cumulative distribution function for Y_i never exceeds the area under the cumulative distribution function for Y_j.

If the decision-maker's utility function is concave (which indicates that the decision-maker is risk averse) and Y_i stochastically dominates Y_j in the second degree, then alternative i will have a larger expected utility, and the decision-maker should prefer alternative i to alternative j. Note, however, that this conclusion does not rely upon the actual utility function (just its shape).

If there exists an alternative that stochastically dominates every other alternative, then that alternative should be preferred.

One limitation of stochastic dominance is that it may happen that, for a pair of alternatives, neither one stochastically dominates the other. Still, even when it cannot identify a single most-preferred alternative, stochastic dominance can be used to eliminate some inferior alternatives from further consideration.

5.5 DECISION TREES: MODELING

A decision tree shows details about the alternatives of a decision and the outcomes of random events and represents the sequence in which decisions and chance events occur. A square node represents a decision (a choice between alternatives), and on its right are branches that correspond to the possible alternatives. A circular node represents a chance event (which cannot be controlled by the decision-maker), and on its right are branches for the possible outcomes. Associated with each outcome is a probability.

The ability to put probabilities on the possible outcomes and calculate expected values makes decision trees very useful. Expected value is the most common measure, although other measures are also available. For instance, Barker and Wilson (2012) presented a method for analyzing decision trees when the outcomes are specified using intervals and when they have multiple attributes.

To draw a decision tree, first identify the decisions to be made and the uncertainties to be considered. The first node on the left should be the first decision that must be made (or the first uncertainty that is resolved before the first decision). Then, add the branches to that node. Then, on each branch, add the next decision or chance node (and its branches) and continue until all of the relevant decisions and uncertainties have been added to every branch. Add the outcome (e.g., the gain or loss that occurs for that sequence of alternatives and events) to the end of every branch on the right-hand side. A single path from the root node on the left-hand side to the end of a branch on the far right represents one possible future.

A decision node may represent a specific choice or a set of choices that are made together. For instance, a decision tree for a situation with two design variables that need to be determined could include two separate decision nodes—one for the first variable with branches for its possible values and one for the second variable with branches for its possible values—or one decision node with branches for all possible combinations of the two variables.

A chance node may represent a specific event or a set of events that are resolved at the same time (with respect to the decision-maker). For instance, a decision tree that incorporates tomorrow's weather could include two separate chance nodes—one for the amount of rain with branches for the possible values and one for the temperature with branches for its possible values—or one chance node with branches for all possible combinations of the two events (e.g., "hot and dry" or "cold and wet").

A chance node represents the resolution of the uncertainty, which occurs when the decision-maker becomes aware of the result (even if the event occurred earlier). Thus, a chance node should be placed after (to the right of) a decision node if the decision-maker must select an alternative before the result of the uncertain event is known. In contrast, a chance node should be placed before (to the left of) a decision node if the result of the uncertain event is known before the decision-maker selects an alternative. In some cases, an uncertain event may have no impact on the outcome for some alternatives; in these situations, the chance node is not necessary on the branches for the alternatives that are not affected.

Example 5.4   Suppose that Joe is designing a medical diagnostic device and is considering using a wavelength-specific high power light-emitting diode (LED) instead of a traditional high-intensity flash lamp source for the device. The LED will cost less, but he is unsure if it will provide adequate light intensity over the lifetime of the device. If Joe chooses the LED, he will conduct accelerated life testing to determine how quickly the LED's optimal power decreases over time due to degradation of the LED (Sawant, 2013). If testing shows that the power decreases too much too soon, then he will have to redesign the device to use the flash lamp, which will increase the development and unit costs.

Assume that the costs of developing and manufacturing the device with a flash lamp are $11,000. The costs of developing and testing the device with the LED are $6,000. If testing shows that the LED performance is adequate, then the additional costs of manufacturing the device with the LED are $3,000. If testing shows that the LED performance is inadequate, then the additional costs of redesigning and manufacturing the device (with the flash lamp) are $8,000. Based on published data about the performance of such LEDs, the engineer believes that the probability that the LED performance will be adequate is 75%.

Figure 5.3 shows a decision tree that can be used to model this decision. Decision trees are usually read from left to right. In this example, either the device with the LED will perform adequately or not. The probability of adequate performance is 75% (0.75); the probability of inadequate performance is 25% (0.25).

Associated with each arrow is the immediate gain or loss associated with that action or outcome. At the far right-hand side are the net gains (losses) associated

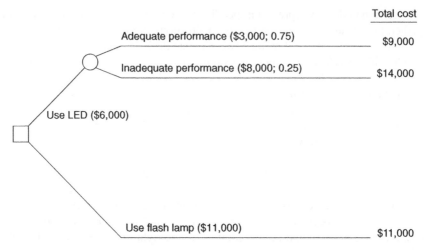

Figure 5.3   A decision tree for the decision described in Example 5.4.

with each outcome. In this example, if Joe decides to use the flash lamp, then the costs will be $11,000. If Joe decides to use the LED and it performs adequately, then the costs will be $6,000 + $3,000 = $9,000 (which is shown at the far right). If Joe decides to use the LED and it performs inadequately, then the costs will be $6,000 + $8,000 = $14,000 (which is shown at the far right).

Note that the node that represents the uncertainty about the LED performance is included only on the "use LED" alternative because it affects the outcome of only that alternative. The cost of using the flash lamp is not affected by the LED performance.

5.6   DECISION TREES: DETERMINING EXPECTED VALUES

A decision tree provides a way to evaluate the expected value of a decision. This calculation proceeds from right to left. The expected value of an uncertain event equals the expected value of the net gains and losses of its outcomes. The expected value of a decision equals the best expected value of its alternatives because the decision-maker can choose the best one.

Example 5.5   In Example 5.4, the expected value of the "use LED" event is $0.75 \times \$9,000 + 0.25 \times \$14,000 = \$10,250$. Figure 5.4 shows the decision tree from Figure 5.3 "rolled up" to the "LED performance" event; the event and its outcomes are removed and replaced with the expected value (shown in Figure 5.4). This removes some details from the decision tree but simplifies further analysis.

The expected value of the "use LED" alternative equals $10,250. The expected value of the "use flash lamp" alternative equals $11,000. Because the "use LED" alternative has the smaller expected cost, Joe will choose that, and the expected value

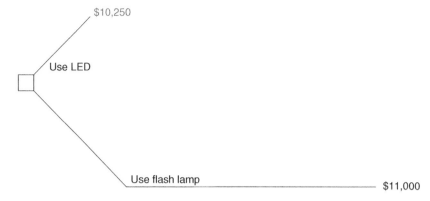

Figure 5.4   The decision tree from Figure 5.3 "rolled up" to the "LED performance" event.

of the decision equals $10,250. The optimal policy is to choose the "use LED" alternative.

If multiple attributes (criteria) will be used to evaluate the outcomes, then the decision-maker should use a utility function to express his preferences about the outcomes. The utility of each outcome on the right-hand side of the tree should be determined. Then, the decision tree can be analyzed (rolled up) to find the policy that provides the greatest expected utility.

Example 5.6   Consider Joe's decision (from Examples 5.4 and 5.5). If development time is also critical, then the time associated with each outcome should be determined (testing the LED will add more time), and Joe should create a utility function for his preferences about cost and time. For instance, suppose testing the LED will add 2 months to the development time, and redesigning and manufacturing the device with the flash lamp will add another month. Then, the three outcomes are (1) the LED has adequate performance, which costs $9,000 and delays development 2 months; (2) the LED has inadequate performance, which costs $14,000 and delays development 3 months; and (3) using the flash lamp costs $11,000 and adds no delay. For the cost attribute, less is better, so the utility of $9,000 equals 1, and the utility of $14,000 equals 0. Suppose Joe believes that the utility of $11,000 equals 0.5. For the development time attribute, a smaller delay is better, so the utility of no delay equals 1, and the utility of 3 months equals 0. Suppose Joe believes that the utility of 2 months equals 0.5. Finally, suppose that Joe believes that weights for the utility of cost and utility of development time should be 0.75 and 0.25.

Given his utility function, Joe determines that the utility of outcome (1) equals 0.875, the utility of outcome (2) equals 0, and the utility of outcome (3) equals 0.625. Then, the expected utility of using the LED equals $0.75 \times 0.875 + 0.25 \times 0 = 0.656$, which is higher than the utility of using the flash lamp. The optimal policy is to choose the "use LED" alternative. The optimality of this policy is sensitive to the utilities that Joe chose, so a sensitivity analysis (cf. Section 5.10) should be conducted.

5.7   SEQUENTIAL DECISION MAKING

In practice, there may be situations in which a decision-maker faces a series of decisions. The decision-maker makes one decision, observes the outcome, makes a second decision, observes its outcome, makes a third decision, and so on. An important principle of decision analysis is that the decision-maker should consider and analyze the future decisions before making the one that needs to be made now. Thus, the decision-maker should already know which alternative should be selected when that decision needs to be made.

In his discussion of football play-calling and decision making, Hurley (1998) concluded that a football coach should never decide what to do on fourth down when his team is on fourth down; the coach should have already made that decision when the team had first down because the plan for fourth down (if the team got to that down) would affect the play-calling on the first three downs.

In risk management, sequential decision making occurs when contingency plans require making decisions after something bad has happened. Decision trees are particularly useful for modeling and analyzing these situations, although the decision tree can become quite large if there are many decisions with many alternatives and possible outcomes.

To model a sequential decision using a decision tree, add a decision node at those places in the tree where the second-stage decision must be made. The path from the initial decision to the second-stage decision should include any chance nodes that will be resolved before the second-stage decision is made. The second-stage decision may be irrelevant to some paths, so it should not be included on them. Like the value at the initial decision node, the value at a second-stage decision node is the optimal of the branches from that node.

Example 5.7   Consider the diagnostic device design decision with the following change: if the LED performance is inadequate, Joe may either redesign the product using the flash lamp, which will cost an additional $8,000, or test a different type of LED, which will cost an additional $1,000. The performance of this LED is also uncertain; it may be adequate or inadequate. If it is adequate, then the additional costs of manufacturing the device with the LED are $3,500. If it is inadequate, then the additional costs of redesigning and manufacturing the device (with the flash lamp) are $8,500. Based on the published data about the performance of such LEDs, the engineer believes that the probability that the performance of the new LED will be adequate is 60%.

When considering whether to use the first LED, he needs to consider what he will do if it is inadequate. Figure 5.5 is a decision tree model of the decision situation. Note that the "Test another?" decision node appears only on the branch in which the performance of the first LED is inadequate because that node is irrelevant if Joe uses the flash lamp or the first LED is adequate.

If the performance of the first LED is inadequate, then the expected cost of testing another LED equals $12,500, and the cost of not testing (and using the flash lamp) is $14,000, so Joe should test another LED (it has the lower cost). This lowers the

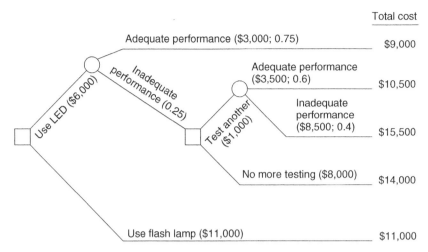

Figure 5.5   A decision tree for the sequential decision described in Example 5.7.

expected cost of using the first LED to $9,875, which is less than the cost of using the flash lamp.

The combination of the best choices at every decision node is called his "policy." Joe will still use the first LED; if it is inadequate, then he will test another; and the expected value of the decision equals $9,875.

5.8   MODELING RISK AVERSION

In NASA's trajectory design problem (mentioned in the Introduction of Chapter 4), one team was more risk averse than the others, which affected the trajectory alternatives that they preferred. In general, a decision-maker's preferences for risky alternatives depend on whether the decision-maker is risk averse. This affects the actions selected to mitigate risks, for a risk-averse decision-maker will usually prefer to avoid or transfer a risk rather than to accept it.

For example, in the St. Petersburg Paradox (first presented by Daniel Bernoulli), a lottery that has an infinite expected monetary value is not considered that valuable by actual gamblers. In this game (or lottery), one pays an initial amount to play, a fair coin is flipped until "heads" appears, and the player is paid 2^n dollars (where n is the number of coin flips). The expected monetary value is $\frac{1}{2}(2) + \frac{1}{4}(2^2) + \frac{1}{8}(2^3) + \cdots$, a series that does not converge. For a truly risk-neutral person, paying any finite amount to play this game should be desirable. However, most people will not pay a large amount because there is a large probability that they will lose money, and their risk aversion makes the lottery worth much less to them. Indeed, paying only $3 to play means that the probability of losing money is 50%.

Thus, when trying to make better decisions, it will be useful to have a way to model the preferences of a risk-averse decision-maker that are (at least approximately) consistent with such behavior. Modeling risk is important because decision-makers do not view gains and losses equally. Risk-averse decision-makers want to avoid bad outcomes. (Extremely risk-averse decision-makers look only at the worst-case scenario.) Utility functions are an established technique for modeling risk.

Utility is a numerical measure of welfare or satisfaction (Brown, 2005). The decision-maker prefers more utility over less. A decision-maker can determine the utility of an outcome based on his preferences and judgments. For instance, a material that is both strong and inexpensive may have a utility of 100 while a weak expensive material has a utility of 0, and a strong but costly material has a utility of 70. A key concept is that utility is relative, not absolute, and it depends on the decision-maker's preferences. The perceived utility of a value will vary between decision-makers and in different situations. There is no single utility function that is valid for all decision-makers and in all situations.

Utility follows from a decision-maker's preferences: because the decision-maker prefers outcome A to B, the utility of A is greater than the utility of B. Given specific conditions about the consistency of the decision-maker's preferences and rules about combining utility values, one can use them to determine an ordering for complex alternatives that is consistent with the decision-maker's preferences. This ordering identifies the alternative that, if selected, would optimize the decision-maker's expected utility.

The ability to evaluate an alternative with multiple possible outcomes and summarize its relative desirability by its expected utility is an important benefit of using a utility function. This provides a scale that allows a decision-maker to compare many alternatives with multiple possible outcomes.

Example 5.8   This example is adapted from one in Luce and Raiffa (1957). Joe may choose one of the two lotteries, each over four possible prizes: (A) a new automobile, (B) a trip to the beach, (C) a computer, and (D) dinner for four at the best restaurant in town. Joe prefers A to B, B to C, and C to D. In the first lottery, every prize is equally likely (the probabilities of winning A, B, C, and D are all 25%). In the second lottery, the probabilities of winning A, B, C, and D are 15%, 50%, 15%, and 20%, respectively, so the probability of the trip has increased. Which lottery should Joe choose?

Luce and Raiffa (1957) provided a set of relevant axioms from which one can justify using expected utility to compare alternatives similar to those in this example. These will be briefly described here.

The first axiom states that (1) given two outcomes, the decision-maker can state which one is preferred and (2) given three outcomes A, B, and C, if the decision-maker prefers A to B and prefers B to C, then he prefers A to C. The second axiom states that a lottery over multiple lotteries is equivalent (to the decision-maker) to a simpler lottery over the outcomes in those lotteries if the probability of each outcome is determined according to the rules of probability. The third axiom states that, if a decision-maker prefers A to B and prefers B to C, then there is a lottery over the outcomes A and C that is equivalent to the outcome B. The fourth axiom extends this idea and states that a lottery in which B is one possible outcome is equivalent to a lottery in which B is replaced by the equivalent lottery over outcomes A and C. The fifth axiom extends transitivity to lotteries. The sixth axiom states that, if the decision-maker prefers A to C, then, for two lotteries over outcomes A and C, the decision-maker prefers the lottery in which A is more likely.

From these axioms, it can be shown that any lottery is equivalent to a simpler lottery involving only the best possible outcome and the worst possible outcome. Moreover, when comparing two lotteries, the decision-maker should prefer the lottery that is equivalent to the simpler lottery with the larger probability of the best possible outcome. (That is, given two lotteries L1 and L2, L1 is equivalent to a simpler lottery SL1, and L2 is equivalent to a simpler lottery SL2. If the probability of the best possible outcome in SL1 is greater than the probability of the best possible outcome in SL2, then the decision-maker should prefer the original lottery L1.) Finally, there exists a utility function that describes the preferences of a decision-maker who accepts these axioms.

Example 5.9 Now, consider Joe's choices from Example 5.8, which are both lotteries over the same four outcomes. Joe's preferences are consistent with all of Luce and Raiffa's axioms. The first step is to find, for outcome B (and then for outcome C), an equivalent lottery over A and D (the best and worst outcomes). The third axiom assumes that such lotteries exist. Joe is indifferent between the trip and a lottery in which the probability of winning the automobile is 60% and winning the dinner is 40%. In other words, B is equivalent to the lottery (0.6 A, 0.4 D). Joe is indifferent between the computer and a lottery in which the probability of winning the automobile is 20% and winning the dinner is 80%. That is, C is equivalent to the lottery (0.2 A, 0.8 D). Note that, in this lottery, the probability of winning the automobile is lower than it is in the lottery that was equivalent to the trip, which reflects the fact that the computer is less valuable to Joe than the trip. Moreover, consider the lottery (0.5 A, 0.5 D), in which the probability of winning the automobile is 50% and winning the dinner is 50%. Joe prefers the trip (B) to this lottery but prefers this lottery to the computer (C).

By the fourth and fifth axioms, we know that, for Joe, the first lottery over all four outcomes is equivalent to a simpler lottery over the best and worst outcomes (the automobile and the dinner) and, in this simpler lottery, the probability of winning the automobile equals $0.25 + 0.25(0.6) + 0.25(0.2) = 0.45$, and the probability of winning the dinner equals $0.25(0.4) + 0.25(0.8) + 0.25 = 0.55$.

Moreover, for Joe, the second lottery is equivalent to a simpler lottery in which the probability of winning the automobile equals $0.15 + 0.50(0.6) + 0.15(0.2) = 0.48$, and the probability of winning the dinner equals $0.50(0.4) + 0.15(0.8) + 0.20 = 0.52$.

Because Joe's preferences are consistent with all six axioms, then Joe should prefer the second lottery because it is equivalent to the second simpler lottery, which has a larger probability of winning the automobile (the best outcome). Joe's preferences can be described by the following utility function: $U(A) = 1$, $U(B) = 0.6$, $U(C) = 0.2$, $U(D) = 0$. (This is not the only utility function consistent with Joe's preferences.) The expected utility of the first lottery is 0.45, and the expected utility of the second lottery is 0.48.

For outcomes involving money, one way to measure utility more precisely is to let the decision-maker compare different risky situations and identify the one that is preferred.

A common risk model is the exponential:

$$U(x) = 1 - e^{-x/R}.$$

The parameter R, called the *risk tolerance*, is used to capture the degree to which the decision-maker accepts risk (Clemen and Reilly, 2001). A decision-maker with this risk model has a constant absolute risk aversion, and the absolute risk aversion equals $1/R$. A larger value of R (smaller $1/R$) is more risk neutral; a smaller value of R (larger $1/R$) is more risk averse.

There are multiple ways to assess the risk tolerance. An organization's risk tolerance may have the same magnitude as its budget (Walls *et al.*, 1995). By examining previous risky decisions, one can determine the risk tolerance that is consistent with these decisions. For instance, this type of analysis revealed that an oil exploration group used a risk tolerance between $20 and $30 million for evaluating and ranking drilling projects (Walls *et al.*, 1995).

More directly, one can estimate a decision-maker's risk tolerance by asking the decision-maker to consider hypothetical decisions. Analyzing these choices will reveal the risk tolerance.

Consider the following decision: Would the decision-maker prefer (over a no-loss, no-gain certainty) a lottery in which there is a 50% chance of a gain of Y and a 50% chance of a loss of $Y/2$? Note that the expected value of this lottery is $Y/4$, so a risk-neutral decision-maker should prefer it. A risk-averse decision-maker should prefer it when the possible loss is small but reject it when the possible loss is large. To determine the risk tolerance, one needs to know the values of Y for which the decision-maker will prefer the gamble over the no-change certainty. The answer should be a range of values of Y from 0 to some maximum value. Let M be the maximum value. Because M is the largest value that makes the lottery desirable, the expected utility of the lottery with $Y = M$ should be 0. Thus, we have to find R such that $0.5(U(M) + U(-M/2)) = 0$. The only feasible answer is the following:

$$R = \frac{M}{2\ln(1 + \sqrt{5}) - 2\ln 2} \approx 1.039M.$$

For instance, if $M = \$4,000$, then $R = \$4,156$. If $M = \$10$, then $R = \$10.39$.

After estimating R for the decision-maker, one can analyze risky decisions in a way that is consistent with the decision-maker's preferences by calculating the utility for every outcome, calculating each alternative's expected utility (instead of the expected monetary value), and identifying the best alternative (the one with the greatest expected utility).

Let $EU(A)$ be the expected utility of an alternative A that has uncertain outcomes. There is a sure value that has a utility equal to $EU(A)$. This value is called the *certainty equivalent* (or cash equivalent) of A and can be denoted as $CE(A)$. In particular,

$$U(CE(A)) = EU(A).$$

If $U(x) = 1 - e^{-x/R}$, then $CE(A) = -R\ln(1 - EU(A))$.

A decision-maker should be indifferent between the risky alternative A and its certainty equivalent $CE(A)$. For a risk-averse decision-maker, the certainty equivalent will be less than the *expected monetary value* of A, which can be denoted $EMV(A)$. (In the diagnostic device design decision, the expected monetary value of using the LED was $-\$10,250$.) The difference between an alternative's expected monetary value and its certainty equivalent is called the *risk premium*, which can be denoted $RP(A)$:

$$RP(A) = EMV(A) - CE(A).$$

Example 5.10   Consider the choice between two gambles: the first (A) has a \$30 gain or a \$1 loss. The second (B) is a \$2,000 gain or a \$1,900 loss. In both, the probability of a gain is 50%, and the probability of a loss is 50%. The expected monetary value of A is $EMV(A) = \$14.50$, and the expected monetary value of B is $EMV(B) = \$50$. It appears that B is better than A. However, a risk-averse decision-maker is likely to choose A because there is no way to lose a lot of money. The risk model is consistent with this behavior.

For instance, if $R = \$4,156$, then the first gamble has an expected utility $EU(A) = 0.5(0.007 - 0.000) = 0.003$, and the second gamble has an expected utility $EU(B) = 0.5(0.382 - 0.580) = -0.099$. Gamble A has a greater expected utility than gamble B does, but gamble B has the greater expected monetary value. The certainty equivalent of gamble A is \$14.47, which nearly equals the expected monetary value because the decision-maker's utility function is nearly linear for small gains and losses. The risk premium is only 3 cents. The certainty equivalent of gamble B is $-\$391.61$, which reflects the decision-maker's risk aversion. Its risk premium is \$441.61. The greater risk premium reflects the fact that gamble B, for this decision-maker, is riskier.

Consider again the lottery discussed in the St. Petersburg Paradox. If the lottery costs \$10 to play, then, for a decision maker who has $R = \$4,156$, the expected utility of the profit equals $\sum_{n=1}^{\infty} \frac{1}{2^n}(1 - e^{-(2^n-10)/R}) \approx 0.000517$, which is positive, so such a decision-maker should be willing to play. (The certainty equivalent is a gain of approximately \$2.15.) If the lottery costs \$20, however, the expected utility of the lottery is approximately -0.00189, and such a decision-maker should be unwilling to play. (The certainty equivalent is a loss of approximately \$7.85, a drop of \$10 because the utility function is nearly linear around 0.)

The exponential utility function is a model of constant absolute risk aversion because the expected utility of the lottery does not depend on the decision-maker's wealth. To model decision-makers who will take larger gambles if they have more wealth, however, a different utility function is needed. Utility functions that model constant relative risk aversion can be used. (The exponential function had constant absolute risk aversion.) The general form has a non-negative parameter α:

$$U(x) = \frac{x^{1-\alpha}}{1-\alpha} \text{ for } x > 0.$$

The constant relative risk aversion equals α. When $\alpha = 0$, the utility function is linear and is appropriate for a risk neutral decision-maker. A larger value of α is appropriate for a more risk-averse decision-maker. For $\alpha = 1$, $U(x) = \ln x$. For $\alpha > 1$, $U(x)$ is always negative but increases toward 0. Note that $U(x)$ is not the utility of the change in the wealth; instead, it is the utility of the resulting wealth x, which is valid as long as wealth remains positive.

Example 5.11   This example is based on one from Clemen and Reilly (2001). Rose has \$10,000 and has the opportunity to invest in a gamble that has the following three outcomes: a 30% chance of gaining \$10,000, a 25% chance of no change, or a 45% chance of losing \$5,000. The expected gain is \$750, and the expected resulting wealth is \$10,750. (The alternative is not investing, which would leave her with \$10,000.)

If Rose's preferences about risk aversion can be models as ln(wealth), then the utility of her current wealth equals 9.2103. The utility of the \$10,000 gain, which would increase her wealth to \$20,000, equals 9.9035. The utility of the \$5,000 loss, which would reduce her wealth to \$5,000, equals 8.5172. The expected utility of the investment is 9.1064, which is less than the utility of her current wealth, so she should, to be consistent with her preferences, avoid the investment.

The certainty equivalent (cash equivalent) of this investment for Rose is the value CE such that $U(\$10,000 + CE) = \ln(\$10,000 + CE) = 9.1064$. The value CE equals $-\$987$, a loss, which again indicates that she should avoid the investment. Although the investment has a positive expected monetary value, it is equivalent to a certain loss to Rose, a risk-averse decision-maker. The risk premium is the difference between the expected monetary value of the lottery and the certainty equivalent. In this case, that difference is \$1,737.

If, however, Rose had \$70,000, the utility of doing nothing equals 11.1563. The expected utility of the investment is 11.1630, and the certainty equivalent is a \$471 increase in wealth, so she should invest. The expected gain is \$750, so the risk premium is now only \$279. More wealth makes her less risk averse.

5.9   ROBUSTNESS

Robustness is related to the extent to which the performance (or feasibility) of an alternative changes due to the impact of external (uncontrollable) variables. This is especially relevant in product design; a robust product is one "that is insensitive to manufacturing, aging, and environmental noises" (Ullman, 1997). A robust design can reduce risk by reducing the likelihood of undesirable outcomes and can be, therefore, a desirable risk management strategy.

Example 5.12   For example, consider the performance of a 4G LTE smartphone. Different wireless carriers offer such phones, but the download speed depends on the carrier and the location. Mossberg (2013) reported the following results of different carriers using an iPhone 5S: in New York City, AT&T averaged nearly 35 megabits per second (mbps), Sprint averaged about 4 mbps, T-Mobile averaged about 7 mbps, and Verizon averaged just over 18 mbps. In the suburbs of Washington, D.C., AT&T averaged 14 mbps, Sprint averaged about 7 mbps, T-Mobile averaged almost 20 mbps, and Verizon averaged 17 mbps. Finally, in Silicon Valley, California, AT&T averaged 10 mbps, Sprint averaged just over 20 mbps, T-Mobile averaged 14 mbps, and Verizon averaged 15 mbps. Thus, the performance (in these three areas) of the four carriers can be compared as follows:

- AT&T: 35, 14, and 10 mbps;
- Sprint: 4, 7, and 20 mbps;
- T-Mobile: 7, 20, and 14 mbps;
- Verizon: 18, 17, and 15 mbps.

These data would indicate that the performance using some carriers (such as AT&T and Sprint) varies greatly in different cities, while the performance using another carrier (such as Verizon) varies little in different cities.

Let $F(x)$ be the performance of alternative x on some attribute. The attribute may be an objective function, or it may be a constraint such that the decision-maker prefers that $F(x)$ should be within the interval T. For example, a designer may want the safety factor of a truss that is being designed to be greater than 2.

Generally there will some uncertainty about $F(x)$ because it depends on the value of one or more external (uncontrollable or unknown) variables. (In the smartphone example, the performance varies by city, which can be considered an external variable for people who travel a great deal.)

Let s be a scenario in which the uncertain variables are realized (the uncertainty is resolved). Then, let $F(x, s)$ be the performance of x in that scenario. Robustness relates to the distribution of $F(x, s)$ over the set S of possible scenarios. The scenarios may span a range of values of an uncertain variable (like the actual dimension of a part) or may be a set of distinct states.

A narrow distribution on $F(x, s)$ means that x is a *robust design* on that attribute. Of course, an alternative that is robust on one attribute (say, cost) may be not robust on another attribute (say, reliability).

It may be possible to predict $F(x, s)$ from analytical engineering models or it may be necessary to perform physical experiments to determine these (using statistical models to fill in the gaps, as in response surface methods).

5.9.1 Variance and Range

A key measure is the variability of $F(x, s)$ over the set S of scenarios. Graphs of the distribution or statistical measures such as the range or variance will give insight into the robustness of an alternative.

If we have a probability distribution $g(s)$ that describes the probability of each scenario s, the mean $\mu(x) = E[F(x, s)]$ and variance $\sigma^2(x) = \text{Var}[F(x, s)]$ can be determined as follows:

$$\mu(x) = E[F(x, s)] = \sum_{s \in S} g(s)F(x, s)$$

$$\sigma^2(x) = \text{Var}[F(x, s)] = \sum_{s \in S} g(s)(F(x, s) - \mu(x))^2.$$

The range $R(x)$ is another useful way to describe the variability of $F(x, s)$ over the set S of scenarios:

$$R(x) = \max_{s \in S} F(x, s) - \min_{s \in S} F(x, s).$$

Example 5.13 Consider the smart phones from Example 5.12. The variance of the performance of the different carriers can be determined from the performance in each city (if we treat the three cities as three samples). For AT&T, the variance equals 180 mbps^2. For Sprint, the variance equals 72 mbps^2. For T-Mobile, the variance equals 42 mbps^2. For Verizon, the variance equals 2.3 mbps^2.

The range of the performance of the different carriers can be determined as well. For AT&T, the range equals $35 - 10 = 25$ mbps. For Sprint, the range equals $20 - 4 = 16$ mbps. For T-Mobile, the range equals $20 - 7 = 13$ mbps. For Verizon, the range equals $18 - 15 = 3$ mbps.

5.9.2 Robust Optimization

When comparing two alternatives, the decision-maker would prefer the alternative that performs better in all scenarios, of course. That is, if the objective is to minimize $F(x)$, alternative y is preferred to alternative x if $F(y, s) < F(x, s)$ for all s in S (this is a type of dominance). Unfortunately, this may not occur, in which case there may be a tradeoff: some alternatives perform better in some scenarios and worse in others. Conceptually, one can consider maximizing robustness, in which case the key is to define "robustness" precisely in order to formulate the objective function.

One possible objective is to optimize the worst-case scenario by finding the alternative x that minimizes the maximum (over s in S) of $F(x, s)$, if minimizing F is desirable. In contrast, if maximizing F is desirable, then the objective is find the alternative x that maximizes the minimum of $F(x, s)$.

Another possibility is to minimize the maximum regret, which is the difference between $F(x, s)$ and $F^*(s) = F(x^*(s), s)$, where $x^*(s)$ is the optimal alternative for that scenario. Minimizing the regret yields an alternative with a performance that is never too far away from the optimal in any scenario. More precisely, the objective function is to minimize the maximum (over s in S) of $|F(x, s) - F^*(s)|$.

Example 5.14   Consider the smart phones from Example 5.12. Maximizing download speed is desirable. Because Verizon has the greatest minimum (15 mbps), it can be considered robust. The performance using the other carriers is less than 15 mbps in at least one city.

The best speed in New York City was 35 mbps, and the regret for each carrier (in that city) is the difference between its download speed and 35 mbps: the regret for AT&T is 0 mbps; for Sprint, 31 mbps; for T-Mobile, 28 mbps; and for Verizon, 17 mbps. In the suburbs of Washington, DC, the best speed was 20 mbps; the regret for AT&T is 6 mbps; for Sprint, 13 mbps; for T-Mobile, 0 mbps; and for Verizon, 3 mbps. In Silicon Valley, the best speed was 20 mbps; the regret for AT&T is 10 mbps; for Sprint, 0 mbps; for T-Mobile, 6 mbps; and for Verizon, 5 mbps. The maximum regret for AT&T is $\max\{0, 6, 10\} = 10$ mbps; for Sprint, $\max\{31, 13, 0\} = 31$ mbps; for T-Mobile, $\max\{28, 0, 6\} = 28$ mbps; and for Verizon, $\max\{17, 3, 5\} = 17$ mbps. AT&T has the minimum maximum regret.

5.9.3   Robust Feasibility

Feasibility robustness describes whether the alternative becomes infeasible in any scenario. More precisely, given an interval T, the decision-maker may require that an alternative is feasible if and only if it satisfies the constraint that $F(x, s)$ is in T for all s in S. Any design that fails to satisfy this constraint is not feasible. In the smartphone example, if a user considers 10 mbps a good speed, then only AT&T and Verizon are feasible carriers in these three cities. Both Sprint and T-Mobile fail to meet that standard in at least one city.

5.9.4   Risk-Based Design

If it is not possible (or desirable) to satisfy the constraint that $F(x, s)$ should be in the interval T for all s in S, then the decision-maker may relax this constraint. If there is a probability distribution over the s in S, then the decision-maker may require instead that a feasible alternative must satisfy the constraint that the probability that $F(x, s)$ is in T is greater than or equal to a specific threshold, which guarantees that the alternative is sufficiently likely to be feasible.

5.9.5   Tradeoff Between Robustness and Optimization

An alternative that has the best expected performance may fail to be robust because the uncertainties lead to high probabilities of failure or because the performance degrades quickly due to the uncertainties. Thus the performance measure or the constraints must be formulated to take into account the uncertainties.

Example 5.15   Consider the truss design problem from Scott and Antonsson (2005) in which the load equals 10 kg. Figure 5.6 shows a schematic of the truss. Colleen, the engineer designing the truss, must select values for the design variables, and the objective functions include maximizing two safety factors (one for bending and the

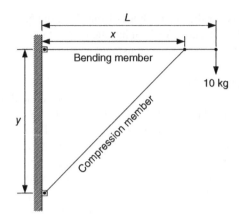

Figure 5.6   A schematic of the truss described by Scott and Antonsson (2005).

other one for compression) and minimizing mass. These outputs are nonlinear functions of the design variables.

Suppose that the truss, after its manufacture and installation, will vary from the nominal design, so there is uncertainty about the actual values of the variables and the truss safety. In particular, suppose that the distance from the wall to the pin has an error ε that is uniformly distributed between -0.01 and 0.01 m. This error affects both $\tilde{x} = x + \varepsilon$, the installed distance from the wall to the pin, and $\tilde{y}$, the installed distance between the lower support and the upper support, which changes both safety factors but not the mass. Note that the error does not affect the actual length of the compression member; thus, $\tilde{x}^2 + \tilde{y}^2 = x^2 + y^2$.

Moving the pin closer to the wall reduces the bending safety factor while moving the pin away from the wall reduces the compression safety factor. The other design variables are t, the thickness of the bending member, h, the height of the bending member, and w, the width of the compression member. The other inputs, which are fixed in this example, are the following: Young's modulus $E = 69 \times 10^9$ Pa, the density $\rho = 2660$ kg/m^3, the yield stress $\sigma = 275 \times 10^6$ Pa, the distance from the lower support to the upper support $y = 0.5$ m, the distance from the supported load to the wall $L = 1$ m, and the supported load $P = 10$ kg.

In the following functions for the safety factor in bending, the safety factor in compression, and the mass, all of the distances are in meters:

$$S_b = \frac{\sigma t h^2}{12P(L - \tilde{x})}$$

$$S_c = \frac{\pi^2 E \, \tilde{x} \, \tilde{y} w^4}{12PL(x^2 + y^2)^{1.5}}$$

$$M = \rho(htL + w^2 \sqrt{x^2 + y^2}).$$

TABLE 5.1   Four Truss Designs. x is the Nominal Distance from Wall to pin (m). w is the Width of Compression Member (mm). PR is the Probability that Both Safety Factors Will be at Least 2.

x (m)	w (mm)	Mass (g)	PR
0.8568	5.3234	141.3	0.00
0.8603	5.3631	142.6	0.67
0.8636	5.4020	144.0	0.84
0.8668	5.4401	145.3	1.00

The desired safety factor is 2; that is, both the bending safety factor and the compression safety factor should be at least 2. Consider the four designs listed in Table 5.1. (Both the thickness t and the height h of the bending member equal 5 mm, but the nominal distance from the wall to the pin x and w, the width of the compression member, is varied as shown in the table.) The first one is the design that minimizes mass while satisfying this constraint if there is no error. Because some error will occur, and one of the two safety factors will be reduced, the probability that this design will satisfy the safety factor constraint equals zero.

The second design minimizes mass while satisfying that both safety factors will be at least 2.05 if there is no error. As long as the error remains small, both safety factors will be at least 2. The probability of this equals 0.67.

The third design minimizes mass while satisfying that both safety factors will be at least 2.1 if there is no error. The probability that the error remains small enough (so that both safety factors will be at least 2) equals 0.84.

The fourth design minimizes mass while satisfying that both safety factors will be at least 2.15 if there is no error. In this case, the error is unlikely to reduce the safety factors below 2, and the probability that both safety factors will be at least 2 equals 1.00.

These designs, therefore, illustrate a tradeoff between performance (minimizing mass) and robustness (maximizing the safety factor). The designs that are more robust (have a higher probability of being safe) also have more mass.

5.10   UNCERTAINTY PROPAGATION: SENSITIVITY ANALYSIS

In addition to uncertainty about future events, which was discussed earlier in this chapter, decision-makers may face uncertainty about the information that they use for making a decision (epistemic uncertainty). This information may be used in decision models such as the MAUT models that were presented in Chapter 3 and the decision trees presented in this chapter.

Uncertainty about the inputs to these models leads to uncertainty about their outputs. A decision-maker should consider this uncertainty and therefore needs methods for determining it. Because the uncertainty is propagated through a model (from its inputs to its outputs), the term "uncertainty propagation" is used for such techniques.

This section discusses *sensitivity analysis*, a basic technique for determining how much the outputs can change. Sections 5.11 and 5.12 present the *method of moments*, which is useful when there is a specific equation that expresses the output as a function of the uncertain input, and *Monte Carlo simulation*, which is an extremely general procedure. Because it relies on knowing the function, the method of moments is a type of intrusive model, whereas Monte Carlo simulation is a type of nonintrusive (or black box) model (cf. Ghosh and Olewnik, 2013).

All of these techniques can be applied to multiple outputs. The techniques presented here are for one output and should be repeated as necessary to study multiple outputs.

Let Y be the relevant output, and let $x_1, \ldots, x_m$ be the uncertain inputs that are needed to determine Y. In general, the output is a function of the inputs, so there is some function f such that $Y = f(x_1, \ldots, x_m)$. In some cases, it may be impossible to write down the function as a mathematical expression, and determining the value of Y requires running a computer program or some other procedure.

The simplest type of sensitivity analysis determines how the output changes as the value of one input variable changes, but the other variables remain at given values. Let $\hat{x}_1, \ldots, \hat{x}_m$ be the given values of the input variables, and let $S_1, \ldots, S_m$ be the ranges of possible values for the input variables. Then, one can determine the sensitivity of the output Y to input variable x_i as follows:

$$\Delta_i(Y) = \max_{x_i \in S_i} f(\hat{x}_1, \ldots, x_i, \ldots, \hat{x}_m) - \min_{x_i \in S_i} f(\hat{x}_1, \ldots, x_i, \ldots, \hat{x}_m).$$

This value can be found by analyzing the function to determine its maximum and minimum directly or by evaluating $f(\hat{x}_1, \ldots, x_i, \ldots, \hat{x}_m)$ at different values of x_i from the range S_i. The output is more sensitive to those input variables that correspond to larger values of $\Delta_i(Y)$.

One can also consider the rate of change by determining the partial derivative $\partial Y / \partial x_i$ or by evaluating $(f(\hat{x}_1, \ldots, \hat{x}_i + \delta_i, \ldots, \hat{x}_m) - f(\hat{x}_1, \ldots, \hat{x}_i, \ldots, \hat{x}_m))/\delta_i$ for appropriate values of δ_i.

Tornado diagrams and spider plots can be used to show how the output variable varies as each input varies over its range of values. See Eschenbach (1992) and Chelst and Canbolat (2012) for more information about constructing these diagrams. (Note that a spider plot is not the same as a spider chart, also known as a radar chart or star plot, which is used to graph the values of multiple attributes on axes that radiate from a common origin.)

Example 5.16 Consider the truss design problem from Example 5.15 (Scott and Antonsson, 2005). Colleen, the engineer designing the truss, must select values for the design variables, and the objective functions include maximizing two safety factors (one for bending and the other one for compression) and minimizing mass. In this example, we will consider the sensitivity of the output variables to uncertainties in

TABLE 5.2   The Impact of Changes to Three Input
Variables on S_b, the Safety Factor in Bending, S_c, the
Safety Factor in Compression, and the Mass M.

Input Variable		S_b	S_c	$M(g)$
t	Min	6.36	10.76	329.49
	Max	6.68	10.76	338.00
	Max–min	0.33	0.00	8.51
h	Min	6.20	10.76	329.49
	Max	6.85	10.76	338.00
	Max–min	0.65	0.00	8.51
w	Min	6.52	9.72	325.67
	Max	6.52	11.87	342.02
	Max–min	0.00	2.15	16.35

three input variables: t, the thickness of the bending member, h, the height of the
bending member, and w, the width of the compression member.

The other inputs, which are fixed in this example, are the following: Young's mod-
ulus $E = 69 \times 10^9$ Pa, the density $\rho = 2660$ kg/m^3, the yield stress $\sigma = 275 \times 10^6$ Pa,
the distance from the wall to the pin $x = 0.82$ m, the distance from the lower support to
the upper support $y = 0.5$ m, the distance from the supported load to the wall $L = 1$ m,
and the supported load $P = 10$ kg. The functions for the safety factor in bending,
the safety factor in compression, and the mass are the same as in the example in
Section 5.9.

Colleen is uncertain if the manufactured truss will meet the specified design variables. She believes that t, h, and w will be in the range [7.8, 8.2] mm, but she is
concerned about how this uncertainty will create uncertainty in the safety factors and
the mass.

Changing one variable at a time over this range yields the results shown in
Table 5.2. Naturally, changes to t and h, which are characteristics of the bending
member, do not affect S_c, the safety factor in compression; changes to w, which is
a characteristic of the compression member, do not affect S_b, the safety factor in
bending. Changes to t or h make a small change to S_b, but changes to w make a
significant change to S_c, although the safety factor is still quite large. Changes to
only t or h change the mass by over 8 g, but changes to w change the mass by over
16 g. The mass is more sensitive to w than to t and h.

5.11   UNCERTAINTY PROPAGATION: METHOD OF MOMENTS

The method of moments requires a mathematical function $Y = f(x_1, \ldots, x_m)$ that
expresses the relationship between the input and the output variables and its first and
second partial derivatives. Each input variable is modeled as a random variable. The
expected value of x_i equals μ_i, and the variance equals $S^2(x_i)$. The method estimates

the expected value and variance of the output variable Y. The Taylor series expansion of the function $f(x_1, \ldots, x_m)$ is the basis of the method of moments, which assumes that the input variables are independent.

The estimators for the expected value and variance of the output variable Y are the following (Modarres, 2006):

$$E(Y) \approx f(\mu_1, \mu_2, \ldots, \mu_m) + \frac{1}{2} \sum_{i=1}^{m} \left[\frac{\partial^2 f(X)}{\partial x_i^2} \right]_{x_i = \mu_i} S^2(x_i)$$

$$\mathrm{Var}(Y) = \sum_{i=1}^{m} \left[\frac{\partial f(X)}{\partial x_i} \right]_{x_i = \mu_i}^{2} S^2(x_i).$$

Example 5.17   Consider again the truss design problem from Example 5.16. The width $w = 8$ mm, and Colleen is not considering any uncertainty in that variable. The uncertainty about the actual value of the variable h is modeled as a random variable that is uniformly distributed over the range [0.78, 0.82] mm. The uncertainty about the actual value of the variable t is modeled in the same way. The expected value of both is 8 mm, and the variance of both is $1/75$ mm^2.

To apply the method of moments to the safety factor in bending, determine the following partial derivatives:

$$\frac{\partial S_b}{\partial h} = \frac{2 \sigma t h}{1000^3 (12P)(L - x)},$$

$$\frac{\partial^2 S_b}{\partial h^2} = \frac{2 \sigma t}{1000^3 (12P)(L - x)},$$

$$\frac{\partial S_b}{\partial t} = \frac{\sigma h^2}{1000^3 (12P)(L - x)}, \text{and}$$

$$\frac{\partial^2 S_b}{\partial t^2} = 0.$$

When each of these evaluated for the given values and the expected values of h and t, they yield the following:

$$\frac{\partial S_b}{\partial h} = 1.6296,$$

$$\frac{\partial^2 S_b}{\partial h^2} = 0.2037,$$

$$\frac{\partial S_b}{\partial t} = 0.8148, \text{and}$$

$$\frac{\partial^2 S_b}{\partial t^2} = 0$$

When h and t equal 8 mm (their expected value), then $S_b = 6.519$.

$$E(S_b) = 6.519 + \frac{1}{2}(0.2037)\frac{1}{75} = 6.520.$$

$$\text{Var}(S_b) = (1.6296)^2\frac{1}{75} + (0.8148)^2\frac{1}{75} = 0.04426.$$

To apply the method of moments to the mass M, determine and evaluate the following partial derivatives:

$$\frac{\partial m}{\partial h} = \frac{\rho t L}{1000^2} = 0.02128,$$

$$\frac{\partial m}{\partial t} = \frac{\rho h L}{1000^2} = 0.02128, \text{ and}$$

$$\frac{\partial^2 m}{\partial h^2} = \frac{\partial^2 m}{\partial t^2} = 0.$$

When h and t equal 8 mm (their expected value), then the mass $M = 0.334$ kg. Because the second derivatives are both zero, the expected value of the mass $E(M) = 0.334$ kg $= 334$ g. The variance of the mass $\text{Var}(M) = (0.02128)^2\frac{1}{75} + (0.02128)^2\frac{1}{75} = 1.208 \times 10^{-5}$ kg^2 $= 12.08$ g^2.

Other numerical techniques for propagating uncertainty have been developed. For example, the equivalent cash flow decomposition technique can use the moments of a stochastic annual cash flow and create a complete distribution of the payback period without simulation (Kim *et al.*, 2013).

5.12   UNCERTAINTY PROPAGATION: MONTE CARLO SIMULATION

Unlike the method of moments, Monte Carlo simulation does not require a mathematical equation; it requires only some procedure (usually implemented as a computer program) that can calculate the output variable(s) given values for the input variables. The method does not require approximating the output with a simpler, surrogate model.

Monte Carlo simulation generates a large number of samples of each uncertain input; using these samples, it generates a large number of samples of each uncertain output. Then, one can view the distribution of the outputs and use a variety of statistical techniques to analyze the results. The text by Fishman (2006) covers the details of various Monte Carlo techniques, including sample generation and variance reduction.

The basic Monte Carlo approach works as follows: Let n be the number of samples. For $i = 1, \ldots, n$, choose a random sample for every input variable and evaluate the output variable to get Y_i, the randomly generated sample. Determine the sample mean $\overline{Y}$ and the sample variance S^2 as follows:

$$\overline{Y} = \frac{1}{n}\sum_{i=1}^{n} Y_i$$

$$S^2 = \frac{1}{n-1}\sum_{i=1}^{n} \left(Y_i - \overline{Y} \right)^2.$$

From these statistics, the $(1 - \alpha)100$ percent confidence interval on the expected value of the output equals $[\overline{Y} - z_{\alpha/2}\frac{S}{\sqrt{n}}, \overline{Y} + z_{\alpha/2}\frac{S}{\sqrt{n}}]$. For a 95% confidence interval, use $z_{0.025} = 1.96$; for a 90% confidence interval, use $z_{0.05} = 1.645$.

Example 5.18   For the truss design problem (considered in Examples 5.16 and 5.17), Colleen generated 5000 samples of h and 5000 samples of t, all selected from a uniform distribution between 7.8 and 8.2 mm. From these samples, she calculated 5000 values for mass and 5000 values for safety of bending. Figures 5.7 and 5.8 display histograms of these results. For the safety factor in bending, the sample mean was 6.524, and the sample variance was 0.04416. This yielded a 90% confidence interval of [6.519, 6.528]. For mass, the sample mean was 0.3338 kg, and the sample variance was 1.197×10^{-5} kg^2. This yielded a 90% confidence interval of [0.3337, 0.3339].

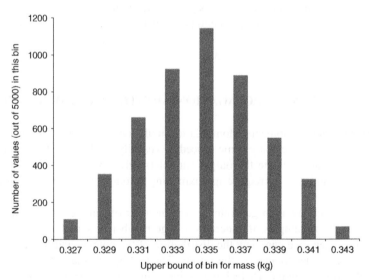

Figure 5.7   A histogram of 5000 values for mass.

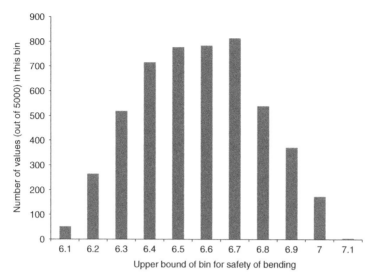

Figure 5.8   A histogram of 5000 values for safety of bending.

Note that these confidence intervals are close to the means estimated using the method of moments.

Monte Carlo simulation can be used to explore the how uncertainties about the attribute values affect the relative desirability of the alternatives. Leber and Herrmann (2012) presented a Monte Carlo simulation technique for doing this and applied it to the problem of selecting and deploying the best technology for use in an airport radiation detection system. Limited experimental testing yielded uncertainty about the performance of the technology on critical tasks; some of the attributes in the decision-making model measured this performance. Leber and Herrmann randomly generated 1000 samples of the uncertain attributes. Each alternative specified particular technologies and how to deploy them. For each set of samples, they determined the overall utility of every alternative and identified the best alternative (the one with the highest overall utility). Then they determined which alternative was the best one most often. They also compared the distribution of the utility for the top six alternatives but saw that no alternative stochastically dominated the others in this case. However, the similarity of the top six alternatives provided guidance to the best technologies to select.

Monte Carlo simulation can also be used to explore the impact of changes to the weights in a multiattribute utility function. Dyer *et al.* (1998) described the multiattribute utility function used to compare alternatives for disposing of surplus weapons-grade plutonium. They randomly generated 5000 sets of 37 weights that were consistent with the ordering of the assessed weights. For each set of sample weights, they ranked the alternatives and then determined each alternative's distribution of ranks in order to show that the rankings generated using the assessed weights were robust because the same alternatives had the best ranking.

EXERCISES

5.1. Consider an uncertain event that will occur in the near future: a baseball or football game, an election, or the weather. Assess your subjective probability for the outcomes of that event. Do the same with a colleague, friend, or classmate. Are your probabilities the same? Why not?

5.2. Consider the example in which Joe must choose between two lotteries with four possible prizes (Example 5.8). Does either lottery stochastically dominate the other?

5.3. Consider the situation in Exercise 2. Suppose that a third lottery is presented to Joe. In this lottery, the probabilities of winning A, B, C, and D are 20%, 20%, 30%, and 30%, respectively. Do either of the first two lotteries stochastically dominate this one?

5.4. When Advanced RISC Machines (now ARM) was founded in 1990, the microprocessor engineering firm faced a decision about how to compete with Intel and other firms in the integrated circuit (chip) business: they could manufacture and sell the chips that they designed or they could license their designs to chip manufacturers (Manjoo, 2013). A key uncertainty related to the yield of a new chip fabrication facility, which would affect the sales and profits. Assume the following: if ARM licenses their designs, then they will make $400 million. If they build a facility to manufacture their chips, they will have to invest $1 billion. The facility's yield is uncertain, which creates uncertainty in their revenue. If the yield remains low, their revenue will be only $100 million. If the yield is moderate, their revenue will be $1 billion. If the yield is excellent, their revenue will be $2 billion. The firm estimates that the probability of low yield equals 0.4, the probability of moderate yield equals 0.5, and the probability of excellent yield equals 0.1. Draw a decision tree corresponding to this decision. What is the expected revenue of the two alternatives? What is the best policy?

5.5. (This problem is based on one in Benjamin and Cornell, 1970.) Mary is designing a cofferdam to reduce the likelihood of flooding at a borrow pit from which embankment material was being taken to build a dam in Chihuahua, Mexico. She considered two different heights for the cofferdam: 3 and 4.5 m. If the cofferdam were 3 m high (which would cost $15,600), then flooding would occur only if the river's flow exceeded 200 m³/s, which had occurred in 43 of the last 45 years. If the cofferdam were 4.5 m high (which would cost $18,600), then flooding would occur only if the river's flow exceeded 550 m³/s, which had occurred in 32 of the last 45 years. The delay caused by flooding would cost the contractor $30,000. Draw a decision tree that includes the above decision and uncertainty. What is the expected total cost of the two alternatives? If Mary wants to minimize the expected total cost, which alternative should she choose (how high should the cofferdam be)?

5.6. (This problem is based on one presented by Toczek, 2012.) Louis owns 1,000 acres (400 hectares) and must make the following decisions: whether to plant corn or soybeans, whether to buy crop insurance, and whether to use fertilizer. (All of these decisions must be made before the upcoming planting season.) Insuring 1,000 acres of corn costs \$35,000; insuring 1,000 acres of soybeans costs \$20,000. Fertilizing 1,000 acres of corn costs \$30,000; fertilizing 1,000 acres of soybeans costs \$10,000. If Louis plants corn and the crop fails, then he will lose \$190,000; otherwise he will gain \$190,000. If Louis plants soybeans and the crop fails, then he will lose \$170,000; otherwise he will gain \$170,000. (These are in addition to the insurance and fertilizer costs.) If Louis uses fertilizer but does not buy insurance, then there is a 5% chance that the crop will fail due to a disaster. If Louis uses fertilizer and buys insurance, then there is no chance that the crop will fail. If Louis does not use fertilizer and does not buy insurance, then there is a 15% chance that the crop will fail due to a disaster or a failure to grow. If Louis does not use fertilizer but buys insurance, then there is a 10% chance that the crop will fail due to a failure to grow. Draw a decision tree that represents Louis's decision situation. What is the best policy? What is Louis's expected profit if he follows that policy?

5.7. Mary is considering two different designs for a bridge across a river than floods every year. The amount of the flood varies from year to year. Assume that the flood amount is either "small," "moderate," "large," or "very large" and that Mary can estimate the probabilities of such floods. When a flood occurs, the bridge could fail, but the likelihood depends on the type of flood. Assume that Mary can estimate, for each bridge design, the probability of the bridge failing in any of the four types of floods. If the bridge fails, it will be rebuilt. Draw a decision tree for this decision problem over a 1-year time horizon in which each branch has two chance nodes: one for the type of flood and the other one for the bridge failure. Draw another decision tree for the same problem in which each branch has a single chance node with eight outcomes (flood type and bridge failure). Finally, draw a third decision tree for the same problem in which each branch has a single chance node with only two outcomes (the bridge failure). In this last tree, how should one calculate the probabilities of each branch of the chance node? (A numerical instance of this problem can be found in Benjamin and Cornell, 1970.)

5.8. (This problem is based on an example described by Hartman (2007), and all values have been converted to present values. In this problem, we will not consider any uncertainties.) Peabody Energy was considering building a power plant in Illinois and believed that demand would increase over time. In the first year, the firm could decide to start construction then, to cancel the project, or delay another year. If they cancelled, they would not gain or lose anything. If they delayed in the first year, then they would face the same decision in the second year. If they delayed in the second year, then they would face the same decision in the third year. If they delayed in the third year, then they would face the same decision in the fourth year, but, in the fourth year, the only two alternatives were to start construction or to cancel the project. If they started construction in the first year, the firm would lose $51 million over 20 years. If they started construction in the second year, the firm would lose $12 million over 20 years. If they started construction in the third year, the firm would gain $12 million over 20 years. If they started construction in the fourth year, the firm would gain $28 million over 20 years. Draw a decision tree that corresponds to the situation faced by Peabody Energy.

5.9. This problem is based on an example described by Hartman (2007). Renesas Electronics is planning to expand a factory in which it makes flash memory. The factory can currently make 9,000 wafers per month. The expansion will increase capacity to 12,000 wafers per month. It can sell everything it makes. The expansion can start now or be delayed. If it is delayed, the firm can decide 3 months from now whether to start expansion at that point or to wait another 3 months (6 months from now). During the expansion, which will take 3 months, the factory will still make 9,000 wafers per month. Because the firm originally planned to start 6 months from now, they will have to pay $2,000,000 extra to start the expansion 3 months early (3 months from now) or $4,000,000 extra to start the expansion 6 months early (now). The profit per wafer in the next 6 months is uncertain and will not be known until after the decision to start now or delay is made. If the expansion is delayed (not started now), then this value will be known before the next decision. The firm estimates that the probability that profit will be $320 per wafer (for the next six months) equals 60%; the probability that profit will be $310 per wafer (for the next 6 months) equals 40%. After 6 months, the profit per wafer will be $300. Because the firm will certainly expand, ignore the cost of expansion. Consider the profit over the next 12 months (the profit from the wafers sold minus any extra cost for starting early). Draw a decision tree that corresponds to the situation faced by Renesas Electronics. Evaluate this tree to determine the optimal policy. What is the expected profit?

5.10. Louis is going skiing. He does not know how many days he will be skiing, but he will need skis every day. He can rent skis at $40 per day, or he can buy skis for $200. He can rent skis for a few days and then buy skis; once he buys some skis, he would not need to rent skis again. Although the number of ski days is unknown, he wants to minimize the total amount spent on skis (under the constraint that he will need skis every day that he skis). There are two ways to model this problem. First, we can model this is as a sequence of decisions: at the beginning of every day, Louis must decide whether to rent or buy, and there is uncertainty at the end of every day about whether he will be back the next day. Second, we can model this as a one-time decision: At the beginning of the first day, Louis picks a specific day on which he will buy skis if he is still skiing. (There is still the uncertainty about how many days he will ski.) Draw decision trees that correspond to these two views of the situation that Louis faces. Because Louis has no probability distribution for the number of days for which he will ski, his objective is to minimize the maximum regret. If Louis will pick a specific day on which to buy skis, which alternative(s) minimize the maximum regret?

5.11. Consider the following game that involves a fair coin (the probability of heads equals 0.5; the probability of tails equals 0.5). The coin will be flipped; if it is heads, the player gets $2,000; if it is tails, the coin will be flipped a second time. If the second flip is heads, the player gets $4,000; if it is tails, the coin will be flipped again. If the third flip is heads, the player gets $8,000; if it is tails, the coin will be flipped again. If the fourth flip is heads, the player gets $16,000; if it is tails, the coin will be flipped again. If the fifth flip is heads, the player gets $32,000; if it is tails, the game ends, and the player gets nothing. Joe (who is risk neutral in this situation) is given the opportunity to play this game under the following conditions: he will pay $3,000 and then win some amount or nothing based on the coin flips. Draw a decision tree for Joe's decision; should he play?

5.12. Consider the game that was described in Exercise 5.11. Rose (who is risk averse in this situation; her risk tolerance is $5,000) is given the opportunity to play this game under the following conditions: she will pay $3,000 and then win some amount or nothing based on the coin flips. Should she play? For Rose, what is the certainty equivalent of playing this game?

5.13. Rose is a risk-averse decision-maker and faces a decision involving the oil rights on a piece of land. A decision analyst helps her determine an appropriate utility function by asking her to consider what she would do in some hypothetical situations. In the first hypothetical situation, she is given the opportunity to take the following gamble: there is a 50% chance of a gain of $200,000 and a 50% chance of a loss of $100,000. In this situation, she would prefer the gamble to doing nothing. In the second hypothetical situation, she is given the opportunity to take the following gamble: there is a 50% chance of a gain of $500,000 and a 50% chance of a loss of $250,000. In this situation, she does NOT prefer the gamble; she prefers to do nothing. If she will model her utility with the following exponential utility function $U(x) = 1 - e^{-x/R}$, then which of the following values of the risk tolerance R yields a utility function that is consistent with her preferences: $50,000, $100,000, $400,000, or $800,000?

5.14. (This problem is adapted from one in Pratt *et al.*, 1995.) Joe has inherited an option on a plot of land and must decide whether to drill on the site before the option expires or abandon the rights. (If he abandons the rights, there is no gain and no loss.) He is not sure if there is oil or not. Drilling will cost $100,000 whether or not there is oil. If oil is found, then it will generate $450,000 in revenue. The likelihood of finding depends on the subsurface structure. If the

subsurface structure is type A, then there is certainly oil. If the subsurface structure is type B, then the probability of finding oil is only 10%. In that area, the
probability of a type A structure is 80%; the probability of a type B structure
is 20%. Before deciding to drill, Joe can decide to pay $10,000 for a seismic
sounding that will reveal whether the subsurface structure is type A or type B.
He can get the results in time to review them before making the drilling decision. (However, he does not have to get the seismic sounding.) Draw a decision
tree that includes the above decisions and uncertainties. Use it to find the optimal policy. In this situation, Joe is risk neutral.

5.15. Suppose Rose has inherited the option described in Exercise 5.14. Use the
appropriate risk tolerance value from Exercise 5.13 to determine what Rose
should do.

5.16. Show that $R = 1.039\,M$ is the appropriate risk tolerance such that $0.5(U(M) +
U(-M/2)) = 0$ (as discussed in Section 5.8). (Hint: make the substitution of
$a = e^{\frac{M}{2R}}$ and solve for a and then R.)

5.17. Consider the four truss designs described in Example 5.15. For each design
and both safety factors, determine the smallest and largest values of each safety
factor across the range of the error. How does the range of the safety factors
vary? Which design has the least range of the safety factors?

5.18. Consider again the ARM example (Exercise 5.4). Assume that the probability
of low yield is 0.4, but the probabilities for moderate yield and excellent yield
are uncertain. For what range of these probabilities does the manufacturing
alternative have a greater expected revenue than the licensing alternative?

5.19. For each of the following statements about ways to propagate uncertainty, state
whether it best describes (1) the method of moments or (2) Monte Carlo simulation:

   (a) Can be used with any type of model
   (b) Requires a model that can be differentiated
   (c) Can require significant computational effort
   (d) Is based on the Taylor series expansion of the model.

5.20. This exercise is based on one in Hartman (2007). A pharmaceutical company
needs to use a supercomputer to run simulation models as part of its research
on cures for AIDS, cancer, and other diseases. The firm expects to perform
thousands of simulation runs per year for the next 3 years. The firm can purchase a supercomputer for $2.5 million; the annual operating and maintenance
costs are $200,000 per year, and the supercomputer can perform 15,000 runs
per year. For every simulation run above 15,000 in a year, the operating costs
rise $1,000 per year to cover the needed overtime. A second alternative is
to outsource the simulation runs to an IT firm that offers supercomputing
services on demand. They will charge the pharmaceutical company $400 per
simulation run. Consider a 3-year time horizon, and assume that the number of

runs per year is the same every year. The firm is not sure how many simulation runs they will need to perform each year. What is the range of total cost if the number of simulation runs varies from 10,000 to 20,000 runs per year? For what range of activity (number of simulation runs per year) is purchasing a supercomputer the lowest cost alternative?

5.21. Consider the supercomputer example from Exercise 5.20. The firm is not sure about some of the relevant costs. The following probability distributions reflect their beliefs about the uncertain costs: the annual operating and maintenance costs are uniformly distributed on the range [$150,000, $250,000]; the additional operating costs for simulation runs above 15,000 per year are uniformly distributed on the range [$500, $1500] (per run per year). Use the method of moments to estimate the mean and variance of the costs if the firm purchases the supercomputer and they perform 20,000 runs per year. Use Monte Carlo sampling to estimate the distribution of costs if the firm purchases the supercomputer and they perform 20,000 runs per year.

5.22. Consider the analysis of a thermocouple that will be used to measure the temperature of a gas stream (Ghosh and Olewnik, 2013). The time $t_{0.99}$ that it will take the thermocouple to reach 0.99 of the gas stream temperature, under certain conditions, depends on the junction density ρ, the thermocouple diameter D, the specific heat capacity c, the convection coefficient h, the initial temperature T_i, and the gas temperature T_∞ as follows:

$$t_{0.99} = \frac{\rho D c}{h} \ln \left(100 - 100 \frac{T_i}{T_\infty} \right).$$

All six inputs are uncertain, so there is uncertainty about the value of the time $t_{0.99}$. Suppose that the uncertainties about all six inputs are modeled as normally distributed random quantities in which the standard deviation equals 4% of the mean. At their mean values, $\rho = 8400 \text{ kg/m}^3$, $D = 0.0007$ m, $c = 400 \text{ J/kg K}$, $h = 200 \text{ W/m}^2\text{K}$, $T_i = 300$ K, and $T_\infty = 470$ K. Use Monte Carlo sampling to determine a 95% confidence interval on the mean of $t_{0.99}$.

5.23. The reliability of a system of systems depends on the reliability of the systems that make up the whole system of systems. Consider, for example, a missile defence system that will, when fielded, include 3 control stations, 5 radar systems, and 12 launcher systems (Tamburello, 2013). The system is considered operational if at least 2 of the 3 control stations, 3 of the 5 radar systems, and 9 of the 12 launcher systems are operational. The key reliability measure is the reliability at the end of a 24-hour mission. Let R_{cs} be the reliability of a control station. Let R_{rs} be the reliability of a radar system. Let R_{ls} be the reliability of a launcher system. Let R_{SOS} be the reliability of the entire missile defence system. This can be calculated as follows:

$$T_{cs} = \sum_{i=2}^{3} \frac{3!}{i!(3-i)!} R_{cs}^i (1 - R_{cs})^{3-i}$$

$$T_{rs} = \sum_{i=3}^{5} \frac{5!}{i!(5-i)!} R_{rs}^i (1 - R_{rs})^{5-i}$$

$$T_{ls} = \sum_{i=9}^{12} \frac{12!}{i!(12-i)!} R_{rs}^i (1 - R_{rs})^{12-i}$$

$$R_{SOS} = T_{cs} T_{rs} T_{ls}$$

Suppose that there is uncertainty about these systems' reliability, and that this uncertainty is modeled as follows: R_{cs} has a beta distribution with $\alpha = 9$ and $\beta = 1$. R_{rs} has a beta distribution with $\alpha = 99$ and $\beta = 1$. R_{ls} has a beta distribution with $\alpha = 48$ and $\beta = 2$. Use Monte Carlo sampling to generate 5000 samples for R_{SOS}. What type of distribution do the sample values for R_{SOS} form? What is the estimated likelihood that R_{SOS} will be at least 0.98?

5.24. Consider the decision of whether to use an LED for a diagnostic device (Example 5.6). The analysis with multiple objectives required Joe to assess a multiattribute utility function. In particular, Joe had to state the utility of a cost of $11,000 and the utility of a delay of 2 months. For what values of these two utilities (which must be between 0 and 1) is the expected utility of using the LED greater than the utility of using the flash lamp? (Assume that the weights on the attributes' utilities remain 0.75 and 0.25.)

REFERENCES

Alpert, M., and H. Raiffa, "A progress report on the training of probability assessors," in D. Kahneman, P. Slovic, and A. Tversky, editors, *Judgment Under Uncertainty: Heuristics and Biases*, Cambridge University Press, Cambridge, England, 1982.

Aughenbaugh, Jason M., and Jeffrey W. Herrmann, "Reliability-Based Decision-Making: A Comparison of Statistical Approaches," *Journal of Statistical Theory and Practice*, Volume 3, Number 1, pages 289–304, 2009.

Aughenbaugh, Jason M., and Chris J.J. Paredis, "The Value of Using Imprecise Probabilities in Engineering Design," *Journal of Mechanical Design*, Volume 128, Number 4, pp. 969–979, 2006.

Barker, Kash, and Kaycee J. Wilson, "Decision Trees with Single and Multiple Interval-Valued Objectives," *Decision Analysis*, Volume 9, Number 4, pages 348–358, 2012.

Benjamin, Jack R., and Allin C. Cornell, *Probability, Statistics, and Decision for Civil Engineers*, McGraw-Hill Book Company, New York, 1970.

Brown, Rex, *Rational Choice and Judgment: Decision Analysis for the Decider*, John Wiley & Sons, Hoboken, New Jersey, 2005.

Chelst, Kenneth, and Yavuz B. Canbolat, *Value-Added Decision Making for Managers*, CRC Press, Boca Raton, Florida, 2012.

Clemen, Robert T., and Terence Reilly, *Making Hard Decisions with DecisionTools*, Duxbury, Pacific Grove, California, 2001.

Cooke, Roger, "The Anatomy of a Squizzel: The Role of Operational Definitions in Representing Uncertainty," *Reliability Engineering and System Safety*, Volume 85, pages 313–319, 2004.

Dempster, Arthur.P., "Upper and Lower Probabilities Induced by a Multivalued Mapping," *The Annals of Mathematical Statistics*, Volume 38, pages 325–339, 1967.

Dyer, James S.; Thomas Edmunds; John C. Butler; and Jianmin Jia, "A Multiattribute Utility Analysis of Alternatives for the Disposition of Surplus Weapons-Grade Plutonium," *Operations Research*, Volume 46, Number 6, pages 749–762, 1998.

Dyer, James S., and Ralph F. Miles, Jr., "An Actual Application of Collective Choice Theory to the Selection of Trajectories for the Mariner Jupiter/Saturn 1977 Project," *Operations Research*, Volume 24, Number 2, pages 220–244, 1976.

Ellsberg, Daniel, "Risk, Ambiguity, and the Savage Axioms," *The Quarterly Journal of Economics*, Volume 75, Number 4, pages 643–669, 1961.

Eschenbach, Ted G., "Spiderplots versus tornado diagrams for sensitivity analysis," *Interfaces*, Volume 22, Number 6, pages 40–46, 1992.

de Finetti, Bruno, "Foresight: its logical laws, its subjective sources," in H.E. Kyburg and H.E. Smokler, eds., *Studies in Subjective Probability*, Wiley, New York, pages 93–158, 1964.

Fishman, George S., *A First Course in Monte Carlo*, Thomson Brooks/Cole, Belmont, California, 2006.

Golany, Boaz, Edward H. Kaplan, Abraham Marmur, and Uriel G. Rothblum, "Nature Plays with Dice – Terrorists Do Not: Allocating Resources to Counter Strategic Versus Probabilistic Risks,"*European Journal of Operational Research*, Volume 192, Number 1, pages 198–208, 2009.

Ghosh, Dipanjan D., and Andrew Olewnik, "Computationally Efficient Imprecise Uncertainty Propagation," *Journal of Mechanical Design*, Volume 135, Number 5, 051002, 2013.

Groen, Frank J., and Ali Mosleh, "Foundations of Probabilistic Inference with Uncertain Evidence," *International Journal of Approximate Reasoning*, Volume 39, pages 49–83, 2005.

Hadar, J., and W.R. Russell, "Rules for Ordering Uncertain Prospects," *The American Economic Review*, Volume 59, pages 25–34, 1969.

Hartman, Joseph C., *Engineering Economy and the Decision-Making Process*, Pearson Education, Upper Saddle River, New Jersey, 2007.

Hurley, W.J., "Optimal Sequential Decisions and the Content of the Fourth-and-Goal Conference," *Interfaces*, Volume 28, Number 6, pages 19–22, 1998.

Jordaan, Ian, *Decisions under Uncertainty: Probabilistic Analysis for Engineering Decisions*, Cambridge University Press, Cambridge, 2005.

Kaplan, Michael, and Ellen Kaplan, *Chances Are: Adventures in Probability*, Viking, New York, 2006.

Kim, Byung-cheol, Euysup Shim, and Kenneth F. Reinschmidt, "Probability Distribution of the Project Payback Period Using the Equivalent Cash Flow Decomposition," *The Engineering Economist*, Volume 58, Number 2, pages 112–136, 2013

Kirkwood, Craig W., *Strategic Decision Making: Multiobjective Decision Analysis with Spreadsheets*, Duxbury Press, Belmont, California, 1997.

Leber, Dennis D., and Jeffrey W. Herrmann, "Incorporating Attribute Value Uncertainty into Decision Analysis," Proceedings of the 2012 Industrial and Systems Engineering Research Conference, Orlando, Florida, May 20–22, 2012.

Luce, R.D., and H. Raiffa, *Games and Decision*, Wiley, New York, 1957.

Lyon, Aidan, "Philosophy of probability," in F. Allhoff, ed., *Philosophies of the Sciences: A Guide*, Wiley-Blackwell, Malden, Massachusetts, 2010.

Manjoo, Farhad, "ARMed for Success in Battle with Intel," *The Washington Post*, page G4, 2013.

Merkhofer, Miley W., "Quantifying Judgmental Uncertainty: Methodology, Experiences, and Insights," *IEEE Transactions on Systems, Man, and Cybernetics*, Volume SMC-17, pages 741–752, 1987.

Modarres, Mohammad, *Risk Analysis in Engineering: Techniques, Tools, and Trends*, Taylor & Francis, Boca Raton, Florida, 2006.

Mossberg, Walter S., "In Battle Over Data Speed, Who is the Fastest in LTE?" *The Wall Street Journal*, page D1, 2013.

Paté-Cornell, M. Elisabeth, "Uncertainties in Risk Analysis: Six Levels of Treatment," *Reliability Engineering and System Safety*, Volume 54, Number 2/3, pages 95–111, 1996.

Pratt, John W., Howard Raiffa, and Robert Schlaifer, *Introduction to Statistical Decision Theory*, The MIT Press, Cambridge, Massachusetts, 1995.

Sawant, Milind M., "Reliability Testing & Bayesian Modeling of High Power LEDs for Use in a Medical Diagnostic Application," dissertation, University of Maryland, College Park, 2013. http://hdl.handle.net/1903/14210, accessed on August 2014.

Scott, Michael J., and Erik K. Antonsson, "Compensation and Weights for Tradeoffs in Engineering Design: Beyond the Weighted Sum," *Journal of Mechanical Design*, Volume 127, pages 1045–1055, 2005.

Shafer, Glenn, *A Mathematical Theory of Evidence*, Princeton University Press, Princeton, New Jersey, 1976.

Spetzler, C.S., and C.-A. S. Staël von Holstein, "Probability Encoding in Decision Analysis," *Management Science*, Volume 22, pages 340–358, 1975.

Swiler, Laura P., Thomas L. Paez, and Randall L. Mayes, "Epistemic uncertainty quantification tutorial," Proceedings of the IMAC-XXVII, Orlando, Florida, February 9–12, 2009.

Tamburello, Robert N., "Evaluation-Focused Reliability Test Program Planning Methodology," Ph.D. dissertation, University of Maryland, College Park, 2013. http://hdl.handle.net/1903/14827.

Toczek, John, "Farm O.R.," *OR/MS Today*, Volume 39, page 14, 2012.

Ullman, David G., *The Mechanical Design Process*, McGraw-Hill, New York, 1997.

von Mises, Richard, *Probability, Statistics, and Truth*, 2nd edition, Macmillan, New York, 1957.

Walley, P., *Statistical Reasoning with Imprecise Probabilities*, Chapman and Hall, New York, 1991.

Walls, Michael R., Thomas G. Morahan, and James S. Dyer, "Decision Analysis of Exploration Opportunities in the Onshore US at Phillips Petroleum," *Interfaces*, Volume 25, Number 6, pages 39–56, 1995.

Weichselberger, Kurt, "The Theory of Interval Probability as a Unifying Concept for Uncertainty," *International Journal of Approximate Reasoning*, Volume 24, pages 149–170, 2000.

6

GAME THEORY

Learning Objectives:

After studying this chapter, the reader will be able to do the following:

1. Analyze a two-player simultaneous, zero-sum game (Section 6.2).
2. Find each player's optimal mixed strategy (Section 6.3).
3. Formulate a resource allocation game as a two-player simultaneous, zero-sum game (Section 6.5).
4. Analyze a two-player, simultaneous, mixed-motive game and find dominated strategies and equilibrium points (Section 6.6).
5. Analyze a two-player Stackelberg game and find the each player's optimal strategy (Section 6.8).

When we consider games, we often think of activities such as chess or tic tac toe (noughts and crosses), where the players alternate their moves. Such games are relatively easy to analyze (unless the state space gets too large, as it does in chess), because, when a player needs to decide which move to make, they know everything that has happened and everything that could happen in the future.

Engineering Decision Making and Risk Management, First Edition. Jeffrey W. Herrmann.
© 2015 John Wiley & Sons, Inc. Published 2015 by John Wiley & Sons, Inc.

In *simultaneous games* such as rock-paper-scissors, however, neither player is sure what the other one will do, but they have to act simultaneously. In the traditional case, each player knows what the other could do, and both players know the *payoff matrix*, which describes the reward (or penalty) that each player will receive (pay) given their joint decisions.

Games occur in engineering as well. For instance, engineering firms often submit bids for projects that are being funded by government agencies. Each bidder must submit documents that thoroughly describe the system that the firm will design and build, its performance and reliability, the purchase and operating costs to the government, and many other details. In such cases, the winning bid is not necessarily the one with the lowest cost because multiple attributes are used to select a supplier. For example, the original process for awarding the USAir Force KC-X tanker contract considered mission capability, proposal risk, and past performance factors as well as cost/price and Integrated Fleet Aerial Refueling Assessment (GAO, 2008). There are multiple players in this situation, including the other firms that could submit bids and the government agency that will select a contractor. A firm that is considering submitting a bid has to consider the potential actions of these other actors, and these other actors make the situation a game.

When a manufacturing firm is designing a family of related products using a product platform, their competition is doing the same. Both firms are trying to maximize their sales in markets of fixed size, so the first firm's sales are affected by not only their products (designed as part of the platform) but also their competitor's products. In this simultaneous game, one can find the dominant strategy for the second firm, which helps the first firm determine how to design their product platform (Karimian and Herrmann, 2009).

Another example of a simultaneous game was presented by Gaver *et al.* (2009), who considered a counterterrorism agent who is searching for a terrorist in a crowd of neutral individuals. The counterterrorism agent must decide how much time to spend investigating each individual encountered. Spending too little time investigating will result in many mistakes, which waste time, but spending too much time investigating reduces the rate at which individuals are investigated. Both cases increase the total time needed to intercept and neutralize the terrorist. Meanwhile, the terrorist is looking for a vulnerable target whose value is greater than a threshold, but the terrorist must select the threshold. Although the terrorist wants to attack a high-value target, if threshold is too high, finding such a target will take too long, which increases the time during which the agent could intercept the terrorist. A game-theoretic model was used to identify the optimal investigation time.

In general, analyzing the risk due to an intelligent adversary requires using game theory. Game theory can improve our understanding of "the nature of the key decisions that intelligent attackers and defenders must make" and emphasizes that "vulnerability and consequence are usually functions of the allocation decisions made by the players, not exogenous numbers or random variables" (Cox, 2009). Cox also provided some examples illustrating the use of game theory in risk analysis.

In the domain of engineering design, when more than one engineer is designing a system and more than one design objective exists, game theoretical methods may be useful for helping the design team resolve conflicts and find "optimal" solutions (Vincent, 1983).

For example, a passenger aircraft design problem can be modeled as a two-player game (Lewis and Mistree, 1998). The first player (aerodynamics) is responsible for the wing and fuselage lift characteristics (such as climb gradients, aspect ratio, and take-off field) and can set (within given bounds) the wing area, the wing span, and the fuselage length. The second player (weight) is responsible for setting the thrust and take-off weight through a fuel balance. Each player needs some information from the other.

Three protocols can be considered (Honda *et al.*, 2012): (1) in a completely *cooperative* protocol, the two designers (players) share all of their information, which allows them to work together to find the best possible performance of the entire system; (2) in a *noncooperative* protocol, neither designer (player) shares any information, and each must decide separately and simultaneously; and (3) in a *leader/follower* protocol (a Stackelberg game), one designer (player) makes a decision and transmits that design to the other designer (player), who then decides.

The noncooperative protocol leads to the worst solutions for the passenger aircraft example, whereas the cooperative protocol leads to the best solutions (Lewis and Mistree, 1998). Unfortunately, the completely cooperative protocol may be difficult to achieve in practice, especially when the members of a design team are distributed at multiple locations. Thus, good sequential processes are needed. Chapter 7 of this textbook discusses such processes, which separate the design problem into subproblems.

Game theory is a well-studied area that focuses on multiple decision-makers who decide independently. The actions of the other decision-makers are (usually) unknown. This type of uncertainty is known as *strategic uncertainty* (Golany *et al.*, 2009). Game theory can be used to determine how players should behave in order to achieve certain ends under certain conditions. It does not, however, describe how humans actually behave in these situations. For an introduction to how they perform and evidence of how quickly they learn to make better choices, see, for example, Camerer (2003).

The results in game theory describe what players should do if they want the optimal guaranteed payoff. Neither player tries to predict what the other one *will* do (the most likely choice); each considers only what the other *could* do (the range of options). Thus, a reasonable goal is to consider the worst that could happen if a particular alternative is selected, and then select the alternative that has the "best" (least bad) worst-case outcome.

Some classic references in game theory are Nash (1951), von Neumann and Morgenstern (1953), and Luce and Raiffa (1957). Raiffa (2007) placed game theory in the context of negotiations, and the collection by Bier and Azaiez (2009) presented applications of game theory to analyzing security threats. Concepts from cooperative game theory have been used to develop an algorithm to solve multiobjective design optimization problems (Freiheit and Rao, 1991).

6.1 GAME THEORY BASICS

The gains (or losses) of the decision-makers are determined by their joint decision. In general, the term "payoff" is used to describe a decision-maker's gain (or loss), and the term "player" is used to refer to a decision-maker. In some cases, the amount that one player gains equals the amount that the other loses; such a situation is called a *zero-sum game*. In a *mixed-motive game*, however, the payoffs to the players are more general. There may be results in which both players gain and others in which they both lose.

A game in *normal form* is a set of n players, n sets of strategies (one set for each player), and n payoff functions (one for each player). Player i will receive a payoff of $M_i(s_1, \dots, s_n)$ if players 1 to n choose strategies s_1 to s_n.

In a two-player game, a strategy pair (s_1^*, s_2^*) is an *equilibrium point* if $M_1(s_1^*, s_2^*) \geq M_1(s_1, s_2^*)$ for any strategy s_1 available to player 1 and $M_2(s_1^*, s_2^*) \geq M_2(s_1^*, s_2)$ for any strategy s_2 available to player 2. That is, a strategy pair is an equilibrium point if neither player can gain by switching to another strategy while the other keeps the same strategy.

Games with equilibrium points may have multiple such points, but not all games have equilibrium points. If a game has no equilibrium point, then both players should be indifferent to their strategies, but using a mixed strategy can increase the expected payoff. A *mixed strategy* is a probability distribution over the set of pure strategies. A player that chooses a mixed strategy determines the probability distribution, which is then used to select a pure strategy at random.

It is common, in two-player games, to show the payoffs as a matrix. Each row corresponds to a strategy for player 1, and each column corresponds to a strategy for player 2, and each cell shows the payoffs to the players if they choose those particular strategies. Note, however, that such a matrix does not completely specify the game because it does not describe who moves first or whether the moves are simultaneous. This additional information is important for analyzing the game. (It will be convenient to discuss two-player games under the assumption that Player 1 is female and that Player 2 is male.)

6.2 ZERO-SUM GAMES

In a *zero-sum game*, the payoff functions sum to a constant, as in the case in which one player must pay the other an amount that depends on their choices and in the case in which there is a single resource that will be allocated to the players. If some players receive more, some must receive less. All of the players are trying to maximize their payoff. In a two-player, zero-sum game, the payoff functions satisfy the following constraint: $M_1(s_1, s_2) + M_2(s_1, s_2) = 0$.

A zero-sum game is *strictly competitive* because it always satisfies the following property: if player 1 prefers payoff $M_1(s_{1a}, s_{2b})$ to payoff $M_1(s_{1c}, s_{2d})$, then player 2 prefers $M_2(s_{1c}, s_{2d})$ to $M_2(s_{1a}, s_{2b})$, and, if the player 1 is indifferent between her payoffs, then player 2 is indifferent between his payoffs. In other words, there is no "win–win" outcome.

If, when considering the uncertainty about what player 2 will do, player 1 is risk averse, then she may want to optimize the worst-case scenario. To perform this, it will be useful to determine, for each and every strategy s_1, the value $M_1^*(s_1) = \min_{s_2}\{M_1(s_1, s_2)\}$ and then choose the strategy that maximizes $M_1^*(s_1)$. By doing this, player 1 guarantees that her payoff will be at least $M_1^*(s_1)$. Player 2 can perform the same type of analysis.

Example 6.1 Consider the following two-player, simultaneous zero-sum game presented in Luce and Raiffa (1957). Each player has two possible strategies. The payoffs for player 1 are the following values:

$$M_1(s_{11}, s_{21}) = 3 \quad M_1(s_{11}, s_{22}) = 1$$
$$M_1(s_{12}, s_{21}) = 2 \quad M_1(s_{12}, s_{22}) = 4.$$

For player 2, $M_2(s_1, s_2) = -M_1(s_1, s_2)$. If player 1 is risk averse, she will determine that $M_1^*(s_{11}) = \min\{3, 1\} = 1$ and $M_1^*(s_{12}) = \min\{2, 4\} = 2$ and then choose strategy s_{12}, which guarantees that she will gain at least 2. If player 2 is also risk averse, he will determine that $M_2^*(s_{21}) = \min\{-3, -2\} = -3$ and $M_2^*(s_{22}) = \min\{-1, -4\} = -4$ and then choose strategy s_{21}, which guarantees that he will lose at most 3. Thus, player 1 gains 2 and player 2 loses 2.

6.3 OPTIMAL MIXED STRATEGIES FOR ZERO-SUM GAMES

If both players are risk neutral, then they may consider mixed strategies. A mixed strategy is a discrete probability distribution over the possible strategies. For example, in the game mentioned in the last section, player 1 may decide to roll a six-sided die and choose strategy 1 if and only if she rolls a six (and choose strategy 2, otherwise). Although both players get to choose a probability distribution, they do not know which strategy will be played because that is the result of a random process.

If player 1 has a set of strategies $\{s_{11}, \dots, s_{1q}\}$, then she chooses a probability distribution $(p_{11}, \dots, p_{1q})$. For instance, in the last example, player 1 could choose $p_{11} = \frac{1}{6}$ and $p_{12} = \frac{5}{6}$. Likewise, player 2 has a set of strategies $\{s_{21}, \dots, s_{2r}\}$, and he chooses a probability distribution $(p_{21}, \dots, p_{2r})$.

The use of mixed strategies creates a new zero-sum game in which the two players choose their mixed strategies (instead of pure strategies). Of course, a player can force the choice of a single pure strategy by setting the corresponding probability to 1 and the probability of any other pure strategy to 0. In this game, the payoff to player

1 is the expected value $\sum_{i=1}^{q} \sum_{j=1}^{r} p_{1i} p_{2j} M_1(s_{1i}, s_{2j})$. Then, player 1 wants to find a probability distribution $(p_{11}, \ldots, p_{1q})$ that maximizes her minimum expected payoff:

$$\text{max} \qquad v$$

$$\text{s.t.} \quad v \le \sum_{i=1}^{q} p_{1i} M_1(s_{1i}, s_{2j}) \, j = 1, \ldots, r.$$

$$\sum_{i=1}^{q} p_{1i} = 1$$

Player 2 has a similar problem, but he wants to find a probability distribution $(p_{21}, \ldots, p_{2r})$ that minimizes player 1's expected payoff (which is the same as maximizing his expected payoff):

$$\text{min} \qquad v$$

$$\text{s.t.} \quad v \ge \sum_{j=1}^{r} p_{2j} M_1(s_{1i}, s_{2j}) \, i = 1, \ldots, q.$$

$$\sum_{j=1}^{r} p_{2j} = 1$$

Both problems are simple linear programming problems. The mixed strategy pair in which both players adopt their optimal mixed strategy is an equilibrium point; neither player can perform better by changing to a different strategy. The minimax theorem discussed in the next section guarantees that the optimal values for these two problems are equal.

Example 6.2   Consider again the two-player game from Example 6.1. The problem for Player 1 can be formulated as follows:

$$\text{max} \qquad v$$

$$\text{s.t.} \quad v \le 3p_{11} + 2p_{12}.$$

$$v \le p_{11} + 4p_{12}.$$

$$p_{11} + p_{12} = 1.$$

The optimal mixed strategy for player 1 is (0.5, 0.5). The probability that she chooses s_{11} is 0.5, and the probability that she chooses s_{12} is 0.5. Her expected payoff is 2.5 no matter what player 2 does. Likewise, the problem for Player 2 can be formulated as follows:

$$\min \quad v$$

$$\text{s.t.} \quad v \geq 3p_{21} + p_{22}.$$

$$v \geq 2p_{21} + 4p_{22}.$$

$$p_{21} + p_{22} = 1.$$

The optimal mixed strategy for player 2 is (0.75, 0.25). The probability that he chooses s_{21} is 0.75, and the probability that he chooses s_{22} is 0.25. His expected payoff is -2.5 no matter what player 1 does.

6.4   THE MINIMAX THEOREM

The minimax theorem (von Neumann, 1928, 1959) is an important result in game theory. Let $\bar{p}_1$ and $\bar{p}_2$ be the probability distributions for players 1 and 2, respectively. Then, the minimax theorem states that

$$\max_{\bar{p}_1} \min_{\bar{p}_2} \sum_{i=1}^{q} \sum_{j=1}^{r} p_{1i} p_{2j} M_1(s_{1i}, s_{2j}) = \min_{\bar{p}_2} \max_{\bar{p}_1} \sum_{i=1}^{q} \sum_{j=1}^{r} p_{1i} p_{2j} M_1(s_{1i}, s_{2j}).$$

That is, for any two-player, simultaneous zero-sum game in which each player has a finite set of strategies, there is a value v, a mixed strategy for player 1 that guarantees her an expected payoff of v and a mixed strategy for player 2 that guarantees him an expected payoff of $-v$. The quantity v is known as the game's *value*.

Example 6.1 is a two-player, simultaneous zero-sum game in which each player has a finite set of strategies. As shown in Example 6.2., if player 1 adopts her optimal mixed strategy, her expected payoff is 2.5. If player 2 adopts his optimal mixed strategy, player 1's expected payoff is 2.5 (and player 2's expected payoff is -2.5). The value of the game is 2.5.

6.5   RESOURCE ALLOCATION GAMES

An interesting class of two-player zero-sum games arises when both players have a finite set of resources that must be allocated to different tasks. Such a problem can occur when a military commander must allocate units to different objectives (cities, bridges, or other targets) at the same time that the other side is doing the same thing. For each objective, the army that has more units there will win that objective. The goal is to win more objectives than the opponent.

A manufacturing firm that must devote resources to developing multiple product families for different market segments has a similar problem. The firm's competitors are doing the same thing, and they will all compete in the marketplace. Spending more resources on product development should lead to a better selling product in each market segment, but the limit on resources requires tradeoffs to be made.

The *Colonel Blotto game* is one version of this game. Each of two players has a finite number of discrete units that must be allocated to a number of objectives, and each player assigns a specific number of units to each objective. They perform this simultaneously. After making their allocations, they determine who won each objective (if the players allocated the same number of units to an objective, neither wins it). The player who wins more objectives wins the game. If the two players win the same number of objectives, the game is a draw. (Various versions exist; in some, the sequence of allocations does not matter because the allocations will be sorted first.)

The number of pure strategies for each player is finite (although possibly huge: if a player has 100 units to allocate to 10 objectives and the sequence matters, there are approximately 4 trillion possibilities). In general, no pure strategy dominates every other one, and winning is intransitive (i.e., there are strategies A, B, and C such that strategy A beats B, B beats C, and C beats A). Of course, some strategies may be dominated and should not be played.

If the winner must pay the loser a certain amount (with no payment in a draw), then the game is a zero-sum game, and there must be an optimal mixed strategy that maximizes the expected payment. The number of pure strategies makes finding this strategy difficult, however.

An example with 107 players competing against each other (in a pairwise manner) in a version with 100 units and 10 objectives was described by Partington (2012). The best pure strategy used was (17, 3, 17, 3, 17, 3, 17, 3, 17, 3), which beat 64 players, lost to 9 others, and drew with the remaining 33.

6.6 MIXED MOTIVE GAMES

Games without the zero-sum property are known as *mixed-motive games*. A zero-sum game is used to model a situation in which all of the players want the same object, which must be divided among them. A mixed-motive game is used to model a situation in which the players want different objects (the "mixed motives"). Some outcomes may be desirable for many or all of the players; some may be undesirable for many or all of the players. In mixed-motive games, there can be "win–win" outcomes (there can also be "nobody wins" scenarios). The military strategy of mutual assured destruction guarantees the attacker that the defender's response would be sufficiently quick and powerful to destroy the attacker even if the attacker also destroys the defender. The "game" of nuclear war is certainly a not a zero-sum game.

The prisoner's dilemma (discussed later) is a famous type of mixed-motive game. (Each prisoner selfishly wants his own freedom and does not care about the other.) Manufacturing companies are often engaged in mixed-motive games with their competition. For instance, consider the situation that CamelBak and Nalgene, leading manufacturers of reusable water bottles, faced in 2008 when consumers began worrying about the presence of bisphenol A (BPA) in their polycarbonate water bottles (Kraft and Raz, 2014). Both firms (and other firms making similar products) had to choose independently whether to replace the polycarbonate with a BPA-free plastic. Each firm would have to invest money to modify their products and processes, but using the BPA-free plastic could provide a marketing advantage (relative to firms that did not use it). Moreover, failing to replace the polycarbonate would reduce sales for both firms as consumers avoided the product altogether. This is not a zero-sum game, for each firms had costs that had no impact on the other one, and the market is fluid: losing one customer did not necessarily mean that the other firm gained a customer. That is, both firms could lose sales (if consumers avoided reusable water bottles), or both firms could gain sales (if consumers were reassured that reusable water bottles were safe). Ultimately, both firms developed water bottles using the BPA-free plastic.

This section will consider a series of simple mixed-motive two-player games with examples based roughly on those in Raiffa (2007). In these games, each player has a set of two alternatives (strategies) and must choose exactly one of them. Both players have perfect information about their own choices and payoffs and the other player's. That is, they both know the same thing. The players must choose simultaneously, and there are no discussions and no agreements ahead of time. Thus, these are noncooperative games.

In our example, we will let the players be known as Joe and Rose. Joe can choose Left or Right, and Rose can choose Up or Down. (These are generic names that correspond to the payoff matrix.) The consequences are shown in the payoff matrix. Each entry shows the payoffs for Rose and Joe in that order. Thus, in Game 1 (Figure 6.1), the entry (126, 77) in the cell Down-Left means that, if Rose chooses Down and Joe chooses Left, then Rose gets a reward (payoff) of 126 and Joe gets 77. (Although expressed in abstract units, the payoffs might be dollars or points or credits of some kind.)

Game 1 (Figure 6.1) is an example of *indeterminancy*. No fixed strategy is better than another. If Rose thinks that Joe will choose Left, then she will choose Down (because her payoff is greater for Down than for Up). Joe, of course, realizes this and therefore chooses Right (because his payoff is greater) under the assumption that Rose will choose Down. Rose figures this out and thus will choose Up, because, if Joe chooses Right, then her payoff is greater. Joe sees this as well and realizes that, if Rose chooses Up, he should choose Left. Because there is no end to this chain of reasoning, neither player can determine what to do.

Game 2 (Figure 6.2) is an example of *dominance* (cf. Section 2.5 in Chapter 2). For Rose, choosing Down is better than choosing Up no matter what Joe chooses. For Joe, choosing Left is better than choosing Right no matter what Rose chooses. For Rose, Down dominates Up. For Joe, Left dominates Right. Therefore, Rose chooses Down, and Joe chooses Left, and the payoffs are 126 to Rose and 77 to Joe.

Game 3 (Figure 6.3) is an example of *iterated dominance*. For Joe, choosing Right is better no matter what Rose chooses. That is, Right dominates Left. For Rose, neither Down nor Up dominates, but Rose knows that Right dominates Left and that Joe will certainly choose Right. In that case, Rose will choose Up, and

Joe

Rose	Left	Right
Up	(46, 55)	(100, 10)
Down	(126, 77)	(55, 97)

Figure 6.1 A two-player game with indeterminancy.

Joe

Rose	Left	Right
Up	(46, 55)	(27, 10)
Down	(126, 77)	(55, 42)

Figure 6.2 A two-player game with dominance.

Joe

Rose	Left	Right
Up	(46, 5)	(27, 10)
Down	(126, 27)	(25, 42)

Figure 6.3 A two-player game with iterated dominance.

the payoffs are 27 to Rose and 10 to Joe. The joint choice (Up, Right) is in equilibrium because neither player has any motivation to change as long as the other stays put.

Game 4 (Figure 6.4) is an example of an *equilibrium* without dominance. For Joe, neither Left nor Right dominates. For Rose, neither Down nor Up dominates. If Rose believes that Joe will choose Left, then she will choose Down, and if Joe believes that Rose will choose Down, then he will choose Left. Neither player has an incentive to change from that joint choice. (Down, Left) is an equilibrium point. Likewise, (Up, Right) is an equilibrium point. Both players can determine these equilibrium points, and both realize that the payoffs for both Joe and Rose in (Down, Left) are better than those in (Up, Right). Thus, Rose will choose Down and Joe will choose Left.

Game 5 (Figure 6.5) is an example of a *social trap*, in which self-interested behavior leads to a suboptimal outcome. For Joe, Right dominates Left. For Rose, Down dominates Up. Joe will choose Right, and Rose will choose Down, and the payoffs are 12 for Rose and 11 for Joe. Both players would have done better with the joint choice (Up, Left), where Rose gains 46 and Joe gains 55.

Joe

Rose	Left	Right
Up	(46, 25)	(97, 67)
Down	(126, 77)	(25, 42)

Figure 6.4 A two-player game with two equilibrium points.

Joe

Rose	Left	Right
Up	(46, 55)	(8, 67)
Down	(126, 7)	(12, 11)

Figure 6.5 A two-player game with a social trap.

The famous *prisoner's dilemma* is also an example of a social trap. Both prisoners are given incentives to confess to reduce their time in prison, so they both perform, although they would both get shorter sentences if neither confessed.

In order to represent this type of game more precisely, let $M_1(s_1, s_2)$ be the payoff to Player 1 and $M_2(s_1, s_2)$ be the payoff to Player 2 if Player 1 chooses strategy s_1 and Player 2 chooses strategy s_2. Then, for Player 1, strategy s_1 dominates strategy b_1 if $M_1(s_1, s_2) \geq M_1(b_1, s_2)$ for all possible Player 2 strategies s_2. For Player 2, strategy s_2 dominates strategy b_2 if $M_2(s_1, s_2) \geq M_2(s_1, b_2)$ for all possible Player 1 strategies s_1.

6.7 BIDDING

When multiple engineering firms submit bids for a project, they are participating in a multiple-player, simultaneous game. In general, analyzing such situations using game theory can be difficult due to the number of players, the rules of the bidding process, and the lack of information about the other players' situations.

A Vickrey auction, a type of *second-price auction*, however, is a special case that has a simple solution. In this auction, there are two or more players who want to buy an item. According to the rules of the auction, the players must submit sealed bids; in effect, their bids are submitted simultaneously. Each bid is a price for the item. The bids will then be revealed, and the item will be sold to the highest bidder, but the price will be the second-highest price.

Suppose Rose is a player (bidder). The item has a value v for Rose. If she wins the auction and pays a price p, then her gain (or loss) is $v - p$. If she does not win the auction, then she neither gains nor loses. Rose's dominant strategy is to bid v (the proof is left as an exercise). She has no incentive to bid anything besides the value that the item has for her. Because every other player has the same incentive, each player's bid should equal the value that the item has for him. Thus, in a second-price auction, every player reveals their private information (the values that the item has for them), and the player with the highest value will win the auction but pay a lower price. No player has any incentive to change, so this is an equilibrium point.

6.8 STACKELBERG GAMES

Unlike simultaneous games, a *Stackelberg game* with two players has two stages: in the first stage, the first player moves (selects an action). Then, after observing the first player's action, the second player moves. Such games are also known as leader-follower games and attacker-defender games. (The name reflects the work of Heinrich von Stackelberg, a German economist, on this topic.)

A Stackelberg game occurs sometimes in the late innings of a baseball game: the manager of the team in the field must decide whether to take out one pitcher and bring in a relief pitcher (who may have a better chance of retiring the player who will be batting next). However, the manager of the team batting has the option to insert a pinch hitter if a relief pitcher is used. The first manager can and should consider the second manager's reaction to his decision when considering what to do.

Stackelberg games have been used to model two-person design teams in which one designer decides what one part of the design will be and then a second designer decides what a second part will be (Lewis and Mistree, 1998; Honda *et al.*, 2012). Stackelberg games have been used to model security problems in which the defender first decides which assets to defend and then the attacker, after observing the defender's actions, decides which assets to attack (cf. Tambe, 2012). Mixed strategies are often effective solutions because, although the attacker knows the probability distribution, he does not know which asset will be defended when the attack occurs.

The analysis of such games, in general, is straightforward for both players if Player 1 is concerned with only optimizing her payoff and Player 2 is concerned with only optimizing his payoff. Player 2 chooses the action that is best for him after observing Player 1's action. For any action that Player 1 can choose, Player 2 has a best response. For each possible action, Player 1 must determine Player 2's best response and use her own payoff as her evaluation of his action. Knowing what Player 2 will do reduces the strategic uncertainty that exists in a simultaneous game.

If Player 2 has multiple responses that are all optimal for him for a given action by Player 1, then Player 1 will still have some uncertainty about Player 2's actions. Player 1 could consider the worst case of these responses and decide to choose the one that has the best worst-case.

Example 6.3   This example is based on a problem written by Toczek (2011). A dice game has four six-sided dice with different numbers on each face. Die A has the following six numbers: 1-1-1-1-7-7. Die B has the following six numbers: 4-4-4-4-4-4.

TABLE 6.1 Probability that Joe Wins if He Chooses First.

Joe's Pick	Rose = A	Rose = B	Rose = C	Rose = D
A		1/3	1/3	1/3
B	2/3		2/3	1/2
C	2/3	1/3		1/3
D	2/3	1/2	2/3	

Die C has the following six numbers: 2-2-2-2-6-6. Die D has the following six numbers: 3-3-3-5-5-5.

Joe and Rose will play a game in which Joe chooses one of the four dice, then Rose chooses a different die, and then they roll the selected dice. The player with the higher number wins. Table 6.1 shows the possible combinations of moves and the probability that Joe will win for each combination.

Joe wants to maximize his probability of winning, and Rose wants to minimize this (this is a zero-sum game). If Joe picks die A, then his probability of winning equals 1/3 no matter which die Rose chooses. If Joe picks die B, then his probability of winning equals 2/3 if Rose chooses A or C and 1/2 if Rose chooses D. For Joe, therefore, die B is better than die A because Rose's best response to die B (which is to choose die D) gives him a higher probability of winning (1/2) than he would have if chose die A. For Joe, die B is also better than die C, but it is equivalent to die D (if he chooses die D, Rose will choose die B, and each one's probability of winning equals 1/2). The complete game is shown in Table 6.1.

Joe's optimal choice is to pick die B or die D, and Rose's best response is to choose the other.

EXERCISES

6.1. In 2013, the US State Department was considering whether to issue a permit for the Keystone XL pipeline, which would carry oil from northern Alberta to the Gulf of Mexico (Mufson, 2013). The environmental impacts of oil spills, which are an important concern, are affected by how oil producers react to the decision: if the permit is denied, they can continue shipping oil by railroad. Oil spills are possible in both modes of transportation (pipeline and railroad). Treat the permitting decision as a two-player game. What type of game is it? Who are the players? What are their strategies?

6.2. Consider a manufacturing firm that is deciding whether to bid on a contract to build a light rail line. The firm knows that multiple competitors are also thinking about submitting a bid. Assume that the firm with the lowest bid will get the contract. Is this a zero-sum game or a mixed-motive game?

6.3. The market entry game models the situation in which many different firms are independently deciding whether to enter into a new market; in some cases, too many of them enter a market, which then becomes worthless, which happened, for example, in 2002 when too many firms decided to build fiber optic communications networks (Camerer, 2003). Consider this zero-sum example. There are 10 firms competing in a market. Each firm must independently and simultaneously decide whether to switch to a new technology. Let m be the number of firms that switch. Any firm that does not switch will lose $m \times \$20,000,000$. Any firm that does switch will gain $(10 - m) \times \$20,000,000$. First, show that this is a zero-sum game. Model this as a two-player game in which the first player is one firm, and the second "player" represents the combined decisions of the other nine players. Does one pure strategy dominate the other? Because the game is symmetric, all of the firms are in the same position. What will the firms do?

6.4. Consider the second-price auction described in Section 6.7. Suppose that the item has a value v for Rose. Show that submitting a bid in which the price equals that value is a dominant strategy for her. (Hint: consider a two-player game in which Rose is one player and the second player is the highest bidder of the other bidders; consider strategy sets that have a range of discrete bid prices from slightly below v to slightly above v; and ignore the payoffs to the other players. Then generalize from this.)

6.5. Rose and Joe agree to play the following zero-sum game. Each must choose Rock or Paper or Scissors. They will choose simultaneously and then reveal their choices. Based on their choices, either Joe will pay Rose some amount or Rose will pay Joe some amount. Rose's payoffs are given in Table 6.2. A positive value is the amount paid from Joe to Rose; a negative amount represents a payment from Rose to Joe. (i.e., a payoff of 2 means that Joe will pay Rose \$2; a payoff of −3 means that Rose will pay Joe \$3.) Both players want to maximize their expected gain (and minimize their expected loss). What is the optimal mixed strategy for Rose? What is Rose's expected gain? What is the optimal mixed strategy for Joe? What is Joe's expected gain?

6.6. (This exercise is based on an example in Cox, 2009.) A defender has two locations (A and B) and can defend only one of them at a time. An attacker will attack exactly one of the two locations. Simultaneously, the defender decides which to defend and the attacker decides which to attack. The cost to the defender depends on which is defended and which is attacked. The defender

TABLE 6.2 Payoff Table for the Game in Exercise 6.5.

Rose's Pick	Joe: Rock	Joe: Paper	Joe: Scissors
Rock	2	−3	4
Paper	−4	6	7
Scissors	−5	−4	1

All payoffs in dollars.

wishes to minimize the cost, whereas the attacker wishes to maximize the cost. If location A is defended and attacked, the cost is 10 units. If location A is defended, but location B is attacked, the cost is 110 units. If location B is defended and attacked, the cost is 20 units. If location B is defended, but location A is attacked, the cost is 80 units. What is the defender's optimal mixed strategy? What is the attacker's optimal mixed strategy? What is the expected cost?

6.7. In the game of rugby (rugby union), a team with the ball but close to their own score line will kick the ball away, and that team (the kicking team) may choose a box kick by the scrum half or a clearance kick by the fly half. The defending team will try to prevent the kick by rushing the scrum half or the fly half. The probability of a successful kick depends on which half attempts the kick and whom the defending team rushes, as shown in Figure 6.6 (the estimates are from Knight, 2011). Note that the kicking team's choice and the defending team's choice are made simultaneously. The kicking team wants to maximize the probability of a successful kick, while the defending team wants to minimize the probability of a successful kick. What is the optimal mixed strategy for the kicking team? What is the optimal mixed strategy for the defending team? What is expected probability of a successful kick?

6.8. Consider an instance of the Colonel Blotto game in which each player has to allocate three units to three objectives. There are 10 pure strategies. (Recall that units cannot be divided.) Identify the dominated pure strategies. Find the pure strategy that has the best worst-case payoff. Is there a mixed strategy that can perform better than this pure strategy?

6.9. Consider the following pressure vessel design example (adapted from Lewis and Mistree, 1998). There are three design variables: the radius R, the length L, and the thickness T (all in inches). The vessel is a hollow cylinder with hollow hemispherical ends. The vessel wall thickness is T inches everywhere. The material density is $\rho = 0.283$ pounds per cubic inch (7.77 g/cm^3). The weight W can be determined as follows:

$$W = \rho\pi \left(\frac{4}{3}(R + T)^3 - \frac{4}{3}R^3 + L(R + T)^2 - LR^2 \right).$$

| | Defenders rush | |
	Scrum half	Fly half
Box kick	0.2	0.8
Clearance	0.95	0.7

Figure 6.6 The probability of a successful kick depends upon which half attempts the kick and whom the defending team rushes (Knight, 2011).

The volume V can be determined as follows:

$$V = \pi \left(\frac{4}{3} R^3 + L R^2 \right).$$

Assume that the possible values for the design variables are limited to the following discrete values: R can be 10, 20, or 30 inches, the length L can be 40, 60, or 80 inches, and the thickness T can be 1, 2, 3, or 4 inches. Moreover, R must be between 5 and 10 T. Rose wants to maximize the volume of the cylinder while Joe wants to minimize the weight. Rose controls the variables R and L; Joe controls the variable T. Consider the following three scenarios:

(a) Rose and Joe will select the values for their design variables simultaneously and independently.

(b) Rose will first select the values for the variables R and L, and then Joe will select a feasible value for the variable T.

(c) Joe will first select a value for the variable T, and then Rose will select feasible values for the variables R and L.

Create the appropriate mixed-motive payoff matrix for the players. In each scenario, which design (values for the three variables) will be selected? Are these designs feasible? What are the volume and weight of these designs? Would Rose prefer to be the first one to decide? Would Joe prefer to be the first one to decide?

6.10. Consider the situation in Exercise 6.9, but now assume that the feasible values for the design variables are all values in the following ranges: $10 \leq R \leq 30$ inches, $40 \leq L \leq 80$ inches, and $1 \leq T \leq 4$ inches. Still, R must be between 5 and 10 T. Which design will be selected in scenarios (a), (b), and (c) from Exercise 6.9?

6.11. Consider the two-player, mixed-motive game shown in Figure 6.7. Each entry is (Payoff to Rose, Payoff to Joe). Are there any dominated strategies? If so, what are they? Are there any equilibrium points? If so, what are they?

6.12. The simplest version of the cake-cutting game can be expressed as follows: two players will split a cake (which stands for a pot of money, a piece of land, or some other resource that can be divided). One player has been identified as the first player, and she will divide the cake into two parts; she can select the sizes

	Joe	
Rose	Left	Right
Up	(104, 203)	(103, 200)
Down	(112, 208)	(105, 204)

Figure 6.7 The two-player, mixed-motive game for Exercise 6.11.

of the two parts (but every bit of the cake is in one of the two parts; that is, the two parts are mutually exclusive and collectively exhaustive). The second player will select which part he takes. The first player wants to maximize the amount of the cake that she gets and so does the second player. What type of game is this? How should the first player divide the cake (i.e., how large should the two parts be)?

6.13. (This is based on a problem in Kirkwood, 1997.) A steel company must renegotiate the labor contract with the union that represents its workers. The steel company must first decide on the offer that it will make, and then the union members will decide whether to accept the offered contract or go on strike. The steel company is considering two alternatives: (1) offer a contract that is the same as the current contract or (2) offer a more generous contract that pays higher salaries and has more benefits. The steel company's future profits are affected by the contract and the union's response as follows: current contract, no strike: profit = $4.5 million; current contract, strike: profit = $3 million; generous contract, no strike: profit = $4 million; and generous contract, strike: profit = $3.5 million. The union will strike if and only if the steel company offers the current contract. What is the optimal strategy for the steel company (which wants to maximize its future profits)? That is, which contract should the steel company offer?

6.14. Rose owns a Christmas tree farm and will sell and ship trees to Joe, who runs a Christmas tree stand. Rose will charge Joe a price of P per tree. Rose can charge Joe $20, $21, $22, $23, $24, or $25 per tree. (If she charges more than $25 per tree, Joe will get his trees somewhere else.) The retail price for Christmas trees in this market is $30, and Joe knows that he will sell somewhere between 300 and 450 trees. After Rose decides on the price that she will charge, Joe has to decide how many trees he will buy from Rose. (Thus, this is a type of Stackelberg game.) Let Q be the number of trees that he buys (where Q is any number between 300 and 450). Rose's revenue will be PQ, the price per tree times the number of trees that Joe purchases. Joe's expected profits, a function of P and Q, will be $-0.1Q^2 + (90 - P)Q - \$9,000$. Rose wants to maximize her revenue, and Joe wants to maximize his expected profits. How much (what price) should Rose charge? How many should Joe buy? What will Rose's revenue be? What will Joe's expected profits be?

REFERENCES

Bier, Vicki M., and M. Naceur Azaiez, editors, *Game Theoretic Risk Analysis of Security Threats*, Springer, New York, 2009.

Camerer, Colin F., *Behavioral Game Theory: Experiments in Strategic Interaction*, Princeton University Press, Princeton, New Jersey, 2003.

Cox, Louis Anthony, Jr. , "Game Theory and Risk Analysis," *Risk Analysis*, Volume 29, Number 8, pages 1062–1068, 2009.

Freiheit, T.I., and S.S. Rao, "A Modified Game Theory Approach to Multiobjective Optimization," *Journal of Mechanical Design*, Volume 113, pages 286–291, 1991.

Gaver, Donald P., Kevin D. Glazebrook, and Patricia A. Jacobs, "Search for a Malevolent Needle in a Benign Haystack," *Game Theoretic Risk Analysis of Security Threats*, Vicki M. Bier and M. Naceur Azaiez, eds., Springer, New York, 2009.

Government Accountability Office (GAO), "Decision: Matter of The Boeing Company," File B-311344, June 18, 2008. http://gao.gov/decisions/bidpro/311344.htm, accessed August 2014, 2008.

Golany, Boaz, Edward H. Kaplan, Abraham Marmur, and Uriel G. Rothblum, "Nature Plays with Dice – Terrorists Do Not: Allocating Resources to Counter Strategic Versus Probabilistic Risks,"*European Journal of Operational Research*, Volume 192, Number 1, pages 198–208, 2009.

Honda, Tomonori, Francesco Ciucci, and Maria C. Yang, "An Information Passing Strategy for Achieving Pareto Optimality in the Design of Complex Systems," *Research in Engineering Design*, Volume 23, Number 1, pages 71–83, 2012.

Karimian, Peyman, and Jeffrey W. Herrmann, "Designing Product Families with Competition: a Design for Market Systems Approach," DETC2009-86422, Proceedings of the ASME 2009 International Design Engineering Technical Conferences & Computers and Information in Engineering Conference, August 30-September 2, 2009, San Diego, California.

Kirkwood, Craig W., *Strategic Decision Making: Multiobjective Decision Analysis with Spreadsheets*, Duxbury Press, Belmont, California, 1997.

Knight, Vince, "To box kick or not to box kick," posted, 2011, http://drvinceknight. blogspot.com/2011/12/to-box-kick-or-not-to-box-kick.html?m=1, accessed August 2014.

Kraft, Tim, and Gal Raz, "The Costly Competition to Sell BPA-Free Bottles," *The Washington Post*, page G2, 2014.

Lewis, K., and Mistree, F., "Collaborative, Sequential, and Isolated Decisions in Design," *Journal of Mechanical Design*, Volume 120 Number 4, pages 643–652, 1998.

Luce, R.D., and H. Raiffa, *Games and Decision*, Wiley, New York, 1957.

Mufson, Steven, "Disaster in Canada Puts Focus on Oil Transportation," *The Washington Post*, page A1, 2013.

Nash, J., "Non Co-Operative Games," *Annals of Mathematics*, Volume 54, Number 2, pages 286-95, 1951.

von Neumann, John, "Zur Theorie der Gesellschaftsspiele," *Mathematische Annalen*, Volume 100, pages 295–320, 1928.

von Neumann, John, "On the theory of games of strategy," translated by Sonya Bargmann, in *Contributions to the Theory of Games*, Volume 4, A.W. Tucker and R.D. Luce, editors, *Annals of Mathematics Studies*, Number 40, pages 13–42, Princeton University Press, Princeton, New Jersey, 1959.

von Neumann, J., and O. Morgenstern, *Theory of Games and Economic Behavior*, Princeton University Press, Princeton, New Jersey, 1953.

Partington, Jonathan, "Colonel Blotto's game," http://www1.maths.leeds.ac.uk/‾pmt6jrp/ personal/blotto.html, accessed August 2014, 2012.

Raiffa, Howard, *Negotiation Analysis: the Science and Art of Collaborative Decision Making*, Harvard University Press, 2007.

Tambe, Milind, *Security and Game Theory: Algorithms, Deployed Systems, Lessons Learned*, Cambridge University Press, New York, 2012.

Toczek, John, "Dice Game," December 2011. http://www.puzzlor.com/2011-12_Dice Game.html, accessed August 2014.

Vincent, T.L., "Game Theory as a Design Tool," *Journal of Mechanisms, Transmissions, and Automation in Design*, Volume 105, pages 165–170, 1983.

7

DECISION-MAKING PROCESSES

Learning Objectives:

After studying this chapter, the reader will be able to do the following:

1. Describe metareasoning and understand its relevance to improving decision making (Introduction).
2. Describe decision-making contexts and identify the decision-making processes that are appropriate for them (Section 7.1).
3. Describe types of decision-making processes, identify their advantages and disadvantages, and identify the situations for which they are appropriate (Sections 7.2–7.5 and 7.11–7.13).
4. Describe the components of decision-making processes, including the analytic-deliberative process (Sections 7.6–7.8).
5. Describe the value of iteration in decision-making processes (Sections 7.7–7.10).
6. Describe the role of search in decision-making processes (Sections 7.14 and 7.15).
7. Analyze a decision-making process as a search (Section 7.14).

Engineering Decision Making and Risk Management, First Edition. Jeffrey W. Herrmann.
© 2015 John Wiley & Sons, Inc. Published 2015 by John Wiley & Sons, Inc.

8. Construct the optimal strategy for a secretary problem (Section 7.16).

9. Describe a composite decision (Section 7.17).

10. Model a composite decision as a separation (Section 7.18).

11. Describe the decisions made during the product development (Section 7.19).

The preceding chapters of this book focused on techniques for choosing an alternative from a given set of alternatives. These alternatives must be identified and evaluated, however, and improving decision making, therefore, requires improving the process that identifies and evaluates alternatives. Thus, our second perspective on decision making is the *decision-making process perspective*, which considers how a decision is made. This perspective describes the process of generating alternatives, collecting information about the alternatives, evaluating the alternatives, and selecting an alternative.

A *decision-making process* is a set of activities through which a decision-maker determines the objectives, identifies and evaluates alternatives, and selects an alternative. There are a wide variety of decision-making processes. The number of participants can range from one person to dozens of people to an entire country (in the case of national elections). The level of analysis can range from almost nothing to in-depth modeling, simulation, and analysis. Some processes have multiple iterations, but others go directly from one step to the next. In some cases, especially when something must be done extremely quickly, there is no time for a formal process, so decision-makers will, based on their experience and expertise, jump immediately to a solution, as studies of naturalistic decision making (NDM) have shown (cf. Klein *et al.*, 2010); this is discussed more in Section 7.11.

Given the variety of decision-making processes, a decision-maker's first step is to choose an appropriate decision-making process. Many decisions have consequences that are so small that no formal technique is needed, and many other decisions are no brainers, but there are still many decisions where a formal process is useful. These include "make-or-break" decisions that are irreversible, involve large investments, affect the safety of others, and have many stakeholders (NRC, 2001).

When selecting a decision-making process, the fundamental tradeoff involves the cost and time of the process versus the number and quality of the alternatives considered and the amount of information used to make the decision. Generating more alternatives and gathering more information usually require more time and money. A low-cost decision-making process will likely consider few alternatives and gather little information about them. The decision-making processes described in this chapter represent different compromises between these competing goals. As Simon (1981) observed, "the design process itself involves management of the resources of the designer, so that his efforts will not be dissipated unnecessarily in following lines of inquiry that prove fruitless."

The numerous activities in the decision-making process can obscure the essential decision that is being made. A myopic view of the decision-making process can lead to poor choices. For instance, in the Boeing headquarters selection decision mentioned in Chapter 1, a focus on absolutely comprehensive information gathering would have wasted time examining undesirable office buildings. Their unusual decision to go public with their search, in contrast, helped generate more information in a short time, although some of it had little value ("Inside Boeing's Big Move," 2001). Boeing wanted a good location for its headquarters and designed its decision-making process to achieve that end. Choices about the decision-making process should be guided by the objective of making a good decision.

Metareasoning refers to thinking about which action to take next during the decision-making process (Russell and Wefald, 1991). Possible actions include searching for alternatives, generating more alternatives, gathering more information, and testing potential solutions. Actions vary on multiple attributes: the amount of time required, the quality of the solution returned, the certainty of the solution being satisfactory, and the usefulness of a partial solution (if the action is interrupted). Each action has some value based on whether it leads to a better solution and the cost of the time needed to perform the action. A rational metareasoning strategy is to perform the action with the maximal expected value until there exist none with a positive value. At that point, the decision-maker should commit to the best solution found so far. Determining the expected value of information (discussed in Chapter 8) is part of metareasoning.

Thinking about how to decide can be useful, although it appears that metareasoning is often done quickly and implicitly. Of course, metareasoning can be taken too far. In a "Dilbert" cartoon from 2007, Scott Adams described some excessive metareasoning: after the pointy-haired manager asked his assistant to setup a meeting with the technology review board to decide how they will decide on new technologies, the assistant went overboard when she first suggested a meeting to decide how they will setup this meeting and then suggested a meeting about scheduling that meeting!

Practically, a heuristic approach to metareasoning may be useful: consider the type of decision-making situation that exists and then choose a decision-making approach that is generally useful in that approach.

Different types of risk management are relevant to this discussion. First, there is the risk of choosing an inappropriate decision-making process, which could lead, on the one hand, to generating too few alternatives and evaluating them inadequately or, on the other hand, to conducting excessive analysis that wastes time and money. The discussion in this chapter addresses this risk directly by describing the pros and cons of different decision-making processes.

Second, problems can occur while executing the selected decision-making process. Understanding common execution problems can help decision-makers avoid these problems. Chapter 9 will discuss this risk.

Third, risk management is a specific type of decision-making process that involves assessing and evaluating the risks involved in an activity, developing alternatives for mitigating that risk, and selecting which ones to adopt. Chapter 9 will discuss this process in detail.

Sections 7.1–7.3 will present some frameworks for classifying decision-making processes, which provide some guidance on choosing an appropriate decision-making process. The chapter continues by presenting a variety of decision-making processes that show some of the options available (Sections 7.4–7.13). Sections 7.14 and 7.15 then discuss the importance of search as a way to consider decision-making processes, and Section 7.16 presents the secretary problem as a special case of decision making in which the process is extremely simple and can be optimized. Chapter 8 expands on the topic of search by focusing on quantitative techniques for determining the expected value of information. Finally, the chapter discusses processes, including product development, that decompose (or separate) a decision into a set of "smaller" decisions (Sections 7.17–7.19). These ideas will lay the foundation for the discussion of decision-making systems in Chapter 10. Chapter 9 discusses the process of managing risk, a type of decision-making process that has a specialized structure.

The discussion of decision-making processes in this chapter does not cover two relevant topics: the presentation of engineering analysis results to decision-makers and the implementation of a decision. Although improving communication skills, in general, is beyond the scope of this book, Chapter 9 does discuss, as part of risk management, the challenges of communicating risk, which is relevant in many situations. Chapter 9 also discusses the importance of considering implementation concerns and the problems that can occur if decision-makers do not.

7.1 DECISION-MAKING CONTEXTS

Decision making occurs in many different situations, and the characteristics of a situation (such as the time available, the degree of consensus, and the decision-maker's expertise) affect the relative usefulness of different decision-making processes. Five decision-making contexts were mentioned in Chapter 2; the following items describe the decision-making process that is appropriate for each context (Snowden and Boone, 2007).

- The first type of decision-making context is the *simple* context, in which clear cause-and-effect relationships are evident to everyone, and there are repeating patterns and consistent events. In this context, one needs proper decision-making processes using clear and direct communication.
- The second type is the *complicated* context, in which cause-and-effect relationships are knowable but not obvious, expert diagnosis is needed, and there are known unknowns. The decision-making process must get expert opinions and listen to possibly conflicting advice.
- The third type is the *complex* context, which is unpredictable and dynamic and full of unknown unknowns and many competing ideas. The decision-making process must be patient, look for patterns, and generate ideas.
- The fourth type is the *chaotic* context, which has high turbulence. This context requires making many decisions but provides no time to think. Decision-makers must look for something that works and reestablish order.

- The fifth type is *disorder*, which is difficult to recognize because multiple ideas and stakeholders create a "cacophony" of many voices. In this situation, decision-makers must detach issues from each other, identify the context that is relevant to each, and respond appropriately.

The risk of choosing the wrong decision-making process can be reduced by correctly identifying the decision-making context and selecting an appropriate decision-making process. If possible, naturally, the most disruptive, disorganized contexts should be avoided. Unfortunately, the context is often beyond the decision-maker's control.

7.2   TECHNICAL KNOWLEDGE AND PROBLEM CONSENSUS

Of the five decision contexts listed in the previous section, the complicated and complex contexts are the ones that are most relevant to engineers most of the time. Choosing and executing an appropriate decision-making process is an important step in these situations. Following Daft (2001), we can identify four primary types of decision-making processes, which will be described briefly here. After introducing these categories, this section will discuss the situations in which each is appropriate.

The *management science approach* relies upon formulating the problem using a mathematical model. This requires identifying the relevant decision variables, including the important constraints, and optimizing an appropriate objective function to find the best solution.

The *Carnegie model* describes decisions as the outcome of a process in which decision-makers form a coalition by talking about the problem, agreeing on the organization's goals, sharing their opinions, defining the problem, and recruiting others who support their position. Then, the coalition searches for a satisfactory solution that uses existing procedures if possible and creates a new solution only if necessary. Optimization is not considered due to the more pressing need to define the problem appropriately and reach consensus. The search for solutions (*problemistic search*) considers only those that are easy to get and will quickly help and ends when the first acceptable solution is found (*satisficing*).

The *incremental decision process model* focuses on the activities that occur during the decision-making process. Mintzberg *et al.* (1976) show that this decision-making process (also known as the strategic decision-making process) is not a simple sequence of tasks but involves iterating between different types of activities that occur in three phases: identification, development, and selection.

The identification phase includes the decision recognition activity and the diagnosis activity. In the decision recognition activity, a decision-making process begins in response to a stimulus such as a creative idea, a worsening problem, or a crisis. In the diagnosis activity, the decision-maker gathers information in order to clarify and define the relevant issues and objectives. (This search for information is distinct from the search for solutions that occurs in the next phase.)

The development phase includes the activities that are most associated with decision-making: search and design. Mintzberg *et al.* described the search activity as one that finds ready-made solutions (thus, it is a type of convergent thinking); the design activity modifies existing solutions or generates new ones (a type of divergent thinking). In the design activity, the designers "begin with a vague image of some ideal solution," enter "a sequence of nested design and search cycles," and "grope along, building their solution brick by brick."

The selection phase is the last step in any one decision, but developing a design "frequently involves factoring one decision into a series of subdecisions, each requiring at least one selection step" (Mintzberg *et al.*, 1976). The selection phase includes screening, evaluation choice, and authorization activities. The screening activity eliminates infeasible alternatives and may be imbedded in the search activity. The evaluation-choice activity may be an individual's judgment, a group decision-making process, or an objective, analytical evaluation. The authorization activity is necessary when the persons performing the evaluation choice must have their selection approved by someone who can authorize the associated expenditures.

In general, the component activities in the incremental decision process involve decision making, implying that making a major decision requires a series of small decisions. Simon (1997) described such a process as a *composite decision*. (This is discussed more in Section 7.17.)

The *garbage can model* describes decision making in an organization that is rapidly growing and changing (Cohen *et al.*, 1972). It is "organized anarchy": there is a great deal of ambiguity, organizational goals are poorly defined, positions have great turnover (people do not stay in the same place for long), and the lack of relevant history means that no one can predict accurately the outcomes of different alternatives. Decisions happen as four "streams" of events (problems, participants, potential solutions, and choice opportunities) interact. A problem is solved when things fall into place; otherwise, it may linger unresolved.

Example 7.1   Sarotte (2009) emphasized the "accidental" nature of the 1989 "decision" to open the German border at the Berlin Wall. During a period of widespread protests, a tired spokesman for the East German Politburo was given an update on travel regulations and mentioned at a news conference that East Germans would be able to exit the country at border crossings. The spokesman, who was not fully aware of the details of the new regulations, gave the impression that East Germans could leave at any time. When this inaccuracy was repeated on West German television, thousands of East Germans watching the broadcasts began gathering at the Berlin Wall checkpoints. Despite assurances from their superiors that no actual policy changes had occurred, East German guards, worried about possible violence, decided to let some persons cross the border. The crowd responded by calling for the gates to be opened, which the guards did, ending the division of Berlin. As West German television stations showed East Germans crossing the border, more East Germans were inspired to do the same. Those with the authority to order violent methods to stop the crowds were unavailable (busy in meetings about other urgent matters or asleep) and unaware of the change on the ground.

Simulation studies of the garbage can model have considered how the individuals in an organization tackle the problems that arrive. When problems arrive slowly, the organization can solve them easily; when problems arrive too fast, they will overwhelm the organization no matter what it does. In between those two cases, the organization will perform better (solve more problems) if problems are solved by the individuals who have the most appropriate combination of skills (Samuelson, 2008; Troitzsch, 2008).

When faced with a problem, the first critical choice is to pick the right decision-making process. One approach for this decision is the contingency decision-making framework for organizations (Daft, 2001). Here we will use product development examples to show the use of the framework, its four decision-making situations (shown in Figure 7.1), and the most appropriate decision-making processes for each one.

In this framework, four different situations arise from looking at two critical characteristics: *problem consensus* and *technical knowledge*. Problem consensus exists when the managers agree about the nature of the problem and the goals to achieve. In other words, there is no disagreement about the "ends" that the organization seeks or what it is trying to accomplish. Technical knowledge exists when the organization understands how to solve problems and achieve its goals. That is, there is no uncertainty about the "means" that the organization can use. This does not imply that the organization can predict the future or that the variability that is inherent in manufacturing and other processes has disappeared. It implies only that the organization has sufficient expertise and valid models that describe the relationships between the decision variables and key performance measures. That is, they know how things work.

In the first decision-making situation, both problem consensus and technical knowledge exist, and the management science approach described by Daft can be used. In product development, this means that it is possible to formulate a valid, relevant mathematical model and use that to optimize the product design. Examples include using structural optimization of an automobile frame to increase crashworthiness and reduce mass (Detwiler *et al.*, 1996) or conducting multidisciplinary

	Problem consensus exists	Problem consensus absent
Technical knowledge exists	Optimization (management science approach)	Coalition building (carnegie model)
Technical knowledge absent	Incremental decision making	Coalition building plus incremental decision making; garbage can model

Figure 7.1 A framework for decision-making processes. The combinations of problem consensus and technical knowledge define four situations. The figure identifies the decision-making processes that are most appropriate for that situation. (Based on Daft, 2001.)

optimization to find the most profitable vehicle design during the early design phase (Fenyes *et al.*, 2002).

In the second decision-making situation, problem consensus does not exist, but technical knowledge does. Proceeding without problem consensus increases the risk that the wrong problem will be solved (the decision will be framed or defined incorrectly). In this situation, the Carnegie model is appropriate, because nothing effective can be done until the organization reaches a consensus about its goals and agrees on the problem definition. In an automobile manufacturing firm, the decision to launch a new vehicle development project based on an initial vehicle concept requires the approval of multiple executives, each with their own perspective on what is good for the firm, so achieving a consensus about the new car's requirements, appearance, and financial viability is crucial (cf. Walton, 1997; Donndelinger, 2006). Of course, the vehicle development project itself is very different and is an example of the next type of decision-making situation.

In the third decision-making situation, problem consensus exists, but technical knowledge does not. Proceeding directly to optimization increases the risk that the solutions generated, although they seem desirable, are actually inferior because the models are incorrect. The incremental decision process model is an appropriate strategy in this situation because it enables the organization to learn as it constructs a solution. This is the most common situation in product development. The product development team's goal is to deliver something that will meet the profitability and performance targets that are set at the beginning of the process. The challenge is that there is great uncertainty about how to meet these targets. There are few validated models for describing how the details of the product design affect performance. The models that exist are quite limited, such as the structural optimization model mentioned earlier. In response to this situation, the product design decision is decomposed into many smaller decisions (Herrmann, 2010), with iteration among the different decisions (Donndelinger, 2006). Thus the incremental decision process model is an appropriate model for this type of decision-making process.

Similarly, de Neufville (1990) described system design as an optimization procedure. However, he noted that it is not a monolithic mathematical program that can be solved directly. Instead, the analyst must first search for a small set of nondominated solutions, conduct sensitivity analysis to determine their robustness, evaluate the solutions in more detail, establish a sequence of configurations so that the system can change over time (if feasible and desirable), and then validate and present the results. The initial screening for a small set of solutions is needed to reduce the effort of the system design process.

In the fourth decision-making situation, neither problem consensus nor technical knowledge exists. In this type of situation, one possible solution is to first build a coalition to define the problem (by applying the Carnegie model) and then to develop a solution to that (by applying the incremental decision process model).

Example 7.2 In the 1990s, Ford made and sold Mercury automobiles that were only superficially different from more popular Ford sedans (Walton, 1997). Consider the problem of the firm's product portfolio and product positioning. Was the similarity (between Mercury and Ford cars) a problem because it failed to distinguish the Mercury line, or was it an effective cost-savings strategy? Could Ford improve Mercury's image if it continued this strategy, or should it eliminate the entire brand (its eventual fate in 2010)? Ford could first build a coalition to define the problem (e.g., improve Mercury's image) and then develop a solution to that (e.g., find an effective combination of marketing strategies and new vehicles).

Sometimes, however, in this situation, decisions will be made in a process that seems almost random, as the garbage can model describes. The following example shows this process.

Example 7.3   Walton (1997) described one engineer's efforts to get a second sheet metal press for the factory that would make the new Ford Taurus. (The factory was already scheduled to receive one press to make another vehicle.) The engineer viewed this as a solution to a vehicle quality problem. Initially, the proposal was rejected based on its cost and the time needed to design and procure the machine. Later, however, a new program manager was appointed, and he supported the proposal. At the same time, an opponent from manufacturing engineering left the development team, and the manufacturing managers suddenly realized that having a backup press would be valuable. In the end, the company making the first press was asked to deliver two of them. This alignment of diverse events not related to the problem is a classic example of the garbage can model.

7.3   OPTIMIZATION: SEARCH AND EVALUATION

The management science approach emphasizes optimization as an appropriate paradigm for decision making in some situations. Optimization does not necessarily mean formulating and solving a complex mathematical program, however. Simpler methods also fit the optimization paradigm, and such methods are more appropriate in some cases.

Bonabeau (2003) categorized decisions using two attributes: the number of alternatives and the complexity of evaluating the alternatives. When the number of alternatives is small and the alternatives are easy to evaluate, it is easy for a human to decide (optimize) using simple approaches. As the number of alternatives increases, then the decision becomes more complex, and a computational approach may be useful to search through the set of alternatives. As the complexity of the evaluation increases, computational models (including decision trees and simulation models) become useful to assist the decision-maker. When the number of alternatives is large and evaluating the alternatives is complex, then formal optimization approaches become useful.

Example 7.4   Choosing the proper material for a component is an important and common design decision. Unfortunately, thousands of different metals, polymers, ceramics, and composites are available, so a computational approach can be helpful.

The CES selector software can search for an appropriate material by finding in its database those that match user-specified criteria such as allowable ranges for density, Young's modulus, cost, carbon content, and other properties.

Example 7.5   The process of choosing trajectories for the Mariner spacecraft missions to Jupiter and Saturn and their moons involved 32 alternatives, but the evaluation was done by the scientists on the science teams. Because the number of alternatives was too large for a direct comparison, computational techniques were used to aggregate the science teams' preferences and rank the alternatives (Dyer and Miles, 1976).

Example 7.6   When Ford Motor Company wanted to improve the utilization of its expensive, full-vehicle prototypes during the development of a new car, it developed and began using an optimization model that could consider thousands of possible prototype configurations and determine which prototypes should be built to minimize prototype costs while meeting testing requirements (Chelst *et al.*, 2001). The number of possible solutions and the complexity of evaluating a solution made optimization an appropriate choice.

7.4   DIAGNOSING RISK DECISION SITUATIONS

Stern and Fineberg (1996) classified decisions about specific, potentially hazardous activities into three categories: (1) unique, wide-impact decisions; (2) repeated, wide-impact decisions; and (3) routine, narrow-impact decisions. (They also considered generic hazard characterizations and decisions about policies for risk analysis, which are not discussed here.) A unique, wide-impact decision is a one-time decision that affects a large number of people. For example, the decision to locate, build, and operate a nuclear waste repository at Yucca Mountain, Nevada, would affect not only the people who live in that part of the Nevada but also those who live near sites around the United States where radioactive waste is currently stored. The Department of Homeland Security's decision to locate a new biological and agricultural research facility in Kansas was a unique decision, although the impact was limited to the area around the facility (GAO, 2009).

   Repeated, wide-impact decisions include those about locating and operating power plants, hazardous waste facilities, and other large-scale construction projects. The impacts are limited to a particular region. For example, Florida Power Corporation's decision to locate a power plant (Stern and Fineberg, 1996) would have aspects that are similar to other decisions to locate power plants.

   Routine, narrow-impact decisions are done frequently in many agencies of different types, from national to local municipalities. These include permits to operate landfills and develop property, approve building designs, and authorize the manufacturing of medical devices.

   Identifying the relevant category of decision should not lead directly to a particular decision-making process, but it can guide those who are diagnosing the decision and planning the process (Stern and Fineberg, 1996). The following steps describe the diagnosis process:

1. Diagnose the kind of risk and state of knowledge.
2. Describe the legal mandate.
3. Describe the purpose of the risk decision.
4. Describe the affected parties and likely public reactions.
5. Estimate resource needs and timetable.
6. Plan for organizational needs.
7. Develop a preliminary process design.
8. Summarize the diagnosis and discuss it within the organization.

The results indicate the nature and level of effort of the analytic-deliberative process (Section 7.8) needed to make the decision.

7.5   VALUES AND ETHICS

Decision-making processes should be guided by the values of the decision-makers, who will have important principles, including ethical norms, that guide their actions.

Keeney (1992) suggested that decision-makers should not, after understanding the decision situation, move directly to generating alternatives. Instead, he recommended *value-focused thinking*, in which a decision-maker specifies the relevant values, which are the principles and objectives that will be used to evaluate the alternatives. Only after identifying the relevant values and the associated attributes, should a decision-maker generate alternatives. Identifying the values first will guide the decision-maker to relevant alternatives. Note that this corresponds to building a means-objective network from the top down and extending it to include alternatives by asking "how can we achieve that objective?" The top-down approach makes it more likely that the alternatives contribute directly to more fundamental objectives.

The task of identifying alternatives is a particularly important opportunity to consider the decision-maker's values and ethical norms. If an alternative involves illegal or unethical behavior or violates the organization's values, then it should be discarded promptly regardless of any other advantages. Vann (2013) provided a long list of books and case studies about ethical decision making in engineering.

Some decisions involve ethical dilemmas in which a decision-maker feels caught between competing principles and objectives. For example, honorable engineers who know that their employers are doing something wrong or making dangerous products want not only to uncover the wrongdoing or hazard in order to protect the public but also to keep their jobs to support their families and avoid the scrutiny and criticism that come from being a "whistleblower" (Sprague, 1998). The Ford engineers who designed the Pinto and the NASA engineers who studied the impact of debris on the space shuttle Columbia faced this type of situation (Birsch, 1994; Gioia, 1994; Roberto *et al.*, 2005). Other dilemmas stem from interpersonal relationships, the conflict between personal gain and the employer's objectives, and the conflict between personal gain and avoiding illegal behavior. Throughout the decision-making process, a decision-maker can evaluate alternatives and determine the right thing to do by analyzing the values of caring, honesty, accountability, promise keeping, pursuit of excellence, loyalty, fairness, integrity, respect for others, and responsible citizenship (Guy, 1990). Systematically considering this set of values can reduce the risk of overlooking important principles and considerations and doing something that one regrets in the future.

7.6   SYSTEMATIC DECISION-MAKING PROCESSES

Various systematic processes for decision making have been described. The decision analysis process (Clemen and Reilly, 2001) has the following seven steps:

1. Identify the decision situation and understand the objectives.
2. Identify the alternatives.
3. Model the problem, the uncertainty, and the preferences.
4. Choose the best alternative.
5. Conduct a sensitivity analysis.
6. Decide if further analysis is needed (if so, go to a previous step).
7. Implement the decision.

Parnell and West (2008) presented a *systems decision process* that was developed for making decisions during the development of complex systems for the military. It has four primary phases:

1. *Problem definition:* Understand the problem originally identified by the decision-maker. Gather information from the stakeholders (also identified by the decision-maker) about the environment, the system objectives, and the requirements. Model the values of the decision-maker and the stakeholders. The decision-maker and stakeholders validate the problem statement. The environment includes technology, economics, politics, organizational issues, legal requirements, ethical considerations, society, nature, and cultural and historical issues.
2. *Solution design:* Generate ideas and alternatives for potential solutions. Enhance the alternatives. Evaluate the alternatives. Gather feedback and ideas from the stakeholders about the alternatives. The decision-maker should approve the alternatives that will be evaluated.
3. *Decision making*: Score the alternatives. Conduct sensitivity analysis to understand the impact of uncertain parameters. Stakeholders provide data and help score the alternatives. The decision-maker selects the solution to implement.
4. *Solution implementation*: Create a plan for implementation. The decision-maker must approve the plan, provide the needed resources, and ensure the cooperation and commitment of the stakeholders.

Morris (1977) gave an engineering decision-making process that includes a role for common sense:

1. Describe the problem (and possibly model it).
2. Define the objective (the most important criteria).
3. Consider the relevant facts and factors in order to identify any constraints.
4. Generate the alternative solutions and choose the best one.
5. Use "horse sense" (a term for common sense that includes drawing on related experience, specific expertise, and one's intuition) to verify that the solution will work, satisfies the constraints, and is the best possible.

The decision analysis cycle (Donndelinger, 2006) has four phases that highlight the importance of considering uncertainty and of gathering more information:

1. In the *deterministic phase*, the decision-maker defines the variables affecting the decision, determines the relationships between them, determines their importance, identifies alternatives, and evaluates their performance.
2. In the *probabilistic phase*, the decision-maker assigns probability distributions to important variables and their values and determines his preferences.
3. In the *informational phase*, the decision-maker determines the economic value of eliminating uncertainty in the important variables and compares this to the cost of collecting the needed information.
4. Finally, the decision-maker makes a *decision* by acting or gathering more information (and returning to the deterministic phase).

NASA's Risk-Informed Decision Making (NASA, 2010), which is suggested for key decisions like system architecture design, emphasizes deliberation and the use of multiple performance measures. It has three parts:

1. The first part identifies alternatives by understanding the stakeholders' expectations, identifying relevant performance measures and constraints, evaluating candidates, and eliminating infeasible alternatives.
2. The second part determines an appropriate approach for analyzing the risks associated with the alternatives, identifies the uncertainties, and determines the distributions of the performance measures for each alternative. The type of risk analysis used will depend on the project scale, the phase of the project life cycle, the amount of detail that is available, and other factors.
3. The third part selects an alternative after developing performance commitments, discussing the relative advantages and disadvantages of the alternatives, and documenting the decision rationale. The decision-makers may require more risk analysis, more information, or revisions to the performance commitments before they can select an alternative. A *performance commitment* is the value of a performance measure that an alternative will exceed with a certain probability;

that is, it is a specific percentile of the distribution of the performance measure for that alternative. Associated with each performance measure is a percentile, and the same percentile is used for all alternatives.

Although these decision-making processes have been presented as sequences of steps, it is important to note that these processes all include the option for iteration. A decision-maker may move forward if the quality of the decision is sufficient but can return to a previous step if some aspects of the decision are unacceptable. The following elements can be used to evaluate the quality (NRC, 2001): Is this decision frame (the problem definition) appropriate? Were creative alternatives generated? Are the information and models used reliable? Are the decision-maker's preferences clear? Is the logic correct? Is the decision-maker committed to act?

7.7   THE DECISION-MAKING CYCLE

The *decision-making cycle* is an iterative decision-making process that is appropriate for those who manage an ongoing project or supervise and schedule operations. This decision-making process was introduced by McKay and Wiers (2004) in their discussion of decision-making in production scheduling. Their decision-making cycle (Figure 7.2) describes the tasks that schedulers perform each day:

1. Situation assessment: what is where.
2. Crisis identification: what needs immediate attention.
3. Immediate resequencing and task reallocation: reactive decisions.
4. Complete scenario update: remapping the future.
5. Future problem identification: what problems can be foreseen.
6. Constraint relaxation and future problem resolution: discounting future problems.
7. Scheduling by rote: dealing with the rest of the problem.

This decision-making process includes problem solving (in the limited sense of finding the answer to a question). The seventh task, scheduling by rote, requires creating a schedule for the work that is not in process, assigning work to resources, and

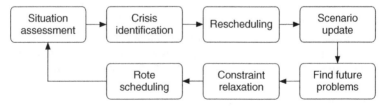

Figure 7.2   Decision making cycle. (Adapted from McKay and Wiers, 2004.)

sequencing the operations subject to the constraints that the scheduler imposes to avoid future problems. Schedule generation algorithms can be useful in this step to reduce the workload of the scheduler and to find solutions that are better than those a human can find (due to the size or complexity of the problem; cf. the discussion of search and evaluation in Section 7.3).

This process also has some similarities to a risk management process because the decision-maker identifies future problems and takes steps to "discount" them by reducing the probability that they will occur and mitigating their impacts if they should happen. Chapter 9 discusses risk management processes in more detail.

7.8 THE ANALYTIC-DELIBERATIVE PROCESS

Those who make decisions about activities that create risks to the public need to consider those risks carefully. An *analytic-deliberative process* focuses attention on analysis and deliberation throughout the decision-making process (Stern and Fineberg, 1996). It also seeks to include a broad set of participants, which is an important part of the discovery decision-making process as well (Nutt, 2003; this process is described in Section 9.8).

The process starts with diagnosing the situation (which is described in Section 7.4). The process moves, as any systematic decision-making process does, from problem formulation to identifying alternatives, evaluating them, and selecting one. The entire time, however, the iteration between analysis and deliberation is happening. Both analysis and deliberation are used to understand the real-world problem in general and understand the risk in particular. (It is similar to the dialogue decision process described in Section 10.3.)

In the analytic part of the process, subject-matter experts use rigorous, accepted methods to derive answers to relevant factual questions in areas such as the natural sciences, mathematics, social science, and law. The analysis activities are based on the assumption that relevant facts can be found through impartial methods. The deliberative part of the process is a formal or informal process in which all of the concerned stakeholders "discuss, ponder, exchange observations and views, reflect on information and judgments concerning matters of mutual interest, and attempt to persuade each other," but it does not require generating a consensus (Stern and Fineberg, 1996). Deliberation may lead to asking additional factual questions that need answers (which restarts the analysis), and the answers to these questions will begin additional deliberation. Ultimately, the responsible organization will make the decision. Although some interested parties may not like the selected alternative, using an analytic-deliberative process attempts to help everyone understand all aspects of the problem and make the decision rationale clear to everyone.

Stern and Fineberg (1996) offered guidelines for organizing an effective yet efficient analytic-deliberative process: include a broad set of participants, inform the participants early about any legal requirements or resource constraints that will put limits on the deliberations, strive to be fair by providing all participants with equivalent resources and information, and build flexibility into the process. Knowing when to stop the process helps avoid unnecessary delays, such as those that can occur during the environmental review of infrastructure projects such as repairing roads, building bridges and power transmission lines, and dredging shipping channels (Howard, 2013).

Example 7.7   When the residents of Cambridge, Massachusetts, and other nearby municipalities raised concerns about plans to ship ethanol (which is flammable) to a fuel storage facility by rail through the area, the resulting process was an analytic-deliberative process (Compaine, 2013). Cambridge politicians opposed the plan, and state legislators passed a law that required the Massachusetts Department of Transportation to conduct a safety study. The agency conducted the study, issued its report about the potentially exposed populations and the ways to reduce the risk to the public, and held public meetings to share information about the study (Massachusetts Department of Transportation, 2013). After this analytical phase, the deliberations began again, and state legislators modified the state budget to prevent the expansion of the fuel storage facility to handle the ethanol. The governor of Massachusetts then vetoed the budget amendment, and the debate continued.

7.9   CONCEPT SELECTION

The value of iteration as an opportunity to generate more alternatives was emphasized by Dieter and Schmidt (2012) in their discussion of the Pugh concept selection method, which can be used during the development of a new product. Concept selection is an important decision in which generating novel solutions is especially useful.

The steps of the Pugh concept selection method (Section 3.1) encourage the generation of new alternatives (design concepts) throughout the decision-making process. The process of comparing the alternative concepts uncovers the strengths and weaknesses of the alternatives, which are organized using the decision matrix and then utilized to generate new alternatives. These new alternatives are compared as the process continues. This iteration avoids the risk of developing an inferior concept in the next part of the development process.

When a design problem can be structured as a number of variables, then one can form a complete design by combining values for the variables. This strategy is the basis for *morphological analysis* (Zwicky, 1948, 1969). For instance, Zwicky structured the design of jet and rocket propulsion systems using six variables: the medium through which the engine moves, the type of motion of the propellant relative to the jet engine, the physical state of the propellant, the type of thrust augmentation, the type of ignition, and the sequence of operations. For each variable, he listed a few alternatives, which yielded 576 possible configurations for the entire system. Morphological analysis can be used to generate a diverse set of alternatives during the conceptual design by separating the system to be designed into different functions (Dieter and Schmidt, 2012). Morphological analysis can also be used as a problem structuring method for analyzing organizations and other social systems (Ritchey, 2006). Typically, in morphological analysis, the values of the individual variables are not evaluated independently; the complete combination is evaluated. If the values of the individual variables can be evaluated independently, then each one is a subproblem, and the subproblems form a separation of the design problem (cf. Section 7.18).

7.10   DECISION CALCULUS

The decision-making processes described here are iterative. A decision-maker may return to a previous step due to changes in the situation, updated information, or the need for more information. One particular form of iteration in decision making involves a decision-maker and an analyst who is supporting the decision-maker by evaluating and ranking alternatives using a mathematical model (such as decision analysis or optimization). Little (1970) called this type of model-based iteration a *decision calculus*. His discussion included the following conversation with an analyst:

Interviewer: "Do you make regular mathematical programming runs for scheduling the refinery?"

Analyst: "Oh yes."

Interviewer: "Do you implement the results?"

Analyst: "Oh no!"

Interviewer: "Well, that seems odd. If you don't implement the results, perhaps you should stop making the runs?"

Analyst: "No. No. We wouldn't want to do that!"

Interviewer: "Why not?"

Analyst: "Well, what happens is something like this I make several computer runs and take them to the plant manager. He is responsible for this whole multi-million dollar plumber's paradise. The plant manager looks at the runs, thinks about them for a while and then sends me back to make a few more with conditions changed in various ways. I do this and bring them in. He looks at them and probably sends me back to make more runs. And so forth."

Interviewer: "How long does this keep up?"

Analyst: "I would say it continues until, finally, the plant manager screws up enough courage to make a decision."

An example of this type of iteration was described by Gensch (2001), who discussed the use of a mathematical model to support the selection of concepts during the new product development at a major manufacturer of heating and cooling systems for large buildings. The firm reused the model to update its plans as new concepts were proposed and ongoing work was completed.

The dialogue decision-making process (Spetzler, 2007; Tani and Parnell, 2013) is a formal process that is, essentially, a decision calculus. This process is described in Section 10.3.

7.11   RECOGNITION-PRIMED DECISION MAKING

The discipline of NDM has studied how people make decisions in familiar real-world contexts (Lipshitz et al., 2001). Based on their study of officers in city fire departments, Klein *et al.* (2010) proposed the *recognition-primed decision* (RPD) *model* to describe experts who have very little time and need to decide quickly. (This could occur, for instance, in the chaotic decision-making context described in Chapter 2.) Experts rely on their situational awareness and seek to achieve certain goals; they do not directly compare two or more alternatives. Based on their experience, tacit knowledge, and ability to recognize patterns and identify anomalies, experts can identify good alternatives immediately. If the chosen alternative performs poorly, however, then it is rejected, and another one is chosen. In addition, to mitigate the risk that an intuitive solution may not work, experts may, before selecting an alternative, perform a mental simulation to evaluate whether that alternative will achieve their goals. Kaempf *et al.* (1996) found that the decision making of naval officers in antiair warfare command-and-control positions on US Navy cruisers was consistent with the RPD model.

7.12   HEURISTICS

Decision-makers use various heuristics to make decisions without analyzing them. The bounded rationality of human decision-makers is an important reason for using heuristics. As mentioned in Chapter 2, humans have developed the skill to use simple heuristics with little information and conduct searches that are appropriate for the environment. For instance, to decide which of two alternatives is greater on some scale (e.g., which city has the larger population or which product is more reliable), the *recognition heuristic* chooses the one that is recognized if the other is not. When faced with multiple alternatives, an engineer may select the most familiar one as a way to reduce uncertainty. The recognition heuristic can perform well, but only in environments (such as sports) where the most successful objects (or people) are those that people most frequently discuss, which increases the likelihood that those objects (or people) will be recognized (Todd and Gigerenzer, 2007).

The *default heuristic* (If there's a default choice, stick with it) describes the decision to choose the default if one is provided (Todd and Gigerenzer, 2007). This can be quite powerful. For instance, consumers are highly likely to use the default software (such as a web browser) that is installed on the computers and laptops that they buy. This leads software manufacturers to seek arrangements with computer manufacturers to be the default software.

A *tallying heuristic* counts the number of ways that one alternative is better than another. The Pugh matrix and Franklin's prudential algebra are versions of this idea. Such approaches can lead to good decisions if the attributes are all related to the decision-maker's objective and are not redundant (Todd and Gigerenzer, 2007).

As mentioned in Chapter 2, using simple rules is sometimes a response to complexity (Simon, 1955, 1978). When faced with a problem that is too large or complex to solve optimally, decision-makers may rely on a simple rule that makes sense based on what they understand. (Another option is to separate the problem into subproblems, as discussed in Section 7.18.) For instance, in some component design situations, the choice of the best material depends only on the *material performance index*, not the part geometry or its functional requirements. Using the material performance index (instead of the complete objective function) simplifies the problem. Ashby (2005) provided material performance indices for a variety of design problems.

7.13 UNCONSCIOUS DECISION MAKING

Finally, decision-makers may use an unconscious decision-making process that has been called *deliberation without attention.*

In studies in which experimental subjects and actual shoppers made simple choices (such as between different towels or different sets of oven mitts) and more complicated choices (such as between different houses or different cars), using conscious thought to decide produced better outcomes for the simple choices, but using unconscious thought to decide produced better outcomes for the complicated choices. In particular, "purchases of complex products were viewed more favorably when decisions had been made in the absence of attentive deliberation" (Dijksterhuis *et al.*, 2006).

These results do not imply that formal decision-making methods are not important. They do show that the human mind is able to compare alternatives using a deliberative process that we do not completely understand. Our systematic decision-making techniques and processes are only approximations of what the human mind does. It is possible that deliberation without attention allows the mind to work without interference. As discussed in Section 2.7, Benjamin Franklin recommended allowing "three or four days consideration" as part of his "prudential algebra." Perhaps he realized that the mind continues to deliberate even when the decision-maker is considering other matters.

Of course, in an organizational setting, using an unconscious decision-making process would be hard to justify. It is certainly not transparent, for instance, and it does not generate alternatives or uncover new information about them. It generates neither the technical knowledge nor the problem consensus discussed in Section 7.2. It requires time that may be unavailable in some contexts.

7.14 SEARCH

When developing the 1996 Ford Taurus, the product development team had to find places inside the car to put many components and subassemblies. For instance, the team considered placing the airbag crash sensors inside the grille opening, on the upper radiator supports, and on a grounding bracket behind the front bumper, among other locations (Walton, 1997). They had to search for a location that was near the front of the car, could be grounded, and did not block the flow of air into the engine compartment. In this search, there was only the need for a feasible location; as soon as one was found, they could stop searching. Walton also described the efforts of the "squeak-and-rattle" engineers who had to identify the causes of noises in the first cars produced at the assembly plant; they literally searched the noisy cars for loose parts.

Effective search processes are crucial to effective decision making. A limited search is a "trap" that causes a decision to fail, and sometimes the failures are huge (Nutt, 2004).

According to Simon (1981), the theory of design is a theory of search. Ideally, this would be a search for the optimal design (or alternative). However, when optimizing is too difficult, then the search is for a satisfactory solution. Indeed, in situations with extreme time pressure, the search may be limited to one solution, as when a skilled decision-maker (such as a firefighter commander) quickly generates a feasible course of action (perhaps by recalling what worked in similar situations) without generating or evaluating any alternatives (Lipshitz *et al.*, 2001).

Example 7.8 The IDEO design process (Nussbaum, 2004; Dubberly, 2005/2013) can be viewed and understood as a search in which different types of decisions must be made. In the observation step, the designers must select some observational techniques (e.g., shadowing). In the brainstorming step, the designers are generating and building on ideas quickly but must still decide which ideas to expand and which to ignore. In the rapid prototyping step, in which mock-ups are used to gather information about the alternatives, the designers must decide which types of models, simulations, and prototypes will be used for which alternatives. In the refining step, the designers decide which alternatives will be eliminated and which will be implemented in the last step.

A search such as the IDEO design process goes through several stages. After recognizing a problem, the decision-maker searches for possible alternatives and uses approximations to eliminate obviously inappropriate alternatives. Essentially, this estimates the probability that an alternative will perform well and discards the alternatives that are unlikely to perform well, which reduces the time and cost of the search process. The search becomes more intensive, and more detailed information is gathered, as some alternatives begin to seem more desirable than the others. Less desirable alternatives do not receive the same amount of scrutiny.

In addition to searching for alternatives, a decision-maker must also search for information about those alternatives. When seeking information, the searcher typically goes through four stages (Zach, 2005): (1) initiation, (2) assessment, (3) exploration, and (4) completion.

In the initiation stage, the task to be done is identified. In the assessment stage, the searcher considers the task in more detail, may discuss it with colleagues, and plans an approach. These actions may lead the searcher to identify other needed inputs. In the assessment stage, the searcher evaluates the resources available for the search, identifies the stakeholders who will be interested in the information found (and the outcome of the decision), and determines the task's importance (which may affect the amount of time allocated to the search).

The exploration stage has two parts: collection and closure. After completing the assessment stage, the searcher decides whether additional input is needed. If so, then the searcher begins collecting information by selecting sources, gathering information, and evaluating the accuracy and completeness of that information. The searcher's next step is to attempt closure by assessing the input and deciding if it is enough. This is affected by the task's importance; a searcher will want more input for more important tasks. The searcher also considers the diminishing returns on gathering more information (additional information will be less relevant and increasingly redundant, and gathering it will consume scarce resources), the time available, and the quality of the information. More information will be gathered while the searcher is not comfortable with the input gathered, and either more time is available or the information is completely inadequate.

If the input is not enough, the searcher may resume collecting information, expand the question, or redefine the task. If the input is enough, the searcher completes the information-seeking process and goes on to make the decision.

The flowchart in Figure 7.3 describes a generic approach to searching during the process of making a decision. Note the multiple decisions that must be made during

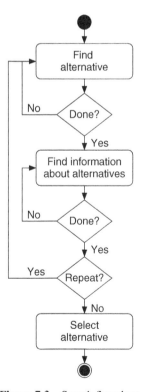

Figure 7.3 Search flowchart.

a search. Making the "Done?" decision and the "Repeat?" decision involves judging whether the alternatives are satisfactory.

During the planning of the Mariner spacecraft missions to Jupiter and Saturn and their moons, the process of choosing trajectories for the two spacecrafts included both types of search. First, engineers from the Jet Propulsion Lab first identified 105 different trajectories. From the 2,624 feasible trajectory pairs, they found 24 desirable alternatives (Dyer and Miles, 1976). They then searched for more trajectory pairs by asking the 10 discipline-specific science teams for their input. This led to removing four trajectory pairs that satisfied no science team while adding 12 more to the list (for a total of 32). The search for information about the alternatives was delegated to the science teams. Each science team ranked the alternatives based on their priorities (preferences) about the importance of different attributes for the trajectories and different levels of risk aversion. This information was aggregated (as discussed in Chapter 4) to form a group ranking. However, the search for alternatives was not quite done, because the preferred trajectory pair was modified to improve its performance on one attribute that was very important to one science team.

The time required to complete a search for a satisfactory solution depends on the density of satisfactory solutions in the search space. Here, the density is the ratio between the number of satisfactory solutions in the search space and the total number of alternatives in the search space. Let p be this density, which can be viewed as the probability that a random selection from the search space is one of the satisfactory solutions. Given n selections, there is a $(1 - p)^n$ probability that none of the randomly selected alternatives is satisfactory. Thus, the probability that at least one of the randomly selected alternatives is satisfactory is $1 - (1 - p)^n$.

Alternatively, if solutions are selected randomly and every solution is equally likely to be selected, then the number of selections before a satisfactory one is found is a random variable with a geometric distribution. Its mean is $(1 - p)/p$. The expected total number of selections including the satisfactory one is $1/p$.

More generally, the problem is to allocate fixed search effort to maximize the probability of finding a satisfactory solution or to devise a plan that minimizes the effort needed to reach a prespecified probability of finding a satisfactory solution.

Washburn (1989) discussed various models of different search processes, including physical searches for stationary and moving targets within a given area. For the case of a stationary target that is at one of many possible discrete locations that are examined one at a time, it can be shown that the optimal search policy is a myopic one: at any step, examine the location that has the largest remaining detection probability. This will minimize the expected time required to find the target.

More precisely, let p_i equal the probability that the target is in location i, q_i equal the probability of not detecting the target when location i is examined, and $n(i)$ be the number of times that the location has already been examined. The remaining detection probability at location i equals $p_i(1 - q_i)q_i^{n(i)}$. If $q_i = 0$, then the remaining detection probability at location i equals p_i the first time it is examined and 0 otherwise. If $q_i > 0$, then the remaining detection probability decreases monotonically each time location i is examined.

7.15 TYPES OF SEARCH IN PRACTICE

In practice, of course, search is usually not modeled as a stochastic process. It is a trial-and-error process that uses heuristics to suggest the paths that should be tried first (Simon, 1981). The previous analytical result suggests that the best way to find something quickly is to look first in the most likely places.

Unfortunately, search in real-world organizations is not so simple. Cyert and March (1992) used the term *problemistic search* to describe searches that organizations conduct in the real world. These searches have three primary characteristics:

1. *Motivated search.* The search is focused on solving a problem. It is not collecting knowledge as a scientific endeavor. There is some existing or anticipated problem that the firm needs to solve. The search will continue until it finds a satisfactory solution or the firm revises the constraints so that an available solution is feasible.

2. *Simple-minded search.* The search begins by looking in two areas. The first area contains solutions that are similar to the existing situation or proposed alternative. The second area involves improvements to the immediate cause of the problem. (For example, if the customer is getting bad parts, then inspect the parts and scrap any bad ones before shipping them.) When a search is not successful looking in these areas, the search becomes more complex. The search looks in more distant areas, and the search looks at areas that are vulnerable as opportunities to get the resources required (by eliminating basic research, e.g., to improve profits).

3. *Bias in search.* The search is influenced by the training and experience of those in the organization, the temptation to use hopes as expectations (which shortens the search), and conflict within the organization.

Example 7.9 The Apollo 13 mission, damaged by an explosion on the way to the moon, included many instances of searching for solutions to unexpected problems. One problem was the buildup of dangerous carbon dioxide caused by the inadequate carbon dioxide scrubber in the lunar module (NASA, 2001/2014). This problemistic search began by considering the lithium hydroxide canisters from the command module, but these had a different shape and would not work directly in the lunar module. Therefore, the search was broadened to design a method to use the canisters in an atypical way with other materials on board, which was successful (see Figure 7.4).

In this case, the search for an innovative carbon dioxide scrubber began due to a random event (the accident), and the astronauts and ground crew were motivated to improve it quickly. When the obvious solution (inserting the canisters from the command module) was found to be infeasible, the search moved to a more complex solution.

Nutt (2005) described and studied five types of search that occur in decision making. These have different combinations of direction setting and uncovering solutions.

Figure 7.4 The improvised lithium hydroxide canister inside the Apollo 13 lunar module. (Photo credit: NASA.)

An "opportunity" search begins with a decision-maker seeing the solution (perhaps, already adopted by peers or competitors) and deciding to take action without considering why the solution is needed. No direction setting is needed (no goal is set), and no formal search occurs.

An "undirected" search also begins with a solution, but the solution has deficiencies (or is politically unacceptable) and is abandoned, which starts a search for a replacement solution that could deliver the original solution's benefits, which were never precisely stated, without its deficiencies. Thus, no specific direction is offered, and such searches led to results that were less likely to be adopted than the results of goal-directed searches.

A "chance" search (also called an "emergent opportunity") describes the process in which an idea and an unsatisfied need accidentally converge (the garbage can model describes how such accidents happen). A goal (the need) was specified, but the emergence of the solution preempts the search for alternatives, especially when the need is related to a large threat. Such searches took less time than the other types.

A "goal-directed" search begins with a specific goal (a desired result). This was the most common search approach observed by Nutt (2005), and goal-directed searches produced results that were more likely to be adopted and completed more quickly than the "results" of opportunity searches. Goals tend to trigger exploration because alternatives (both off-the-shelf solutions and innovative ideas) are judged primarily by their impact on performance.

A "problem-directed" search begins with a specific problem that needs to be solved. Such searches produced results that were not as good as the results of goal-directed searches (the results were less likely to be adopted, and the searches took more time).

Nutt (2005) concluded that goal-directed searches are the most effective way to search because they clarify the expected benefits up front, unlike undirected searches. That is, a goal-directed search reduces the risk that time and effort will be wasted on a "wild goose chase." Problem-directed searches are less effective because they limit the search to solutions that can remove the problem and because blaming and self-protection take resources away from productive activities. A problem-directed search can be preempted if an emergent opportunity happens to appear, but this is not as effective.

7.16 SECRETARY PROBLEM

In the classic decision-making problem, all of the alternatives (and the relevant attributes) are available when the decision-maker decides. There are cases, however, when decisions must be made about alternatives sequentially. Alternatives must be accepted or rejected one by one. In other cases, a decision-maker may decide to halt a search in the middle, going with the best so far and not looking any further.

Consider, for instance, Rose, who is driving down an expressway on a trip through an unfamiliar area. A highway sign informs her that there are five exits in the next 50 km (30 miles). She is hungry and tired and wants to stop to eat and rest at one of these next five exits, but she does not want to explore every exit, and she is certainly not going to turn around and go back to a previous exit. Instead, she will stick with the exit that she chooses. As she approaches each exit, billboards and other signs provide her with information about the restaurants and other facilities at that exit. She can decide to exit there or can keep going down the highway. If she passes the first four exits, she will have to stop at the fifth. In this problem, she has to accept or reject each exit without knowing anything about the future exits (except that they exist).

A similar problem can occur when evaluating applicants for an open position. This has been called the secretary problem, the candidate problem, the job search problem, the parking spot problem, the beauty contest problem, the house selling problem, the optimal stopping problem, and the house hunting problem. The following description is based on Chun (2000).

Let T be the number of applicants for a position, which is known at the beginning. The applicants are interviewed sequentially in a random order. The decision-maker can rank all the applicants interviewed so far from best to worst without ties (but knows nothing about the applicants not yet interviewed). Each applicant must be rejected or accepted immediately after the interview. The decision to reject or accept an applicant is based only on the relative ranks of the applicants interviewed so far. A rejected applicant cannot be accepted later (because they will leave and take a job somewhere else).

The decision-maker wants the best applicant. The decision-maker is not interested in merely finding someone who meets some specific criteria. Accepting one of the first applicants may result in losing a better applicant who is still waiting to be interviewed. (If the decision-maker merely wants an acceptable applicant, then the problem is much simpler: the first applicant who meets the specified requirements should be accepted.)

Solving this problem requires finding a policy that maximizes the probability of selecting the best applicant in the entire group. Selecting someone besides the best applicant is considered a "bad" outcome, so this policy reduces the risk that this will occur.

First, let a "candidate" be the best of the applicants interviewed so far. Note that not all applicants are candidates. After the decision-maker has interviewed m alternatives out of a total of T, then the probability that the best one of those interviewed so far is the best of the entire group is $p_1(m) = m/T$. The probability that the best one so far is the kth best in the entire group (where $k \leq T - m + 1$) can be calculated as follows:

$$p_k(m) = p_{k-1}(m)\frac{T - m - k + 2}{T - k + 1}.$$

After the decision-maker has interviewed m applicants and has $n = T - m$ to go, the optimal policy is to stop if and only if the current applicant is a candidate (the best so far) and the following condition is true:

$$S(m, n) = \sum_{j=1}^{n} \frac{1}{m + j - 1} \leq 1.$$

Example 7.10 Suppose that $T = 10$ applicants are interviewing for a position. The sum $S(m, n)$ decreases as follows:

$S(1,9) = 2.8. S(2,8) = 1.8. S(3,7) = 1.3. S(4,6) = 0.99. S(5,5) = 0.75. S(6,4) = 0.54.$ $S(7,3) = 0.38. S(8,2) = 0.24. S(9,1) = 0.11.$ Because the first three terms are greater than 1, the decision-maker should not accept the first, second, or third applicant. Thus, the decision-maker should interview the first three applicants and automatically reject them. The first applicant who is better than the first three should be accepted. (This will be a candidate.)

If, in this example, the fourth applicant is not better than all of the first three, this applicant is not a candidate and should be rejected. If the fifth applicant is better than all of the first three, this applicant must be better than the fourth applicant. Therefore, this applicant is a candidate and should be accepted.

The initial number that should be considered and automatically rejected increases as the total number increases, as listed in Table 7.1. The decision-maker accepts the first applicant who is better than those automatically rejected. While this strategy does not guarantee that the decision-maker will get the very best applicant, it does maximize the probability of this. It gives some idea of when the decision-maker has searched "enough." The best of the automatically rejected applicants becomes the benchmark that is used to determine when a future applicant should be accepted. The worst-case situation is that, by bad luck, the best applicant was one of those automatically rejected and the worst applicant is the last one interviewed and will be selected.

The results of a small simulation study indicate how well decision-maker could do. In 720 random sequences of 10 applicants, this policy chose the best one 266

TABLE 7.1 Number of Applicants to Interview and Reject Automatically.

Total Number of Applicants	Number Rejected	Percentage Rejected (%)
5	2	40
10	3	30
15	5	33
20	7	35
25	9	36
30	11	37
35	13	37
40	15	38
45	16	36
50	18	36

TABLE 7.2 Quality of the Applicant Selected in 720 Random Sequences of 10 Applicants.

Rank of Applicant Selected	Frequency	Percentage (%)
1	266	36.9
2	144	20.0
3	88	12.2
4	54	7.5
5	43	6.0
6	29	4.0
7	29	4.0
8	24	3.3
9	21	2.9
10	22	3.1

times (37% of the trials). Table 7.2 lists how often each applicant (identified by their rank in the entire group) was selected. Following the optimal policy makes selecting the best applicant 10 times more likely than selecting the worst applicant.

Although the preceding paragraphs referred to "applicants" who were "interviewed," the same rule holds for job offers that are received, expressway exits that are approached, and so forth. The "applicants" are the alternatives that arrive (or appear) one by one; the "interview" is the process of evaluating one alternative.

7.17 COMPOSITE DECISIONS

The earlier sections in this chapter have discussed the process of making a decision and have noted that this process requires making decisions. The decision-maker must choose a process, first of all, select relevant objectives, guide the search for alternatives and information, decide when to stop searching and gathering information, and make other choices that affect the progress of the decision-making process.

This section and the next two sections reinforce the notion that making one decision requires making many decisions. They emphasize, however, the logical decomposition of a decision, especially in situations that involve designing a product or a system or making a complex plan. The subdecisions involve components that make up the complete system or plan. The decision that concerns the entire system or plan is a *composite decision*.

For instance, Petroski (1992) described the many decisions involved in planning a vacation: selecting a mode of transportation (drive, take a bus, take a train, and take an airplane); selecting a time to leave; if driving, selecting a route and when and where to stop; if flying, selecting which flight to which airport and how to get to their hotel; and picking a hotel. The vacation plan is a composite decision that involves all of these decisions about components of the plan.

Example 7.11 Simon (1997) described another composite decision: the design of a new battleship for the British Navy. The composite decision involved the following component decisions:

1. The First Sea Lord and the Assistant Chief of Naval Staff determine the features that the ship should have (speed, radius of action, offensive qualities, and armor protection).
2. The Director of Naval Construction and the Controller develop ideas for the ship and estimate the size and cost of these.
3. The Sea Lords select one of these alternatives.
4. The Director of Naval Construction determines the ship's approximate dimensions and shape.
5. The Engineer-in-Chief arranges the equipment needed to move the ship while the Director of Naval Ordnance determines the positions of the weapons systems.
6. The Director of Torpedos designs the torpedo armament, and the Director of Electrical Engineering designs the electrical machinery, lighting, and other systems.
7. The Director of Naval Equipment decides on the boats that the ship will carry and the anchors and cables; the Director of the Signal Department designs the communications equipment; the Director of the Navigation designs the means for navigating the ship; and other groups design other parts of the ship. (Altogether, 14 departments are involved.)
8. When conflicts appear between different systems, the directors meet, discuss the problems, and agree on compromises.
9. The Board approves the completed design.

In general, according to Mintzberg *et al.* (1976), developing a design "frequently involves factoring one decision into a series of subdecisions, each requiring at least one selection step."

Decomposition is a natural strategy for attacking large problems. Cognitive limitations force human decision-makers to decompose problems into subproblems. Many writers have documented these cognitive limitations (see, e.g., Simon, 1981). Fallin and Thurston (1994) presented a structured methodology for decomposing a multivariable, multiobjective design problem. In practice, however, the decomposition is created in an informal, heuristic way.

Decomposition occurs in a wide variety of problem domains. In manufacturing facilities, the manufacturing planning and control systems are decomposed into modules that solve a variety of problems that range from aggregate production planning to master production scheduling and material requirements planning and down to detailed shop floor scheduling (see, e.g., Hopp and Spearman, 2001; Vollmann et al., 1997).

The usefulness of decomposition does not, however, imply that every decision should be decomposed completely. An important cost of decomposition is the potential inferiority of the alternatives chosen (when evaluated using more fundamental performance measures).

Holt et al. (1960) captured the conflict between the desire to make complex decisions all at once and the desire to reduce the effort of making decisions in their description of an ideal decision making system: "First, management wants good decisions–the goal is to select those that are less costly and have the more desirable outcomes. Second, since making decisions takes time, talent and money, we do not seek the very best decision without some regard to the cost of research. Rather, management wants decision-making methods that are easy and inexpensive to operate. Third, it would be desirable, if the techniques were available, to handle large and complex problems more nearly as wholes, in order to avoid the difficulties that occur when problems are treated piecemeal. Fourth, it is certainly advantageous to use fully the knowledge and experience available within the firm. Intimate knowledge of the decision problem is indispensable to improvement in decision-making methods."

7.18   SEPARATION

The simplest type of composite decision is one that involves multiple, independent components. For example, a vacation plan may require three components: selecting flights to and from the destination city, selecting a rental car, and selecting a hotel. Many composite decisions are not so simple, however, and the decisions about the components (the *subdecisions*) may interact. For instance, the subdecisions are not independent if the traveler can get a package deal by purchasing from the airline a vacation package that also includes a rental car and a hotel.

A *separation* is an abstraction of a composite decision in which the composite decision, considered as a design optimization problem, is replaced by a set of linked subproblems that may have precedence constraints between them (Karimian and Herrmann, 2009; Herrmann, 2010).

The concept of separation is similar (but not identical) to the idea of decomposition-based design optimization. Both replace a design optimization

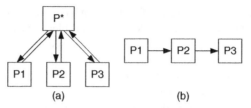

Figure 7.5 (a) A typical decomposition scheme has multiple first-level subproblems (P1, P2, P3) that receive inputs from a second-level problem (P*), which also coordinates their solutions. (b) Separation yields a sequence of subproblems. Solving one provides the input to the next.

problem with a set of subproblems. In a typical decomposition approach, however, a second-level problem must be solved to coordinate the subproblem solutions in an iterative manner (see Figure 7.5).

Separation, in contrast, does not require subsequent coordination. It is a decentralized and sequential approach related to the concept that is called *factorization* by Pahl and Beitz (1996). A large problem is replaced by a set of subproblems. The solution to one subproblem will provide the inputs to one or more subsequent subproblems. However, there is no higher-level problem to coordinate the solution. Note that the separation does not have to be a simple sequence of subproblems; it may have subproblems that are solved in parallel at places. A given separation specifies a partial order in which the subproblems are solved. A different order of subproblems would be a different separation.

The objective functions of the subproblems are surrogates for the original problem's objective function. These surrogates come from substituting simpler performance measures that are correlated with the original one, eliminating components that are not relevant to that subproblem, or from removing variables that will be determined in another subproblem. The subproblems may have constraints that are means to the original objective function (cf. Section 2.2).

As mentioned earlier, separation replaces a large optimization problem with a set of smaller ones, as decomposition does. However, the subproblems in a separation do not have to correspond strictly to different disciplines. In particular, note that, unlike the multiple-discipline-feasible (MDF) and individual-discipline-feasible (IDF) techniques (Hulme and Bloebaum, 2000; Allison *et al.*, 2007), separation does not iterate until the solution converges. This is a key distinctive feature of separation. Moreover, a separation does not include the special recursive structure of dynamic programming (cf. Bradley *et al.*, 1977). Finally, despite the similar name, separation is not the same as separable programming, a branch of mathematical programming that uses a linear program to approximate a nonlinear optimization problem in which the objective function and the constraints are sums of single-variable functions (Stefanov, 2001).

Example 7.12   The preliminary design of an unmanned aerial vehicle (UAV) can be separated into three subproblems that are solved in sequence: (1) determine the

UAV's maximum take-off weight to meet mission, range, and other requirements, (2) determine the wing area and engine thrust to meet speed and other performance requirements, and (3) determine the characteristics of the autopilot (Sadraey, 2010). The results of each step are needed to complete the next one. The detailed design of the UAV tail can be separated into three problems: in the first subproblem, the UAV design engineer selects the tail configuration; after this, two other subproblems (design the vertical tail and design the horizontal tail) can be done in parallel (Sadraey, 2010).

Example 7.13   Flight planning optimization attempts to find a route (a track along the ground), a profile (the altitudes along that track), and the speed for each segment of the route. The overall objective is to minimize the total cost of fuel, overflights, and other items. Although one could formulate this as a single trajectory optimization problem, a common approach in practice separates the problem into two subproblems: (1) optimize the route with a rule-based profile and then (2) optimize the profile and speed of that route.

A *catalog design* task requires an engineer to design a system by selecting existing components for specified functions. Computer systems, piping networks, hydraulic systems, and heat exchanger networks are typical applications (Carlson-Skalak *et al.*, 1998). In some cases, the configuration of the components is fixed, so the overall catalog design task can be separated into subproblems (one for each type of component) that can be solved in parallel.

Example 7.14   The design of a machine that can transfer bodily fluids from one specimen container to another for medical testing may require, after the configuration is determined, selecting trays that can hold containers, a robotic arm to handle the containers, a vortexer that can mix the specimens before transfer, a pipette, and a barcode scanner. These do not need to be designed, but the design team must select the appropriate components from among those that are available from suppliers. Designing the machine is a composite decision that can be represented as the separation shown in Figure 7.6.

Systems engineering development processes include both top-down and bottom-up approaches (Blanchard and Fabrycky, 1998). These are two different types of separations for system design problems. Different approaches can be used for the same problem. Although they solved the same facility layout redesign problem, some teams of engineers used a top-down approach, and other used a bottom-up approach in a study described by Gralla and Herrmann (2014). Examples 7.15 and 7.16 are cases of top-down separations in other domains.

Example 7.15   Manheim (1966) described the separation of a highway location problem, which, given the two ends of the highway, must specify the centerline of the highway from one end to the other and the shape of the road (its cross-section

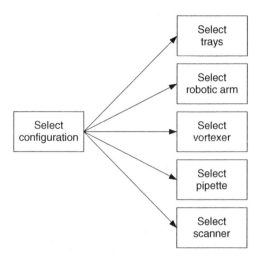

Figure 7.6 The separation of a machine design decision. After the configuration is selected, the components are selected independently.

Figure 7.7 The separation of a highway design decision. Each subproblem is solved in sequence.

and relationship to the ground surface) at regular intervals along this path. The highway design procedure separated the problem into three subproblems that are solved sequentially: select a "band of interest," select a location, and select a specific design, as shown in Figure 7.7.

Example 7.16 Wertz and Larson (1999) described the process of designing a space mission architecture as a series of decisions. This separation requires solving the following subproblems: determining the orbit and constellation, allocating pointing and tracking functions between the payload and spacecraft elements, selecting the elements needed to support communications and control, designing the spacecraft, choosing a launch and orbit transfer system, and planning the logistics of maintaining the space mission. These are not independent, but there are various arrangements of the subproblems that can be followed to complete the design.

Within a separation, the solution to one subproblem may generate constraints that the solutions to other subproblems must satisfy. When developing the 1996 Taurus, Ford decided that the new car would use the automated fixtures already in use at the assembly plants (Walton, 1997). This decision about the manufacturing process constrained the wheelbase of the car and the location of the door hinges, which in turn determined the location of the window glass that dropped into the doors, which determined the size of the sail, which affected the look of the car, the locations of speakers and outside rearview mirrors, and the functioning of the climate control system.

Constraints exclude solutions that are infeasible with respect to one or more of the many different conditions that a successful design must satisfy. In decision making, constraints are important because they reduce the search effort (often by identifying the boundary between sets where good solutions are likely and sets where they are not).

For example, if the objective is to maximize profit, one can formulate a design problem with no constraints. In this approach, the evaluation of profit must penalize any unreasonable solution. For instance, if the power tool is too heavy, few customers will buy the tool, and sales and profit will be low. While theoretically possible, this approach clearly results in a huge search space and a complex objective function. Thus, the computational effort will be extremely large.

In contrast, including constraints (such as an upper bound on the weight of the power tool) limits the search space and simplifies the objective function, which makes solving the problem much easier. When designing a production line, instead of optimizing an objective function that includes the cost of equipment and the costs associated with cycle time and work-in-process inventory, an industrial engineer may simply set an upper bound on equipment utilization in order to keep cycle time and work-in-process inventory levels to a reasonable level. Section 2.2 listed additional examples of constraints (from Hazelrigg, 1996) that simplify design problems.

When the subproblems are solved by different decision-makers, separating a problem in a way that yields a high-quality solution is, in general, a difficult problem that falls into the category of *mechanism design* (Myerson, 2008).

The order in which the subproblems are solved can affect the quality of the design that is ultimately selected. The objectives used in the subproblems can also affect the quality (Karimian and Herrmann, 2009). Examples 7.17 and 7.18 show these phenomena.

Example 7.17   A passenger aircraft design problem can be separated into two subproblems (Lewis and Mistree, 1998). The first subproblem (Aerodynamics) concerns the wing and fuselage lift characteristics such as climb gradients, aspect ratio, and take-off field. Solving that requires setting the wing area, the wing span, and the fuselage length. The second subproblem (Weight) requires setting the thrust and take-off weight through a fuel balance. Solving the aerodynamics problem first and then the weight subproblem generates one design, and solving the weight problem first and then the aerodynamics subproblem generates a different design.

Example 7.18   This example was developed by Paul Collopy and presented by Hazelrigg (2012). As part of the process of designing a new airplane, one engineering team designed the landing gear, and a second team designed the tail. Both teams were given cost and weight constraints, and each was evaluated on how well it met its cost and weight targets. The landing gear team generated two alternatives:

the first one was too heavy but very inexpensive and the second had an acceptable weight but just barely met the cost constraint. Meanwhile, the other team generated two alternatives for the tail: the first one was too expensive but very lightweight and the second had an acceptable cost but just barely met the weight constraint. Both teams picked their second choices (which were optimal given the objectives), but the total cost and weight of these exceeded the total cost and weight of the first "infeasible" alternatives. They would have produced a lighter, less-expensive plane by picking their first alternatives. This dilemma occurred because the objectives of the subproblems that the teams solved led them to solutions that were inferior when combined.

7.19   PRODUCT DEVELOPMENT PROCESSES

Product development organizations seek to make good decisions. In practice, they decompose a design problem into a series of subproblems (a separation), and design engineers and other members of the team must try to satisfy a variety of constraints and make tradeoffs between multiple competing objectives.

It is convenient to view a product as a hierarchy of subsystems, subassemblies, and components. Because designing a product requires designing all of these elements, a product development project involves a hierarchy of decisions. A decision at one level sets targets and constraints or provides information for decisions at another level. A typical example is aircraft design (see, for instance, Kalsi *et al.*, 2001). The conceptual design phase selects wing area, fuselage length, wingspan, take-off weight, and installed thrust, and the detailed design steps must respect these constraints. Setting these constraints makes component (or subsystem) design easier although the constraints prevent system-level optimization (cf. Hazelrigg, 1996, and Keeney, 1992).

Product development requires a wide variety of decisions, including the following 12 interdependent types of decisions (Krishnan and Ulrich, 2001):

1. Selecting the opportunities to pursue.
2. Selecting the assets to share across products.
3. Determining the core product concept.
4. Setting the target values of the attributes.
5. Determining the values of key design parameters.
6. Creating the physical form and industrial design.
7. Selecting the desired variants of the product.
8. Determining the product architecture.
9. Selecting who designs the components.
10. Determining the assembly precedence relations.
11. Selecting the configuration of the supply chain.
12. Selecting who produces and assembles the product.

Because making good decisions requires expertise and an organization of people can be experts in only a few things, a manufacturing firm specializes in a certain class of products. It focuses its attention on the market for that class of products, the technologies available to produce that class, and the regulations relevant to that class.

Because the design problem is highly complex, product development teams decompose the problem into a product development process, which provides the mechanisms for linking a series of design decisions that do not explicitly consider profit.

For example, at an American sports clothing and accessories company, the process for bringing new products to market is a series of phases, each of which ends with a decision to move forward. A decision to change a product starts a prestudy phase that leads to a go/no-go decision (move forward or cancel the project). Up to four more phases follow: the concept study phase, the detailed development phase, the final development phase, and the industrialization phase. Each one ends with a go/no-go decision (move forward or repeat that phase). After the last phase, the product is launched (released).

The following nine steps are the primary activities that many product development processes accomplish (Schmidt *et al.*, 2002):

1. Identify the customer needs.
2. Establish the product specification.
3. Define alternative concepts for a design that meets the specification.
4. Select the most suitable concept.
5. Design the subsystems and integrate them.
6. Build and test a prototype; modify the design as required.
7. Design and build the tooling for production.
8. Produce and distribute the product.
9. Track the product during its life cycle to determine its strengths and weaknesses.

This list (or any other description that uses a different number of steps) is an extremely simple depiction that not only conveys the scope of the process but also highlights the inherent decomposition. Iteration can occur within each step as possible solutions are generated, evaluated, and revised (Cross and Roozenburg, 1992). There are many other ways to represent product development processes and the component tasks, including the use of schedules or a design structure matrix (Smith and Eppinger, 2001).

The first six steps listed above form a separation of profit maximization problem. Associated with each step are a subproblem and some constraints:

1. Identify the customer needs. Which customer requirements should the product satisfy to maximize sales? Constraints: product line and market segment.

2. Establish the product specification. Which product performance targets (including cost) should the product meet to satisfy the customer requirements? Constraints: customer requirements and available technologies.
3. Define alternative concepts and select the most suitable concept for a design that meets the specification. Which set of product features best satisfies the product performance targets? Constraints: product performance targets and available technologies.
4. Design the subsystems and integrate them. Which shapes and materials can be used to make the product features? Constraints: conceptual design, manufacturing feasibility, safety, and government regulations.
5. Build and test a prototype; modify the design as required. Does the selected design meet the product performance targets? Constraint: product performance targets.
6. Design and build the tooling for production. Which tools and manufacturing processes can be used to manufacture the product? Constraints: shape and material of components.

The above descriptions are deliberately brief and general to show the idea. Note that this decomposition starts with the assumption that maximizing profit relies upon maximizing sales.

Manufacturing firms understand that design decisions (although made early in the product life cycle) have an excessive impact on the profitability of a product over its entire life cycle. Consequently, product development organizations have created and used concurrent engineering practices for many years (see Smith, 1997, for a historical view). Many types of tools and methods (such as cross-functional product development teams and design for manufacturing guidelines) have been created, adopted, and implemented to improve decision-making. Cooper (1994) identified three generations of formal approaches to product development, all of which involve decomposition.

It should be noted, however, that decomposition is not the only way to describe product development. As an alternative to decomposing a system design problem into subproblems, Hazelrigg (1996) proposed creating and refining system design models to express how detailed design variables affect the overall system performance. This approach suggests that a product development process would end with using the model to find the optimal design. State-of-the-art *design for market systems* approaches motivated by the *decision-based design* (DBD) framework (Hazelrigg, 1998; Shiau and Michalek, 2009) include enterprise models that add variables from the marketing and manufacturing domains to models with conceptual design variables and adapt existing decomposition techniques to solve them (Fenyes *et al.*, 2002; Renaud and Gu, 2006; Michalek *et al.*, 2006; Williams *et al.*, 2008). The *model-based systems engineering* paradigm also emphasizes using comprehensive system design models for making tradeoffs and finding superior system designs (Ogren, 2000; Estefan, 2007).

EXERCISES

7.1. NASA, the European Space Agency, and other partners committed in 2013 to keeping the International Space Station (ISS) operational through 2020 (Achenbach, 2013). Consider the decision of whether to continue operating the ISS beyond 2020, which affects not only the space agencies but also the contractors that support the operations and scientific researchers who do zero-gravity experiments on the ISS. Which type of decision process would be appropriate for making this decision?

7.2. In 2013, the Washington Metropolitan Area Transit Authority (WMATA) faced a decision about how to fix ongoing water leaks that damaged equipment and limited service on one line (Hedgpeth, 2013). WMATA tried various short-term solutions, including diverting and pumping the water, but then began looking for long-term solutions, including drilling wells and installing a protective waterproof liner. WMATA hired an engineering firm to find possible solutions and brought in experts from other cities to review their plans. Which type of decision-making process is this? Is it appropriate for the situation (given the level of technical knowledge and problem consensus)?

7.3. The decision to sell *The Washington Post* involved multiple decisions (Timberg and Yan, 2013): the CEO and the publisher agreed to sell the paper (instead of letting it decline gradually or reducing staff drastically), the CEO decided to consult the board of directors, the CEO decided to hire an investment firm to find potential buyers, and the CEO agreed to accept the buyer's offer. Which parts of the incremental decision-making process presented in Section 7.2 correspond to which of these activities?

7.4. As part of the process of selecting a site for a new hospital in Prince George's County, Maryland, the Dimensions Healthcare System Board of Directors chose, from the four sites being considered, to endorse two of the sites (Dimensions Healthcare System, 2013). The two rejected sites were unacceptable because of their location and because they had multiple owners (Spivack, 2013). The two selected sites met the site selection criteria, including factors related to size, location, site development costs, and future development potential. After this decision, negotiations regarding the financial terms for each location began. The Board of Directors still needed to select one site for submitting its application to the Maryland Health Care Commission. Which parts of the incremental decision-making process presented in Section 7.2 correspond to which of these activities?

7.5. In 2013, the US State Department was considering whether to issue a permit for the Keystone XL pipeline, which would carry oil from northern Alberta to the Gulf of Mexico (Mufson, 2013). How should this decision situation be classified: as a unique, wide-impact decision; a repeated, wide-impact decision; or a routine, narrow-impact decision?

7.6. In July 2013, the California Department of Toxic Substances Control issued a draft expansion permit that would allow the expansion of a landfill that accepts toxic wastes that are not allowed in most landfills (Wozniacka, 2013). How should this decision situation be classified: as a unique, wide-impact decision; a repeated, wide-impact decision; or a routine, narrow-impact decision?

7.7. In 2013, the Federal Communications Commission (an independent government agency in the United States) began the process of deciding whether to allow passengers on airplanes to use their cellphones while airborne (Knutson *et al.*, 2013). The process involved numerous activities. For each of the following, identify whether it is part of the analytic process or part of the deliberative process: (a) conducting studies about whether cellphones pose a safety threat to aircraft, (b) drafting a rule and inviting comments from the public about it, and (c) meeting to decide whether to approve the rule.

7.8. In the process to select exterior colors for the 1996 Ford Taurus, paint suppliers proposed their latest colors while Ford personnel went to conferences of color professionals, boat shows, fashion shows, spring break, and other events to identify color trends (Walton, 1997). Is this a search for alternatives or a search for information?

7.9. On June 12, 1969, General Samuel Phillips, the Apollo program director, who needed to decide whether Apollo 11 would launch as scheduled in July, chaired a meeting with NASA managers and contractors, who described the status of different systems (Nelson and Men, 2009). In what way was this meeting a search?

7.10. When selling her family's house, McLay (2013) assumed that the problem fit the assumptions of the secretary problem and estimated that they would receive at most six offers on the house. What is the smallest number of offers that they should consider before accepting one?

7.11. (This question was motivated by an example in Chun, 2000.) A mining company is searching for mineral deposits in a new region. The company has enough money to build only one mine. They have identified 15 sites to explore. They can explore sites one at a time. Once they explore a site, they must decide immediately whether or not to build a mine there. If they build a mine there, then they stop searching. If they do not build a mine there, then they will move on to explore the next site. Because some other firms will build a mine on an explored site before too long, the mining company is facing a secretary problem. The mining company wants to maximize the probability of getting the best of these 15 sites. What is the minimum number of sites that should be explored? That is, which site is the first that could be selected?

7.12. How do real-world decisions combine aspects of classical multicriteria decisions and the secretary problem?

7.13. Rose is designing a new full-service automobile maintenance facility for a car dealership. How could she separate this design decision into many separate decisions?

7.14. Public health emergency preparedness planners in the state of New York needed to design a warehouse to store medical supplies that would be delivered from a stockpile if a large-scale bioterrorism attack occurred. In particular, besides the usual building construction issues, they needed to determine the location in the warehouse and layout for three areas (receiving, storage, and shipping) and make sure that each area had enough space for the expected supplies. Suggest a separation of this design problem that makes the design process easier.

7.15. Engineering teams solved a satellite design problem that included three design variables (payload mass, velocity change, and payload power) that affected the performance of three highly coupled subsystems: payload and orbital, power, and propulsion (Austin-Breneman *et al.*, 2012). One team optimized the design variables sequentially, one at a time. Describe the advantages and disadvantages of this particular separation.

7.16. A design team developed three concepts for a motorcycle helmet that includes LEDs on the back of the helmet to indicate the turn signal (Hsu *et al.*, 2013). The first concept would wire the helmet's turn signals directly to the motorcycle's electrical system, the second concept would use a wireless connection to the motorcycle's existing signals, and the third concept would use a wireless connection to the motorcycle's turn signal switch. The design team was concerned about cost, battery life, safety, ease of use, aesthetics, head mobility, ergonomics, weight, manufacturing, and implementation. Explain how making this decision early in the product development process would simplify the design process. What is the drawback of making this decision early?

7.17. The space mission analysis and design process (Wertz and Larson, 1999) includes the following steps:

1. Define broad objectives and constraints of the space mission.
2. Estimate quantitative mission needs and requirements related to the broad objectives and constraints.
3. Define alternative mission concepts that state broadly how the mission will work.
4. Define alternative mission architectures (for each mission concept) that define the subsystems (elements) that can meet the requirements of that mission concept.
5. For each mission concept, identify the system drivers, the key parameters that influence overall cost and performance.
6. Characterize mission concepts and architectures by defining, in detail, what the system is and what it does.

7. Identify critical requirements, the key requirements that determine the cost and performance.

8. Evaluate mission utility by quantifying how well the system design meets the critical requirements and broad objectives.

9. Define a mission concept (select a baseline system design).

10. Define specific system requirements.

11. Allocate (flow down) requirements to system elements.

How is this process similar to the decision-making processes discussed in this chapter? What is the "big" decision being made? Which steps are generating alternatives? Which steps are generating information for evaluating the alternatives? Which steps are making decisions? What are those decisions?

7.18. Field Marshal Lord Alanbrooke, a commander in the British Army during World War II, would, when evaluating proposed operations, ask the following practical questions: "Where will it be? Who will do it? Are there enough forces, equipment, training?" (Kennedy, 2013). At what point in the incremental decision process model would such questions be appropriate?

7.19. Model the secretary problem with five applicants using a decision tree and use it to find the policy that maximizes the probability that the decision-maker will select the best applicant. Note that all five possible sequences of the relative quality (such as 5th, 1st, 3rd, 2nd, and 4th) are equally likely. The uncertainty resolved during each interview is that applicant's quality relative to those already interviewed. After the decision-maker selects an applicant, assume that any uncertainty about whether that applicant is the best is resolved. (*Hint:* let the value of the best applicant be 1 and the value of every other candidate be 0; the expected value equals the probability that the applicant selected is the best.)

REFERENCES

Achenbach, Joel, "2013: a Space Conundrum," *The Washington Post*, page A1, September 15, 2013.

Allison, James T., Michael Kokkolaras, and Panos Y. Paplambros, "On Selecting Single-Level Formulations for Complex System Design Optimization," *Journal of Mechanical Design*, Volume 129, pages 898–906, 2007.

Ashby, Michael F., *Materials Selection in Mechanical Design*, 3rd edition, Elsevier, Amsterdam, 2005.

Austin-Breneman, Jesse, Tomonori Honda, and Maria C. Yang, "A Study of Student Design Team Behaviors in Complex System Design," *Journal of Mechanical Design*, Volume 134, Number 12, 124504, 2012, doi: 10.1115/1.4007840.

Birsch, Douglas, "Whistle blowing, ethical obligation, and the Ford Pinto case," in *The Ford Pinto Case: A Study in Applied Ethics, Business, and Technology*, Douglas Birsch and John H. Fielder, editors, State University of New York Press, Albany, New York, 1994.

Blanchard, Benjamin S., and Walter J. Fabrycky, *Systems Engineering and Analysis*, 3rd edition, Prentice Hall, Inc., Upper Saddle River, New Jersey, 1998.

Bonabeau, Eric, "Don't Trust Your Gut," *Harvard Business Review*, Volume 81, Number 5, pages 116–123, 2003.

Bradley, Stephen P., Arnoldo C. Hax, and Thomas L. Magnanti, *Applied Mathematical Programming*, Addison-Wesley Publishing Company, Reading, Mass., 1977.

Carlson-Skalak, Susan, Michael D. White, and Yong Teng, "Using an Evolutionary Algorithm for Catalog Design," *Research in Engineering Design*, Volume 10, pages 63–68, 1998.

Chelst, Kenneth, John Sidelko, Alex Przebienda, Jeffrey Lockledge, and Dimitrios Mihailidis, "Rightsizing and Management of Prototype Vehicle Testing at Ford Motor Company," *Interfaces*, Volume 31, Number 1, pages 91–107, 2001.

Chun, Young H., "Sequential Search and Selection Problem Under Uncertainty," *Decision Sciences*, Volume 31, Number 3, pages 627–648, 2000.

Clemen, Robert T., and Terence Reilly, *Making Hard Decisions with DecisionTools*, Duxbury, Pacific Grove, California, 2001.

Cohen, Michael, James March, and Johan Olsen, "A Garbage Can Model of Organizational Choice," *Administrative Science Quarterly*, Volume 17, Number 1, pages 1–25, 1972.

Compaine, Ben, "Cambridge Discovers the Limits of its Green Virtue," *The Wall Street Journal*, page A15, July 20, 2013.

Cooper, Robert G., "Third-Generation New Product Processes," *Journal of Product Innovation Management*, Volume 11, Number 1, pages 3–14, 1994.

Cross, Nigel, and Norbert Roozenburg, "Modelling the Design Process in Engineering and in Architecture," *Journal of Engineering Design*, Volume 3, Number 4, pages 325–337, 1992.

Cyert, Richard M., and James G. March, *A Behavioral Theory of the Firm*, Blackwell Publishers Inc., Malden, Massachusetts, 1992.

Daft, Richard L., *Organization Theory and Design*, 7th edition, South-Western College Publishing, Mason, Ohio, 2001.

Detwiler, Duane, Shantaram Ekhande, and Mark Kistner, "Computer aided structural optimization of automotive body structure," SAE Technical Paper 960523, 1996, doi:10.4271/960523, online at http://papers.sae.org/960523/.

Dieter, George E., and Linda C. Schmidt, *Engineering Design*, 5th edition, McGraw-Hill, Boston, 2012.

Dijksterhuis, Ap, Maarten W. Bos, Loran F. Nordgren, and Rick B. van Baaren, "On Making the Right Choice: The Deliberation-Without-Attention Effect," *Science*, Volume 311, Number 5763, pages 1005–1007, 2006.

Dimensions Healthcare System, "Dimensions Healthcare System narrows potential new hospital site to two locations," press release, July 25, 2013. Available online at http://www.dimensionshealth.org/wp-content/uploads/2011/12/For-Immediate-Release-DHS-Narrows-Site-to-Two-Locations-FINAL2.pdf, accessed July 27, 2013.

Donndelinger, Joseph A., "A decision-based perspective on the vehicle development process," Chapter 19, in *Decision Making in Engineering Design*, K. Lewis, W. Chen, and L.C. Schmidt, editors, ASME Press, New York, 2006.

Dubberly, Hugh, "How do you design? A compendium of models," http://www.dubberly.com/articles/how-do-you-design.html, March 18, 2005, accessed December 12, 2013.

Dyer, James S., and Ralph F. Miles, Jr., "An Actual Application of Collective Choice Theory to the Selection of Trajectories for the Mariner Jupiter/Saturn 1977 project," *Operations Research*, Volume 24, Number 2, pages 220–244, 1976.

Estefan, Jeff A., "Survey of Model-Based Systems Engineering (MBSE) methodologies," Jet Propulsion Laboratory, California Institute of Technology, Pasadena, California, 2007.

Fallin, T. Wade, and Deborah L. Thurston, "Decision decomposition for the lifecycle of the design process," in *Advances in Design Automation*, Volume 2, DE-Vol. 69–2, pages 383–392, The American Society of Mechanical Engineers, New York, 1994.

Fenyes, Peter, Joseph Donndelinger, and Jing-Fang Bourassa, "A new system for multi-disciplinary analysis and optimization of vehicle architectures," AIAA-2002-5509, 9th AIAA/ISSMO Symposium on Multidisciplinary Analysis and Optimization, Atlanta, Georgia, September 4–6, 2002.

Gensch, Dennis, "A Marketing-Decision-Support Model for Evaluating and Selecting Concepts for New Products," *Interfaces*, Volume 31, Number 3, Part 2, pages S166–S183, 2001.

Gioia, Dennis A., "Pinto fires and personal ethics: a script analysis of missed opportunities," in *The Ford Pinto Case: A Study in Applied Ethics, Business, and Technology*, Douglas Birsch and John H. Fielder, editors, State University of New York Press, Albany, New York, 1994.

Government Accountability Office (GAO), "Observations on DHS's analyses concerning whether FMD research can be done as safely on the mainland as on Plum Island," GAO-09-747, July, 2009.

Gralla, Erica L., and Jeffrey W. Herrmann, "Design team decision processes in facility design," in Proceedings of the 2014 Industrial and Systems Engineering Research Conference, Y. Guan and H. Liao editors, Montreal, Canada, June 1–3, 2014.

Guy, Mary E., *Ethical Decision Making in Everyday Work Situations*, Quorum Books, New York, 1990.

Hazelrigg, George A., *System Engineering: an Approach to Information-based Design*, Prentice Hall, Upper Saddle River, New Jersey, 1996.

Hazelrigg, George A., "A Framework for Decision-Based Engineering Design," *ASME Journal of Mechanical Design*, Volume 120, pages 653–658, 1998.

Hazelrigg, George A., *Fundamentals of Decision Making for Engineering Design and Systems Engineering*, 2012. Online at http://www.engineeringdecisionmaking.com/

Hedgpeth, Dana, "Water troubles on the Red Line," *The Washington Post*, page B1, September 5, 2013.

Herrmann, Jeffrey W., "Progressive Design Processes and Bounded Rational Designers," *Journal of Mechanical Design*, Volume 132, Number 8, 081005, 2010.

Holt, Charles C., Franco Modigliani, John F. Muth, and Herbert A. Simon, *Planning Production, Inventories, and Work Force*, Prentice-Hall, Inc., Englewood Cliffs, New Jersey, 1960.

Hopp, Wallace J., and Mark L. Spearman, *Factory Physics*, 2nd edition, Irwin McGraw-Hill, Boston, 2001.

Howard, Philip K., "Why it takes so long to build a bridge in America," *The Wall Street Journal*, page A11, November 23, 2013.

Hsu, Jeremy, Adam Kopp, Michael Murray, Isaac Ro, and Andrew Sabelhaus, "Turning heads: arrow head helmet," Department of Mechanical Engineering Design Day, University of Maryland, May, 2013.

Hulme, K.F., and C.L. Bloebaum, "A Simulation-Based Comparison of Multidisciplinary Design Optimization Solution Strategies Using CASCADE," *Structural and Multidisciplinary Optimization*, Volume 19, Number 1, Pages 17–35, 2000.

"Inside Boeing's big move," *Harvard Business Review*, Volume 79, Number 9, pages 22–23, 2001.

Kaempf, George L., Gary Klein, Marvin L. Thordsen, and Steve Wolf, "Decision Making in Complex Naval Command-And-Control Environments," *Human Factors*, Volume 38, Number 2, pages 220–231, 1996.

Kalsi, Monu, Kurt Hacker, and Kemper Lewis, "A Comprehensive Robust Design Approach for Decision Trade-Offs in Complex System Design," *Journal of Mechanical Design*, Volume 123, pages 1–10, 2001.

Karimian, Peyman, and Jeffrey W. Herrmann, "Separating Design Optimization Problems to Form Decision-Based Design Processes," *Journal of Mechanical Design*, Volume 131, Number 1, 011007, 2009.

Keeney, Ralph L., *Value-Focused Thinking: a Path to Creative Decisionmaking*, Harvard University Press, Cambridge, Massachusetts, 1992.

Kennedy, Paul, *Engineers of Victory*, Random House, New York, 2013.

Klein, Gary, Roberta Calderwood, and Anne Clinton-Cirocco, "Rapid Decision Making on the Fire Ground: The Original Study Plus a Postscript," *Journal of Cognitive Engineering and Decision Making*, Volume 4, Number 3, pages 186–209, 2010.

Knutson, Ryan, Gautham Nagesh, and Jack Nicas, "Cellphone calls on planes? Debate is cleared for takeoff," *The Wall Street Journal*, page B1, November 22, 2013.

Krishnan, V., and Karl T. Ulrich, "Product Development Decisions: A Review of the Literature," *Management Science*, Volume 47, Number 1, pages 1–21, 2001.

Lewis, K., and F. Mistree, "Collaborative, Sequential, and Isolated Decisions in Design," *Journal of Mechanical Design*, Volume 120, Number 4, pages 643–652, 1998.

Lipshitz, Raanan, Gary Klein, Judith Orasanu, and Eduardo Salas, "Focus Article: Taking Stock of Naturalistic Decision Making," *Journal of Behavioral Decision Making*, Volume 14, pages 331–352, 2001.

Little, John D.C., "Models and Managers: The Concept of a Decision Calculus," *Management Science*, Volume 16, Number 8, pages B-466–B-485, 1970.

Manheim, Marvin L., *Hierarchical Structure: A Model of Design and Planning Processes*, The MIT Press, Cambridge, Massachusetts, 1966.

Massachusetts Department of Transportation, "Ethanol safety study," http://www.massdot.state.ma.us/planning/Main/CurrentStudies/EthanolSafetyStudy.aspx, accessed August 14, 2013.

McKay, Kenneth N., and Vincent C.S. Wiers, *Practical Production Control: A Survival Guide for Planners and Schedulers*, J. Ross Publishing, Boca Raton, Florida, 2004. Co-published with APICS.

McLay, Laura, "The secretary problem is a useful model for selling a house," Punk Rock Operations Research, June 10, 2013. http://punkrockor.wordpress.com/2013/06/10/the-secretary-problem-is-a-useful-model-for-selling-a-house/, accessed June 26, 2013.

Michalek, Jeremy J., Oben Ceryan, Panos Y. Papalambros, and Yoram Koren, 2006, "Balancing Marketing and Manufacturing Objectives in Product Line Design," *ASME Journal of Mechanical Design*, Volume 128, Number 6, pages 1196–1204.

Mintzberg, Henry, Duru Raisinghani, and André Théorêt, "The Structure of Unstructured Decision Processes," *Administrative Science Quarterly*, Volume 21, Number 2, pages 246–275, 1976.

Morris, George E., *Engineering: A Decision-Making Process*, Houghton Mifflin Company, Boston, 1977.

Mufson, Steven, "Disaster in Canada puts focus on oil transportation," *The Washington Post*, page A1, July 9, 2013.

Myerson, Roger B., "Perspectives on Mechanism Design in Economic Theory," *American Economic Review*, Volume 98, Number 3, pages 586–603, 2008.

NASA, "Apollo 13," http://science.ksc.nasa.gov/history/apollo/apollo-13/apollo-13.html, June 29, 2001; accessed June 11, 2014.

NASA, *Risk-Informed Decision Making Handbook*, NASA/SP-2010-576, Version 1.0, April 2010.

National Research Council (NRC), *Theoretical Foundations for Decision Making in Engineering Design*, National Academy Press, Washington, 2001.

Nelson, Craig, Rocket Men: *The Epic Story of the First Men on the Moon*, Viking, New York, 2009.

de Neufville, Richard, *Applied Systems Analysis*, McGraw-Hill, New York, 1990.

Nussbaum, Bruce, "The power of design," *Business Week*, May 17, 2004.

Nutt, Paul C., "Breaking Out of the Failure Mode with Best Practice Decision-Making Processes," *International Journal of Business*, Volume 8, Number 2, pages 169–201, 2003.

Nutt, Paul C., "Expanding the Search for Alternatives During Strategic Decision-Making," *Academy of Management Executive*, Volume 18, Number 4, pages 13–28, 2004.

Nutt, Paul C., "Search During Decision Making," *European Journal of Operational Research*, Volume 160, Number 3, pages 851–876, 2005.

Ogren, Ingmar, "On Principles for Model-Based Systems Engineering," *Systems Engineering*, Volume 3, Number 1, pages 38–49, 2000.

Pahl, Gerhard, and Wolfgang Beitz, *Engineering Design: a Systematic Approach*, Ken Wallace, editor, translated by Ken Wallace, Luciënne Blessing, and Frank Bauert; Springer, London, 1996.

Parnell, Gregory S., and Paul D. West, "Systems decision process overview," in *Decision Making in Systems Engineering and Management*, G.S. Parnell, P.J. Driscoll, and D.L. Henderson, editors, John Wiley & Sons, Inc., Hoboken, New Jersey, 2008.

Petroski, Henry, *To Engineer is Human*, Vintage Books, New York, 1992.

Renaud, J. E., and X. Gu, "Decision-based collaborative optimization of multidisciplinary systems," in *Decision Making in Engineering Design*, K. Lewis, W. Chen, and L.C. Schmidt, editors, ASME, New York, pages 173–186, 2006.

Ritchey, T., "Problem Structuring Using Computer-Aided Morphological Analysis," *Journal of the Operational Research Society*, Volume 57, Number 7, pages 792–801, 2006, Special Issue: Problem Structuring Methods.

Roberto, Michael, Richard M.J. Bohmer, Amy C. Edmondson, and Erika Ferlins, "Columbia's Final Mission: A Multimedia Case," Harvard Business School Teaching Note 305–033, June 2005.

Russell, Stuart, and Eric Wefald, "Principles of Metareasoning," *Artificial Intelligence*, Volume 49, pages 361–395, 1991.

Sadraey, M., "A systems engineering approach to unmanned aerial vehicle design," AIAA 2010–9302, 10th AIAA Aviation Technology, Integration, and Operations (ATIO) Conference, Fort Worth, Texas, September 13–15, 2010.

Samuelson, Douglas A., "Understanding Organizational Anarchy," *OR/MS Today*, pages 34–38, 2008.

Sarotte, Mary E., "How it went down," *The Washington Post*, November 1, 2009.

Schmidt, Linda C., Guangming Zhang, Jeffrey W. Herrmann, George E. Dieter, and Patrick F. Cunniff, *Product Engineering and Manufacturing*, 2nd edition, College House Enterprises, Knoxville, Tennessee, 2002.

Shiau, C.-S. N., and Jeremy J. Michalek "Should Designers Worry About Market Systems?" *ASME Journal of Mechanical Design*, Volume 131, Number 1, page 011011, 2009.

Simon, Herbert A., "Behavioral Model of Rational Choice," *Quarterly Journal of Economics*, Volume 69, Number 1, pages 99–118, 1955.

Simon, Herbert A, "Rational decision-making in business organizations," in *Nobel Lectures, Economics 1969–1980*, A. Lindbeck, editor, pages 343–371, World Scientific Publishing, Singapore, 1978.

Simon, Herbert A., *The Sciences of the Artificial*, 2nd edition, MIT Press, Cambridge, Massachusetts, 1981.

Simon, Herbert A., *Administrative Behavior*, 4th edition, The Free Press, New York, 1997.

Smith, Robert P., "The Historical Roots of Concurrent Engineering Fundamentals," *IEEE Transactions on Engineering Management*, Volume 44, Number 1, pages 67–78, 1997.

Smith, Robert P., and Steven D. Eppinger, "A Predictive Model of Sequential Iteration in Engineering Design," *Management Science*, Volume 43, Number 8, pages 1104–1120, 2001.

Snowden, David J., and Mary E. Boone, "A Leader's Framework for Decision Making," *Harvard Business Review*, Volume 85, Number 11, pages 69–76, 2007.

Spetzler, Carl S., "Building decision competency in organizations," in *Advances in Decision Analysis: From Foundations to Applications*, W. Edwards, R.F. Miles, Jr., and D. von Winterfeldt, editors, Cambridge University Press, Cambridge, 2007.

Spivack, Miranda S., "Sites for new Pr. George's hospital complex are narrowed to 2," *The Washington Post*, page B1, July 26, 2013.

Sprague, Robert L., "The Voice of Experience," *Science and Engineering Ethics*, Volume 4, Number 1, pages 33–44, 1998.

Stefanov, Stefan M., *Separable Programming: Theory and Methods*, Kluwer Academic Publishers, Dordrecht, Netherlands, 2001.

Stern, Paul C., and Harvey V. Fineberg, editors, *Understanding Risk: Informing Decisions in a Democratic Society*, National Academy Press, Washington, DC, 1996.

Tani, Steven N., and Gregory S. Parnell, "Use the appropriate decision process," in *Handbook of Decision Analysis*, G.S. Parnell, T.A. Bresnick, S.N. Tani, and E.R. Johnson, editors, John Wiley & Sons, Inc., Hoboken, New Jersey, 2013.

Timberg, Craig, and Jia L. Yang, "The Post's most improbable move quickly became the clear path," *The Washington Post*, page A1, August 7, 2013.

Todd, Peter M., and Gerd Gigerenzer, "Environments that Make us Smart: Ecological Rationality," *Current Directions in Psychological Science*, Volume 16, Number 3, pages 167–171, 2007.

Troitzsch, Klaus G., "The Garbage can Model of Organisational Behaviour: A Theoretical Reconstruction of Some of its Variants," *Simulation Modelling Practice and Theory*, Volume 16, Number 2, Pages 218–230, 2008.

Vann, W. Pennington, "Engineering ethics references," http://www.niee.org/biblio-1.htm, accessed December 21, 2013.

Vollmann, Thomas E., William L. Berry, and David C. Whybark, *Manufacturing Planning and Control Systems*, 4th edition, Irwin/McGraw-Hill, New York, 1997.

Walton, Mary, *Car: A Drama of the American Workplace*, W.W. Norton & Company, New York, 1997.

Washburn, Alan R., *Search and Detection*, 2nd edition, Operations Research Society of America, Arlington, Virginia, 1989.

Wertz, James R., and Wiley J. Larson, editors, *Space Mission Analysis and Design*, 3rd edition, Microcosm Press, Torrance, California, and Kluwer Academic Publishers, Dordrecht, The Netherlands, 1999.

Williams, Nathan, Shapour Azarm, and, P.K. Kannan, "Engineering Product Design Optimization for Retail Channel Acceptance," *ASME Journal of Mechanical Design*, Volume 130, Number 6, page 061402, 2008.

Wozniacka, Gosia, "Calif. recommends expansion of hazardous dump," Associated Press, July 2, 2013. http://news.yahoo.com/calif-recommends-expansion-hazardous-dump-193528498.html, accessed July 11, 2013.

Zach, Lisl, "When is Enough Enough? Modeling the Information-Seeking and Stopping Behavior of Senior Arts Administrators," *Journal of the American Society for Information Science and Technology*, Volume 56 Number 1, Pages 23–35, 2005.

Zwicky, Fritz, *The Morphological Method of Analysis and Construction*, California Institute of Technology, Pasadena, California, 1948.

Zwicky, Fritz, *Discovery, Invention, Research—Through the Morphological Approach*, The Macmillan Company, Toronto, 1969.

8

THE VALUE OF INFORMATION

Learning Objectives:

After studying this chapter, the reader will be able to do the following:

1. Calculate the expected value of perfect information relevant to a decision with uncertainty (Sections 8.1 and 8.3).
2. Calculate the expected value of imperfect information relevant to a decision with uncertainty (Sections 8.2 and 8.3).
3. Estimate the relative value of testing different alternatives (Section 8.4).
4. Estimate the relative value of measuring different uncertain attributes (Section 8.5).

Information about a product or a system that is being developed is usually valuable. When Ronnie Harker, a Royal Air Force test pilot, flew an early version of the North American P-51 Mustang in 1942, he realized that its mediocre performance at high altitudes was due to an underpowered engine, and that using a different engine (the more powerful Rolls-Royce Merlin 61) would significantly improve the fighter. His suggestion, when adopted, allowed the Allies to deploy the P-51 (shown in Figure 8.1) as a long-range daytime escort over Europe during World War II, which increased

Engineering Decision Making and Risk Management, First Edition. Jeffrey W. Herrmann.
© 2015 John Wiley & Sons, Inc. Published 2015 by John Wiley & Sons, Inc.

Figure 8.1   Four US Army Air Force North American P-51 Mustang fighters. (Photo credit: United States Army Air Force.)

Figure 8.2   The littoral combat ship USS Freedom (LCS 1) off the coast of Southern California. (Photo credit: James R. Evans, United States Navy.)

the effectiveness of their strategic bombing campaign against the German industrial sector (Kennedy, 2013).

More recently, testing prototypes of a littoral combat ship (shown in Figure 8.2) led to over 150 design changes, including adding more crew, adding a walkway around the bridge, and making one version longer to add room for more ballast (Nissenbaum, 2013).

Sometimes, however, the information gathered may not clarify the issue. The design of a reinforced concrete school building specified concrete with 4% of entrained air and a design strength of 3500 psi (Benjamin and Cornell, 1970). Tests on the material used during construction showed up to 10% air and a strength of 2100 psi for the concrete cylinders. The construction firm faced a risky decision: replacing the structure would have delayed completion a year, but accepting the present structure involved the chance that the structure would fail in the future, and the firm would have been liable for the damages. More testing was ordered, but the load tests did not clarify the issue: the structure showed no signs of distress during 16 tests using a superimposed load on the beams and slabs. Moreover, the relationships between beam capacity and concrete cylinder strength were unknown, and most of the structure did not need to meet the specified design strength.

In other cases, the cost of the information may exceed its value, and the decision-maker should proceed without it. For instance, in 2013, the US Department of Defense (DOD) waived the requirement for a prototype during the development of a helicopter (the VXX) that would be used to transport the President and other government officials. The DOD determined that, in this case, prototypes of critical subsystems (including communications systems) would increase development costs by nearly $1 billion and delay the time required to field an aircraft by 16 months but provide no benefit. Building and testing a prototype helicopter would yield information and improvements to the aircraft and save $542 million, but this would cost approximately $3 billion and delay the time required to field an aircraft by at least 16 months (GAO, 2013/2014). Given these estimates, the best prototyping strategy was no prototype.

As part of the decision-making process, the decision-maker may wish that more information (data) about an uncertain quantity was available. If the data were available, then they could be used to update the decision-maker's beliefs about the uncertain quantity. The techniques of *inference* can be used to estimate parameters based on the data. Bayesian methods are extremely useful and powerful, especially when estimating the parameters of a probability distribution. The general approach is to model the decision-maker's prior knowledge as a probability distribution and then update the distribution using Bayes' theorem. Some examples of this will be presented in this chapter. Classical estimation techniques (from statistics) are relevant for cases where little-to-no prior information is available. A complete discussion of inference is beyond the scope of this chapter, but excellent studies are available (Pratt *et al.*, 1995; Jordaan, 2005).

Test information is often used to estimate the failure rate of a component. The Bayesian approach begins with a prior distribution for the failure rate and then uses Bayes' theorem to update that distribution based on the test results. In general, this updating can be a difficult computational problem. In some cases, however, the updating has a simple form. For instance, if the prior distribution on a failure rate is a gamma distribution, then observing a number of failures over a total time leads to another gamma distribution with updated parameter values (Modarres, 2006).

When precise probabilities are not available, a decision-maker can use *evidence theory* (Dempster–Shafer theory) and evidence combination rules for combining imprecise probability statements (evidence) from multiple sources (Dempster, 1967; Shafer, 1976). (Imprecise probabilities were introduced in Section 5.3.)

These rules generate new imprecise probabilities from the evidence. The purpose of this is similar to the purpose of Bayesian updating although the calculations are different. An important limitation is that different evidence combination rules will give different results, especially when the evidence is conflicting, but guidelines have been developed to suggest the conditions under which different rules are most appropriate (Rao and Annamdas, 2013). Formal extensions of Bayesian theory for uncertain evidence have been developed as well (Groen and Mosleh, 2005).

The focus of this chapter is the decision to gather information (or not). The analysis of this decision is a type of *preposterior analysis.*

In a decision with uncertainty, more information may help a decision-maker by providing better estimates of the performance or outcomes associated with an alternative. It may help a decision-maker develop a more accurate understanding of the distribution of the outcome by resolving some of the uncertainty. Whether a product will pass a qualifying test is uncertain. If the probability of success depends on the quality of the material, and the quality of material is itself uncertain, then there is a lot of uncertainty about the test outcome. Determining the quality of the material will reduce the uncertainty about the test results.

Simply waiting for some uncertainties to become resolved is one way to gain information. In some cases, however, a decision-maker has the opportunity to spend some resources to gain information about the uncertain value. If the cost of gaining information is high, however, it may be better to go ahead without the information.

Of course, misleading information can be harmful and lead a decision-maker to select a poor alternative. This can happen if the decision-maker receives incorrect information but believes that it is correct or if the decision-maker has an incorrect understanding of how the information is relevant.

False positives and false negatives are examples of imperfect information. A *false positive* occurs when the results of a test indicate that a condition is present when it is actually absent. A *false negative* occurs when the results of a test indicate that a condition is absent when it is actually present. *Receiver operating characteristic* (ROC) *curves* describe how a threshold-based test changes the likelihood of false positives and false negatives. When setting the threshold, a decision-maker must make a tradeoff between the costs of false positives and false negatives. For example, an eye pressure threshold is used to determine whether a patient has glaucoma (Swets *et al.*, 2000). If the eye pressure exceeds the threshold, then the patient is diagnosed as having glaucoma and begins receiving treatment. Unfortunately, the eye pressure is imperfect information because the eye pressure in healthy eyes (and the eye pressure in the presence of glaucoma) varies among patients. A low threshold results in more diagnoses (which increases false positives), but a high threshold reduces the number of diagnoses (which increases false negatives and reduces true positives). The relationship between false positives and false negatives can be visualized with a ROC curve (Figure 8.3). The value of the test changes as the threshold is changed. Each point on the ROC curve corresponds to a different threshold, which affects the probability of a true positive (if the condition is actually present) and the probability of a false positive (if the condition is absent). A different test that had both fewer false positives and fewer false negatives would be even more valuable because it would

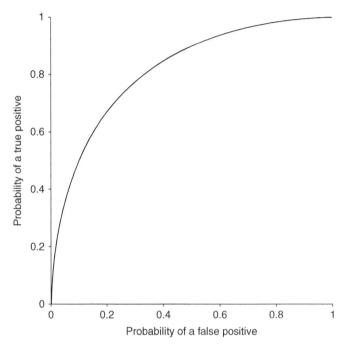

Figure 8.3   A receiver operating characteristic (ROC) curve, based on the example in Swets *et al.* (2000).

be more accurate. The accuracy of a ROC curve is measured by calculating the area under the curve. As the curve moves up, the probability of a false negative decreases (for a given false-positive rate), and the test is more accurate.

The *economic value of information* describes the expected benefit that the decision-maker would realize from having the information (Lawrence, 1999). This quantity can be used by the decision-maker to determine whether resources should be spent to get the information. Information is valuable if it leads to a better decision. The net value after subtracting the cost of gathering the information from the expected value of the information is known as the *expected net gain* of the information.

Example 8.1   Consider the following example of construction (based roughly on an example from de Neufville, 1990). Developers in the San Francisco Bay area plan to build on 350 acres (140 hectares) of reclaimed land. They can build now or wait to build after preloading the site to accelerate consolidation. The major uncertainty is the condition of the soil, which may be insufficiently consolidated. If they build now and the soil is bad (insufficiently consolidated), they will incur an extra $1,000,000 in repair costs. If they build now and the soil is good (consolidated), they will incur no extra repair costs. If they wait, then they are sure that the soil will be consolidated (there is no risk), but they will incur $300,000 in preloading costs and lost revenue due to the delay. An expert estimates that the probability that the soil is bad is 25%

(thus, the probability that the soil is good is 75%). The developers can get perfect information about the condition of the soil for $100,000. Should they purchase the information?

Section 8.1 discusses how to calculate the expected value of perfect information, and Section 8.2 discusses how to calculate the expected value of imperfect information. Section 8.3 describes the value of information about ambiguous probabilities. Section 8.4 discusses the value of information when trying to select the truly best alternative (the selection problem). Section 8.5 describes a technique for determining the relative value of information about specific attributes used to evaluate alternatives.

The techniques described in this chapter generally assume that precise probability distributions for uncertain quantities can be determined. When precise information is not available, the techniques can still be useful using approximate values and conducting a sensitivity analysis to get a range for the value of the information being considered.

8.1   THE EXPECTED VALUE OF PERFECT INFORMATION

We can analyze a situation similar to Example 8.1 by computing the expected value of the information. Given a decision situation L, before gathering some information, let the expected value of the optimal strategy be $EV^*(L)$. The opportunity to gather information creates a new decision situation LI. Let the expected value of the optimal strategy for that decision be $EV^*(LI)$. The *expected value of perfect information* (EVPI) is the expected increase in the value of the situation:

$$EVPI = EV^*(LI) - EV^*(L).$$

Determining the EVPI of a decision situation involves three steps:

EVPI Step 1. Consider a general decision situation that has a set A of alternatives and an unknown X that can be any one of t different values. The probability that $X = j$ is p_j for $j = 1, \ldots, t$. This probability does not depend on the decision-maker's choice. If alternative i in A is chosen and the unknown quantity $X = j$, then there is some remaining uncertainty about the outcome that can be expressed with the following conditional probability: let w_{ij} be the number of possible outcomes and let q_{ijk} be the probability that the value of the outcome equals y_{ijk} for $k = 1, \ldots, w_{ij}$. Figure 8.4 shows a decision tree that captures the key aspects of this situation. From this, we can determine $EV^*(L)$, the expected value of the decision with no information about X:

$$EV^*(L) = \max_{i \in A} \sum_{j=1}^{t} \sum_{k=1}^{w_{ij}} p_j q_{ijk} y_{ijk}.$$

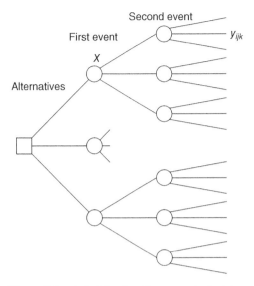

Figure 8.4   A decision tree for a generic decision.

EVPI Step 2. The decision-maker can get information about X before the decision
must be made. If the information is perfect, then the decision-maker accurately
knows the value of X before selecting an alternative. Figure 8.5 shows a decision
tree that captures the key aspects of the situation with perfect information. The
following equation determines $EV^*(LI)$, the expected value of the decision with
perfect information about X:

$$EV^*(LI) = \sum_{j=1}^{t} p_j \max_{i \in A} \left\{ \sum_{k=1}^{w_{ij}} q_{ijk} y_{ijk} \right\}.$$

This formula reflects the fact that the uncertainty in X does not disappear but is
resolved before the decision-maker chooses. There is an optimal choice for
each possible value of X.

EVPI Step 3. Determine the EVPI as $EVPI = EV^*(LI) - EV^*(L)$. The decision-
maker should be willing to pay any amount less than or equal to the EVPI
for the perfect information. Paying more than the EVPI would be an inferior
decision.

If the unknown X is the only uncertainty worth considering, then the above calculations can be simplified. Let y_{ij} be the outcome if the decision-maker chooses
alternative i and the unknown quantity $X = j$. Then,

$$EV^*(L) = \max_{i \in A} \sum_{j=1}^{t} p_j y_{ij},$$

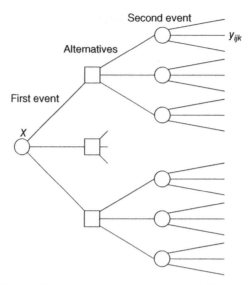

Figure 8.5   A decision tree for a generic decision with perfect information about the unknown quantity X.

and

$$\text{EV}^*(LI) = \sum_{j=1}^{t} p_j \max_{i \in A} y_{ij}.$$

8.2   THE EXPECTED VALUE OF IMPERFECT INFORMATION

If the information about X is imperfect, then there is still some uncertainty about X. The decision-maker will get the imperfect information, then make a decision, and then the uncertainty about X and any other uncertainties will be resolved. Figure 8.6 shows a decision tree that captures the key aspects of the situation with imperfect information. The *expected value of imperfect information* (EVII) is the gain in the situation from having the imperfect information before selecting an alternative.

EVII Step 1. This is the same as EVPI Step 1, which calculates $\text{EV}^*(L)$.

EVII Step 2. Consider the distribution of the imperfect information, which must be given or assessed based on past experience. Let $p_{h|j}^I$ be the probability that the information says that $X = h$ when actually $X = j$ for $h = 1, \dots, t$ and $j = 1, \dots, t$. From this, the decision-maker can calculate the following probabilities: let $\hat{p}_h$ be the probability that the information says that $X = h$ for $h = 1, \dots, t$, and let $p_{j|h}^C$ be the probability that actually $X = j$ if the information

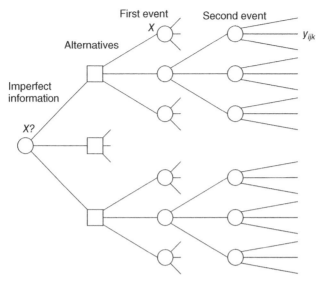

Figure 8.6 A decision tree for a generic decision with imperfect information X? about the unknown quantity X.

says that $X = h$ for $h = 1, \ldots, t$, and $j = 1, \ldots, t$. The conditional probabilities can be determined by Bayes' theorem.

The following determines $EV^*(LII)$, the expected value of the decision with imperfect information about X:

$$\hat{p}_h = \sum_{j=1}^{t} p_j p^I_{h|j}.$$

$$p^C_{j|h} = \frac{p_j p^I_{h|j}}{\hat{p}_h}.$$

$$EV^*(LII) = \sum_{h=1}^{t} \hat{p}_h \max_{i \in A} \left\{ \sum_{j=1}^{t} \sum_{k=1}^{w_{ij}} p^C_{j|h} q_{ijk} y_{ijk} \right\}.$$

EVII Step 3. Determine the EVII as $EVII = EV^*(LII) - EV^*(L)$. The EVII is the most that the decision-maker should pay for this imperfect information; if the imperfect information costs more than this, the decision-maker is better off without it.

In general, $EV^*(L) \le EV^*(LII) \le EV^*(LI)$, and $0 \le EVII \le EVPI$. That is, imperfect information helps the decision-maker some, and perfect information helps more.

If the unknown X is the only uncertainty worth considering, then the calculation in Step 2 can be simplified. Let y_{ij} be the outcome if the decision-maker chooses alternative i and the unknown quantity $X = j$. Then,

$$EV^*(LII) = \sum_{h=1}^{t} \hat{p}_h \max_{i \in A} \left\{ \sum_{j=1}^{t} p_{j|h}^C y_{ij} \right\}.$$

The EVII increases (and approaches the EVPI) as the quality of the information improves (as $p_{j|j}^I$ approaches 1). Of course, the decision-maker must have some idea of how good the information is; otherwise, it is impossible to determine its value. The EVPI is an upper bound on EVII; thus, in situations where the information is imperfect but the quality is uncertain, the decision-maker at least knows that the EVII cannot be greater than the EVPI, which requires less data to calculate.

The analysis here of EVII and EVPI assumes that the decision-maker is risk-neutral, so calculating these quantities is straightforward. If the decision-maker is risk averse, then the analysis must calculate $EU^*(L)$, the expected utility of the decision without information, and then find the maximum value of the cost of the information, such that the expected utility of the decision with the information is not less than $EU^*(L)$ (for a complete and rigorous discussion, see Lawrence, 1999).

Example 8.2   Consider again Example 8.1. In this decision, the only uncertainty being considered is the current condition of the soil. This is the unknown X, and it has two possible values: (1) good or (2) bad. The probabilities are $p_1 = 0.75$ and $p_2 = 0.25$. The alternatives are to (1) build now or (2) wait. There are four outcomes (which are the changes in profit from the baseline): $y_{11} = \$0$, $y_{12} = -\$1{,}000{,}000$, and $y_{21} = y_{22} = -\$300{,}000$.

EVPI Step 1.

$$EV^*(L) = \max_{i=1,2} \sum_{j=1}^{2} p_j y_{ij}$$

$$= \max\{-\$250{,}000, -\$300{,}000\}$$

$$= -\$250{,}000.$$

With no information, the best option is to build now, with an expected loss of $250,000. Figure 8.7 displays a decision tree of the situation with no information.

EVPI Step 2. Suppose that the developers can get perfect information about the condition of the soil. There is a 25% chance that the soil is bad (in which case, they will wait) and a 75% chance that the soil is good (in which case, they will build now with no risk of extra cost). Figure 8.8 displays a decision tree of the situation with perfect information. The expected loss in this situation is $75,000:

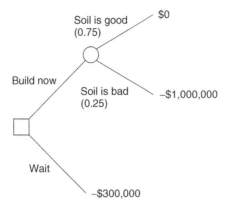

Figure 8.7 A decision tree for the construction decision with no information.

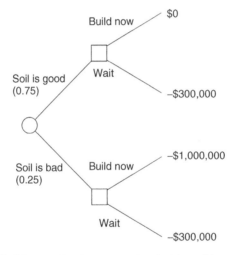

Figure 8.8 A decision tree for the construction decision with perfect information.

$$\text{EV}^*(LI) = \sum_{j=1}^{2} p_j \max_{i=1,2} \{y_{ij}\}$$

$$= 0.75 \max\{0, -\$300,000\} + 0.25 \max\{-\$1,000,000, -\$300,000\}$$

$$= -\$75,000.$$

EVPI Step 3. The EVPI = $\text{EV}^*(LI) - \text{EV}^*(L)$, which equals $-\$75,000 - (-\$250,000) = \$175,000$ in this case. The developers should be willing to pay up to $175,000 for perfect information.

The developers can also get imperfect information from testing samples of soil obtained from borings, but the test is not perfect. Data about the results of previous tests have been used to justify the following statements about its accuracy:

- If the soil is good, there is a 90% chance that the test will say that the soil is good (and a 10% chance that the test will say that the soil is bad).
- If the soil is bad, there is an 80% chance that the test will say that the soil is bad (and a 20% chance that the test will say that the soil is good).

EVII Step 1. $EV^*(L) = -\$250,000$.

EVII Step 2. Let $h = 1$ if the test says that the soil is good and $h = 2$ if the test says that the soil is bad. Hence, $p'_{1|1} = 0.9$ and $p'_{2|1} = 0.1$; $p'_{1|2} = 0.2$ and $p'_{2|2} = 0.8$. From this information, the probability of each outcome of the test and the conditional probabilities for the soil status given the test results can be determined using Bayes' theorem:

$$\hat{p}_1 = 0.75(0.9) + 0.25(0.2) = 0.725$$
$$\hat{p}_2 = 0.75(0.1) + 0.25(0.8) = 0.275$$
$$p^C_{1|1} = \frac{0.75(0.9)}{0.725} = \frac{27}{29}$$
$$p^C_{2|1} = \frac{0.25(0.2)}{0.725} = \frac{2}{29}$$
$$p^C_{1|2} = \frac{0.75(0.1)}{0.275} = \frac{3}{11}$$
$$p^C_{2|2} = \frac{0.25(0.8)}{0.275} = \frac{8}{11}.$$

Figure 8.9 displays a decision tree of the situation with imperfect information. These lead to the following expected value of the decision with imperfect information:

$$EV^*(LII) = 0.725 \max\left\{\frac{27}{29}(0) + \frac{2}{29}(-\$1,000,000), -\$300,000\right\}$$
$$+ 0.275 \max\left\{\frac{3}{11}(0) + \frac{8}{11}(-\$1,000,000), -\$300,000\right\}$$
$$= 0.725(-\$68,965) + 0.275(-\$300,000)$$
$$= -\$132,500$$

If the test says that the soil is good, then they should build now if they want to minimize the expected cost. The chance of building on bad soil drops to 2/29, and the expected cost of building in this case is $68,965. If the test says that the soil is bad, then they should wait, incurring the cost of $300,000. Thus, the expected cost is $132,500.

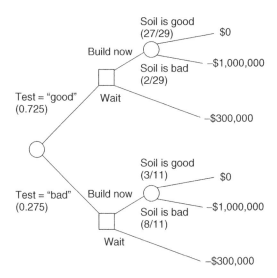

Figure 8.9   A decision tree for the construction decision with imperfect information.

EVII Step 3. The EVII = EV*(*LII*) − EV*(*L*), which equals −$132,500 − (−$250,000) = $117,500 in this case. The developers should be willing to pay up to $117,500 for this imperfect information. Note, of course, that the imperfect information is worth less than the perfect information (i.e., EVII < EVPI).

As mentioned earlier, the EVII depends on the quality of the information. In particular, the EVII changes as $p_{1|1}^I$ and $p_{2|2}^I$ change (note $p_{2|1}^I = 1 - p_{1|1}^I$ and $p_{1|2}^I = 1 - p_{2|2}^I$). Table 8.1 shows the EVII for combinations of $p_{1|1}^I$ and $p_{2|2}^I$. When both equal 1, then the information is perfect, and the EVII equals the EVPI, which is an upper bound on the EVII. When both equal 0, although the information is always wrong, the EVII again equals the EVPI because the decision-maker, who is aware of the information quality, can use the wrong information to make a better decision. This situation is similar to getting information from someone who always lies; the information that the liar gives is still useful because the opposite of what the liar says is always true. The lowest EVII occurs when the sum $p_{1|1}^I$ plus $p_{2|2}^I$ equals (or is close to) 1. Then, the probability that the test says the soil is *good* is the same for both actual soil conditions (because $p_{1|2}^I = 1 - p_{2|2}^I = p_{1|1}^I$). The result thus gives the decision-maker no information about the actual soil condition.

Example 8.3   This example is based on a problem written by John Toczek. A dice game has four six-sided dice with different numbers on each face. You and three friends will play a simple game, where you will each roll one of the dice, and the highest number wins. For convenience, let us label the dice A, B, C, and D.

TABLE 8.1 The Expected Value of Imperfect Information (EVII) in Thousands of Dollars for the Construction Example for Different Values of $p_{1|1}^I$ and $p_{2|2}^I$.

$p_{2|2}^I$	$p_{1|1}^I$										
	0	0.1	0.2	0.3	0.4	0.5	0.6	0.7	0.8	0.9	1
0	$175.0	$152.5	$130.0	$107.5	$85.0	$62.5	$40.0	$17.5	$0.0	$0.0	$0.0
0.1	$157.5	$135.0	$112.5	$90.0	$67.5	$45.0	$22.5	$0.0	$0.0	$0.0	$17.5
0.2	$140.0	$117.5	$95.0	$72.5	$50.0	$27.5	$5.0	$0.0	$0.0	$12.5	$35.0
0.3	$122.5	$100.0	$77.5	$55.0	$32.5	$10.0	$0.0	$0.0	$7.5	$30.0	$52.5
0.4	$105.0	$82.5	$60.0	$37.5	$15.0	$0.0	$0.0	$2.5	$25.0	$47.5	$70.0
0.5	$87.5	$65.0	$42.5	$20.0	$0.0	$0.0	$0.0	$20.0	$42.5	$65.0	$87.5
0.6	$70.0	$47.5	$25.0	$2.5	$0.0	$0.0	$15.0	$37.5	$60.0	$82.5	$105.0
0.7	$52.5	$30.0	$7.5	$0.0	$0.0	$10.0	$32.5	$55.0	$77.5	$100.0	$122.5
0.8	$35.0	$12.5	$0.0	$0.0	$5.0	$27.5	$50.0	$72.5	$95.0	$117.5	$140.0
0.9	$17.5	$0.0	$0.0	$0.0	$22.5	$45.0	$67.5	$90.0	$112.5	$135.0	$157.5
1	$0.0	$0.0	$17.5	$40.0	$62.5	$85.0	$107.5	$130.0	$152.5	$175.0	$175.0

Die A has the following six numbers: 1-1-1-1-7-7. Die B has the following six numbers: 4-4-4-4-4-4. Die C has the following six numbers: 2-2-2-2-6-6. Die D has the following six numbers: 3-3-3-5-5-5. When all four dice are rolled, the probability that A wins equals 1/3, and the probabilities for the all other dice equal 2/9.

Suppose that the winner will get $10. Suppose Joe picks A, and Rose picks D. You have to choose between B and C, and then Louis will have whichever die is left. Is it worth anything to you to have Joe and Rose roll their dice before you pick?

The expected value of the game with no information is the maximum of the expected value of choosing B, which is $(2/9)$ $10 = $2.22, and the expected value of choosing C, which is $(2/9)$ $10 = $2.22.

To determine the expected value of the game with perfect information about Joe and Rose's results, there are three cases to consider:

1. Joe rolls a 7. The probability of this outcome is 1/3. You will definitely lose no matter which die you choose and what you roll.
2. Joe rolls a 1, and Rose rolls a 3. The probability of this outcome is 1/3. If you choose B (and Louis gets C), you win if and only if Louis rolls a 2. The conditional probability of this outcome is 2/3. If you choose C (and Louis gets B), you win if and only if you roll a 6. The conditional probability of this outcome is 1/3. Thus, choosing B is better than choosing C.
3. Joe rolls a 1, and Rose rolls a 5. The probability of this outcome is 1/3. If you choose B (and Louis gets C), you will surely lose (to Rose or Louis). If you choose C (and Louis gets B), you win if and only if you roll a 6. The conditional probability of this outcome is 1/3. Thus, choosing C is better than choosing B.

At this point, it seems clear that knowing Joe's roll and Rose's roll affects your optimal choice. With the information about their rolls, your probability of winning increases to $(1/3)(0) + (1/3)(2/3) + (1/3)(1/3) = 1/3$, so the expected value of the decision with this information is $3.33. Therefore, the expected value of this perfect information equals $3.33 - $2.22 = $1.11. You should be willing to pay up to $1.11 to have Joe and Rose roll before you choose.

Note that, in the decision with the information, Joe's probability of winning is still 1/3, Rose's probability of winning is still 2/9, but Louis's probability of winning decreases to 1/9 (and his expected value drops from $2.22 to $1.11). Because you are hurting Louis if you get the information, you should pay him for the privilege.

8.3   EXPERIMENTATION TO REDUCE AMBIGUITY

Part of the decision-making process is deciding how much information to gather, and, in general, a decision-maker can use this type of analysis to determine the expected value of reducing uncertainty through experimentation. *Decision ambiguity* is a special case in which the probabilities of uncertain events are themselves uncertain. In general, this occurs when the decision-maker is unsure of the probabilities. More information allows for a better (less uncertain) estimate of the probability, but information costs money, so the decision-maker needs to decide how much to gather.

Example 8.4   Consider a lottery that has two steps: first, one of the three coins will be selected at random, and then the selected coin will be flipped. Rose, the player, must decide whether to play after the coin is selected. She must pay \$10 to play, but she will win \$20 if the coin lands "heads" (and get nothing if the coin lands "tails"). The coins are indistinguishable but perform differently: the probability of heads with the first coin is 0.1, the probability of heads with the second coin is 0.5, and the probability of heads with the third coin is 0.7.

After a coin has been selected, Rose is unsure about the probability of a heads. That is, the probability is ambiguous: the probability that it equals 0.1 is 1/3, the probability that it equals 0.5 is 1/3, and the probability that it equals 0.7 is 1/3. Because the coins are equally likely to be selected, the total probability of heads is 13/30, so the expected value of playing is (13/30)(\$10) + (17/30)(−\$10) = −\$1.33. Rose will decline to play, so the expected value of the decision EV*(L) = \$0.

Now, suppose that Rose has the opportunity to flip the selected coin before deciding to play to reduce the ambiguity. If she can flip the selected coin sufficiently many times, then, based on the frequency of heads, she would be nearly certain which coin was selected and would know her probability of winning. This would be an example of (nearly) perfect information about the probability (but it does not reduce the uncertainty about the result of the coin flip).

If, however, she can flip the selected coin only N times (where N is not large), then the experimental coin flips are imperfect information. The expected value of the coin flips can be determined as follows:

Let p_i be the probability that coin i will be heads when flipped, $i = 1, \ 2, \ 3$.

Let $P_{ijk} = \binom{j+k}{j} p_i^j (1 - p_i)^k$ be the probability that, when coin i is flipped $j + k$ times, j heads and k tails will occur.

Using Bayes' theorem and the fact that the coins are equally likely, we can determine the probability that coin i was selected given that j heads and k tails did occur:

$$P'_{i|jk} = \frac{P_{ijk}}{P_{1jk} + P_{2jk} + P_{3jk}} = \frac{\binom{j+k}{j} p_i^j (1 - p_i)^k}{\sum_{h=1}^{3} \binom{j+k}{j} p_h^j (1 - p_h)^k}.$$

After $j + k$ experimental coin flips that yield j heads and k tails, the posterior probability of heads equals $\sum_{i=1}^{3} P'_{i|jk} p_i$. She then needs to decide whether to play; she will play if the expected value of the game is positive.

For example, suppose Rose flips the selected coin one time before deciding whether to play. Figure 8.10 displays a decision tree of the situation with this

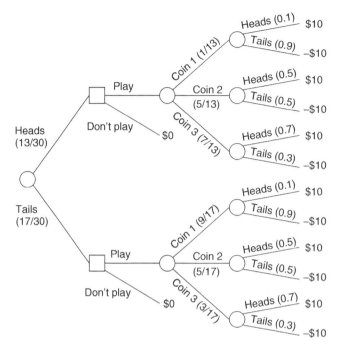

Figure 8.10 A decision tree for the coin flip game with imperfect information.

imperfect information. Suppose that the result is heads ($j = 1$ and $k = 0$), with only one flip, $P_{i10} = p_i$ for all three coins; therefore,

$$P'_{1|10} = 0.1/(0.1 + 0.5 + 0.7) = 1/13$$

$$P'_{2|10} = 0.5/(0.1 + 0.5 + 0.7) = 5/13$$

$$P'_{3|10} = 0.7/(0.1 + 0.5 + 0.7) = 7/13.$$

The ambiguity about the probability of heads has been reduced but not eliminated: the probability that it equals 0.1 is 1/13, the probability that it equals 0.5 is 5/13, and the probability that it equals 0.7 is 7/13. The posterior probability of heads equals $\frac{1}{13}(0.1) + \frac{5}{13}(0.5) + \frac{7}{13}(0.7)$, which is approximately 0.577. The expected value of the game is $1.54, so Rose will play.

In contrast, if the result of the one experimental coin flip is tails ($j = 0$ and $k = 1$), $P_{i01} = 1 - p_i$ for all three coins; therefore,

$$P'_{1|01} = 0.9/(0.9 + 0.5 + 0.3) = 9/17$$

$$P'_{2|01} = 0.5/(0.9 + 0.5 + 0.3) = 5/17$$

$$P'_{3|01} = 0.3/(0.9 + 0.5 + 0.3) = 3/17.$$

TABLE 8.2   The Expected Value of Imperfect Information (EVII) in the Coin Flip Game.

Number of Coin Flips (N)	Expected Value of Imperfect Information (EVII)
1	$0.67
2	$0.71
3	$0.97
4	$1.08
5	$1.09
6	$1.20
7	$1.23
8	$1.24
9	$1.28
10	$1.29
11	$1.30
12	$1.31
13	$1.31
14	$1.32
15	$1.32

Again, the ambiguity about the probability of heads has been reduced but not eliminated: the probability that it equals 0.1 is 9/17, the probability that it equals 0.5 is 5/17, and the probability that it equals 0.7 is 3/17. The posterior probability of heads equals $\frac{9}{17}(0.1) + \frac{5}{17}(0.5) + \frac{3}{17}(0.7)$, which is approximately 0.324. The expected value of the game (given this imperfect information) is a loss of $3.53, so Rose would not play, so the expected value of the decision equals 0.

Therefore, the total expected value of the situation with one coin flip $\mathrm{EV}^*(LII) = \frac{13}{30}(\$1.54) + \frac{17}{30}(0)$, which is approximately $0.67. The EVII = $0.67 − $0 = $0.67.

In general, let V be the value of winning ($20 for Rose), and let C be the cost of playing ($10 for Rose). Then, the expected value of the game without the experimental coin flips

$$\mathrm{EV}^*(L) = \max \left\{ 0, \sum_{i=1}^{3} \frac{1}{3} p_i V - C \right\}$$

and the expected value of the game with N experimental coin flips

$$\mathrm{EV}^*(LII_N) = \sum_{j=0}^{N} \sum_{i=1}^{3} \frac{1}{3} P_{i,j,N-j} \max \left\{ \sum_{h=1}^{3} P'_{h|j,N-j} p_h V - C, 0 \right\}.$$

The expected value of the imperfect information from N experimental coin flips is the difference between these quantities. In this example, because $\mathrm{EV}^*(L) = \$0$, $\mathrm{EVII} = \mathrm{EV}^*(LII)$.

After Rose calculates these quantities (shown in Table 8.2), she determines that the expected value of the imperfect information from 10 experimental coin flips is

$1.29, so she would pay up to $1.29 for the results of that experiment. In particular, if four or more heads appear in the 10 experimental coin flips, then she should play the game. The expected value of the imperfect information from 15 experimental coin flips is only $1.32, however, and the expected value of perfect information about the coin is $1.33.

In this case, the experimental coin flips are valuable because the coins are quite different. If the three coins had a very similar probability of heads, then the experimental coin flips would have much less value. For instance, if the probabilities were 0.45, 0.5, and 0.6, then the expected value of the imperfect information from 15 experimental coin flips is only 9 cents.

This example assumes that there are a finite number of different coins, but the approach can be extended to the case of a coin with an unknown probability of heads (the actual coin is one of many possibilities).

8.4 EXPERIMENTATION TO COMPARE ALTERNATIVES

In general, the ability to make a correct selection depends on the quality of the information about the performance or value of each alternative. When uncertainty about the performance exists, the decision-maker may consider gathering information by taking measurements or samples or running simulation models of the alternatives. Because gathering information requires resources, the decision-maker will want to allocate resources in a way that increases the likelihood that the information gathered will lead to the truly best alternative. The *selection problem* requires finding the best alternative when performance is a random variable, and an alternative's true performance must be estimated using experimentation. In some studies, this problem is known as choosing the best of several "treatments" or "processes" (Pratt *et al.*, 1995).

For example, a photovoltaics engineering firm may develop a computer simulation to estimate the energy losses within a photovoltaic array and evaluate the system's overall performance (Bucciarelli, 1994). The model can be used to compare different systems that are being considered for a particular installation, but it takes time to run. Moreover, if the model included random elements (for the weather or component failures, for instance), then its output is different every time it is run. More simulation runs provide more information about the photovoltaic system's true performance, but this requires time and resources.

Given a set of sample data collected from observations (such as measurements, evaluations, or simulation runs), the decision-maker can, for each alternative, create (using classical statistical approaches or by updating a prior using Bayes' theorem) a probability distribution that expresses his beliefs about the true value of the alternative. If the decision-maker selects the alternative i that has the greatest expected value, but some other alternative has the greatest actual value, then an *opportunity loss* occurs. The opportunity loss equals the difference between the actual value of the truly best alternative and the actual value of i, the selected alternative. The expected value of perfect information (EVPI) about the alternatives' actual values equals the expected value of the conditional loss (Pratt *et al.*, 1995).

If we express this using the terms from Section 8.1, $EV^*(L) = v_i$, the value of the selected alternative, and $EV^*(LI) = \max\{v_1, \ldots, v_n\}$, the value of the best alternative. Thus, $EVPI = \max\{v_1, \ldots, v_n\} - v_i$.

Unfortunately, in general, the EVPI cannot be determined exactly, but one can use a Monte Carlo technique (cf. Section 5.12) to draw samples $v_1, \ldots, v_n$ of the n alternatives' values (from the decision-maker's distributions) and calculate sample values for $x = \max\{v_1, \ldots, v_n\} - v_i$. The average of these samples for x is an estimate for EVPI.

Example 8.5 Consider a situation in which there are four alternatives (1, 2, 3, and 4). Based on a small number of observations about the value of each alternative, Rose (the decision-maker) forms a normal distribution to express her beliefs about each one's true value. The mean and variance of each normal distribution is given in Table 8.3. Based on this, she selects alternative 4 because it has the greatest mean.

A Monte Carlo simulation drew 500 samples from each of the four distributions. These were used to calculate 500 sample values for $x = \max\{v_1, v_2, v_3, v_4\} - v_4$. The average of these samples for x was 3.2, which is an estimate for EVPI.

If resources are available to gather more information about the alternatives, the decision-maker will want to allocate these resources in a way that increases the likelihood that the information gathered will lead to the truly best alternative. There are multiple approaches to determine good allocations. These include the indifference zone (IZ) approach, the expected value of information procedure (VIP), and the optimal computing budget allocation (OCBA) algorithm (Bechhofer *et al.*, 1995; Chen, 1996; Chick and Inoue, 2001; Kim and Nelson, 2006; Branke *et al.*, 2007; Chen *et al.*, 2008). These are normally used as sequential approaches. At each step, the relative benefit of gathering more observations (collecting samples or performing simulation runs) about each alternative is estimated, these values are used to determine which alternatives should be observed and how many observations should be collected, and then the collected data are used to update the alternatives' performance. In some versions, the calculations are done after each observation. The process stops when the total number of observations reaches the upper bound (due to the limited resources available) or when the benefit of gathering more observations becomes sufficiently small. There are tradeoffs among the procedures: some are more efficient (more likely

TABLE 8.3   The Distributions for the Values of the Four Alternatives.

Alternative	Mean	Variance
1	94.7	508.4
2	147.1	316.4
3	164.2	16.4
4	167.1	40.9

to identify the truly best alternative for a given level of computational effort) and some are more "controllable" (easier to set parameter values to obtain a desired level of correct selection). Computational results presented by Branke *et al.* (2007) demonstrated the strengths and weaknesses of these procedures.

The OCBA approach begins by evaluating every alternative a small number of times. This provides enough data to calculate a sample mean and sample variance for the performance measure for each alternative. Then, using this data, the OCBA procedure, when used in its fully sequential mode, estimates the approximate probability of correct selection (PCS) if another sample is taken for each alternative. That is, it estimates the approximate PCS if the first alternative is evaluated again, the approximate PCS if the second alternative is evaluated again, the approximate PCS if the third alternative is evaluated again, and so forth. The alternative that gives the greatest estimated approximate PCS when evaluated is then evaluated once to get another data point. The sample mean and variance for this alternative are updated, and the procedure estimates the approximate PCS for each alternative again. This continues until the resources for evaluating alternatives are completely consumed.

The following procedure is based on the one presented by Branke *et al.* (2007), although the notation has been simplified in a few places. The decision-maker's objective is to select the system that has the maximum system performance. The EAPCS$_i$ is the estimated approximate probability of correct selection, which determines the allocation of the next simulation replication. This version includes a computing budget that cannot be exceeded, but other stopping rules can be used.

Let k be the number of alternative systems, one of which will be selected. Let B be the total number of simulation replications that can be run. $\Phi_v(x)$ is the cumulative distribution function of the standard t distribution ($\mu = 0$, $\kappa = 1$) with v degrees of freedom.

1. For $j = 1, \ldots, k$, run n_0 independent replications of system j, measure the system's performance in each replication, set $n_j = n_0$, and determine the sample mean $\bar{x}_j$ and the sample variance $\hat{\sigma}_j^2$ of the performance.

2. Set the total number of simulation replications run $N = kn_0$.

3. Renumber the systems so that system k has the largest sample mean.

4. For $j = 1, \ldots, k - 1$, calculate $d_{jk} = \bar{x}_k - \bar{x}_j$.

5. For $i = 1, \ldots, k$, do the following:

   (a) Set $n_i^* = n_i + 1$; for $j \neq i$, set $n_j^* = n_j$.

   (b) For $j = 1, \ldots, k - 1$, calculate $\tilde{\lambda}_{jk}^{-1} = \dfrac{\hat{\sigma}_j^2}{n_j^*} + \dfrac{\hat{\sigma}_k^2}{n_k^*}$ and

$$v_{jk} = \frac{[\hat{\sigma}_j^2/n_j^* + \hat{\sigma}_k^2/n_k^*]^2}{[\hat{\sigma}_j^2/n_j^*]^2/(n_j^*-1) + [\hat{\sigma}_k^2/n_k^*]^2/(n_k^*-1)}.$$

   (c) Calculate

$$\text{EAPCS}_i = \prod_{j=1}^{k-1} (1 - \Phi_{v_{jk}}(\tilde{\lambda}_{jk}^{1/2} d_{jk})).$$

6. Let i^* be the system with the greatest value of $EAPCS_i$. Run one independent replication of system $j = i^*$, measure the system's performance in that replication, increase n_j by 1, and update the sample mean $\bar{x}_j$ and the sample variance $\hat{\sigma}_j^2$ of the performance. Increase N by 1. If $N < B$, return to Step 3.
7. Select the system with the greatest $\bar{x}_j$.

Example 8.6 Consider again the situation from Example 8.5. Table 8.3 lists the sample mean and variance of the observations initially gathered (these were used to form the distributions used to estimate the EVPI). Three observations of each alternative (system) were made. System 4 has the largest sample mean and would be selected if no more observations were made. Given the data, the OCBA procedure can be used to estimate the approximate PCS if no more observations were made; the result is 0.636. If one more observation of a system were made, the PCS would increase. The estimated approximate PCS values ($EAPCS_i$) for systems 1, 2, 3, and 4 are 0.644, 0.664, 0.642, and 0.659, respectively. Another observation from system 1 or system 3 would increase the PCS approximately only 0.008 or 0.006. In contrast, another observation from system 2 or system 4 would increase the PCS approximately 0.028 or 0.023. Thus, more observations from these systems will be more valuable. In particular, the OCBA procedure will run another replication from alternative 2, which has the greatest $EAPCS_i$.

8.5 EXPERIMENTATION TO COMPARE ALTERNATIVES WITH MULTIPLE ATTRIBUTES

When the utility of an alternative depends on multiple attributes and these attributes are uncertain due to randomness in the processes used to evaluate the attributes, then an "experiment" is an information-gathering activity that provides a value for one attribute of one alternative and can therefore reduce the uncertainty about the true attribute value.

For example, the Domestic Nuclear Detection Office (DNDO) of the US Department of Homeland Security collaborated with the US Customs and Border Protection (CBP) to evaluate different radiation detection systems to be used in airports in the United States to screen passengers and luggage that arrive from overseas and detect, identify, and localize illicit radiological or nuclear material. Multiple criteria were used for selecting a specific detection system for an operational demonstration. These criteria included the probability that the detection system would detect different types of radiological and nuclear material, including plutonium, uranium, and radionuclides used in industry and medicine. Testing was conducted to evaluate the ability of different systems to detect each material. In particular, test samples with different materials were passed through the detection system, and the system's performance was measured by the success rate (the number of times that it detected that material divided by the number of trials with that material). This rate was used to estimate the probability that the detection system would detect that material, and this estimate had uncertainty based on the number of trials. Of course, the time and resources available to test the different systems and different materials was limited; running more trials with one material in order to reduce the uncertainty associated with that attribute would limit the number of trials with other materials.

The uncertainty about an alternative's total utility depends on the uncertainty about the attribute values. If resources are available to gather more information about the attributes, the decision-maker will want to allocate these resources in a way that reduces the uncertainty about the alternative's total utility.

Consider a case in which the total utility of alternative i is the weighted sum of m attributes:

$$U_i = \sum_{j=1}^{m} k_j u_j(x_{ij}).$$

Assume that the single-attribute utility functions are linear functions such that, for $j = 1, \dots, m$,

$$u_j(x_{ij}) = a_j + b_j x_{ij}.$$

Then, after rearranging the terms, we can express the total utility as a linear function:

$$w_j = k_j b_j, \quad j = 1, \dots, m$$

$$K = \sum_{j=1}^{m} k_j a_j$$

$$U_i = K + \sum_{j=1}^{m} w_j x_{ij}.$$

Let σ_{ij}^2 be the variance of probability distribution that represents the uncertainty about x_{ij} and let σ_i^2 be the variance of probability distribution that represents the uncertainty about U_i. These are related as follows:

$$\sigma_i^2 = \sum_{j=1}^{m} w_j^2 \sigma_{ij}^2.$$

Because more information will reduce the uncertainty in the attribute values (the variance), it also reduces the uncertainty in the total utility. In some cases, when the resources available for gathering information about the attribute values are limited, the decision-maker must decide where to use the resources. For instance, the decision-maker may want to minimize the variance of the total utility (but this is not the only possibility).

If an "important" attribute (one with a large value of w_j) also has a large variance σ_{ij}^2, then spending resources to gather information about this attribute should reduce the variance of the total utility. In some cases, an important attribute will have a small variance but a less important attribute will have a large variance. In this case, a compromise may be most effective.

To illustrate this point, consider a case in which the uncertainties about the true attribute values are expressed with normal distributions based on prior information. New observations can be acquired; the values are random due to measurement error, but they are normally distributed with a known variance. Thus, there is a conjugate prior that is easy to update with new data, and we can determine the impact of new data on the variance of the posterior distributions for the attribute values and the total utility.

To simplify the presentation, it will be useful to define the "precision" τ of an uncertain quantity as the reciprocal of its variance. That is, in general, $\tau = 1/\sigma^2$. First, we will consider the general situation of updating (using Bayes' theorem) beliefs about the unknown mean of a normal distribution.

Suppose that the prior distribution for the unknown mean μ is normally distributed with its mean equal to μ_0 and its variance equal to σ_0^2. If n observations are taken from a measurement process that is normally distributed with its mean equal to μ and its variance equal to σ^2 (note that the variance of this process is known), then the posterior distribution for the unknown mean μ is normally distributed. Let $\tau_0 = 1/\sigma_0^2$ be the precision of the prior distribution. Let $\tau = 1/\sigma^2$ be the precision of the measurement process. Let $\bar{x}$ be the average of the n observations (the sample mean). The precision of the posterior distribution is $n\tau + \tau_0$, and the mean and variance of the posterior distribution are

$$\frac{n\tau\bar{x} + \tau_0\mu_0}{n\tau + \tau_0}, \frac{1}{n\tau + \tau_0}.$$

Note that more observations increase the precision and reduce the variance of the posterior distribution. Because the reduction does not depend on the results of the observations, it can be predicted before the samples are collected.

Now we return to our problem with multiple attributes. Suppose that the prior distribution for the unknown true attribute value x_{ij} is normally distributed with its mean equal to $\hat{\mu}_{ij}$ and its variance equal to $\hat{\sigma}_{ij}^2$. Let $\hat{\tau}_{ij} = 1/\hat{\sigma}_{ij}^2$ be the precision of the prior distribution. Suppose that n_{ij} observations are taken from a measurement process that is normally distributed with its mean equal to x_{ij} and its variance equal to σ_i^2 (note that the variance of this process is known and the same for all of the alternatives, which is a simplifying assumption). Let $\tau_i = 1/\sigma_i^2$ be the precision of the measurement process. Let $\bar{x}_{ij}$ be the average of the n_{ij} observations (the sample mean). The posterior distribution for the unknown attribute value x_{ij} is normally distributed. Because the precision of the posterior distribution is $n_{ij}\tau_i + \hat{\tau}_{ij}$, the mean and variance of the posterior distribution are

$$\frac{n_{ij}\tau_i\bar{x}_{ij} + \hat{\tau}_{ij}\hat{\mu}_{ij}}{n_{ij}\tau_i + \hat{\tau}_{ij}}, \frac{1}{n_{ij}\tau_i + \hat{\tau}_{ij}}.$$

The posterior distribution for the total utility of alternative i is also normally distributed. The mean and the variance of this posterior distribution equal

$$K + \sum_{j=1}^{m} w_j \times \frac{n_{ij}\tau_i \bar{x}_{ij} + \hat{\tau}_{ij}\hat{\mu}_{ij}}{n_{ij}\tau_i + \hat{\tau}_{ij}}, \sum_{j=1}^{m} \frac{w_j^2}{n_{ij}\tau_i + \hat{\tau}_{ij}}.$$

More observations reduce the variance of the posterior distribution. Because this reduction does not depend on the results of the observations, it can be predicted before the samples are collected and can be used to plan which attributes should be measured.

Example 8.7   Consider a decision in which the utility function has two attributes and the weights on those attributes are $w_1 = 0.75$ and $w_2 = 0.25$. The variance of the prior uncertainty in the first attribute is 0.5 (the precision equals 2), and the variance of the prior uncertainty in the second attribute is 4 (the precision equals 0.25). The variance of the prior uncertainty in the total utility equals 0.53125. The variance of the first attribute measurement error is 4 (the precision equals 0.25), and the variance of the second attribute measurement error is 8 (the precision equals 0.125). Suppose that the decision-maker has enough resources to make a total of 20 observations of both attributes. If 10 observations of the first attribute are made, then the precision of posterior uncertainty in the first attribute will increase to $2 + 10(0.25) = 4.5$; the variance will decrease to 0.222. If 10 observations of the second attribute are made, then the precision of posterior uncertainty in the second attribute will increase to

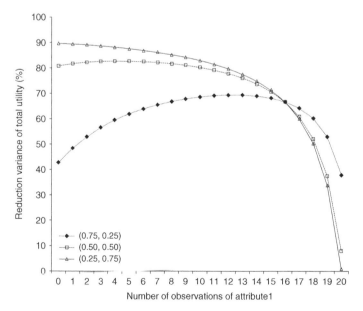

Figure 8.11   The percent reduction in the variance of the total utility in three scenarios $(w_1, w_2) = (0.75, 0.25)$, $(w_1, w_2) = (0.5, 0.5)$, and $(w_1, w_2) = (0.25, 0.75)$.

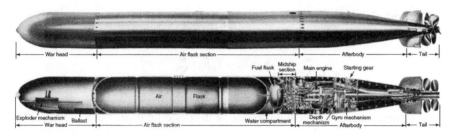

Figure 8.12 Mark 14 torpedo side view and interior mechanisms. (Image credit: United States Navy.)

$0.25 + 10(0.125) = 1.5$; the variance will decrease to 0.667. Thus, the variance of the posterior uncertainty in the total utility will decrease to 0.1667. A search over all of the possible allocations will show that taking 12 observations of the first attribute and 8 observations of the second attribute will reduce the variance of the posterior uncertainty in the total utility to 0.1625, which is the best possible with 20 total observations. Of course, the best allocation depends on the relative importance of the attributes. Figure 8.11 displays the percent reduction in the variance of the total utility for this example in three scenarios $(w_1, w_2) = (0.75, 0.25)$, $(w_1, w_2) = (0.5, 0.5)$, and $(w_1, w_2) = (0.25, 0.75)$. The uncertainty about the first attribute is low, but when it is important ($w_1 = 0.75$), it is helpful to spend some resources to measure it. When the two attributes are equally important ($w_1 = 0.5$) or when the second attribute is more important ($w_1 = 0.25$), measuring the first attribute is not productive, and it is more useful to spend the resources to measure the second attribute, which has more uncertainty.

EXERCISES

8.1. At the beginning of World War II, the US Navy's Mark 14 torpedo (shown in Figure 8.12) had numerous performance and reliability problems. The Navy's submarines used the torpedoes in attacks on enemy warships and merchant marine vessels. The torpedo's problem had not been fixed because insufficient testing had yielded little useful information about the root causes (a weak contact pin, a faulty magnetic exploder, and a tendency to run deeper than set), and testing had been limited because the torpedoes were expensive (Kennedy, 2013). Describe the value that testing the torpedoes has. How would the beginning of a war increase this value?

8.2. Consider the coin flip game presented in Example 8.4. Show that the expected value of perfect information about the coin is $1.33. If Rose were offered a choice between paying 50 cents for one experimental coin flip or paying $1.50 for five experimental coin flips, which should she choose? Why?

8.3. Consider the coin flip game presented in Example 8.4. Show that the variance of the distribution about the probability of heads decreases after the result of one experimental coin flip. Which result (heads or tails) reduces the variance most?

8.4. This example is based on a case described by Gold (2013). Louis is considering installing solar panels on the roof of his home in Sun City, Arizona. If he goes forward, he will pay the installation firm $70 a month for 20 years but will save money on his electric bill. The amount he will save depends on the amount of sun that Sun City will receive. Every day of sun will save him $3.50. He assumes that the number of days of sun in the next 20 years will be similar to the sunshine in the past, but he is not sure how many days of sun that Sun City normally receives every year. In round numbers, he would estimate the probability distribution as follows: the probability of 200 days of sun is 15%; the probability of 250 days of sun is 25%; the probability of 300 days of sun is 40%; and the probability of 350 days of sun is 20%. What is the expected value of perfect information about how many days of sun that Sun City normally receives every year? (Consider the entire 20-year time horizon.)

8.5. Rose wants to buy a used car. She is considering two cars: (1) the first is from a car dealership whom she trusts, and (2) the second is owned by Joe, who bought the car a few years ago from someone else. The cars are equivalent to Rose. The price of the first car is $10,000, but Joe is offering to sell his car to Rose for only $9000. Rose is sure that the first car is in good shape and will not require any major repairs. She is unsure about Joe's car. She estimates that there is a probability of 0.25 that Joe's car has structural damage that will require major repairs that will cost $3000. She can buy from CARFAX a vehicle history report that will accurately tell her whether the car has any structural damage and will need these major repairs. (Thus, it is perfect information.) Rose is risk neutral in this context. What is the expected value of the perfect information in the vehicle history report?

8.6. CARFAX will charge Rose $30 for the vehicle history report. The expected value of the information in the vehicle history report depends on Rose's assessment of the probability p that Joe's car has structural damage (e.g., $p = 0.25$). For what range of this probability p is the vehicle history report worth the $30 price?

8.7. (This is based on a problem written by John Toczek.) Joe is sick. He may have a cold, the flu, or a bacterial infection. The probability of a cold is 0.5, the probability of flu is 0.2, and the probability of a bacterial infection is 0.3. If his illness is a cold, Joe will miss five days of work, which will cost him $500 (lost income). If his illness is the flu, Joe will miss 8 days of work, which will cost him $800 (lost income). If his illness is a bacterial infection (and he does not treat it), Joe will miss 12 days of work, which will cost him $1200 (lost income). Joe (who is not sure what is wrong with him) has to decide whether or not to go to the doctor. The cost to go to the doctor will be $200. If his illness is a cold or the flu, he will still miss work (the number of days missed and the lost income will not be reduced). However, if he has a bacterial infection, the doctor will prescribe antibiotics, which will cost $50, but he will miss only 2 days of work, which costs Joe $200 in lost income. Before deciding to go to the doctor, Joe can take his temperature, which may be "normal" or "high." Joe knows that, if he has a cold, then the temperature will certainly be "normal"; if he has the flu, the temperature will certainly be "high"; if he has a bacterial infection, the temperature will certainly be "high." Thus, taking his temperature is imperfect information about his illness. If it were "high," the probability of flu is 0.4, and the probability of a bacterial infection is 0.6. What is the expected value of this imperfect information (taking his temperature)?

8.8. (This problem is adapted from one in Pratt *et al.*, 1995.) Joe has inherited an option on a plot of land and must decide whether to drill on the site before the option expires or abandon the rights. He is not sure if there is oil or not. Drilling will cost $100,000 whether or not there is oil. If oil is found, then it will generate $450,000 in revenue. The likelihood of finding depends on the subsurface structure. If the subsurface structure is type A, then there is certainly oil. If the subsurface structure is type B, then the probability of finding oil is only 10%. In that area, the probability of a type A structure is 80%; the probability of a type B structure is 20%. Before deciding to drill, Joe can decide to pay for a seismic sounding that will reveal whether the subsurface structure is type A or type B. He can get the results in time to review them before making the drilling decision. The results of the seismic sounding are perfectly accurate. Joe is risk neutral in this situation. What is the expected value of the information generated by the seismic sounding?

8.9. Instead of the seismic sounding, Joe could pay a geologic consultant for a field inspection that will yield information about the subsurface structure. The consultant gives Joe the following information about the accuracy of his inspection: if the subsurface structure is truly type A, then there is a 85% probability that the inspection will indicate that subsurface structure is type A; if the subsurface structure is truly type B, then there is a 50% probability that the inspection will indicate that subsurface structure is type B. Joe is risk neutral in this situation. Joe can get the results of the inspection in time to review them before making the drilling decision. What is the expected value of the imperfect information generated by the field inspection?

8.10. This exercise is based on an example from Benjamin and Cornell (1970). As part of the process of creating a foundation for a building, Mary must decide whether to purchase a large number of 40-foot (12-m) steel piles or a large number of 50-foot (15-m) steel piles, which will be driven into ground where the depth of the bedrock is either 40 or 50 feet. The alternatives are the different piles. The possible states of nature are the different depths of the bedrock. Each alternative and state-of-nature combination has a different cost. All include the cost of the pile and the pile driving.

- If she chooses the 40-foot pile and the bedrock is 40 feet deep, then there is no additional cost.
- If she chooses the 40-foot pile and the bedrock is 50 feet deep, then the additional costs include those for the idle equipment and crew and the cost of splicing and welding the pile to the correct length. The total extra cost will be $400,000.
- If she chooses the 50-foot pile and the bedrock is 40 feet deep, then the additional cost is that for cutting off the pile to the correct length and scrapping the unnecessary piece. The total extra cost will be $100,000.
- If she chooses the 50-foot pile and the bedrock is 50 feet deep, then there is no additional cost.

Mary believes that the probability that the bedrock depth is 40 feet equals 0.7 and the probability that the bedrock depth is 50 feet equals 0.3. Mary can proceed without acquiring more information, pay for a sonic test to determine (perhaps inaccurately) the depth (and then order the piles), or pay to drill a hole that will determine accurately the depth (and then order the piles). The sonic test will cost $20,000; drilling the test hole will cost $50,000. If the bedrock is truly 40 feet deep, then the outcome of the sonic test is as follows. The probability that the test says 40 feet equals 0.6; the probability that the test says 45 feet (13.5) equals 0.3; and the probability that the test says 50 feet equals 0.1. If the bedrock is truly 50 feet deep, then the outcome of the sonic test is as follows. The probability that the test says 40 feet equals 0.1; the probability that the test says 45 feet equals 0.2; and the probability that the test says 50 feet equals 0.7. What is the expected value of the imperfect information provided by the sonic test? What is the expected value of the perfect information provided by drilling a hole? What should Mary do if she wants to minimize the expected total cost?

8.11. Consider the pile ordering problem again. Suppose that Mary has the option, if the sonic test indicates that the bedrock is 45 feet deep, to drill a hole to determine the depth of the bedrock before ordering the piles. At this point (after the sonic test indicates a depth of 45 feet), what is the value of this perfect information? Why has it changed from the amount in the previous problem? Would including this option make the sonic test the best option?

8.12. The reliability of a system of systems depends on the reliability of the systems that make up the whole system of systems. Consider, for example, a missile defense system that will, when fielded, include 3 control stations, 5 radar systems, and 12 launcher systems (Tamburello, 2013). The system is considered operational if at least two of the three control stations, three of the five radar systems, and nine of the twelve launcher systems are operational. The key reliability measure is the reliability at the end of a 24-h mission. Let R_{cs} be the reliability of a control station. Let R_{rs} be the reliability of a radar system. Let R_{ls} be the reliability of a launcher system. Let R_{SOS} be the reliability of the entire missile defense system. This can be calculated as follows:

$$T_{cs} = \sum_{i=2}^{3} \frac{3!}{i!(3-i)!} R_{cs}^{i}(1-R_{cs})^{3-i}$$

$$T_{rs} = \sum_{i=3}^{5} \frac{5!}{i!(5-i)!} R_{rs}^{i}(1-R_{rs})^{5-i}$$

$$T_{ls} = \sum_{i=9}^{12} \frac{12!}{i!(12-i)!} R_{ls}^{i}(1-R_{ls})^{12-i}$$

$$R_{SOS} = T_{cs}T_{rs}T_{ls}.$$

Suppose that there is uncertainty about R_{cs} and R_{ls}, but R_{rs} is known to be 0.99. The prior distribution for R_{cs} is as follows: $P\{R_{cs} = 0.86\} = 0.1$, $P\{R_{cs} = 0.88\} = 0.3$, $P\{R_{cs} = 0.90\} = 0.4$, $P\{R_{cs} = 0.92\} = 0.2$. The prior distribution for R_{ls} is as follows: $P\{R_{ls} = 0.92\} = 0.1$, $P\{R_{ls} = 0.94\} = 0.1$, $P\{R_{ls} = 0.96\} = 0.6$, and $P\{R_{ls} = 0.98\} = 0.2$.

The firm developing the missile defense system must decide whether to redesign the control system and launcher system (which will cost \$5 million) so that the system-of-systems reliability meets the target, which is 0.97, or go ahead with the current systems into operational testing, which will determine R_{SOS}, the reliability of the entire missile defense system. If $R_{SOS} \leq 0.97$, the firm will have to spend \$10 million to rework the systems so that the system-of-systems reliability meets the target. (Note that R_{SOS} is uncertain because of the uncertainties about R_{cs} and R_{ls}.) Before making this decision, the firm has the opportunity to conduct some tests of the control system. They can conduct 5 or 10 tests. The result of each test is a "success" or "fail." The probability of passing one test (a "success") equals R_{cs}. Based on the test results (the number of successes), which are imperfect information about R_{cs}, they will update their beliefs about R_{cs} and then decide whether to redesign or go ahead. (They will use Bayes' theorem to update their beliefs about R_{cs}.) What is the expected value of the imperfect information if they conduct five tests of the control system? What is the expected value of the imperfect information if they conduct 10 tests of the control system? (Answering these questions involves many calculations; using a spreadsheet or a programming language may be useful.)

8.13. Consider the ROC curve discussed at the beginning of this chapter (and shown in Figure 8.3). Each point on the ROC curve corresponds to a different threshold. Which points correspond to low thresholds? Which points correspond to high thresholds?

8.14. For the construction example (Examples 8.1 and 8.2), prove that the EVII always equals 0 when $p_{1|1}^{I} + p_{2|2}^{I} = 1$.

TABLE 8.4   The Distributions for the Net Present Values of the Three Alternatives.

Alternative	Mean	Standard Deviation
1	$55,000	$20,000
2	$45,000	$15,000
3	$60,000	$12,000

8.15. A food manufacturer in Baltimore, Maryland, wanted to install an automated system for checking their processed food for low-density polyethylene (LDPE) and other harmless but undesirable contaminants before it was sent to storage tanks (from which it would be piped into jars and tubs). The analysis of three different technologies considered the installation cost, the capacity (amount screened per unit time), and the cost of false negatives (which occur when the detection technology fails to detect a contaminant). Assume that the firm developed a value function based on these factors and that research into the performance and costs of these technologies yielded distributions for the net present values of the three alternatives (expressed in dollars). The parameters of these normal distributions are shown in Table 8.4. Right now, the firm would choose the third alternative (because it has the greatest expected net present value), but they are also considering conducting some tests and doing research to make sure that they choose the best one. As discussed in Section 8.6, use Monte Carlo sampling to draw samples of the alternatives' values and estimate the EVPI about the alternatives' true values.

8.16. Consider Example 8.6. What factors make another observation from system 2 or system 4 more valuable than another observation from system 1 or system 3?

REFERENCES

Bechhofer, R.E., T.J. Santer, and D.M. Goldsman. *Design and Analysis of Experiments for Statistical Selection, Screening, and Multiple Comparisons*, John Wiley and Sons, Inc., New York, 1995.

Benjamin, Jack R., and C. Allin Cornell, *Probability, Statistics, and Decision for Civil Engineers*, McGraw-Hill Book Company, New York, 1970.

Branke, Jürgen, Stephen E. Chick, and Christian Schmidt, "Selecting a Selection Procedure," *Management Science*, Volume 53, Number 12, pages 1916–1932, 2007.

Bucciarelli, Louis L., *Designing Engineers*, The MIT Press, Cambridge, Massachusetts, 1994.

Chen, Chun-H., "A Lower Bound for the Correct Subset-Selection Probability and its Application to Discrete Event Simulations," *IEEE Transactions on Automatic Control*, Volume 41, Number 8, pages 1227–1231, 1996.

Chen, Chun-H., Donghai He, Fu Michael, and Loo H. Lee, "Efficient Simulation Budget Allocation for Selecting an Optimal Subset," *INFORMS Journal on Computing*, Volume 20,
Number 4, pages 579–595, 2008.

Chick, Stephen E., and Koichiro Inoue, "New Two-Stage and Sequential Procedures for Selecting the Best Simulated System," *Operations Research*, Volume 49, Number 5, pages
732–743, 2001.

Dempster, Arthur P., "Upper and Lower Probabilities Induced by a Multivalued Mapping,"
Annals of Mathematical Statistics, Volume 38, Number 2, pages 325–339, 1967.

Gold, Russell, "Solar Groups Seek Tea-Party Support," *The Wall Street Journal*, page A3, July
3, 2013.

Government Accountability Office (GAO), "Department of Defense's waiver of competi-
tive prototyping requirement for the VXX Presidential Helicopter Replacement Program,"
GAO-13-826R, September 6, 2013. http://www.gao.gov/assets/660/657446.pdf, accessed
May 23, 2014.

Groen, Frank J., and Ali Mosleh, "Foundations of Probabilistic Inference with Uncertain
Evidence," *International Journal of Approximate Reasoning*, Volume 39, pages 49–83,
2005.

Jordaan, Ian, *Decisions under Uncertainty: Probabilistic Analysis for Engineering Decisions*,
Cambridge University Press, Cambridge, 2005.

Kennedy, Paul, *Engineers of Victory*, Random House, New York, 2013.

Kim, Seong-H., and Barry L. Nelson, "Selecting the best system," in *Handbook in Operations Research and Management Science*, Vol 13, S.G. Henderson and B.L. Nelson, editors,
Elsevier, Oxford, 2006, pages 501–534.

Lawrence, David B., *The Economic Value of Information*, Springer, New York, 1999.

Modarres, Mohammad, *Risk Analysis in Engineering: Techniques, Tools, and Trends*, CRC
Press, Boca Raton, Florida, 2006.

de Neufville, Richard, *Applied Systems Analysis*, McGraw-Hill, New York, 1990.

Nissenbaum, Dion, "Navy's Ship of the Future Faces Rough Budgetary Seas," *The Wall Street
Journal*, page A1, November 13, 2013.

Pratt, John W., Howard Raiffa, and Robert Schlaifer, *Introduction to Statistical Decision
Theory*, The MIT Press, Cambridge, Massachusetts, 1995.

Rao, Singiresu S., and Kiran K. Annamdas, "A Comparative Study of Evidence Theories in the
Modeling, Analysis, and Design of Engineering Systems," *Journal of Mechanical Design*,
Volume 135, 061006, 2013.

Shafer, Glenn, *A Mathematical Theory of Evidence*, Princeton University Press, Princeton, NJ,
1976.

Swets, John A., Robyn M. Dawes, and John Monahan, "Better Decisions Through Science,"
Scientific American, Volume 283, pages 82–87, 2000.

Tamburello, Robert N., "Evaluation-Focused Reliability Test Program Planning Methodology," Ph.D. dissertation, University of Maryland, College Park, 2013. Available online at
http://hdl.handle.net/1903/14827.

9

RISK MANAGEMENT

Learning Objectives:

After studying this chapter, the reader will be able to do the following:

1. Identify the components of a risk management process (Section 9.1).
2. Describe the role of decision making in risk management (Section 9.1).
3. Identify similarities in risk management processes (Sections 9.1 to 9.4).
4. Use the potential problem analysis process to identify risks and select risk mitigation strategies (Section 9.2).
5. Describe how preventive actions, buffers, and contingency actions reduce risk (Section 9.2).
6. Identify the similarities and differences of precursors and warnings (Sections 9.5 and 9.6).
7. Describe two types of systems for monitoring warnings and precursors (Sections 9.5 and 9.6).
8. Describe the characteristics of good risk communication (Section 9.7).
9. Write effective risk communication messages (Section 9.7).
10. Identify possible causes of bad decisions (Section 9.8).

Engineering Decision Making and Risk Management, First Edition. Jeffrey W. Herrmann.
© 2015 John Wiley & Sons, Inc. Published 2015 by John Wiley & Sons, Inc.

11. Suggest actions to prevent bad decisions (Section 9.8).
12. Describe the process of learning from failure (Sections 9.9 and 9.10).

"That's the risk you take." In everyday conversation, the term "risk" means the chance that something "bad" will happen. There are risks associated with the use and operation of the products and systems that engineers design, so engineers must consider the relevant risks and strive to reduce them. Moreover, product development processes and other activities have risks, and those who plan and manage the activities must strive to reduce those risks. At the organizational level, business continuity and disaster recovery planning is an important risk management activity. Risks can cover health and safety, financial, privacy, and other hazards, as the following examples demonstrate.

In November, 2013, the Tokyo Electric Power Company (TEPCO) began extracting 122,640 fuel rods from a nuclear reactor (Unit Number 4) at the Fukushima Daiichi nuclear plant, which was damaged in the catastrophic 2011 Tohoku earthquake and tsunami, and moving them to a nearby storage building (Harlan, 2013). Because the fuel rods were stored in a pool of water 30 m (100 feet) above the ground, the risk of a nuclear meltdown (which could occur if the concrete basin holding the water and the fuel rods were damaged) remained excessive. The goal of the operation was to eliminate that potential problem.

The operation itself, however, contained risks, which had to be reduced. The workers wore protective clothing, and the crane used had redundant wires and brakes so that it would not drop any fuel rods if another earthquake occurred. When the operation began, it was not known how many, if any, of the fuel rods were damaged, which could expose the radioactive material inside them. (For more about the decommissioning process and the associated risks, see Strickland, 2014.)

After Proctor and Gamble introduced single-dose laundry detergent capsules in Italy, a poison control center in Milan reported hundreds of cases in which young children were accidentally exposed to the detergent (sometimes after biting into the capsules). The Milan officials advised the company to change the packaging to make it opaque (which would be less attractive to children) and harder to open. After the changes were made, the rate of reported poison cases due to their capsules fell by 60% (Ng, 2013), and the company changed the packaging used in the United States as well.

Bidding for a construction project involves a financial risk. For instance, companies submitting bids for a light-rail line in Maryland could spend up to $10 million to prepare a detailed bid for the project, which would lead to a contract worth more than $6 billion over 40 years (Shaver, 2013a). A firm that bid but lost would be out millions of dollars. The firm that won the contract would certainly recover the cost of the bid but would face new financial risks. They would need to design and construct the light-rail line without delays or cost overruns because the contract would limit the reimbursement for those costs. Moreover, the annual payments for operating and maintaining the light-rail line could be reduced if the trains were not sufficiently reliable and clean.

A large power tool manufacturer discovered, after thousands of drills had been manufactured overseas but while the drills were still in transit on a ship, that these drills had an unreliable component. With a brand-new, high-profile product, a larger-than-normal failure rate would not only incur excessive warranty costs but also damage the brand's reputation. To mitigate the short-term and long-term financial risks, the company decided to reduce the likelihood that customers would buy unreliable drills by "auditing" the drills after they reached the firm's warehouse (Rinder, Maayan, private communication, 2013). This costly process involved unpacking every drill, testing its clutch settings and speeds, and then, if the drill passed the test, returning it to its original packaging before shipping it to distribution centers and retailers.

The use of unmanned aerial systems and vehicles for activities within the United States has worried privacy advocates who feared that unmanned aerial vehicles (UAVs) could acquire information that would collect private information about US citizens. To reduce that risk, the Federal Aviation Administration (FAA) planned to require test site operators to establish policies that comply with the Fair Information Practice Principles, which require providing notice, allowing choice and consent about the use of information, allowing access to the information, securing the data, and enforcing these principles (FAA, 2013; FTC, 2013).

In general, we view *risk* as the distribution of possible outcomes, which can be expressed in many ways. The Australia/New Zealand Standard for Risk Management defined *risk* as " … the possibility of something happening that impacts on your objectives. It is the chance to either make a gain or a loss. It is measured in terms of likelihood and consequence" (Standards Australia and Standards New Zealand, 2004). Thus, the risk can be described as a set of possible outcomes, and with each outcome a probability is associated. That is, the risk is a probability distribution.

The examples at the beginning of this section described the likelihood of something undesirable occurring. Although undesirable outcomes are the ones usually considered, risks also include the likelihood of something good occurring. Submitting a proposal (similar to other investments of time and resources) may have an uncertain outcome, but some of the possible outcomes are desirable.

Risk management occurs during the design of a system and in ongoing operations. Risk management leads to making decisions about whether to do something (or which action to take) to reduce risk. If one considers risk as a probability distribution over the possible outcomes, then risk management can be seen as the selection of an action to modify that probability distribution. "The purpose of risk management is to ensure that adequate measures are taken to protect people, the environment, and assets from harmful consequences of the activities being undertaken, as well as balancing different concerns, in particular, HES (health, environment, and safety) and costs. Risk management includes measures both to avoid the occurrence of hazards and reduce their potential harms" (Aven and Vinnem, 2007).

Risk management involves "coordinated activities to prevent, control, and minimize losses incurred due to a risk exposure, weighing alternatives, and selecting appropriate actions" (Modarres, 2006). That is, risk management involves decision making. In many cases, an organization will identify "a risk," by which they mean a specific bad outcome that could happen. To manage that risk, the organization must decide on one (or more) of the following actions: (1) avoiding the risk by abandoning the planned action or eliminating the root cause or the consequences, (2) reducing the likelihood of the root cause or decreasing its consequences by modifying the planned action or performing preventive measures, (3) transferring the risk to another organization, or (4) assuming (accepting) the risk without mitigating it. One can also view the possibilities as modifying the background environment, modifying the exposure, modifying the effects, and compensating for the effects (Morgan, 1981).

Unfortunately, some individuals fail to manage risk effectively. In particular, they fail to invest in measures that should reduce their risk. They underestimate or ignore the likelihood that something bad will happen; they use short time horizons (which make investments in risk reduction look undesirable); they do not have the money to invest in risk reduction; they do not want to do something that is different from the norm in their community; and they may assume that someone (such as the federal government) will compensate them if they do suffer a loss (Kunreuther, 2006). Failing to mitigate the risk of low-probability, high-impact events (e.g., by improperly underestimating the probability of a "black swan") while optimizing efficiency can lead to disaster (Taleb, 2007, 2013).

In engineering, risk management should be part of the design process from the very beginning. According to Apollo engineering and development director Maxime Faget, "If I am an engineer, I better damn well understand what reliability and what failure means, otherwise I am not an engineer....We had redundant valves, quad-redundant valves, everything else. I basically said the best way to deal with risk management is in the basic conceptual design, get the damn risk out of it" (quoted in Nelson, 2009).

Using a checklist is a simple risk management process. For example, reviewing a checklist for design for manufacturing (DFM) and design for assembly (DFA) can help a design engineer avoid manufacturing and assembly problems (or redesigning the part after the manufacturing engineers point out its objectionable features). Checklists (similar to other procedures for routine decision making) work well when the risks are well understood, and the techniques for reducing them are well known. Checklists can also guide one through a complicated process step by step, which reduces the risk of forgetting something important (Gawande, 2010).

To mitigate the risk that a manufacturing concern will make a selected styling design infeasible, which would increase the time (and cost) of developing a new vehicle, Toyota uses a *set-based concurrent engineering* process in which they create full-scale models and analyze the manufacturability of multiple styling designs (Sobek *et al.*, 1999). If one of the designs does run into serious problems, then they can use one of the remaining designs, and they would not have to start over.

A firm that designs and manufactures medical devices or other products that can be hazardous may establish a *master harms list*, which identifies all relevant harms associated with a product's component failures; it is an investment that makes the process of identifying harms more efficient (Amor, 2013). A committee of subject matter experts can generate the list for a family of similar products, but the product development team must use the list, which can be provided using a template or form so that using the list is not overly time consuming or complex. The firm must also have a process for updating the list as product designs and technologies change and new hazards appear.

More generally, designing safe products is called *system safety design*. For example, to develop a rehabilitation robot exoskeleton for treating shoulder injuries, the design engineers must design a fail-safe control system that ensures that the exoskeleton never moves the patient at an excessive velocity, never moves the patient outside their safe position range, and never applies excessive torque to the patient (Roderick and Carignan, 2007). The solution involved adding additional sensors and multiple emergency stops.

Manufacturing operations also need risk management. Clothing retailers in Europe and North America responded to disasters in the Bangladesh garment manufacturing industry by collaborating in 2013 to hire safety inspectors and create a set of standards for fire and structural safety inspections (Alliance for Bangladesh Worker Safety, 2013a). The retailers included Carter's, The Children's Place, Costco, Gap, J.C. Penney, Jordache, Kohl's, L.L. Bean, Macy's, Nordstrom, Sears, Target, and Wal-Mart. This collaboration setup a risk management process in which safety inspectors monitor the conditions in Bangladesh garment factories that supply these retailers and report unsafe conditions (based on the standards developed). The program also includes fire and building safety training programs for factory management and workers and a "hotline" for workers to report unsafe conditions. The retailers agreed to avoid purchasing garments from unsafe factories that endanger their workers (Alliance for Bangladesh Worker Safety, 2013b). Thus, the process gives factory owners an incentive to reduce the risk of a fire or structural accident, and the retailers reduce the risk that a fire or structural accident will disrupt their supply chain operations.

For extremely large construction projects, establishing and executing an effective risk management process is especially important. For instance, because cost overruns frequently occur on large infrastructure projects, the risk management process for the expansion of the Panama Canal includes a cost and schedule simulation model for predicting the likelihood of cost and schedule overruns due to a variety of risk factors (Alarcón et al., 2011).

From the problem-solving perspective, risk management is a type of decision under uncertainty because there is uncertainty about what will happen. The choice can be analyzed using the techniques discussed in Chapter 5 in order to find the "optimal" level of risk, which is the point that minimizes the total expected costs of the bad outcomes and the actions taken to reduce their likelihood. A more risk-averse approach is to identify the actions that reduce the risk to an "acceptable" level. (Section 2.9 discussed risk acceptance.) If all of the risks are acceptable, then the product or system or process is considered safe. When the uncertain outcome depends upon the actions of an intelligent adversary, game theory (discussed in Chapter 6) can be used to determine the best way to minimize risk.

From the problem-solving perspective, discussions of risk management typically assume that the context is a complicated one in which there is time for the analysis needed to understand and evaluate the risks (cf. Section 7.1). Managing risk in a simple context requires formulating appropriate policies, but managing risk in more dynamic contexts will be less formal (similar to the heuristics and recognition-primed decision-making processes discussed in Sections 7.11 and 7.12). The decision-making cycle (Section 7.7) is a type of risk management process, and the analytic-deliberative process (Section 7.8) can be used for making decisions about activities that create risks to the public. Because risk management depends upon information about the risks, the techniques for determining the value of information (discussed in Chapter 8) can be applied to improve risk management.

This chapter will consider risk management as a decision-making process that involves gathering information, evaluating alternatives, deciding what to do, and monitoring the outcome (Section 9.1). It will discuss a practical risk management process that any decision-maker can use (Section 9.2) and formal risk management processes (Sections 9.3 and 9.4). Sections 9.5 and 9.6 discuss the role of precursors and warnings. Section 9.7 describes effective risk communication techniques. Section 9.8 considers the risk of a bad decision. Sections 9.9 and 9.10 describe how one can learn from failures that do occur. Specific risk assessment techniques, which provide information about the risk of a system failure, are beyond the scope of this book.

Because risk management processes usually include monitoring operations that trigger risk mitigation actions if risks increase, risk management processes can be viewed as a type of feedback control system. The risk management process senses the risk, determines if it is unacceptably high, and takes actions (inputs) to modify the activity in a way that should reduce the risk.

9.1   RISK MANAGEMENT PROCESS

Standard descriptions of risk management typically include the following activities (shown in Figure 9.1): risk framing, risk assessment (risk identification, risk analysis, and risk evaluation), risk treatment, monitoring and review, and communication and consultation. In general, these activities require in-depth knowledge about the organization's operations and the relevant risks.

Risk framing (also known as *risk management planning*) establishes the context in which the organization operates, including legal requirements (NIST, 2011). Risk framing produces the *risk management strategy* that specifies how an organization will assess, mitigate, and monitor risks. Risk framing may determine risk tolerance, set risk acceptance criteria, and define the scope of the other risk management activities. It may identify the assumptions that affect how decision-makers assess, mitigate, and monitor risks.

Risk identification generates a list of all of the risks by considering the events, threats, and vulnerabilities that might affect the organization's objectives. This activity also identifies their causes and impacts. The risk identification may require gathering information from a variety of experts and references, especially when the product

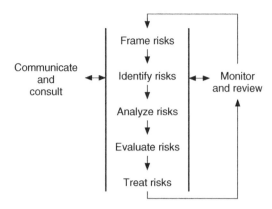

Figure 9.1 A risk management process (adapted from ISO 31000).

or system is an unfamiliar innovation. In a large, heterogeneous organization, a survey sent to key members of the primary units can be used to generate an initial list of risks. Identifying undesirable scenarios includes describing how barriers that contain hazards could fail. Hazards include chemical, biological, thermal, mechanical, electrical, ionizing radiation, nonionizing radiation, and information such as computer viruses (Modarres, 2006). In normal operations, barriers prevent exposures to these hazards, but barriers can fail to degradation or damage. Risk identification should be systematic so that it covers all aspects of an activity over its entire life cycle, and the results should be carefully organized and thoroughly documented (Goncalves and Heda, 2014).

Risk analysis examines the causes of those events, their consequences (both good and bad), and the likelihood of those consequences. Qualitative and quantitative techniques have been developed. Probabilistic risk assessment (PRA) techniques, developed initially for nuclear power applications, can be used to estimate the likelihood of undesirable scenarios and the severity of the consequences that result and to identify the components that contribute most to the risk, the uncertainties in these assessments, and the benefits of mitigation strategies (Modarres, 2006). PRA is a model-based approach that uses functional block diagrams, master logic diagrams, event trees, and fault trees to identify the initiating events and determine the consequences of those events. Risk analysis also identifies the factors (including existing controls such as inspection processes) that influence the consequences and their likelihood. When possible, expressing all of the consequences on the same scale (such as cost) makes comparing the risks easier. In some cases, it may be necessary to combine different types of consequences (such as financial, health and safety, and reputation) into an aggregate measure. At this step, a *risk reporting matrix* (risk matrix) may be generated to display the likelihood and consequences of different risks (considered separately). This type of chart is discussed more in Section 9.7. Over time, the relative likelihood of different risks may change; for instance, human errors have become a more common cause of aircraft crashes while engine failures and collisions have become less common (Achenbach *et al.*, 2014).

The ways to describe uncertainties can be grouped into six levels of sophistication, from simply identifying the potential hazards and failure modes to displaying a family of risk curves (Paté-Cornell, 1996). A wide variety of techniques for estimating likelihoods are available. In the context of product design, testing prototypes or analyzing data about past failures may be sufficient for estimating the likelihood of a component or product failure. Extreme value theory can be used to generate a distribution for the minimum or maximum of a series of independent, identically distributed (i.i.d.) random variables. When the number of variables is large, then the distribution is a Gumbel, Frechet, or Weibull extreme value distribution (Bier *et al.*, 1999). Such distributions can be useful when considering waves, floods, and other natural phenomenon in which only the most extreme (severe) event is of interest.

Risk evaluation compares the risks and the relevant risk acceptance criteria (cf. Section 2.9) to determine which are acceptable and which are unacceptable. Risk acceptance criteria include relative risk acceptance criteria and absolute risk acceptance criteria (Modarres, 2006). An absolute risk acceptance criterion specifies the acceptable risk directly. A relative risk acceptance criterion specifies the acceptable risk as a multiple of other risks. Unacceptable risks should be treated to reduce their likelihood or consequences. This activity also prioritizes the risks so that the most serious ones get proper attention and resources.

Risk treatment (also known as *risk response planning*) identifies possible ways (treatment alternatives) to mitigate (reduce) the unacceptable risks, determines how the risk treatment alternatives would mitigate the risk, and selects which treatments to implement. The categories of treatment alternatives include (1) avoiding the risk by abandoning the planned action or eliminating the root cause or the consequences, (2) reducing the likelihood of the root cause or decreasing its consequences by modifying the planned action or performing preventive measures, (3) transferring the risk to another organization, or (4) assuming (accepting) the risk without mitigating it.

For instance, consider the risks that Proctor and Gamble faced when it discovered that children were biting into single-dose laundry detergent capsules. The firm could avoid the risk by halting the production and sales of these capsules. They could reduce the likelihood of the risk by changing the packaging. They could reduce the consequences by changing the ingredients in the detergent so that it was not dangerous when consumed. They could transfer the financial risks by purchasing liability insurance that would pay for the medical treatment of anyone made ill by the detergent and for any fines or damages from legal action against the firm. Finally, they could accept the risk by changing nothing.

Monitoring and review (also known as *risk monitoring and control*) requires verifying that the selected risk mitigation actions are implemented, evaluating their impact to determine whether the risks are indeed decreasing, and looking for precursors and other signals that some risks might be increasing. For example, in the Netherlands, because the dikes that protect low-lying areas from floods can degrade over time, they must be tested periodically to determine that they still meet flood protection requirements. Inadequate dikes must be reinforced, and dike maintenance and repair in the Netherlands costs approximately 1.5 billion euros every year (Eijgenraam *et al.*, 2014).

Risk management processes occur in many domains and take on many forms. The international standard ISO 31000 (Risk Management—Principles and Guidelines) places risk management in the context of a risk management framework, which is the decision-making system that will perform risk management in an organization. The ISO standard emphasizes that an organization may use different risk management processes at different levels. The framework itself must be designed, implemented, monitored, and improved as needed. In the context of information systems, NIST (2011) described a multitiered approach in which risk management is conducted at the organization, business process, and information system levels. Different sets of personnel perform the processes at each level, and the risk management decisions at one level are influenced by the risk management decisions at the higher levels.

In the context of engineering design, the *failure mode and effects analysis* (FMEA) process is a risk management process that focuses on how the components of a product (or a system) can fail and what happens if they do (Stamatis, 2003). The FMEA process first identifies the failure modes for the components (e.g., a pipe in a machine may burst, a router in a computer network may stop working, or a machine in a production line may jam). This activity is risk identification. The process continues by determining, for each failure mode, the probability that it will occur (occurrence), the probability that it will not be detected if it occurs (detection), and the consequences on the component and on the complete product (or system) if it occurs and is not detected (severity). This activity is a type of risk analysis. Typically, these three factors (the severity, the occurrence, and the detection) are combined to get an overall risk priority number (RPN), and those failure modes with RPNs that are too large need to be addressed (treated) if possible (cost and other attributes need to be considered as well). This activity is risk evaluation. Finally, in the FMEA process, actions to address the high-priority failure modes are chosen; these actions (changes to the product or system design) should lower a failure mode's severity, reduce its likelihood, or improve the ability to detect it. This activity is risk treatment. Management must monitor the design process to make sure that these actions (design changes) are completed in a way that actually reduces the corresponding risk. This activity is risk monitoring and review.

9.2   POTENTIAL PROBLEM ANALYSIS

Kepner and Tregoe (1965) presented a practical approach to risk management that focuses on analyzing potential problems in a planned activity. Essentially, this process recommends reducing the probability of causes of bad events and reducing their impact through preventive actions, buffers, and contingency plans. This process, like other risk management processes, considers different causes of bad outcomes as independent events that can be treated (mitigated) independently. This process does not require in-depth risk assessment calculations, and it concentrates more on the risk mitigation actions, but it is conceptually the same as the process described in Section 9.1.

A *preventive action* is an action that one can take now, before the activity begins, to prevent a future problem. In particular, it is meant to eliminate or reduce the probability that the root cause of a problem occurs. Because a potential problem may have several possible causes, multiple preventive actions may be needed. A *contingency action* is an action that one can take during the activity in response to something undesirable happening to prevent additional problems (i.e., to prevent the situation from getting worse). A contingency action could be triggered by a precursor or other warning that signals a likely imminent bad event (these are discussed more in Sections 9.4 and 9.5). Providing the means to perform a contingency action may require preparation (such as installing equipment). Moreover, contingency actions may have potential problems that need to considered and prevented.

A *buffer* is a reserve of some extra resource (people, material, money, or time) that is set aside before the activity begins and used during the activity only if needed. (The buffer contains the extra resources that are above and beyond the expected amount needed.) Acquiring the buffer is a necessary preparation for the contingency action of using it if it is needed.

In general, the key is to consider the entire chain of possible events and consequences to identify opportunities to interrupt the flow of events that leads to a serious loss by eliminating or reducing the probability of something bad happening. An event tree can be a useful tool for describing the range of possibilities.

For instance, many types of equipment include a large red emergency stop button (kill switch or e-stop) that can halt the equipment if a dangerous situation occurs. Pressing the button is a contingency action, but installing this button is a necessary preparation, and training operators to use it properly is a preventive action. The button's prominence causes another potential problem: the button could be accidentally pushed, which could be costly. Installing a protective cover over the button is a preventive action, because the cover prevents an operator or bystander from accidentally pushing the button. The cover increases the time needed to push the button, however, so the protective cover must be easy to open to prevent a dangerous delay.

Dangerous activities require those involved to consider potential problems continuously. In 1969, the crew of the Apollo 9 mission tested the lunar module (shown in Figure 9.2). The mission included a test of the Apollo spacesuit, which was designed to allow the astronauts in the lunar module to return to the command module if something went wrong. Using the spacesuit to return the command module was a contingency action that could prevent a catastrophe. During the Apollo 9 mission, however, the astronaut testing the spacesuit was ill, which led the mission commander to limit spacesuit testing in order to prevent the potential problem of the astronaut being sick while in the suit, which could be life-threatening. In particular, this reduced the likelihood of the astronaut being sick.

The *potential problem analysis process* has the following steps:

1. Anticipate potential problems
2. Set priorities (based on the probability, seriousness, and invisibility of the problem)
3. Anticipate possible causes (and assess their probabilities)

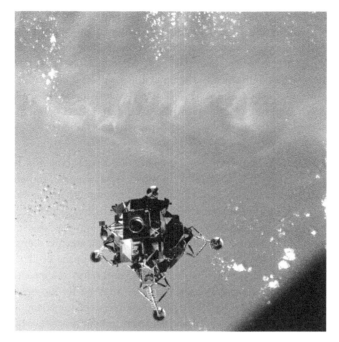

Figure 9.2 The lunar module during the Apollo 9 mission. (Photo credit: NASA.)

4. Take preventive actions
5. Set contingency actions
6. Set controls, including triggers and monitoring
7. Implement plan.

This process is guided by the following key questions:

- What could go wrong?
- What is each problem? (What, where, when, in what degree?)
- How risky is each problem?
- How serious are the consequences? (Are they fatal, damaging, or annoying?)
- How likely is it?
- What are the possible causes of each problem?
- How likely is each possible cause?
- How can a possible cause be prevented?
- How can its effects be minimized (through buffers)?
- How can the most serious potential problems be handled?

The decision-making cycle (McKay and Wiers, 2004) is a similar type of risk management process (this was discussed in Chapter 7). Recall that after resolving any crises and updating his understanding of the situation, the smart decision-maker then looks for future problems and identifies constraints that can be relaxed in order to reduce the likelihood and impact of future problems. For instance, in the domain of scheduling a factory, the scheduler considers when new products, new processes, or new materials will be introduced, when machines will be upgraded or moved, and even adverse weather. Then, the scheduler may request that critical operations be done at times when these potential problems would not affect them or when those with the knowledge and skills to solve problems will be available.

Example 9.1 Consider the design and construction of a production line to make rear axle assemblies that will be installed in trucks (tractor units). In particular, suppose that a truck manufacturing firm had been purchasing rear axle assemblies from a supplier but decided to manufacture them in its own factory when the current contract with the supplier ended. Given a budget for equipment purchases, information about the expected production (based on forecasted demand), the steps required to assemble the rear axle, the cost, the size, and capabilities of the needed equipment, and other relevant data, the production line design team selected appropriate production and material handling equipment and created a layout for the production line. As the team neared the end of the design phase and prepared to present their work to the firm's executives, they reviewed their risk management process, which included the following actions.

First, they identified a set of potential problems, including cost overruns, delays in installation and startup, insufficient capacity, and excessive work-in-process inventory. For each potential problem, they considered the possible causes and consequences.

1. Cost overruns could occur if equipment were more expensive than expected, but this was unlikely because the design team received specific quotes for the equipment that they want to install. Because large cost overruns were unlikely, this was not a serious problem.

2. Cost overruns and delays could occur if the installation and startup process ran into problems integrating the production equipment with the material handling equipment. For most of the equipment, this was unlikely, because the design team chose equipment similar to equipment used elsewhere in the factory (indeed, their equipment selection decisions included similarity as one attribute). The testing station, however, required a new type of machine, and the team believed that installing and debugging that equipment were likely to delay the overall installation and startup process. This could be a serious problem because the manufacturing firm would have no way to produce or purchase rear axles after the end of the supplier's contract.

3. The team is also concerned about the production line's capacity, which depended upon the equipment productivity (number of units per hour) being greater than demand. The first possible cause considered was lower-than-expected productivity. Their productivity estimate was based

on assumptions about the number of production hours per month, the processing times at each station, the availability of the equipment, the rate of defects, and the frequency and time of changeovers (between different versions of the axle). Because the factory has not previously assembled these axles, there is uncertainty about these quantities, and after modeling and propagating this uncertainty through their model, the team believed that it was likely that productivity would not be sufficient for the greater production volumes that were required in the second year of production. This could be a serious problem, because a shortage of rear axles would limit the sales of trucks. Greater-than-expected demand for trucks is another cause of this potential problem because the demand for rear axles would exceed the capacity of the production line. This particular cause is considered unlikely, but it would be a serious problem.

4. The team was also concerned that disruptions would lead to excessive inventory between stations. The possible causes included processing time variability and machine breakdowns. Because many of the operations are automatic, processing time variability was considered low, and other disruptions were considered unlikely because most of the equipment is familiar. The unfamiliar testing equipment was not the production bottleneck, so the excess capacity there would prevent inventory problems. Moreover, excessive inventory is not considered a serious problem (relative to the other potential problems).

From this list of potential problems, the team considered the testing station and the insufficient capacity to be the most important to address. To reduce the likelihood that the installation of the testing machine would cause delays, they proposed expediting its purchase, trying it with extra rear axles as soon as possible, and hiring a specialist to be on-call to troubleshoot the machine if necessary. These actions were meant to prevent the potential problem (delaying production). The team recommended that the firm negotiate an option to extend the supplier's contract that could be used if the installation were behind schedule 3 months before the scheduled production start date.

The design team identified some contingency plans for the potential problem of insufficient capacity. They suggested that, if necessary, extra shifts could be run because the factory had a capacity buffer (it did not run 24 hours a day), process improvement projects could be executed to improve the capacity of bottleneck equipment, and faster (but more expensive) equipment could be purchased and installed.

To monitor these risks, the team planned to create a detailed installation and startup schedule and track the progress on a daily basis so that they would know when it fell behind schedule. In addition, they planned to verify the values used in the productivity calculations during installation and startup and adjust their estimates as necessary; significantly lower values would trigger the contingency actions.

9.3   RISK MANAGEMENT GUIDE FOR DOD ACQUISITION

The process of acquiring a system for use by the Department of Defense (known as program development) requires managing risk. The most important objectives are the program cost, schedule, and performance objectives. According to the "Risk Management Guide for DOD Acquisition" (Department of Defense, 2006), a risk has three components: (1) a future root cause that, if eliminated or corrected, would prevent a potential consequence from occurring, (2) the probability (or likelihood) that the future root cause will occur, and (3) the consequence (or effect) of the future root cause.

Moreover, risks (potential problems in the future) are not the same as *issues* (problems that exist now). If the root cause has already occurred, then it has created an issue that needs to be resolved (it is no longer a risk). Program managers use resources to solve current issues (issue management) and to mitigate future potential root causes and their consequences (risk management). For example, the fact that a program is currently behind schedule is an issue (not a risk).

The risk management process includes the following activities (shown in Figure 9.3): risk identification, risk analysis, risk mitigation planning, risk mitigation plan implementation, and risk tracking. These are similar to the activities discussed in Section 9.1.

The DOD guide emphasizes the pervasive nature of risks, which can occur at any time in a program's life cycle, can affect the objectives of any stage of the program, and can be associated with every feature of a program. Every person (including the program manager, systems engineer, test manager, financial manager, contracting officer, and logistician) is responsible for identifying risks throughout the program life cycle.

Risk management planning develops the methods that will be used for identifying, assessing, and mitigating risks. These methods form the activities of the risk management process.

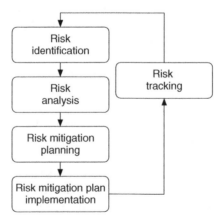

Figure 9.3   The DOD risk management process   (adapted from Department of Defense, 2006).

9.4 RISK MANAGEMENT AT NASA

The National Aeronautics and Space Administration (NASA) Risk-Informed Decision Making Handbook (NASA, 2010) discusses the coordination of risk-informed decision making (RIDM) and continuous risk management (CRM). RIDM is a decision-making process for key decisions that "uses a diverse set of performance measures (some of which are model-based risk metrics) along with other considerations within a deliberative process to inform decision making." These "key decisions," which include system design decisions, supplier selection, and budget allocation, are difficult because of their significance, the complexity of understanding the consequences, the presence of substantial uncertainty, multiple criteria, and multiple stakeholders.

The RIDM process has six steps (1–6) organized into three parts (I–III):

I. Identification of alternatives
   1. Understand stakeholder expectations and derive performance measures
   2. Compile feasible alternatives
II. Risk analysis of alternatives
   3. Set the framework and choose the analysis methodologies
   4. Conduct the risk analysis and document the results
III. Risk-informed alternative selection
   5. Develop risk-normalized performance commitments
   6. Deliberate, select an alternative, and document the decision rationale.

Five roles support the RIDM process: (1) stakeholders, who are affected by the decisions but are outside the organization, (2) risk analysts, who quantify the risks in the areas of safety, performance, cost, and schedule, (3) subject matter experts, who provide information about specific topics, (4) technical authorities, who provide oversight in the areas of engineering, safety and mission assurance, and health and medicine, and (5) the decision-maker, who has the responsibility to make the decision.

The CRM process identifies, analyzes, tracks, communicates, and controls risks. According to NASA, "RIDM and CRM are complementary risk management processes that operate within every organizational unit. Each unit applies the RIDM process to decide how to meet objectives and applies the CRM process to manage risks associated with implementation. In this way, RIDM and CRM work together to provide comprehensive risk management throughout the entire life cycle of the project."

In particular, RIDM "initializes" CRM by providing the risk analysis for the alternative that is being implemented. CRM then tracks these risks while attempting to reduce them to acceptable levels. Ideally, risks should decrease over time as controls are implemented and uncertainties are resolved. CRM, in turn, leads to further decision making when new risks appear and new alternatives for risk mitigation are developed.

9.5 PRECURSORS

In July, 2013, during a spacewalk outside the International Space Station (ISS), an astronaut experienced water in the helmet of his spacesuit (shown in Figure 9.4); this was an unexpected event, but the ISS crew concluded that the problem was the drink bag, which was replaced. A week later, during the next spacewalk, the same astronaut, wearing the same spacesuit, "experienced a large amount of water [1 to 1.5 liters] inside the helmet area, originating somewhere behind the crewmember's head near the neck/lower head area. The presence of this water created a condition that was life threatening" (NASA, 2013/2014). Fortunately, the astronaut was able to return to the ISS and remove the spacesuit before any harm occurred. The water problem on the first spacewalk was a precursor; it indicated the presence of a hazard never before seen. Unfortunately, the root cause of the problem was not identified, and the problem occurred again; fortunately, no one was harmed, and a more thorough failure analysis was conducted.

A precursor indicates that the likelihood of a hazard has increased, but that does not guarantee that it will happen. For instance, should a plume of ash automatically trigger evacuations? Popocatepetl (the "smoking mountain") is a volcano about 64 km (40 miles) from Mexico City, Mexico. It had a violent eruption in 2000, so, in April, 2012, when it began to spew rock and ash, Mexican authorities raised the volcano alert level and urged citizens to monitor the situation closely and prepare for possible evacuations. No violent eruption occurred, however, and the alert level was reduced in September, 2012. (It did erupt several times in 2013.)

Manufacturing firms depend on knowing the prices of their raw materials in order to make good product design and production planning decisions. When a fire destroyed the largest sugar terminal in a Brazilian port in 2013, analysts saw that

Figure 9.4 Extravehicular mobility unit (EMU) with water in helmet during post-EVA 23 screening test. (Photo credit: NASA, 2013/2014.)

the resulting decrease in exports would likely increase prices in the future after a year in which sugar production was high due to dry weather (Josephs, 2013). The destruction of the terminal was a precursor for higher sugar prices.

Example 9.2 In some cases, the increased risk can estimated quantitatively, as it was when an inspection at the Davis–Besse nuclear power plant in Ohio revealed some leaks. (In the following, "accident sequence precursor" is abbreviated as "ASP," and "core damage probability" is abbreviated as "CDP.") According to the Nuclear Regulatory Commission (2004/2013), "During an inspection of the control rod drive mechanism (CRDM) nozzles in February 2002, the licensee discovered that three nozzles were leaking through axial cracks, and that one of the leaking nozzles had begun to develop a circumferential crack. During repair of one of the leaking nozzles, the nozzle became loose in the reactor pressure vessel (RPV) head. Subsequent investigation revealed that a cavity had formed around that nozzle in the low-alloy steel portion of the RPV head, leaving only the stainless steel-clad material as the reactor coolant pressure boundary over an area of approximately 16.5 square-inches [107 square centimeters]."

"The conditions at Davis–Besse were identified by the licensee and reported to the NRC before any radioactive material was released or any accident or event occurred. The NRC required the plant to remain shutdown until all significant deficiencies had been corrected."

"The ASP analysis calculated a ΔCDP of six in one thousand (6×10^{-3}) from the degraded conditions that existed at Davis–Besse before February 2002. Based on the preliminary analysis, this event would be a 'significant' precursor which is the highest category (i.e., an increase in core damage probability of greater than one chance in a thousand) in the Agency's annual Performance and Accountability Report to Congress. This risk at Davis–Besse represents one of the higher risk conditions analyzed by the ASP program."

Precursors are a source of valuable information for risk management. Understanding the causes of precursors and their frequency can help one assess a risk and identify possible risk treatments (Bier *et al.*, 2004). Not all precursors lead to accidents, but precursors occur more often, so it might be easier to estimate their rate, which can be used to estimate the accident rate. Understanding why some precursors lead to accidents and others do not (the *exacerbating factors* and the *mitigating factors*) can provide valuable insights. The general process of identifying accident precursors includes the following activities (Tamuz, 2004):

1. Aggregating data about precursors
2. Detecting signals of potentially dangerous events
3. Gathering information about the events
4. Interpreting and analyzing this information to classify events and look for patterns
5. Making decisions and implementing changes that reduce risk

6. Compiling and storing data for later use
7. Disseminating information to those who are at risk.

Within this general risk management framework, there are many different methods for identifying accident precursors, and different systems have been constructed in health care, aviation, and nuclear power generation. The choice of how to gather information is a key distinction between different systems. Some systems, such as the Aviation Safety Reporting System (ASRS), use a voluntary reporting system. Others use a surveillance system that directly observes operations.

In a voluntary reporting system, those who observe safety-related events (unsafe conditions or unusual situations that are precursors) file reports about what happened. Gathering useful information requires designing a system that has few barriers to reporting. For instance, punishing those who report violations of safety rules would reduce the number of reports; providing some limited immunity, however, helps create a culture in which learning can occur and risks are reduced (Tamuz, 2004).

Surveillance systems tend to have more reliable counts of safety-related events (because they do not rely on humans choosing to file reports). For instance, the FluView report (CDC, 2014) provides data about influenza testing, hospitalizations, and mortality on a weekly basis. Unfortunately, the precise statistics generated by surveillance systems provide no narratives for understanding the factors that lead to safety-related events.

The value of a precursor can be determined by considering the Bayesian network that relates the precursor, intermediate events, and system failure. Given this information, it is possible to determine the probability of system failure if the precursor does not occur and the probability of system failure if the precursor does occur. Moreover, it is possible to determine which intermediate event is more likely if system failed and the precursor did occur.

Example 9.3   Consider a system S that has two subsystems (A and B). If either subsystem fails, then system S fails. In addition, there is a precursor P, which affects the likelihood of A or B failing. That is, the probability that subsystem A fails depends on whether P has occurred, and the probability that subsystem B fails depends on whether P has occurred. Figure 9.5 shows the Bayesian network for this situation. For introductions to Bayesian networks, see Pearl (1988) and Jensen and Nielson (2007). The following calculations can be done using only the definition of conditional probabilities, however. Software such as the Bayes Net Toolbox is available for doing the calculations automatically and more efficiently, but evaluating large networks can be a computational challenge even with modern software packages.

The following information about the relationships is given: the probability that P occurs during one operation is 0.05. The conditional failure probabilities for subsystems A and B are given in Table 9.1. From this, it is possible to determine that the probability that system S fails during operation equals 0.619. If P does not occur, the probability that system S fails equals 0.6. If P does occur, however, the probability that system S fails equals 0.98.

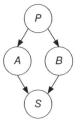

Figure 9.5   The Bayesian network for a situation in which a precursor P affects the states of two subsystems A and B, which affect the state of the system S.

TABLE 9.1   **The Conditional Probabilities for Subsystems A and B.**

	A Fails	A Operates	B Fails	B Operates
P	0.9	0.1	0.8	0.2
Not P	0.2	0.8	0.5	0.5

Each value is the conditional probability that A (or B) fails (or operates) given that P has occurred (not occurred).

Moreover, consider the investigation of a failed system. Given that system S failed, suppose that Rose, the owner of the system, wants to know which subsystem failed so that it can be repaired or replaced. Knowing which subsystem failure is more likely will reduce the expected time looking for the problem. Given that S failed, the probability that A failed equals 0.380, and the probability that B failed equals 0.832 (it is possible that both failed). If S failed and P did not occur, the probability that A failed equals 0.333, and the probability that B failed equals 0.833. If S failed and P did occur, however, the probability that A failed equals 0.918, and the probability that B failed equals 0.816. Thus, observing the precursor significantly changes the likelihood that subsystem A failed. If she knows that P occurred, then Rose is more likely to find the failure if she starts by checking subsystem A. (All of the probabilities listed here are determined by applying Bayes' theorem.)

9.6   WARNINGS

Warnings are part of the information flow in risk management (and are related to risk communication). They provide risk managers with information that should make them aware that a problem has occurred (and a contingency plan should be initiated) or that the root cause of a risk has become more likely (i.e., the probability has increased, or the distribution of the consequence has changed). Some warnings are messages that something bad has happened. For example, public health and homeland security officials rely upon various environmental sensors and syndromic surveillance systems for detecting events that would signal a bioterrorism attack. Homeowners depend on smoke detectors to notify them if a fire has started (although other less-dangerous events, such as burned food, can create smoke as well). Other warnings, such as weather advisories, are about precursors. They indicate that the risks have increased. A report about the results of a bridge inspection may contain a warning that corrosion or other factors have weakened structural components, and the risk of a bridge collapse has, therefore, increased.

A warning system can be highly automated, with alarms that are generated automatically whenever a sensor (or combination of sensors) has a reading that signals an imminent threat. A smoke detector starts beeping when smoke particles enter it, and a tsunami warning system issues alerts when a detection buoy senses extraordinary temperatures and pressures from the bottom of the sea.

A good warning system will communicate information quickly enough that the risk manager can act by implementing a contingency plan or employing a buffer in time to prevent serious consequences. In addition, a good warning system will provide accurate information about the threat.

Unfortunately, warnings are often imperfect information. That is, there can be false positives (sounding an alarm when it is unnecessary) and false negatives (failing to alarm when necessary). (These were also discussed in Chapter 8.)

The measures of *sensitivity* and *specificity* can be used to evaluate a warning system or other similar imperfect information. The measures depend on data about the number of true positives, false positives, true negatives, and false negatives, collected over time or for a population.

The number of actual positives equals the number of true positives plus the number of false negatives. The sensitivity equals the number of true positives divided by the number of actual positives. The number of actual negatives equals the number of true negatives plus the number of false positives. The specificity equals the number of true negatives divided by the number of actual negatives. The *positive predictive value* (PPV) equals the number of true positives divided by the total number of true positives and false positives. The PPV measures the likelihood that result is true given a positive test result.

Let TP be the number of true positives. Let FP be the number of false positives. Let TN be the number of true negatives. Let FN be the number of false negatives. Then, we can express the sensitivity and specificity as follows:

$$\text{Sensitivity} = TP/(TP + FN).$$

$$\text{Specificity} = TN/(TN + FP).$$

$$\text{PPV} = TP/(TP + FP).$$

The designer of a warning system that relies upon thresholds to determine whether to issue a warning must consider how much evidence is needed to conclude that a threat is real (Choo, 2009). A lower rate of false negatives (a greater sensitivity) will unfortunately increase the rate of false alarms (false positives that decrease specificity).

The best threshold could be determined by considering the various costs. The cost of a false positive depends on the resources that are mobilized when an alarm sounds, but the cost of a false negative depends on the harm and damage that occurs when a real threat is missed. The warning system designer can set a threshold that minimizes the expected cost (or maximizes expected utility).

A detection system's receiver operating characteristic (ROC) curve describes how increasing the detection probability is correlated with increasing the probability of false alarms. Such curves were initially developed in studies of radar workers in World War II (Washburn, 1989).

Given certain assumptions about the noise in the signal that is used to detect the threat, a detection system can be analyzed as follows: let x be the scaled alarm threshold ($-\infty < x < \infty$), let $\Phi(x)$ be the cumulative distribution function of a standard normally distributed random variable, and let d be the detection system's signal-to-noise ratio (Washburn, 1989). The probability of false alarms equals $1 - \Phi(x)$, and the detection probability equals $1 - \Phi(x - \sqrt{d})$. The value d is also the reciprocal of the squared coefficient of variation (SCV) of the signal (which is random due to the noise). A larger value of d is desirable because it implies that one can tune the detection system so that it can achieve a larger detection probability with a low probability of false alarms.

9.7 RISK COMMUNICATION

In a risk management process, those who provide information about alternatives to decision-makers often face the problem of describing the uncertainties about the outcomes. This is the general problem of *risk communication*. For example, a research & development (R&D) department may need to explain that the performance of an advanced technology (which the firm hopes will actually work and be ready in time for the development of a new product or manufacturing process) is not guaranteed; there is a chance that it will not work, and there is a chance that it will be delayed. Failing to describe this uncertainty may lead to overly high expectations, which could cause future problems for the R&D department if the technology does not work or is not ready on time (Matheson and Matheson, 2007).

The following are the *elements of risk communication* (Modarres, 2006):

- The nature of the risk
- The nature of the benefits
- The uncertainties in the risk assessment
- The risk management options available.

The nature of the risk describes the hazard, its size, and its severity; the urgency of the situation; whether the risk is increasing or decreasing; and the relative risk of different locations and populations. The nature of the benefits describes who will benefit from accepting the risk and the quantity and quality of the expected benefits.

Describing the uncertainties in the risk assessment requires explaining the methods used to assess the risk and the uncertainties and the importance of the uncertainties. Describing the risk management options includes reviewing the actions taken so far to reduce the risk, listing the actions that individuals and organizations can take to reduce their risk, and the expected effectiveness (reduction in risk) and costs of these actions.

There may be multiple ways to describe a risk. For instance, after Typhoon Haiyan struck the Philippines in November, 2013, the risk of typhoons in that country was presented on three maps by Clark et al. (2013): the first showed the paths of 27 typhoons that struck the nation in the last 5 years, the second showed the relative number of typhoon strikes in different parts of the country, and the third showed the prevalence of steep slopes (which make landslides more likely) in different parts of the country. In addition, they included a chart of the number of deaths from storms per year from 1970 to 2012. In three of those 43 years, the number of deaths exceeded 2,000; in 32 years, the number of deaths was less than 1,000. These graphics expressed the typhoon risk in different ways. The number of typhoons and deaths are absolute measures, while the other two maps expressed the relative risk of different provinces.

A natural mode for communicating about an uncertain event is to use a word that describes the likelihood that the event will occur. Such words include the terms "doubtful," "unlikely," "possible," and "almost certain." Unfortunately, although some are more imprecise than others, these words convey vague uncertainties. For example, although the term "tossup" describes a probability that may be between 0.4 and 0.6, the term "likely" describes a probability that may be between 0.5 and 1.0, and the terms "unlikely," "improbable," and "doubtful" all describe the same range of probabilities (Wallsten et al., 1986).

A basic problem in risk communication is the challenge of representing an uncertain value. When a probability distribution for the uncertain value is available, there are multiple ways to represent it, including a probability density function (e.g., the "bell curve" of a normally distributed random value), a cumulative distribution function, or a box plot (a box-and-whiskers plot). Because it simplifies the distribution to a small number of values, a box plot is a useful way to compare multiple distributions. For instance, Figures 9.6 and 9.7 show the cumulative distribution functions and box plots for four normal distributions that have the means and variances listed in Table 8.3. (In Figure 9.7, the ends of the whiskers are the 2nd and 98th percentiles of the distribution, but other varieties of box plots are also used.)

The most challenging version of risk communication is concerned with how government agencies and others describe risks to the public. Weather forecasters, for instance, have to analyze the output of different weather models (which may give different results) and describe what might happen to those who are reading, watching, and listening. The messages are expressed in familiar terms such as "a 40 percent chance of rain tomorrow," "a frost advisory," and "a tornado warning has been issued for our area." Among the decision-makers are the residents who must decide what

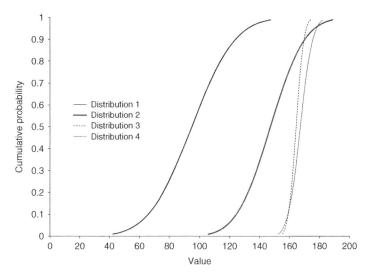

Figure 9.6   Cumulative distribution functions for the four distributions in Table 8.3.

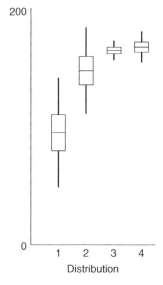

Figure 9.7   Box plots for the four distributions in Table 8.3. The ends of the "whiskers" represent the 2nd and 98th percentiles.

to wear, how to protect their plants and crops, and whether to take shelter in a basement or cellar. Other decision-makers include emergency managers who must decide whether to activate emergency plans.

The National Highway Traffic Safety Administration (NHTSA) provides 5-Star Safety Ratings, which are a qualitative, relative risk measure, to share information about the crash protection and rollover safety of new vehicles (NHTSA, 2014). A car that has a rating with more stars is safer than a car that has a rating with fewer stars.

The University of Maryland Police Department issues "crime alerts" that are "important notifications for recent crimes reported in the campus and surrounding area." The department also generates uniform crime reports that are delivered monthly for the FBI's crime reporting program. Information about particular crimes and statistics about criminal activity over time provide the students, staff, and faculty with information about the risk of being a victim of crime so that they can decide what to do and how to be safe.

In general, risk communication should follow these fundamental rules (Modarres, 2006):

1. Accept and involve the public as a legitimate partner
2. Plan carefully and evaluate performance
3. Listen to the public's specific concerns
4. Be honest, frank, and open
5. Co-ordinate and collaborate with other credible sources
6. Meet the needs of the media
7. Speak clearly and with compassion.

The following factors affect the effectiveness of risk communication (Brandeau *et al.*, 2008): whether the officials providing information are trusted, credible, polite, respectful, and confident; whether the message is accurate, precise, accessible, and consistent, and whether it suggests taking action or just provides information; the relative risk of subgroups; and the age, special needs, information needs, economic status, language, alertness, and preparedness of the public.

Certain practices characterize effective risk communication (Modarres, 2006):

- Know the audience and the best way to reach them
- Involve experts who can explain the risk assessment
- Involve people with expertise in risk communication
- Provide information from credible sources
- Share the responsibility for effective risk communication with all involved parties
- Distinguish between science and value judgments
- Use a transparent, open risk analysis process
- Provide perspective for the risk by comparing the risk to similar risks.

The way that risk information is communicated affects how individuals use it when deciding what to do (Zhong and Kim, 2011). The following are the key attributes: (1) the information source and frequency, (2) the message content, (3) the message style, and (4) the transmission channel. Information from official, familiar information sources that is repeated in a predictable way is more likely to change the perception of danger. The information should answer the following questions: What is the risk? Which geographical area or location is threatened? What protective actions are possible? When does (or will) the risk occur? How much time is left before the impact? Who is issuing the warning? Information communicated with an appropriate message style is more likely to change the perception of danger and provoke responses. The message style includes its consistency, continuity, certainty, urgency, sufficiency, specificity, clarity, and accuracy. Although broadcast media (newspapers, television, radio, and social media) are convenient for government agencies and others who need to reach a large number of people quickly, information delivered through personal channels influences risk perception more.

In the health care setting, communicating risks to patients is much different, of course, because there is a very small audience, but it remains challenging (Paling, 2003). If a patient believes that the physician is both competent and caring, the patient will trust the physician and will be more likely to understand the risks. Visualizing probabilities is an important task. Paling presented some innovative techniques, and Gigerenzer and Edwards (2003) emphasized the use of natural frequencies. For instance, to discuss the quality of a mammogram, they suggest, "Eight out of every 1000 women have breast cancer. Of these eight women with breast cancer seven will have a positive result on mammography. Of the 992 women who do not have breast cancer some 70 will still have a positive mammogram."

When discussing a low-probability, high-consequence extreme event, it is important to communicate clearly its likelihood without using expected values that may conceal its severity (Bier *et al.*, 1999). This allows relevant risk acceptance criteria to be considered. Because of risk aversion, an activity in which the probability of an extremely bad outcome is too large will be rejected even if the expected losses are low. Moreover, there may be uncertainty about the event's likelihood, which should encourage the risk manager to collect more information and generate a better estimate or avoid the activity by invoking the precautionary principle (which was discussed in Chapter 2).

A risk reporting matrix such as the one shown in Figure 9.8 is often used to compare different risks along the dimensions of likelihood and consequences. (Figure 9.8 uses the format described in Department of Defense, 2006.) Associated with each combination of likelihood and consequences is the relative risk level ("low," "moderate," or "high"). Classifying each risk using this type of matrix allows one to distinguish the most critical risks, which need mitigation if at all possible, from those that can be accepted. Risk mitigation activities should reduce the likelihood or consequences of the risks until they are all acceptable, and risk reporting matrices can be used to visualize the changes.

Within an organization that uses such table, the likelihood rows should have standard values. In the version for DOD acquisition, "1" is called "not likely" and means approximately 10%. The value "2" is called "low likelihood" and means approximately 30%. The value "3" is called "likely" and means approximately 50%. The value "4" is called "highly likely" and means approximately 70%. The value "5" is called "near certainty" and means approximately 90%. Others use different scales with a different number of distinct values and ranges from "impossible" to "frequent."

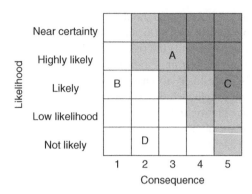

Figure 9.8 A risk reporting matrix (adapted from Department of Defense, 2006) with four hypothetical root causes. The white boxes are "low risk," the light grey boxes are "medium risk," and the dark grey boxes are "high risk."

The scale of consequences should also be well defined. In the version for DOD acquisition, a "1" means that the consequence will have minimal or no impact on technical performance, schedule, or cost. A value of "2" is a small (e.g., 1%) increase in cost, a minor reduction in technical performance, or a delay that is so short that the program will still be able to meet key dates. This continues to a value of "5," which is a severe degradation in technical performance (the system cannot meet key performance requirements), the inability to meet key program milestones, or a cost increase that exceeds the allowable budget. Other scales describe the consequences as "negligible," "marginal," "critical," and "catastrophic" or by the level of morbidity and mortality: "none," "minor," "severe," and "deadly."

In Figure 9.8, four hypothetical root causes are noted. Risk A denotes a root cause that is "highly likely" and has consequences that correspond to a value of "3." This combination is in the moderate risk range. Risk B denotes a root cause that is "likely" and has consequences that correspond to a value of "1." This combination is in the low risk range. Risk C denotes a root cause that is "likely" and has consequences that correspond to a value of "5." This combination is in the high risk range. Risk D denotes a root cause that is "Not Likely" and has consequences that correspond to a value of "2." This combination is in the low risk range.

Other visualizations of risk include probability distributions, the imposed constraint risk matrix, and the band-aid chart (NASA, 2010). A band-aid chart (shown in Figure 9.9) is similar to a box plot, but the horizontal width of the boxes represents key percentiles of the distribution. A process decision program chart can be used to show the risks associated with different tasks in a project and the countermeasures being used to mitigate the risks (Straker, 1995).

Some risk visualizations can be quite bad, unfortunately, as Example 9.4 shows.

Example 9.4 A pamphlet about invasive pneumococcal disease printed by a pharmaceutical company included a graphic that was intended to show that adults with diabetes, heart disease, and lung disease have a greater risk for developing invasive

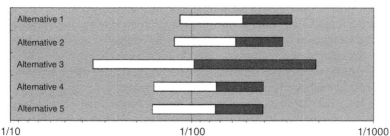

Figure 9.9   A notional band aid chart that shows the distribution of a performance measure (*X*) for different alternatives. (Image credit: NASA, 2010.)

pneumococcal disease than healthy adults (Merck Sharp & Dohme Corp., 2013). The graphic used icons of different sizes for the different risks. (The icon was a generic male figure similar to those used on signs for restrooms.) The national rate for inva- sive pneumococcal disease is 12.9 per 100,000 (CDC, 2011/2014). According to the pamphlet, the risk for adults with diabetes is three times the risk for healthy adults, but the icon used for adults with diabetes was twice as tall as the icon used for healthy adults (and thus had four times the total area). The risk for adults with heart disease (and adults with lung disease) is six times the risk for healthy adults, but the icon used for adults with heart disease (and the icon for adults with lung disease) was nearly four times as tall as the icon used for healthy adults (and thus had nearly 16 times the total area). The sizes of the icons are larger for the groups with higher risk, but the dimensions (the height and the area) did not correspond to the quantitative change in risk.

9.8   MANAGING THE RISK OF A BAD DECISION

When evaluating a decision retrospectively, it is important to distinguish between the choice and the outcome. It may be impossible to eliminate all disastrous (or even unwanted) outcomes, and, in that case, a bad outcome is possible. Although the mul- tifaceted nature of rationality makes it difficult to call a decision absolutely irrational (as discussed in Chapter 2), it is sometimes possible to see, with the benefit of hind- sight, where a decision-maker went wrong. (Of course, sometimes a decision-maker performs poorly but is lucky enough to avoid a disaster.)

The features of a good decision include the six elements of *decision quality*: an appropriate frame for the decision; creative, feasible alternatives; useful, reliable information; clearly specified objectives; logical and correct reasoning; and the decision-maker's commitment to action (cf. Matheson and Matheson, 2007).

Bad decisions have many causes because decision making is complex. A decision is the selection of the best alternative; a decision is a process of searching for alterna- tives and gathering information; and a decision is part of a decision-making system.

Avoiding bad decisions, therefore, would seem to require a large amount of effort. One could, in principle, spend a lot of time studying the decision to be made to make sure that the formulation is the correct one (in the context of the organization), that the process being used is the right one, and that the alternative selected is indeed the best one. Spending so much effort on every decision would be extreme, however, and would likely lead to "analysis paralysis." Engineers must make many decisions every day and cannot analyze every one of them the same way.

When the stakes are high, however, more care is needed, and a risk management approach may provide a way to balance the need to make a decision efficiently and avoid a bad decision. As discussed in Sections 9.1 and 9.2, managing risk involves identifying the risks (the potential problems), analyzing them (determining their likelihood and consequences), evaluating them (determining which are acceptable), treating (mitigating) the unacceptable risks by taking preventive actions or preparing contingency plans, and monitoring the risks as the decision-making process proceeds.

Two important questions follow: What are the risks in decision making? What can be done to mitigate these risks? Studies of decision-making failures have identified a variety of problems that can occur, and those wishing to make better decisions can move in the right direction by avoiding these. The following paragraphs discuss the problems that can occur in different parts of the decision-making process.

9.8.1 Selecting a Process

Problems can occur when decision-makers choose inappropriate decision-making processes or manage them poorly. Some decision-makers have a limited ability to perform their job because they do not know proper decision-making methods (Simon, 1997). Some decision-makers choose a decision making style that is inappropriate for the situation (Snowden and Boone, 2007). Different decision-making contexts are discussed in Chapter 7. In general, an idea imposition process (discussed later in this chapter) is an inferior decision-making process (Nutt, 2002). Merchant (2013) described how companies typically misuse their budgeting process, which leads to obsolete plans, inappropriate allocations of funds, wasteful spending, and other poor decisions.

9.8.2 Managing the Process

Some decision-makers do not understand the information flow and decision making within the organization and do not understand their role in the decision-making system. They fail to maintain information responsibility (Drucker, 1988). In some cases, subordinates who have insufficient clout or inadequate enthusiasm to do a good job may manage the decision-making process (Nutt, 2002). Some decision-makers fail to involve or adequately consult all of the interested and affected parties, who therefore have little opportunity to contribute to the deliberations, may not understand the rationale for the decision, and may consider the responsible organization to be biased (Stern and Fineberg, 1996).

In product development organizations that use formal design reviews (or "gates") to control the progress of projects, some senior managers cancel gate meetings, fail to show up, fail to make decisions and allocate resources, and allow some projects to bypass gates (Cooper, 2008).

Some decision-makers fail to define the scope of tasks allocated to others and do not determine the scope of tasks assigned to themselves (Busby, 2001). For example, a study at an automobile company concluded that 64% of those on product development teams believed that their teams had the right to decide which features will be standard; unfortunately, 83% of those in the marketing group believed that their group had that right. Similarly, 77% of those on product development teams believed that they had the right to decide which colors will be offered, while 61% of those in the marketing group believed that their group had that right (Rogers and Blenko, 2006).

Decision making sometimes takes too much time because (1) some decision-makers guard their power by insisting on making too many decisions, which delays the process; (2) some decision-makers are afraid of choosing the wrong thing (and receiving the blame) and therefore postpone decisions until there is enough information to identify the best alternative; and (3) some decision-makers postpone decisions because they do not know how to deal with complicated decisions (Russo, 2006). Others, however, rush their decisions (Nutt, 2004).

When used by an analyst, quantitative decision aids (including decision analysis and probabilistic risk assessment) may yield results that the decision-maker does not use (Brown, 2005). Of course, analysts may not be skilled due to a lack of training or ability, but a more fundamental problem occurs because the analyst has many priorities:

- Analysts are interested in using methods that they understand and with which are comfortable
- Analysts want to maintain their professional standing
- Analysts want to receive an economic gain
- Analysts want to serve the decision-maker.

The first three of the above could lead to a mismatch between the analyst's priorities and the decision-maker's priorities. Inappropriate priorities for the analyst can lead to the following types of problems: asking the wrong question, overlooking relevant knowledge, using bad data, producing inappropriate output, and miscommunicating the output.

9.8.3 Generating Alternatives

Some decision-makers prematurely accept the first idea that appears and fail to search for other, possibly innovative (but not well-known) alternatives (Nutt, 2002). They may do this when the idea is suggested by a powerful person whom they do not want to disregard or when they are overwhelmed and just want to move forward (Nutt, 2003). Some decision-makers are unable to generate alternatives without seeing preexisting solutions (Nutt, 2004). Some fail to generate alternatives because they rush their decisions (Nutt, 2004) or consider only the political considerations (Nutt, 2002). Groups may generate and consider too few alternatives due to groupthink (Janis, 1971).

9.8.4 Selecting Objectives

The objectives of the decision-maker and the corresponding attributes used to evaluate alternatives are extremely important. Unfortunately, the presence of multiple factors that influence decision-making can lead to confusion and different interpretations of what designers should be doing. For example, a study of Volvo engineers responsible for the final development of new engines revealed that some engineers believed that their job was to make the engine meet performance specifications, a second set thought that they needed to resolve tradeoffs between performance categories, and a third set focused on providing the customer with a good driving experience through a superior engine (Sandberg, 2001).

Some decision-makers pursue a misleading, unstated, or unknown direction or pursue a proposed direction without verifying that the stakeholders agree with that direction (Nutt, 2002). Ignoring the values of the stakeholders may lead to unethical choices. Some decision-makers use a relevant but incomplete set of objectives (Drucker, 1967). Some decision-makers use too many objectives, which leads to excessive and unproductive discussions about their relative importance (Matheson and Matheson, 2007).

As discussed in Chapter 10, the mechanisms linking decision-makers to the overall corporate goals are constraints and incentives such as schedules, rewards, and penalties. That is, the decision-making system is "loosely coupled." This simplifies decision making because individual decision-makers do not have to spend time trying to decipher possibly complex relationships to determine exactly how the alternatives in front of them affect overall corporate goals, but this distance allows individual decision-makers to use inappropriate objectives and rules, which leads to short-sighted actions. Moreover, decision-makers may have conflicts among loyalties to the individual, the unit, and the organization (Simon, 1997).

9.8.5 Evaluating Alternatives

Selecting the right alternative depends on evaluating the alternatives correctly and considering the uncertainties that exist. Inaccurate evaluations arise from many sources. Some decision-makers use information that is inaccurate or inadequate to assess the risks or use information that does not address the concerns of the interested and affected parties (Stern and Fineberg, 1996). Some decision-makers believe that a new situation is similar to the ones that previously occurred, and some ignore important constraints or minimum goals (Drucker, 1967). Others ignore ethical dilemmas such as conflicts of interest (Nutt, 2002). Some decision-makers have limited knowledge about the facts and considerations that are relevant (Simon, 1997). Because of "bounded awareness," some decision-makers fail to see, seek, use, or share relevant and accessible information (Bazerman and Chugh, 2006). They do not tell others the assumptions that they can make, the normal requirements, and the exceptional circumstances that can occur, and they compound the error by failing to involve others in the decision (Busby, 2001). The members of a group may fail to share information due to groupthink or ignore the information presented by individuals (cf. Chapter 4).

Pattern recognition and emotional tagging processes can distort decision-making. Campbell *et al.* (2009) identified three problems that affect the evaluation process:

1. Inappropriate self-interest: "the presence of inappropriate self-interest typically biases the emotional importance we place on information, which in turn makes us readier to perceive the patterns we want to see. Research has shown that even well-intentioned professionals, such as doctors and auditors, are unable to prevent self-interest from biasing their judgments of which medicine to prescribe or opinion to give during an audit."
2. Distorting attachments: Decision-makers become "attached to people, places, and things, and these bonds can affect the judgments we form about both the situation we face and the appropriate actions to take." Attachments are certainly important in personal relationships, but they can interfere in technical and professional situations where more objective criteria should govern decision-making.
3. Misleading memories: "These are memories that seem relevant and comparable to the current situation but lead our thinking down the wrong path. They can cause us to overlook or undervalue some important differentiating factors."

Unlike a clear and present danger, uncertainty about a risk (an ambiguous threat) can discourage the evaluation of risk mitigation alternatives. For instance, the uncertainty about the damage caused by the foam strike at launch (along with misleading memories of previous harmless foam strikes) led to ineffective information gathering and risk assessment during the final mission of the space shuttle Columbia (Roberto *et al.*, 2005).

Some decision-makers misuse evaluation by wasting time and resources on evaluating, defending, and justifying the selected solution instead of comparing multiple alternatives (Nutt, 2002). Others delay the process by insisting on better models and more information beyond that which is really necessary. Others deliberately provide incorrect information (such as excessive budget estimates) to protect their own turf; when everyone does this, the whole organization suffers (Matheson and Matheson, 2007).

9.8.6 Selecting Alternatives

Even when given accurate, relevant information, decision-makers can select the wrong alternative for many reasons. Some rely on inappropriate "rules of thumb," some fail to avoid biases, and some fail to organize the relevant information in a systematic way (Russo and Schoemaker, 1989). Some decision-makers will refuse to halt an under-performing activity because they originally initiated it (a phenomenon known as "escalation of commitment"; Schmidt *et al.*, 2001). Some decision-makers accept the first claim that appears or use the wrong objectives to make the decision. Selecting an alternative that involves illegal or unethical behavior or violates the organization's values may lead to unwanted trouble in the future.

9.8.7   Other Problems

Problems can occur when implementing a decision as well. Some decision-makers fail to see that the decision is implemented correctly (Drucker, 1967), while others must resort to using edicts and persuasion to implement solutions (thereby failing to manage the social and political reaction to a decision) because they used a poor decision-making process (Nutt, 2002). Personnel changes may lead to revisiting decisions that were previously made although the situation is otherwise unchanged (Chelst and Canbolat, 2012). In some cases, individuals insincerely agree to implement something and then fail to do so, but no one holds them accountable because corporate norms prevent confrontation (Matheson and Matheson, 2007).

In general, human errors can lead to bad decisions. Humans unintentionally slip and lapse when conducting routine actions, they make mistakes by applying the wrong rules or failing to solve problems, and they violate procedures when they seek to satisfy other needs (Reason, 1990).

Finally, organizations need to learn how to make good decisions, but some organizations discourage learning by punishing bad outcomes and never looking back (Nutt, 2002). Section 9.9 will discuss learning from failures in more detail.

9.8.8   Mitigating Decision Risks

For some of the above risks, it is clear how a decision-maker can mitigate the risk. For instance, to avoid the risks associated with letting subordinates manage the decision-making process, the decision-maker should lead the process directly (although some tasks can be delegated).

In particular, the following "safeguards" can reduce the risks of inappropriate self-interest, distorting attachments, and misleading memories (Campbell *et al.*, 2009): (1) inject fresh experience or analysis by "exposing the decision maker to new information and a different take on the problem"; (2) introduce further debate and challenge, which "works best when the power structure of the group debating the issue is balanced"; and (3) impose stronger governance by requiring that a decision be ratified at a higher level, which can stop a decision that is based on a distortion.

In general, avoiding decision-making risks means designing and executing an appropriate decision-making process. For instance, reducing of risk of *idea imposition* (prematurely adopting the first powerful claim that appears) requires a thorough decision-making process in which the decision-maker considers competing claims, as the following paragraphs discuss.

9.8.9   Overcoming Idea Imposition

Nutt (2003) concluded that debacles such as the design of the Denver International Airport all followed a decision-making process in which "a claim suggested by a powerful claimant is adopted" and then "identified, evaluated, and installed" without debate, for no one questions the claim that is being imposed on the organization. According to Nutt, the claim identifies "the arena of action, topic to be addressed, and,

by its exclusion, topics to be ruled out." Thus, accepting a claim influences the scope
of the debate and prevents people from proposing other views and better alternatives.

After adopting the first claim, the decision-maker must spend effort to defend the
selection and persuade others to implement it. To avoid these problems, Nutt suggested the following "discovery decision-making process":

1. Investigate and reconcile competing claims: the decision-maker should continue searching after the initial claim appears and should look for undisclosed
   or hidden concerns and considerations (other claims) by getting the input of a
   cross-section of informed people. Although getting this input can be a long and
   costly effort, it is better than cleaning up a bad decision.
2. Understand the forces who can block action and implementation: the
   decision-maker should inhibit idea imposition by including others through
   direct and indirect participation.
3. Set directions indicating desired results: the decision-maker should use these
   directions to indicate the objectives and how they are related, which will guide
   the search for ideas.
4. Uncover ideas: the decision-maker should search for solutions, which will be
   easier and less controversial if the previous steps have been executed properly.
5. Evaluate options: the decision-maker should get information about the alternatives in order to document and verify their benefits with respect to the desired
   direction without political overtones. Then, the alternatives can be compared
   objectively to determine the best one. Finally, the decision-maker should consider risk appropriately, without ignoring it or overanalyzing it.

9.9 LEARNING FROM FAILURES

Failure analysis is a well-established topic in the area of engineering design (Becker
and Shipley, 2002). The process involves inspecting the failure, developing a complete case history, determining the root causes of the failure with a detailed examination of the failed component and other analysis, and writing a technical report that
describes the results of the investigation (Dieter and Schmidt, 2014). This process
can lead to changes that make operations less risky. For instance, the investigation of
the 1996 crash of TWA Flight 800 determined that flammable vapors in a fuel tank
exploded, and this insight led to a new rule (issued in 2008) that required airlines to
lower the oxygen levels in aircraft fuel tanks as they empty.

When organizations make bad decisions, then it is important to learn from that failure. Learning can be difficult, however, because a culture of intolerance can inhibit
discussing and learning from failures, bad luck can make a good process seem like
a failure, and hindsight can make an unfortunate outcome seem preordained (Nutt,
2002). Although good processes are more likely to produce good outcomes, it is
important to distinguish between bad outcomes and bad processes (which can, if one
is very lucky, still produce a good outcome).

Besides the knowledge gained from the failures that occur during testing, which are, to some extent, expected, engineers can also learn from unexpected failures of systems that are in operation. A few examples follow.

Example 9.5 The Amarube Trestle in Kami, Japan, was the scene of a deadly train accident caused by a poorly designed decision-making system. This brief discussion of the accident, its cause, and the lesson to be learned is based on a longer description in Hatamura (2009). On December 28, 1986, an alarm informed train dispatchers on that line that the wind velocity was great enough to make crossing the trestle unsafe. Because they did not have actual wind velocity information, however, they called a station close to the trestle, which reported that the wind velocity was not that great. As the doomed train approached the Amarube Trestle, the alarm sounded again, and again the dispatchers called to check on the wind but did not activate the warning lights. The need to check also introduced unnecessary delays that reduced their ability to warn the train. Because the warning lights were not on, the train went onto the trestle, and a very strong gust blew the cars off the trestle. The system was poorly designed; a system in which a very strong wind measurement immediately activates the warning lights would be safer. In general, warning systems should not include humans, who can ignore safety signals (alarms).

Example 9.6 Petroski (1992) described the story of the de Havilland Comet, which was the first commercial jet aircraft; it was introduced in 1952, but no prototypes were ever built. Within 2 years, three planes exploded at altitude. After investigating the accidents, researchers concluded that the cabin had exploded. An underwater experiment with one plane repeatedly pressurized and depressurized the cabin as it would in the air until a fatigue crack developed in the corner of a square window. The failure was previously unknown because the aircraft previously built and tested had not been tested in this way. Petroski concluded that "failures are the accidental experiments that contribute to the engineer's experience, just as the colossal mistakes of chess masters should be lessons for students of the game." Moreover, "finding the true causes of failure often takes as much of a leap of the analytical imagination as original design concepts."

Nevil Shute, the author of *On the Beach*, worked at de Havilland as an engineer and wrote a book called *No Highway*, which was about a fictional plane called the Reindeer, which is also subject to early fatigue problems. His book was basis of the 1951 film *No Highway in the Sky*, in which James Stewart stars as the engineer who discovers its flaw.

Example 9.7 Petroski (2005) described the 1999 Texas A&M Bonfire collapse and the investigation by a special commission, which issued a final report in 6 months. The commission studied various causes, including the failure of the center pole, unstable soil, a damaged cross tie, sabotage, and defective components. Finite element analysis was used to simulate the bonfire stack. According to Petroski, "the report shows the structural collapse to be a classic case of design evolution and engineering hubris." The Bonfire grew in size, complexity, number of people, and number of problems, and precursors (structural collapses in 1957 and 1994 and shorter burn times before collapse) were ignored. The report concluded that a combination of factors caused the failure: (1) slightly sloping ground, (2) logs more crooked than usual, (3) upper-tier logs wedged between lower-tier logs, (4) upper tiers built out farther than in past years, (5) no steel cables wrapped around the lowest tier. These problems, in turn, were due to four "root causes": (1) a lack of adequate engineering analysis, (2) a lack of documentation of crucial details of the design, (3) the university did not acknowledge the magnitude of the danger, and (4) student organizations did not heed warnings that it was unsafe (including injuries during construction). "No specific individuals" were found to blame.

The iterative process of design, build, and redesign has always provided engineers with opportunities to learn. The changes that occur over years in an everyday product (like a pencil) happen because engineers and inventors learn from the failures of old designs and create better ones (Petroski, 1990). The dome of St. Peter's Basilica in Rome (designed by Michelangelo and completed in 1624) is a singular notable example (Figure 9.10 is a modern photograph of the church). After the dome was constructed, it began to crack, and a series of improvements were made, with new problems leading to new solutions, which generated knowledge and yielded best practices that could be used elsewhere (Wells, 2010). In some cases, a systematic approach is taken. For instance, engineers working for Under Armour and for Lockheed Martin went through a 2-year process of trial and error (involving a wind tunnel, six mannequins, and a world-class speed skater) to find the best fabrics for and best places for zippers and seams in speedskating suits to be used in the 2014 Winter Olympics (Maese, 2013).

There are many causes of failures. The following 10 categories of failure are sorted in increasing order of potential influence (Hatamura, 2009):

1. Ignorance
2. Carelessness
3. Ignoring procedures
4. Misjudgment
5. Insufficient research and examination
6. The unknown
7. Changes in constraints
8. Poor planning
9. Inappropriate sense of values
10. Poor organizational operation.

Figure 9.10   St. Peter's Basilica, Rome, Italy. (Photo credit: Jill Renuart.)

McKaig (1962) listed three primary reasons for building failures: ignorance, care-lessness, and greed. To be more specific, he included the following list of "causes of failure":

1. Ignorance during design, construction, or inspection
2. Ignorance during supervision and maintenance
3. Improper assumption of authority
4. Competition without supervision
5. Lack of precedent
6. Lack of sufficient preliminary information
7. Economy in first cost
8. Economy in maintenance
9. Negligence by an engineer or architect
10. Risk taking by a contractor or superintendent
11. Lack of proper coordination in production of plans
12. Unusual occurrences such as earthquakes, extreme storms, and fires.

If an organization learns from its failures, it may experience a period in which every decision is good and every design succeeds. However, danger is lurking because a string of successful designs can yield complacency and overconfidence, which can lead an engineer to introduce innovations such as lower cost, more efficient designs and processes that reduce safety factors (Petroski, 2012). Thus, there is a cycle in which failures lead to learning, which leads to success, which leads to failure.

9.10   TRANSFORMING FAILURE INFORMATION

Stories about failures such as the Amarube Trestle, the Comet, and the Texas A&M Bonfire are potentially valuable, but information about failures must be transformed into knowledge to be truly useful (Hatamura, 2009). This transformation requires the following activities:

1. Describing the failure
2. Recording the failure information
3. Transmitting the failure information
4. Learning the failure information
5. Experiencing failure.

Consider, for instance, the aftermath of the 2011 accident at Fukushima, Japan. The Investigation Committee established by the Japanese cabinet investigated the accident site, interviewed hundreds of witnesses and experts, and reviewed the current prevention, preparedness, and response plans. Their policy recommendations included many about the risk assessment procedures, risk communication, regulatory structure, nuclear power plant safety, the power company (TEPCO), and other relevant issues. The committee, which Yotaro Hatamura chaired, recognized that creating and sharing a detailed record was needed to learn from the accident. When interviewed about the process, Hatamura highlighted this objective, "In the majority of cases, in order to find out the cause of an accident, in order to find out what happened, the focus is on determining responsibility. But if you do so, you lose the chance to learn from the accident" (Hatamura, 2012). The Investigation Committee's final recommendation called for an extended investigation and for recording "the results of a comprehensive investigation … and collection of testimonies of … stakeholders and victims; investigating the adequacy of relief, support and reconstruction programs for the victims; or transferring the facts showing how extensive and serious the damage by a nuclear disaster could be." Moreover, the country has the responsibility to "transfer the whole picture … to future generations based on the recorded results of comprehensive investigation of the Fukushima nuclear disaster" (Investigation Committee, 2012).

Unfortunately, it is hard to transmit failure information, which changes over time in the following ways (Hatamura, 2009): it attenuates, it is simplified, it is distorted, it is made into a myth, it is localized, it does not move up and down the organization, and it is not accumulated.

Hatamura (2009) explained that "the correct method of self-learning is one that utilizes knowledge learned from one's own experiences and from those of others. … failures are encountered through which learning and experience build up.

Learning from others' failures enhances this knowledge. These two sources of knowledge shape the generalized experience. Once failure is encountered with this self-study method, generalized knowledge can be used ... and this illuminates the way forward. ... Success can be achieved in a shorter time when failure information is sublimated into a form of knowledge, the aforementioned generalized experience."

McKaig (1962), in the preface to his book on building failures, stated, "Only if the reasons for a failure are understood and published have we who play a professional role in construction truly done all we can to prevent a recurrence." His addition to the record is a collection of examples of concrete failures, steel failures, failures caused by alterations, foundation failures, negligence and ignorance, lack of precedent, aging buildings, and failures due to wind, fire, and explosion. He continued, "Experience can be a very expensive teacher, and fortunately we do not have to relive all the experiences of those who went before us."

EXERCISES

9.1. A system such as a dam or dike is "designed for the N-year flood" if the probability (in 1 year) of a flood that exceeds its capacity is $1/N$ (Benjamin and Cornell, 1970). If the sizes of annual floods are independent, then consider how many "50-year" floods will happen over a period of 50 years. What is the probability that no such floods will occur? What is the probability that exactly one such flood will occur? What is the probability that exactly two such floods will occur? What is the probability that three or more such floods will occur? In what part of a risk management process is information like this generated?

9.2. For the risky scenarios described in the introduction to this chapter (TEPCO, light-rail line bids, power tool manufacturer, and the regulation of unmanned aerial systems by the FAA), identify possible actions in the following categories: (1) avoiding the risk by abandoning the planned action or eliminating the root cause or the consequences, (2) reducing the likelihood of the root cause or decreasing its consequences by modifying the planned action or performing preventive measures, and (3) transferring the risk to another organization.

9.3. Joe is preparing to present his team's design concept to the executives who will evaluate the design and decide whether to approve the project. Joe has analyzed the potential problems related to the presentation in the executive conference room, and the biggest risk is that he would not be able to use the AV equipment correctly. Identify preventive actions, buffers, and contingency actions that can help Joe prevent this potential problem.

9.4. When developing the 1996 Ford Taurus, the product development team encountered delays with the development of new complex reflector headlamps, so their leader decided that they should also develop an optic plate lamp as a replacement if the new headlamps were not ready on time (Walton, 1997). How does the choice to develop a backup headlamp prevent a potential problem?

9.5. In the 1990s, the Ford assembly plant in Atlanta ran the body shop at a rate of 80 cars per hour, although the final assembly line needed only 68 per hour, so that it could stockpile dozens of automobile bodies that could be used when the body shop was not working due to machinery breakdowns (Walton, 1997). How does the choice to create these stockpiles prevent a potential problem?

9.6. In 2013, Honda recalled 143,083 vehicles of 2007 and 2008 Honda Fit in the United States because of a potential problem with the master power window switch on the driver's door, which could overheat and cause a fire (American Honda Motor Company, 2013). The company recommended that customers park their cars outside until they have the switch inspected and replaced. How does this recommendation prevent a potential problem?

9.7. A food manufacturer in Baltimore, Maryland, wanted to install an automated system for checking their processed food for low-density polyethylene (LDPE) and other harmless but undesirable contaminants before it was sent to storage tanks (from which it would be piped into jars and tubs). Uncertainty about the capacity and accuracy of the system led them to suggest renting some equipment and constructing a prototype system to evaluate its performance (capacity and accuracy). How does installing the system prevent a potential problem? How does the prototype prevent a potential problem?

9.8. During the construction of the Brooklyn Bridge, a long catwalk was used to access the top of one tower. To manage the risk of the catwalk failing, installed at one end was a sign that read "Safe for only 25 men at one time. Do not walk close together, nor run, jump, or trot. Break step!" How does the decision to restrict the use of the catwalk prevent a potential problem?

9.9. After the Tacoma Narrows bridge collapse in 1940, bridge designers reacted in different ways (Wells, 2010): some designed heavier and stiffer bridges, but others found designs (such as the First Severn Crossing, built in 1966) that could pre-empt the problem of aeroelastic flutter by stabilizing itself. Which one is a preventive action? Which one is a contingency action?

9.10. For the Apollo missions, NASA installed on the spacecraft's nose a launch escape tower (shown in Figure 9.11) that could ignite and take the astronauts away from the Saturn V rocket if a catastrophe occurred on the launch pad. How does this launch escape tower prevent a potential problem?

9.11. The Great Shakeout is an annual earthquake drill. On October 17, 2013, as part of that year's event, the University of Maryland sent an email to the campus community to "practice earthquake protective actions." How does an earthquake drill mitigate risk? Is an earthquake drill a preventive action or a contingency action? How does an earthquake drill prevent a potential problem?

9.12. As Cyclone Phailin approached northeastern India, at least 64,000 people left their homes, a dry bulk cargo facility closed and sent all of it ships to sea, and emergency managers sent a rescue force to the area (Sullivan and Pradhan, 2013). How do these actions prevent potential problems?

Figure 9.11   The top of the Saturn V rocket used for the Apollo 11 mission. (Image credit: NASA.)

9.13. In areas that are prone to floods, residents resort to building on high ground above flood levels, creating artificial hills to create high ground, or creating dikes to contain the flood waters (Plate, 2002). Are these preventive actions or contingency actions? Do these actions reduce the likelihood of floods or reduce the consequences of floods? In addition, when a flood does occur, residents may close openings with sandbags or brick walls or move belongings to higher parts of a building. Are these preventive actions or contingency actions?

9.14. A severe solar storm (a coronal mass ejection) could disable satellites and create strong ground currents that travel through pipelines, power lines, and telecommunications cables and could disable these systems and other infrastructure. The impacts include disrupting local radio communications, disorienting GPS satellites, interrupting the air traffic control communications with planes flying over the North Pole, damaging high-voltage transformers, causing long-term power outages, which could have enormous financial impacts, and harming astronauts in space (Plumer, 2013). Identify each of the following as a preventive action, a buffer, or a contingency action:

(a) Given a warning, electric grid operators reroute currents to minimize the impact.

(b) Airlines reroute flights away from the North Pole, an especially vulnerable area.

(c) Electric grid operators stockpile transformers to replace those that are damaged.

(d) Electric grid operators install capacitors to block dangerous ground currents.

(e) Space agencies build and launch more satellites that monitor solar activity.

9.15. Consider the potential problem of large asteroids hitting the earth. NASA and other organizations have developed ideas for defending the planet by managing this risk (Ianotta, 2013). For each of the following, identify its role in an asteroid impact risk management system:

(a) Developing, launching, and operating a satellite that, from a position near Venus, looks for asteroids approaching Earth.

(b) Using ground-based telescopes and amateur astronomers to identify asteroids.

(c) Installing infrared sensors on commercial geosynchronous satellites.

(d) Counting the number of large asteroids in parts of the asteroid belt that are easy to view from Earth.

(e) Launching a probe (a kinetic impactor) that hits an incoming asteroid and deflects its course away from Earth.

(f) Launching a spacecraft (a gravity tractor) that hovers near an incoming asteroid and deflects its course away from Earth.

(g) Launching a rocket with nuclear weapons so that its blast deflects the asteroid's course away from Earth.

(h) Defining a plan that defines who would direct an asteroid deflection mission.

9.16. Full-scale tests of the HealthCare.gov web site were conducted just 2 weeks before its launch in October, 2013, and provided little time to correct the problems that were discovered, but the site launched as scheduled anyway, and thousands of visitors experienced problems when accessing the site (Somashekhar and Goldstein, 2013). Testing is part of which step in a risk management process? In general, is a decision to launch a web site on schedule despite poor test results a decision to avoid, reduce, transfer, or accept the risk that the web site will not work properly? What other risk treatment options could have been considered?

9.17. In Brazil, the generation of electricity using wind turbines was growing rapidly in 2013. For example, a wind farm with more than 400 wind turbines

was built in the state of Bahia, Brazil (Forero, 2013). Brazil has some areas
with winds that are ideal for generating electricity, and, because the winds are
stronger during a drought, building wind farms manages the risk associated
with hydropower, which is naturally limited during a drought. Is building wind
farms a decision to avoid, reduce, transfer, or accept the risk of running short
of electricity?

9.18. The accident at the Amarube Trestle was caused when a gust of wind blew
a train off the tracks. According to Hatamura (2009), after the accident, the
threshold for the wind alarm was lowered from 25 m/s to 20 m/s. How will this
change affect the number of false alarms?

9.19. A tsunami early warning system is designed to sound a warning when the threat
of a tsunami has increased. For instance, the triggering event of a system in
Indonesia is an earthquake with a moment magnitude greater than the critical
threshold of 7.2 Mw (Seng, 2013). What are the expected benefits and costs of
decreasing the threshold? What are the expected benefits and costs of increasing the threshold?

9.20. Consider the potential problem of severe solar storms. Airlines can divert
planes if they get a warning, but a diversion costs the airlines money because
the planes fly longer paths and consume more fuel. Solar storms that are
spotted by satellites may not hit the earth. Should the airlines always divert
their planes when solar storms are spotted? Why or why not? Recommend a
policy for the airlines.

9.21. Food inspectors in the United States Food and Drug Administration (FDA)
blocked certain shipments of Mimolette cheese in 2013 after finding too many
cheese mites on the rinds of the cheese, which is produced in France (Dennis,
2013). Describe the FDA's food inspection process as a risk management process. What role in this process do food inspectors process? What type of risk
management activity is the choice to refuse the import of certain shipments?
Assume that the inspectors use a simple threshold rule for determining whether
a particular shipment of Mimolette cheese has too many cheese mites. What is
the cost of a false negative? What is the cost of a false positive? Given these
costs, should the FDA use a low or high threshold?

9.22. The Quebec Bridge, a heavy steel bridge over the St. Lawrence River, collapsed
during construction in 1907 and killed 74 men. Before the disaster, the responsibility for both the design and the construction were given to one firm, and
bridge components were increasingly misaligned (Wells, 2010). Describe why
both events were precursors of the disaster.

9.23. In 2013, *The Washington Post* reported that the Washington Suburban Sani-
tary Commission (WSSC), which serves 1.8 million people in two Maryland
counties, had 350 miles (560 km) of prestressed concrete cylinder pipe in use
as water mains (Shaver, 2013b). These large but relatively unreliable water
mains (with diameters as large as eight feet) carry pressurized water, and nine

exploded between 1996 and 2013. One explosion led to flooding on a major road, and another blew out doors and walls in an office park. Due to laws restricting the release of information about critical infrastructure, WSSC has not released information about the locations of these mains. Assume that you live in the WSSC service area. What risks do these mains pose to you? What options do you have for managing these risks?

9.24. The prestressed concrete pipes have reinforcing wires. The wires can crack when they corrode, which weakens the pipe; therefore, cracking wires are a precursor for a pipe explosion. WSSC was using a break-detection system to detect when the reinforcing wires cracked, and WSSC planned to shut down and repair any pipe in which they detected cracking wires (Shaver, 2013b; Weil, 2013). Explain how this system serves as a risk management process. What is the cost of a false positive? What is the cost of a false negative? How would the relative costs affect how WSSC officials set the threshold for reacting to a warning?

9.25. In July, 2013, after a warning of cracking wires, WSSC officials reacted by warning residents that they would need to shut off water to over 100,000 residents for as long as 5 days in order to repair the damaged section of the water main before it exploded (Weil, 2013; Shaver and Halsey, 2013). Residents stockpiled water, restaurants, shops, and hotels at the National Harbor complex closed, and firefighters deployed tank trucks to the affected area. Within 48 hours, however, workers had fixed and closed a broken valve, which allowed the water main repair to occur without a major shutdown, although mandatory water restrictions remained in place. After the fact, the WSSC spokesman stated that they believed that the broken valve could not be fixed: "No one thought these guys were going to pull this off" (Halsey and Shaver, 2013). Some residents and county officials complained that they were not told about this possibility. Should WSSC have mentioned the possibility of fixing the broken valve? Why or why not?

9.26. Rose sends emergency messages to Enormous State University's faculty, staff, and students. Suppose that a hazardous material spill occurs in the chemistry building on a normal day of classes. (This building has classrooms, laboratories, and offices.) Rose needs to send an effective risk communication message soon after the spill is reported. Which *types* of information should she include in this message?

9.27. Consider the pneumococcal disease risk graphic described in Example 9.4. Create a better graphic that more clearly shows the increase in risk.

9.28. Consider the scales on the risk reporting matrix discussed in Section 9.7. Scales from 1 to 5 were used for describing the likelihood of a risk and its consequences. What type of measurement scales are these? Would it be appropriate to multiply these numbers?

9.29. Some descriptions of FMEA suggest using ordinal scales from 1 to 10 for the severity, the occurrence, and the detection measures. Is it appropriate to multiply these numbers? Suggest a technique for comparing different risks that have been evaluated on these three measures.

9.30. The Pipeline & Hazardous Materials Safety Administration (part of the United States Department of Transportation) has published data (PHMSA, 2014) about significant pipeline incidents, their causes, and their impacts (fatalities, injuries, and property damage). Assume that this historical data (about all pipeline systems) is sufficient for estimating the risks of significant pipeline incidents in the future. Use the data about the seven types of causes (corrosion, excavation damage, etc.) to create three risk reporting charts: one that describes the fatality risks, one that describes the injury risks, and one that describes the property damage risks. (Note that the fatalities, injuries, and property damage data should be expressed per incident.) How do the risks of the different types of incidents compare?

9.31. The St. Petersburg Paradox described in Chapter 5 has an infinite expected monetary value. Suppose that Joe, tempted by this fact, is considering paying $150 to play the game. How would you describe the risk that he faces? For instance, what is the probability that he will lose money?

9.32. McKaig (1962) described building failures from the first half of the 20th century. What role does his book play in the process of learning described by Hatamura? Would his book be as useful if it described the failures of medieval cathedrals? Why or why not?

REFERENCES

Achenbach, Joel, Scott Higham, and Ashley Halsey III, "From a Mysterious One-Off, Lessons for Air Safety," *The Washington Post*, page A1, 2014.

Alarcón, Luis F., David B. Ashley, Angelique Sucre Keith R.M. de Hanily, and Ricardo Ungo, "Risk Planning and Management for the Panama Canal Expansion Program," *Journal of Construction Engineering and Management*, Volume 137, Number 10, pages 762–771, 2011

Alliance for Bangladesh Worker Safety, "Alliance for Bangladesh Worker Safety helps to establish common set of fire and safety standards for garment factories in Bangladesh," http://www.bangladeshworkersafety.org/wp-content/uploads/2013/November%20Press%20Release.pdf, accessed August 2014, 2013a.

Alliance for Bangladesh Worker Safety, "Statement of purpose by leaders of the Alliance for Bangladesh Worker Safety," http://www.bangladeshworkersafety.org/wp-content/uploads/Alliance-Action-Plan-Package-FINAL.pdf, accessed August 2014, 2013b.

American Honda Motor Company, "Statement by American Honda regarding master power window switch recall: 2007–2008 Honda Fit," http://www.honda.com/newsandviews/article.aspx?id=7262-en. accessed August 2014, 2013.

Amor, David, "Streamlining risk management in medical devices: establishing a master harms list," http://www.mddionline.com/blog/devicetalk/streamlining-risk-management-medical-devices-establishing-master-harms-list, accessed August 2014, 2013.

Aven, Terje, and Jan E. Vinnem, *Risk Management: With Applications from the Offshore Petroleum Industry*, Springer-Verlag, London, 2007.

Bazerman, Max H., and Dolly Chugh, "Decisions without Blinders," *Harvard Business Review*, pages 88–97, 2006.

Becker, William T., and Roch J. Shipley, *ASM Handbook*, Volume 11: *Failure Analysis and Prevention*, ASM International, Materials Park, Ohio, 2002.

Benjamin, Jack R., and Allin C. Cornell, *Probability, Statistics, and Decision for Civil Engineers*, McGraw-Hill Book Company, New York, 1970.

Bier, Vicki M., Yacov Y. Haimes, James H. Lambert, Nicholas C. Matalas, Rae Zimmerman, "A Survey of Approaches for Assessing and Managing the Risk of Extremes," *Risk Analysis*, Volume 19, Number 1, pages 83–94, 1999.

Bier, Vicki M., Howard Kunreuther, and James R Phimister, *Accident Precursor Analysis and Management: Reducing Technological Risk through Diligence*, National Academies Press, Washington, 2004.

Brandeau, Margaret L., Gregory S. Zaric, Johannes Freiesleben, Frances L. Edwards, and Dena M. Bravata, "An Ounce of Prevention is Worth a Pound of Cure: Improving Communication to Reduce Mortality During Bioterrorism Responses," *American Journal of Disaster Medicine*, Volume 3, Number 2, pages 65–78, 2008.

Brown, Rex, "The Operation was a Success But the Patient Died: Aider Priorities Influence Decision Aid Usefulness," *Interfaces*, Volume 35, Number 6, pages 511–521, 2005.

Busby, J.S., "Error and Distributed Cognition in Design," *Design Studies*, Volume 22, pages 233–254, 2001.

Campbell, Andrew, Jo Whitehead, and Sydney Finkelstein, "Why Good Leaders Make Bad Decisions," *Harvard Business Review*, pages 60–66, 2009.

Centers for Disease Control and Prevention, "Active bacterial core surveillance report, Emerging Infections Program Network, Streptococcus pneumoniae, 2010," 2011, http://www.cdc.gov/abcs/reports-findings/survreports/spneu10-orig.pdf, accessed August 2014.

Centers for Disease Control and Prevention, "2013-2014 influenza season week 4 ending January 25, 2014," http://www.cdc.gov/flu/weekly/index.htm, accessed August 2014.

Chelst, Kenneth, and Yavuz B. Canbolat, *Value-Added Decision Making for Managers*, CRC Press, Boca Raton, Florida, 2012.

Choo, Chun W., "Information Use and Early Warning Effectiveness: Perspectives and Prospects," *Journal of the American Society for Information Science and Technology*, Volume 60, Number 5, pages 1071–1082, 2009.

Cooper, Robert G., "The Stage-Gate Idea-to-Launch Process–Update, What's New, and Nexgen Systems," *Journal of Product Innovation Management*, Volume 25, Number 3, pages 213–232, 2008.

Clark, Patterson, Richard Johnson, Laris Karklis, Jason Samenow, and Julie Tate, "In the Path of the Storm Again," *The Washington Post*, Page A8, 2013.

Dennis, Brady, "Gut-Wrenching Punch to Lovers of French Cheese," *The Washington Post*, Page A1, 2013.

Department of Defense, "*Risk Management Guide for DOD Acquisition,*" 6th edition (Version 1.0), 2006.

Dieter, George E., and Linda C. Schmidt, "Techniques of failure analysis," supplement to *Engineering Design*, 5th edition, http://highered.mcgraw-hill.com/sites/dl/free/0073398144/934758/Ch14TechniquesOfFailureAnalysis.pdf, accessed August 2014.

Drucker, Peter F., *The Effective Decision*, Harvard University Graduate School of Business Administration, Boston, Massachusetts, 1967.

Drucker, Peter F., "The Coming of the New Organization," *Harvard Business Review*, Volume 66, Number 1, pages 45–53, 1988.

Eijgenraam, Carel, Jarl Kind, Carlijn Bak, Ruud Brekelmans, Dick den Hertog, Matthijs Duits, Kees Roos, Pieter Vermeer, Wim Juijken, "Economically Efficient Standards to Protect the Netherlands Against Flooding," *Interfaces*, Volume 44, Number 1, pages 7–21, 2014.

Federal Aviation Administration (FAA), *Roadmap for Integration of Civil Unmanned Aircraft Systems* (UAS) *in the National Airspace System* (NAS), 1st edition, http://www.faa.gov/about/initiatives/uas/media/UAS_Roadmap_2013.pdf, accessed August 2014, 2013.

Federal Trade Commission (FTC), "Fair Information Practice Principles," http://ftc.gov/reports/privacy3/fairinfo.shtm, accessed August 2014, 2013.

Forero, Juan, "Perfect Winds Blowing Brazil to New Era of Renewable Energy," *The Washington Post*, Page A1, 2013.

Gawande, Atul, *The Checklist Manifesto: How to Get Things Right*, Metropolitan Books, New York, 2010.

Gigerenzer, Gerd, and Adrian Edwards, "Simple Tools for Understanding Risks: From Innumeracy to Insight," *British Medical Journal*, pages 741–744, 2003.

Goncalves, Marcus, and Raj Heda, *Risk Management for Project Managers: Concepts and Practices*, ASME Press, New York, 2014.

Halsey III, Ashley, and Katherine Shaver, "WSSC Keeps the Water Running," *The Washington Post*, Page A1, 2013.

Harlan, Chico, "In Japan's Nuclear Cleanup, a High-Wire Step," *The Washington Post*, Page A14, 2013.

Hatamura, Yotaro, editor, *Learning from Design Failures,* Springer, 2009.

Hatamura, Yotaro, "Was Fukushima an accident waiting to happen?" http://www.pbs.org/wgbh/pages/frontline/health-science-technology/japans-nuclear-meltdown/yotaro-hatamura-was-fukushima-an-accident-waiting-to-happen/ 2012, accessed August 2014.

Iannotta, Ben, "Capturing an Asteroid," *Aerospace America*, pages 44–51, 2013.

Investigation Committee on the Accident at Fukushima Nuclear Power Stations of Tokyo Electric Power Company, "Final report on the accident at Fukushima Nuclear Power Stations of Tokyo Electric Power Company: Recommendations," 2012. http://www.nirs.org/fukushima/SaishyuRecommendation.pdf, accessed August 2014.

Janis, Irving L., "Groupthink," *Psychology Today*, Volume 5, Number 6, pages 43–46, 1971.

Josephs, Leslie, "Good Weather is Bad for Sugar Prices," *The Wall Street Journal*, page B5, 2013.

Kepner, Charles H., and Benjamin B. Tregoe, *The Rational Manager: a Systematic Approach to Problem Solving and Decision Making*, McGraw-Hill, New York, 1965.

Kunreuther, Howard, "Disaster Mitigation and Insurance: Learning from Katrina," *The ANNALS of the American Academy of Political and Social Science,* Volume 604, pages 208–227, 2006.

Maese, Rick, "Under Armour is Working on the Fastest Suit on Ice for Sochi," *The Washington Post*, page A1, 2013.

Matheson, David, and James E. Matheson, "From decision analysis to the decision organization," in W. Edwards, R.F. Miles, Jr., and D. von Winterfeldt, eds., *Advances in Decision Analysis: From Foundations to Applications*, Cambridge University Press, Cambridge, 2007.

McKaig, Thomas H., *Building Failures: Case Studies in Construction and Design*, McGraw-Hill Book Company, Inc., New York, 1962.

McKay, Kenneth N., and Vincent C.S. Wiers, *Practical Production Control: a Survival Guide for Planners and Schedulers*, J. Ross Publishing, Boca Raton, Florida, 2004. Co-published with APICS.

Merchant, Kenneth A., "Companies Get Budgets All Wrong," *The Wall Street Journal*, page R5, 2013.

Merck Sharp & Dohme Corp., "Are You at Risk for Any of These Diseases?," *Pneumococcal Disease* 2013.

Modarres, Mohammad, *Risk Analysis in Engineering: Techniques, Tools, and Trends*, CRC Press, Boca Raton, Florida, 2006.

Morgan, Granger M., "Choosing and Managing Technology-Induced Risk," *IEEE Spectrum*, pages 53–60, 1981.

NASA, "Risk-Informed Decision Making Handbook," NASA/SP-2010-576, Version 1.0, April 2010.

NASA, "International Space Station (ISS) EVA suit water intrusion high visibility close call," December 20, 2013, http://www.nasa.gov/sites/default/files/files/Suit_Water_Intrusion_Mishap_Investigation_Report.pdf, accessed February 27, 2014.

National Highway Traffic Safety Administration (NHTSA), "5-Star Safety Ratings Frequently Asked Questions," http://www.safercar.gov/Vehicle+Shoppers/5-Star+FAQ, accessed January 30, 2014.

National Institute of Standards and Technology (NIST), "Managing information security risk," NIST Special Publication 800–39, Gaithersburg, Maryland, March 2011.

Nelson, Craig, *Rocket Men: The Epic Story of the First Men on the Moon*, Viking, New York, 2009.

Ng, Serena, "Safety experts raise concerns over popular laundry packs," *The Wall Street Journal*, page A1, *November* 19, 2013.

Nuclear Regulatory Commission, "Davis-Besse preliminary accident sequence precursor analysis," available online at http://www.nrc.gov/reactors/operating/ops-experience/vessel-head-degradation/news/2004/09-16-04-ml0426005320.pdf, dated September 16, 2004, accessed January 21, 2013.

Nutt, Paul C., *Why Decisions Fail*, Berrett-Koehler Publishers, Inc., San Francisco, 2002.

Nutt, Paul C., "Breaking out of the Failure Mode with Best Practice Decision-Making Processes," *International Journal of Business*, Volume 8, Number 2, page 169–201, 2003.

Nutt, Paul C., "Expanding the Search for Alternatives During Strategic Decision-Making," *Academy of Management Executive*, Volume 18, Number 4, pages 13–28, 2004.

Paling, John, "Strategies to Help Patients Understand Risks," *British Medical Journal*, pages 745–748, 2003.

Paté-Cornell, M.E., "Uncertainties in Risk Analysis: Six Levels of Treatment," *Reliability Engineering and System Safety*, Volume 54, Number 2/3, pages 95–111, 1996.

Petroski, Henry, *The Pencil: a History of Design and Circumstance*, Knopf, New York, 1990.

Petroski, Henry, *To Engineer is Human*, Vintage Books, New York, 1992.

Petroski, Henry, *Pushing the Limits*, Vintage Books, New York, 2005.

Petroski, Henry, "Things Happen," *Mechanical Engineering*, pages 38–41, 2012.

Pipeline & Hazardous Materials Safety Administration (PHMSA), "Significant pipeline incidents by cause," http://primis.phmsa.dot.gov/comm/reports/safety/SigPSIDet_1994_2013_US.html?nocache=1582, accessed August 2014.

Plate, Erich J., "Flood Risk and Flood Management," *Journal of Hydrology*, Volume 267, pages 2–11, 2002.

Plumer, Brad, "How Business is Coping with Big Risks from Outer Space," *The Washington Post*, Page G1, 2013.

Reason, James, *Human Error*, Cambridge University Press, Cambridge, 1990.

Roberto, Michael, Richard M.J. Bohmer, Amy C. Edmondson, and Erika Ferlins, "Columbia's Final Mission: A Multimedia Case," Harvard Business School Teaching Note 305–033, June 2005.

Roderick, Stephen, and Craig Carignan, "Designing safety-critical rehabilitation robots," in A. Lazinica, editor, *Rehabilitation Robotics*, 2007.

Rogers, Paul, and Marcia Blenko, "Who has the D? How Clear Decision Roles Enhance Organizational Performance," *Harvard Business Review*, pages 53–61, 2006.

Russo, Edward J., "Why so Slow?" *Industrial Engineer*, page 36, 2006.

Russo, Edward J., and Paul J.H. Schoemaker *Decision Traps: Ten Barriers to Brilliant Decision-Making and How to Overcome Them*, Bantam/Doubleday/Dell Publishing Group, New York, 1989.

Sandberg, Jorgen, "Understanding Competence at Work," *Harvard Business Review*, Volume 73, Number 3, pages 24–28, 2001.

Schmidt, Jeffrey B., Mitzi M. Montoya-Weiss, and Anne P. Massey, "New Product Development Decision-Making Effectiveness: Comparing Individuals, Face-to-Face Teams, and Virtual Teams," *Decision Sciences*, Volume 32, Number 4, pages 575–600, 2001.

Seng, Denis, and Stanley Chang, "Tsunami Resilience: Multi-Level Institutional Arrangements, Architectures and System of Governance for Disaster Risk Preparedness in Indonesia," *Environmental Science and Policy*, Volume 29, pages 57–70, 2013.

Shaver, Katherine, "Pursuit of Private Firms for Md. Purple Line Approved," *The Washington Post*, Page B1, 2013a.

Shaver, Katherine, "Md. Suburbs have Some of the Nation's Worst Water Mains," *The Washington Post*, Page A1, 2013b.

Shaver, Katherine, and Ashley Halsey III, "Pr. George's Braces for Water Loss," *The Washington Post*, Page A1, 2013.

Simon, Herbert A., *Administrative Behavior*, 4th edition, The Free Press, New York, 1997.

Snowden, David J., and Mary E. Boone, "A leader's Framework for Decision Making," *Harvard Business Review*, Volume 85, Number 11, pages 69–76, 2007.

Sobek, Durward K., Allen C. Ward, and Jeffrey K. Liker, "Toyota's Principles of Set-Based Concurrent Engineering," *Sloan Management Review*, pages 67–83, 1999.

Somashekhar, Sandhya, and Amy Goldstein, "Tests Began too Late, Health Site Builders Say," *The Washington Post*, Page A1, 2013.

Stamatis, D.H., *Failure Mode and Effect Analysis: FMEA from Theory to Execution*, ASQ Quality Press, Milwaukee, Wisconsin, 2003.

Standards Australia and Standards New Zealand, "Risk Management," AS/NZS 4360, 2004.

Stern, Paul C., and Harvey V. Fineberg, editors, *Understanding Risk: Informing Decisions in a Democratic Society*, National Academy Press, Washington, D.C., 1996.

Straker, David, *A Toolbook for Quality Improvement and Problem Solving*, Prentice Hall, London, 1995.

Strickland, Eliza, "Fukushima's Next 40 Years," *IEEE Spectrum*, pages 46–53, 2014.

Sullivan, Brian K., and Bibhudatta Pradhan, "Powerful Typhoon Nears India, Forcing Large-Scale Evacuation," *The Washington Post*, Page A11, 2013.

Taleb, Nassim N., *The Black Swan: The Impact of the Highly Improbable*, Random House, New York, 2007.

Taleb, Nassim N., "The fourth quadrant: a map of the limits of statistics," in John Brockman, editor, *Thinking*, HarperCollins, New York, 2013.

Tamuz, Michal, "Understanding accident precursors," in V.M. Bier, H. Kunreuther, and J.R Phimister, editors, *Accident Precursor Analysis and Management: Reducing Technological Risk through Diligence*, National Academies Press, Washington, 2004.

Wallsten, Thomas S., David V. Budescu, Amnon Rapoport, Rami Zwick, and Barbara Forsyth, "Measuring the Vague Meanings of Probability Terms," *Journal Of Experimental Psychology: General*, Volume 115, Number 4, pages 348–365, 1986.

Walton, Mary, *Car: A Drama of the American Workplace*, W.W. Norton & Company, New York, 1997.

Washburn, Alan R., *Search and Detection*, 2nd edition, Operations Research Society of America, Arlington, Virginia, 1989.

Weil, Martin, "Water to be Shut off in Prince George's," *The Washington Post*, Page B1, 2013.

Wells, Matthew, *Engineers: A History of Engineering and Structural Design*, Routledge, London, 2010.

Zhong, Wei, and Yushim Kim, "Searching for sweet spots of communication during an emergency situation: pandemic influenza outbreaks and public risk communication," National Public Management Research Conference, Syracuse, New York, June 2–4, 2011.

10

DECISION-MAKING SYSTEMS

Learning Objectives:

After studying this chapter, the reader will be able to do the following:

1. Identify two classes of decision-making systems (Section 10.1).
2. Describe the stages through which a decision-making system progresses (Section 10.1).
3. Describe how an organization influences its decision-makers (Section 10.2).
4. Describe different decision-making roles (Section 10.3).
5. Identify the functions of the participants in a dialogue decision process (Section 10.3).
6. Describe the function of information in a decision-making system (Sections 10.4 and 10.7).
7. Explain the tradeoffs involved in centralizing and decentralizing decision making in an organization (Section 10.5).
8. Describe the relationship between the structure of an organization and the structure of the systems that it designs (Section 10.5).

Engineering Decision Making and Risk Management, First Edition. Jeffrey W. Herrmann.
© 2015 John Wiley & Sons, Inc. Published 2015 by John Wiley & Sons, Inc.

9. Explain why a product development organization is a decision-making system (Section 10.6).
10. Describe different ways to organize a product development organization and identify the strengths and weaknesses of each (Section 10.7).
11. Explain why a product development organization is like a factory (Section 10.8).

The last part of our discussion of engineering decision making will consider the third perspective: decision-making systems. This perspective considers the people who perform the decision-making process and the flow of information.

A product development organization is a decision-making system (Herrmann and Schmidt, 2002), and this perspective looks at the human actors who design products and systems. As Bucciarelli (1994) wrote, "the process of designing is a process achieving consensus among participants with different interests in the design. ... The process is necessarily social and requires the participants to negotiate their differences and construct meaning through direct, and preferably face-to-face, exchange."

This perspective also provides another context for and more insight into the decision-making methods and processes discussed in earlier chapters. According to Bucciarelli (1994), "their true meaning and value [are], namely, how they function to provide a framework for negotiation."

Traditional decision analysis has focused on helping a decision-maker make an important decision for which expending the resources for an in-depth study is justified, but this limits the impact of better decision making. Considering an organization as a decision-making system in which decisions emerge from the activities of many people — "an ecology of patterns of behavior" (Matheson and Matheson, 2007) — provides a new view of decision analysis in which modifying the behaviors of individuals allows better decisions to emerge. Instead of using decision analysis for isolated studies to help only the most powerful decision-makers, an organization can create a culture of good decision making, and decision analysts can provide better tools to everyone, assisted by the abundance of inexpensive but powerful information technology (Matheson and Matheson, 2007).

Section 10.1 discusses two classes of decision-making systems, and Section 10.2 reviews how organizations influence the decisions of their members. Section 10.3 describes the different roles in decision-making, Section 10.4 highlights the importance of information flow, and Section 10.5 discusses organizational structure. Section 10.6 describes product development organizations, and Section 10.7 discusses the flow of information in product development and different types of product development teams. Section 10.8 describes the similarities between product development organizations and factories. Chapter 11 will turn from describing organizations as decision-making systems to discussing how one can model and improve decision-making systems.

10.1   INTRODUCTION TO DECISION-MAKING SYSTEMS

Organizations include families, professional societies, government agencies, small businesses, and large product development organizations. An organization can be as small as a team or as large as a national government. More generally, an organization is "the pattern of communications and relations among a group of human beings, including the process for making and implementing decisions" (Simon, 1997).

Organizations are decision-making systems. As Simon (1997) wrote, "[The] whole mass of decisions that are continually being made in a complex organization can be viewed as an organized system. Particular decision-making processes aim at finding courses of action that are feasible or satisfactory in the light of multiple goals and constraints; and decisions reached in any one part of the organization enter as goals or constraints for decisions being made in other parts."

Two important types of decision-making systems are control systems and transformation systems. A *control system* is a decision-making system that continually monitors the state (status) of another system and makes decisions that determine the instructions (inputs) that should be sent to the other system so that it meets its goals. A *transformation system* is a decision-making system that receives information from external sources and then makes decisions that generate new information that someone else will use. In a design setting, this information is assembled into a coherent document that describes the system design (Conway, 1968). From the decision-making point of view, however, the document (whatever its form) is simply a means of recording the decisions that are made.

Both types of systems involve decision making, which creates information from other information, so their operations are quite similar. The distinction made here focuses on the different purposes of the two types of systems. Organizations include both types of systems.

For example, within a manufacturing firm, a production planning office is a control system because the production managers continually monitor the status of the machines, workers, and jobs in the factory, decide what should be done to optimize the factory's performance, and generate production schedules and other instructions that (in theory, at least) govern what the factory will do.

When a manufacturer is designing and building new railcars for a transit authority (similar to a subway system), representatives from the manufacturer, the transit authority, and the Federal Transit Administration work together as a Safety and Security Certification Committee (SSCC) (Vitek, 2013). Throughout the life cycle of the railcar (from design to operation), the SSCC uses a risk management process to monitor the status of safety hazards that the safety engineer identifies and make decisions about whether mitigations proposed to reduce the risks are acceptable. Thus, a SSCC is a type of control system.

An architecture firm is a transformation system because it receives work from clients, who specify their wants, and the firm decides on a design for the client. This is, of course, a composite decision and thus requires various individuals in the firm to decide on different components of the design. The design (a set of blueprints or a computer model) is then sent to the contractor, who will oversee the building's construction. It is important to note that this decision-making system yields designs, not buildings. The construction system that transforms raw materials into finished buildings uses designs as instructions, but construction is not part of the decision-making system.

Similarly, the design of software is also a transformation: "the knowledge of user requirements has to be translated into knowledge about computing systems" (Endres and Rombach, 2003). Similar to product development, software development uses many different software design processes (Dubberly, 2005/2013).

Gioia (1994) described the recall investigation process at Ford in 1973: field reports of accidents were sent to the recall coordinator, who reviewed them and decided which should go to a preliminary department-level review. At this review, the members of the field recall office voted on each case to recommend a recall (or not). The recommended cases went to higher levels in the organization for further deliberation. This can be seen as a transformation system that transforms information about accidents into recommendations for recalls. (It is also part of a larger control system that monitors accidents and issues recalls.)

The Federal Aviation Administration (FAA) Air Traffic Control System Command Center's Collaborative Decision Making (CDM) program is a control system because it monitors the weather and runway closures, receives information from the commercial airlines' operational control centers, and then decides when to issue ground delays and how to allocate arrival slots to the airlines, who then decide which flights should get those slots and which should be cancelled (Chang *et al.*, 2001).

Over time, as it matures, a decision-making system typically moves through three stages (Holt *et al.*, 1960). In the first stage, when an organization is small, skilled managers make decisions as situations arise. In the second stage, the complexity of the operations increases, and the firm installs a system of decision making. For routine decisions, heuristics or simple rules guide decision making. In the third stage, the firm seeks to improve decision making by implementing decision support tools. Often these tools help decision-makers treat problems in a more integrated manner.

In the end, however, different organizations have different structures and decision-making and information flow patterns due to the differences in their environment and their tasks. Thus, there is no single best structure for every organization. The study of how the variables that describe the internal structure of an organization (e.g., whether different departments have different objectives, whether they collaborate to achieve common goals, and how they resolve conflict) are related to the variables that describe the organization's environment is called *contingency theory* (Lawrence and Lorsch, 1967).

10.2   MECHANISMS OF ORGANIZATION INFLUENCE

Generally, the mechanisms linking decision-makers to the overall corporate goals are constraints and incentives such as schedules, rewards, and penalties. That is, the decision-making system is "loosely coupled" (Simon, 1997). In a manufacturing firm, therefore, increasing profit is merely an indirect influence on most decision-makers in the firm. Instead, an organization influences the decisions of the individuals in the organization in the following ways (Simon, 1997):

- The organization divides work among its members. This assignment causes each person to focus on a specific task and the corresponding decisions.
- The organization establishes certain practices that specify how a task shall be done, which means that the person performing the task does not have to decide.
- The organization transmits decisions by establishing systems of authority and influence, through supervisors and advisors and social relationships. Authority permits a decision made by one person to influence the behavior of others; thus specialization in decision making can occur.
- The organization establishes channels of communication, both formal and informal. The formal ones (including reports both written and oral) typically match the formal structures, whereas the informal ones correspond to the social relationships.
- The organization trains and indoctrinates its members so that each person acquires the knowledge, skill, and loyalties needed to make decisions that promote the organization's goals.

The formal plan of organization affects behavior because individuals respect the authority that created the plan, and it provides a framework for individuals to understand the organization's goals and their individual role in solving the complex problem.

For instance, the FAA's CDM program that was mentioned in Section 10.1 influences the decisions of the airlines by establishing a formal channel of communication for the airlines to notify the FAA of their schedule changes and defining everyone's roles and responsibilities in the decentralized decision-making process (Chang *et al.*, 2001).

In some cases, the coupling to organizational objectives can be made explicit. For example, Reinertsen (1997) discussed methods that use sensitivity analysis to estimate how development expenses, unit costs, product performance, and development delays affect the profitability of a product development project. This analysis can be aggregated to understand how these factors affect the profitability of the entire enterprise. This approach can help engineers make project management and product and process design decisions by estimating the "bottom line" impact of those changes.

10.3 ROLES IN DECISION-MAKING SYSTEMS

The persons in a decision-making system have different roles. Five different roles were identified by Rogers and Blenko (2006):

1. those who *recommend alternatives* by gathering, analyzing, and presenting information to the decision-maker;

2. those who *provide input* by providing, when consulted, information about the
    alternatives;
3. those who *agree* by verifying that an alternative is feasible with respect to their
    domain (e.g., compliance with safety and environmental regulations) and veto-
    ing those alternatives that are not;
4. the one who *decides*, is responsible for the decision, and has the authority to
    implement it; and
5. those who *perform* the decision by implementing the desired actions.

Example 10.1 Consider a maintenance planning system that transforms work
requests from the factory into work orders for the maintenance technicians. The
actors are the maintenance supervisor, the coordinator, the maintenance planner, and
the safety manager (Hingle, 2013). Each person has a distinct role. The maintenance
planner *provides input* by identifying the personnel and equipment required and
estimating the expected time to complete the maintenance task. The safety manager
agrees by verifying that the maintenance plan is not dangerous. The coordinator *recommends an alternative* by generating a production schedule that will accommodate
the maintenance activities. The maintenance supervisor *decides* by approving the
schedule and assigns work to the maintenance technicians who *perform* the work.

A different set of roles was presented by Spetzler (2007):

1. the *decision-makers* who are responsible for making the decision and allocating
    the required resources;
2. the *decision staff* who gather information, generate and evaluate alternatives,
    facilitate the decision-making process, and communicate the decision to those
    who must implement it; and
3. the *content experts and implementers* who provide facts about the alternatives
    and their consequences (especially practical knowledge that only the imple-
    menters have).

Compared with the roles described by Rogers and Blenko (2006), Spetzler's
decision-makers include the one who *decides*; Spetzler's *decision staff* are those who
recommend alternatives; and Spetzler's *content experts and implementers* are those
who provide input, those who agree, and those who perform the decision (as shown
in Figure 10.1).

The *dialogue decision process* (Spetzler, 2007; Tani and Parnell, 2013) is a
good example of a process in which different persons have clearly defined roles.
Two groups participate in the process: the decision board and the project team. The
decision board includes the stakeholders who must accept the decision. They have the
power to block implementation of the decision, so they must be part of the process.
They also have the power to implement the decision, so their approval should be sufficient for implementation. On the project team are the analysts and staff who facilitate

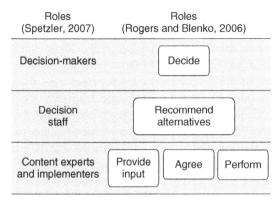

Figure 10.1   The decision roles of Spetzler (2007) include the roles identified by Rogers and Blenko (2006).

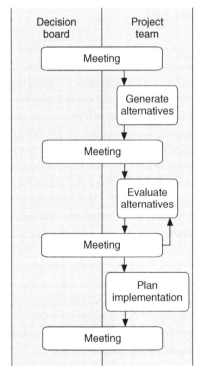

Figure 10.2   The dialogue decision process.

the decision process, have relevant information, and can perform the decision analysis.

The two teams meet multiple times as shown in Figure 10.2. (The number of meetings is an unfortunate problem with the process.) There are four key meetings. At the first, the decision board agrees on the statement of the problem. After the project team generates alternatives, they present these alternatives to the decision board at the second meeting, where the decision board reviews them, adds or eliminates alternatives, and agrees that the project team should evaluate those that remain. After the project team evaluates the remaining alternatives and generates new alternatives that combine the best aspects of the original ones, the project team presents their insights to the decision board at the third meeting. The decision board may ask for more analysis, in which case this part of the process resembles a decision calculus (which is discussed in Chapter 7). The decision board selects an alternative, and the project team creates an implementation plan, which the decision board reviews and approves at the last meeting in the process. In this process, the decision board is the decision-maker, and the project team members are the decision staff. The project team may call on content experts to get information.

10.4   INFORMATION FLOW

Decisions are based on information provided by others in the organization. A decision, once made, influences, to some extent, future decisions. The decisions are interconnected in a complex web. Top-down communication is one form of the information flow, as a supervisor gives policies and directions to subordinates. Other flows are also important for getting the relevant facts to a decision-maker, as in gathering intelligence from where operations are occurring (on the factory floor or the battlefield). One decision leads to information that is used to make another, and so forth until each decision is an assembly of many decisions.

The British administration of India (from the mid-1700s to the mid-1900s) provides a good example of formal information flow (Drucker, 1988). The administration had nine provincial political secretaries. Each one had over 100 district officers that reported to him. Each month, each district officer wrote a report about four clearly identified tasks, including what he expected to happen, what happened, why it happened, what was going to happen, and what he was planning to do. Each political secretary responded to this report with detailed comments to the district officer. (This decision-making system is a type of control system.)

In space mission development, the mission sponsors provide information about the available time, funding limits, and other constraints; users and operators provide information about the mission's broad objectives and performance requirements; and the engineers generate and evaluate mission concepts and detailed designs (Wertz and Larson, 1999).

The formal flow of information through official documents can unfortunately be insufficient (Curtis, 1990). For example, although the marketing group may produce documents that list the customer's requirements (or specifications), the designers will often need to communicate informally with the marketing group to understand these documents.

10.5   THE STRUCTURE OF DECISION-MAKING SYSTEMS

Information processing studies from economics claim that the hierarchical nature of corporations (including those that design and produce goods) evolved naturally out of the need to process information efficiently. In particular, the economic benefits of centralized decision-making motivated the rise of large organizations (Malone, 1997). Centralized decision-makers can integrate diverse kinds of remote information efficiently and make better decisions than unconnected local decision-makers.

Hierarchies are structured so that agents of an enterprise can reduce the time necessary for completing tasks and reduce the risks associated with making decisions based on the imperfect or incomplete information (Borland and Eichberger, 1998). More generally, hierarchical structures are the basis of our world, both physical and human (see Simon, 1981, for a detailed discussion). Organisms are made of systems that are composed of subsystems and components. A hierarchy is a way to organize an enterprise, especially one that needs to solve a complex problem. It provides structure, regular routines, and rewards such as power and status (Leavitt, 2003).

There are at least two reasons for decentralizing decision making, however, even if the superiors are more highly trained. The superiors have limited time and cannot afford to waste time on less important things. In addition, sending the superiors the required information and transmitting the information from the superiors back to the subordinates can be costly.

Beyond the important influence of hierarchical structures, the structure of a decision-making system reflects the nature of the decisions that it addresses. In particular, the structure of a design organization will "mirror" the structure of the system that it designs (Colfer and Baldwin, 2010). The communication between the units, in turn, reflects the interfaces between the subsystems. The organization's structure affects the system design, which, in turn, can affect the organization's structure. Over time, these co-evolve.

For example, an electronic device manufacturer may have a team of engineers who design the system hardware, a team of system programmers who design the operating system, and individual developers who design the individual applications that run on the device. The engineers and system programmers have to communicate about the hardware–operating system interface, and the system programmers and developers have to communicate about the operating system–application interface. Additional examples were provided by Gulati and Eppinger (1996).

This phenomenon, also known as Conway's Law, implies that a decision-making system is limited by its ability to generate only solutions that reflect its structure (Conway, 1968). Because the current structure might have emerged from (or been influenced by) the structure of previous solutions it was required to generate, it is likely that the structure will resemble the structure of previous solutions. If the structure of the system that is being designed changes during the development process, then the structure of the organization that is developing the system should also change, and the new organizational structure should reflect the new system structure.

This phenomenon creates not only some advantages — the organization can produce familiar solutions efficiently — but also some disadvantages: it will be hard to generate extremely novel solutions efficiently, if at all. The mirroring phenomenon was not seen, however, in design organizations in which everyone can directly influence every part of the design and can directly communicate to the others (Colfer and Baldwin, 2010).

10.6 PRODUCT DEVELOPMENT ORGANIZATIONS

In a market economy, manufacturing firms serve the interest of their community by employing workers, purchasing materials, producing goods, generating profits, and not harming the community. Guiding the activities of a firm are the ethical standards of the community, the firm's civic responsibilities, regulatory constraints, and the values and consciences of the owners and executives. Making a profit is certainly an important objective to a manufacturing firm. If it loses money over a long period, it will have to shut down, and it would not accomplish its objectives.

Within a manufacturing firm, the product development organization is the set of people who plan, design, and test new products that will, when manufactured and sold, generate revenue for the manufacturing enterprise. (The manufacturing and assembly processes must be designed as well.) Fundamentally, then, a product development organization transforms information about the world (e.g., technology, customer needs and preferences, and regulations) into information about products and processes that will generate profits for the firm. It performs this transformation through decision making (Herrmann and Schmidt, 2002).

Example 10.2   During World War II, the Admiralty's Department of Miscellaneous Weapons Development (DMWD) regularly turned ideas for weapons and other devices into effective systems like the Hedgehog anti-submarine weapon (Kennedy, 2013) or "plastic" protective plating for shielding the bridges on merchant vessels (Pawle, 1957). The inputs included formal requests from other organizations within the Admiralty, the concepts generated by the department's engineers and scientists, and ideas submitted by well-meaning civilians. Given a promising concept, the department conducted research and then developed and tested solutions, iterating quickly and repeatedly until they had designed and demonstrated an effective, practical device or weapon that was ready for mass production (or shown that the idea was a dud). The DMWD was successful in part because its leaders rejected the slow bureaucratic, conscientious routines that were no longer suitable for a nation at war.

Given the importance of profit to a firm's survival, product development organizations naturally want to generate profitable product designs subject to the relevant regulatory and ethical constraints and other conditions that the firm's owners impose based on their values. Hazelrigg (1998) proposed a framework for product development in which the firm chooses the product's price and design to maximize the expected utility of the design, where the utility function reflects not only the profits but also the inherent uncertainty and the corporation's tolerance for risk.

A more practical approach is a high-level estimate of profitability based on unit costs, development costs, marketing costs, sales price, and projected sales. This can be used for deciding whether to begin a product development project (cf. Walton, 1997). In some firms, this type of model, called a "product profit model" (Smith and Reinertsen, 1991), is used during the product development to understand how changes in costs and sales (changes that result from design decisions) affect profitability.

In practice, product development organizations have sought to develop profitable product lines through the decomposition of a complex problem into a sequence of steps that a variety of experts perform (as discussed in Chapter 7). Some of these steps solve more manageable subproblems. This decomposition is a natural way to overcome human limitations and find satisfactory solutions directly.

Within the organization, product development teams report periodically to a group of more senior personnel who have decision-making authority over all aspects of the project. Product development review systems come in many forms. Typically, the project review and oversight group formally reviews each project at predetermined points in the development process (e.g., stage-gate or phase review; see also McGrath, 1996; Reinertsen, 1997). Normally, many different project teams are operating at any one time.

10.7 INFORMATION FLOW IN PRODUCT DEVELOPMENT

Reinertsen (1997) suggested that an organization generates new information by testing new ideas. Both successes and failures generate information, so testing uncertain ideas is a good policy. For example, a rocket manufacturing firm may design, prototype, and test novel concepts and learn how to improve existing products and create innovative ones.

As mentioned earlier, a product development organization generates new designs by making decisions, and the decision-makers generate and share information as they work. (The different types of decisions were listed in Section 7.19.)

One advantage of viewing product development as a decision-making system (in particular, a transformation system) is the focus on information-processing and decision-making flows instead of personnel reporting relationships. This view can be used to help organization members understand the flows of information and decisions in the same way that an organization chart describes administrative authority relationships and that a process plan (routing) describes the flow of material through a factory.

Different processes launch different sets of information-processing and decision-making activities. Each step requires information exchange and decision making. In the decision-making system, individuals make decisions based on information received from other units and information processed internally by other members of the same unit.

As discussed in Section 10.3, there are different roles in decision-making systems, and some participants make decisions and some do not. A decision-maker gets some information, makes a decision, and consequently generates new information.

The "make a decision" step may involve sending information to and receiving information from others. For example, a design engineer of a product development team may send a solid model of a component to the testing group, where a finite element analysis expert determines how the part will behave and returns a report to the designer.

Various types of decisions are interrelated and coupled with the information flow. Management decisions that affect the management and scheduling of the design process set constraints on design decision making by limiting the time and funds available to generate, evaluate, and compare alternatives. Design decisions such as the product architecture have significant project management implications. Decision making requires information, generates information, and determines who gets which information.

Although the hierarchical organization chart is a natural way to structure a product development organization, it is not the best way to structure information flow in a product development process. Product development activities generate information such as drawings, solid models, test results, and process plans. The flow of information from one activity to another creates precedence constraints between activities (cf. Smith and Eppinger, 2001).

If information flow were restricted to the paths on the organization chart, the product development process would operate using a "throw-it-over-the-wall" mentality in which each business unit performs their part of the development process alone, making decisions suited to their objectives, and then passes the design in progress to the next business unit. Good product development practice led designers away from that restrictive model years ago (Smith, 1997). It is especially important that the product and the manufacturing process be designed concurrently.

These considerations show how the information flow in a product development organization can differ substantially from information flow in other types of organizations, which have different functions and different structures.

Under the pressure of time and budget constraints, product development organizations have found that information must flow through channels outside the organization chart. One common solution is to form interdisciplinary project teams, which are ad hoc groups created for specific product development projects. Many product development textbooks mention the different forms of product development teams. For instance, Schmidt *et al.* (2002) described functional, modified-functional, balanced, and independent teams.

Reinertsen (1997) described three ways to organize a product development organization and discussed the strengths and weaknesses of each.

The *functional organization* is the traditional hierarchy with departments full of specialists. This organization exploits an economy of scale and can be efficient, reducing the cost of product development. However, this organization can be slow and has large communication costs, which inhibit communication between different departments. In this setting, a mechanism for integrating design with manufacturing and other concerns is required; such mechanisms include getting the approval of every area, assigning liaison personnel who transfer information between different areas, and establishing committees that include representatives from different areas (Smith, 1997).

The *autonomous team* has members from many areas, and the team leader is the supervisor for the team members. The team can work quickly to reduce the time to complete a project especially when team members are willing to be flexible and work outside their specialty. Thus, the team can adjust capacity rapidly. Such teams are quickest when there is little market risk or technical risk. Mitigating such risks would require communicating with experts in the firm, whom the isolated team does not have. Moreover, the team may lack a company-wide perspective.

In the *hybrid organization* (sometimes known as a *matrix organization*), team members have two superiors, which requires a careful definition of who has what authority. The team members are representing their home department and bring a variety of perspectives. The interdisciplinary cross-functional product development team includes team members who come from multiple business units and have different levels of experience and decision-making authority. The members may represent the production, marketing, finance, maintenance, and regulatory compliance departments, for example. Such teams meet regularly to share project-related information, and members communicate information between the team and their respective business units. The team will dissolve when the new product has been established in the marketplace, and responsibility for the product will return to the appropriate place in the organization. Such an organization can lower unit cost, because the manufacturing representative can look for manufacturing cost problems and consult with peers in the manufacturing department. Similarly, this can improve product performance by because representatives from marketing communicate the customer's preferences, and the team can get access to technical experts.

One advantage of the project team approach is that team members (who will eventually be on multiple teams) have a greater chance of becoming aware of the key objectives of all relevant business units because they are no longer insulated from these units. Because project teams are temporary, the communication channels mentioned before lack the permanence and stature of an organization chart reporting line. Moreover, individuals use different networks (which include different sets of people) to get different types of information (Curtis, 1990). Still, over time, this collection of channels, along with the relationships formed on interdisciplinary project teams, makes a network through which information flows. This network overcomes the limitations of the organization's hierarchical structure, and it more accurately represents the organization's behavior.

Of course, the members of the team may disagree about which design alternatives are best. For instance, in automotive design, industrial designers, who tend to prefer designs that are aesthetically pleasing, have good proportions, and are symmetric, may clash with human factors engineers, who prefer designs in which drivers and passengers of all shapes and sizes have good visibility and can reach the controls, and structural engineers, who prefer designs that meet the relevant safety standards (Rogers, 2013). Selecting the best alternative when different objectives conflict is a recurring challenge in product development. Multicriteria decision making techniques (similar to those discussed in Chapter 3) can be useful.

10.8 THE DESIGN FACTORY

A single product development project requires many related activities and decisions. A product development organization may concurrently execute different activities in the same project. This resembles a factory that simultaneously fabricates different components that will be combined in a single final assembly. Moreover, the organization conducts multiple projects that yield a stream of new products over time.

Of course, this organization (similar to a factory or production line) has queues because tasks and decisions wait for the attention of the persons who must complete them. There are many reasons for queues, including variability and insufficient capacity. Hopp and Spearman (2001) discussed the influence of variability, and Hall (1991) described the behavior of queues. Reinertsen (1997) suggested the following suggestions for reducing queues in product development organizations:

- Add capacity by adding full-time or part-time staff, working overtime, providing better tools (computer-aided analysis, for example), more or better support staff, and training.
- Manage demand by limiting the number of active projects, spacing arrivals, reducing the scope of projects, and reusing solutions.
- Reduce variability by controlling the arrival process, reusing solutions, and standardizing tasks.
- Implement control systems that remove the queue from the critical path, monitor queues, reserve time at bottleneck resources, and plan capacity.

In addition, like traditional factories, product development organizations perform many nonvalue-added operations, unfortunately. For example, although design reviews can be an effective way to reduce the risk of creating an inferior design, preparing and participating in unnecessarily formal and extended presentations can waste time and generate little useful information. Likewise, documentation standards that yield specific instructions for mass production may add unnecessary paperwork when designing and fabricating prototypes that are used for testing. There are often many opportunities for improvement.

EXERCISES

10.1. Consider the government of a country, state, province, county, or other jurisdiction with which you are familiar. For each of the decision-making roles mentioned in Section 10.3, identify the persons who perform that role.

10.2. Answer the following questions about this government:
   (a) Is it a control system or a transformation system?
   (b) How does it influence its decision-makers?
   (c) What type of information is used and generated by the decision-makers?

(d) Is decision making centralized or decentralized? Is that justified?

(e) Does the structure of the organization reflect the structure of its outputs?

10.3. Describe an experience in which you were part of a product development team. Which type of team was it? What were the advantages and disadvantages of its structure?

10.4. For each of the following elements of a product development organization, identify an element of a factory that best corresponds to it:

(a) An engineer's email inbox

(b) Engineers

(c) Design information

(d) Making a design decision

REFERENCES

Borland, Jeff, and Jurgen Eichberger, "Organizational Form Outside the Principal-Agent Paradigm," *Bulletin of Economic Research* Volume 50, Number 3, 0307–3378, pp 201–227, 1998.

Bucciarelli, Louis L., Designing Engineers, The MIT Press, Cambridge, Massachusetts, 1994.

Chang, Kan, Ken Howard, Rick Oiesen, Lara Shisler, Midori Tanino, and Michael C. Wambsganss, "Enhancements to the FAA Ground-Delay Program Under Collaborative Decision Making," *INTERFACES*, Volume 31, Number 1, pages 57–76, 2001.

Colfer, Lyra, and Carliss Y. Baldwin, "The Mirroring Hypothesis: Theory, Evidence and Exceptions," Working Paper 10–058, Harvard Business School, 2010.

Conway, Melvin, "How Do Committees Invent?" *Datamation*, Volume 14, Number 4, pages 28–31, 1968.

Curtis, Bill, "Empirical studies of the software design process," in D. Diaper, D. Gilmore, G. Cockton, and B. Shackel, eds., *Human-Computer Interaction* (INTERACT '90), Proceedings of the IFIP TC 13 Third International Conference on Human-Computer Interaction, pages xxxv-xl, Cambridge, August 27–31, 1990.

Drucker, Peter F., "The Coming of the New Organization," *Harvard Business Review*, Volume 66, Number 1, pages 45–53, 1988.

Dubberly, Hugh, "How do you design? A Compendium of Models," http://www.dubberly.com/articles/how-do-you-design.html, March 18, 2005, accessed December 12, 2013.

Gioia, Dennis A., "Pinto fires and personal ethics: a script analysis of missed opportunities," in Douglas Birsch and John H. Fielder, editors, *The Ford Pinto Case: A Study in Applied Ethics, Business, and Technology*, State University of New York Press, Albany, New York, 1994.

Gulati, Rosaline K., and Steven D. Eppinger, "The coupling of product architecture and organizational structure decisions," Working Paper Number 3906, Massachusetts Institute of Technology, Sloan School of Management, May 28, 1996.

Hall, Randolph W., *Queueing Methods for Services and Manufacturing,* Prentice Hall, Englewood Cliffs, 1991.

Hazelrigg, George A., "A Framework for Decision-Based Engineering Design," *Journal of Mechanical Design*, Volume 120, pp. 653–658, 1998.

Herrmann, Jeffrey W., and Linda C. Schmidt, "Viewing product development as a decision production system," DETC2002/DTM-34030, Proceedings of the 14th International Conference on Design Theory and Methodology Conference, ASME 2002 Design Engineering Technical Conferences and Computers and Information in Engineering Conference, Montreal, Canada, September 29-October 2, 2002.

Hingle, Justin, "Maintenance planning system analysis," unpublished report, University of Maryland, April 26, 2013.

Holt, Charles C., Franco Modigliani, John F. Muth, and Herbert A. Simon, *Planning Production, Inventories, and Work Force*, Prentice-Hall, Inc., Englewood Cliffs, New Jersey, 1960.

Hopp, Wallace J., and Mark L. Spearman, *Factory Physics*, 2nd edition, Irwin McGraw-Hill, Boston, 2001.

Kennedy, Paul, *Engineers of Victory*, Random House, New York, 2013.

Lawrence, Paul R., and Jay W. Lorsch, *Organization and Environment: Managing Differentiation and Integration*, Harvard University, Boston, 1967.

Leavitt, H.J., "Why Hierarchies Thrive," *Harvard Business Review*, Volume 81, Number 3, pages 96–102, 2003.

Malone, Thomas W., "Is Empowerment Just a Fad? Control, Decision Making, and IT," *Sloan Management Review*, pages 23–35, 1997.

Matheson, David, and James E. Matheson, "From decision analysis to the decision organization," in W. Edwards, R.F. Miles, Jr., and D. von Winterfeldt, eds., *Advances in Decision Analysis: From Foundations to Applications*, Cambridge University Press, Cambridge, 2007.

McGrath, Michael E., *Setting the PACE in Product Development*, Butterworth-Heinemann, Boston, 1996.

Pawle, Gerald, *The Secret War: 1939–1945*, William Sloane Associates, Inc., New York, 1957.

Reinertsen, Donald G., *Managing the Design Factory: A Product Developer's Toolkit*, The Free Press, New York, 1997.

Rogers, Christina, "Does This Car Come in My Size?" *The Wall Street Journal*, page D1, 2013.

Rogers, Paul, and Marcia Blenko, "Who Has the D? How Clear Decision Roles Enhance Organizational Performance," *Harvard Business Review*, pages 53–61, 2006.

Schmidt, L.C., G. Zhang, J.W. Herrmann, G. Dieter, and P.F. Cunniff, *Product Engineering and Manufacturing*, 2nd Edition, College House Enterprises, Knoxville, Tennessee, 2002.

Simon, Herbert A., *The Sciences of the Artificial*, 2nd edition, MIT Press, Cambridge, Massachusetts, 1981.

Simon, Herbert A., *Administrative Behavior*, 4th edition, The Free Press, New York, 1997.

Smith, Robert P., "The Historical Roots of Concurrent Engineering Fundamentals," *IEEE Transactions on Engineering Management*, Volume 44, Number 1, pages 67–78, 1997.

Smith, Robert P., and Steven D. Eppinger, "A Predictive Model of Sequential Iteration in Engineering Design," *Management Science*, Volume 43, Number 8, pages 1104–1120, 2001.

Smith, P.G., and Reinertsen, D.G., *Developing Products in Half the Time*, Van Nostrand Reinhold, New York, 1991.

Spetzler, Carl S., "Building decision competency in organizations," in W. Edwards, R.F. Miles, Jr., and D. von Winterfeldt, eds., *Advances in Decision Analysis: From Foundations to Applications*, Cambridge University Press, Cambridge, 2007.

Tani, Steven N., and Gregory S. Parnell, "Use the appropriate decision process," in G.S. Parnell, T.A. Bresnick, S.N. Tani, and E.R. Johnson, eds., *Handbook of Decision Analysis*, John Wiley & Sons, Inc., Hoboken, New Jersey, 2013.

Vitek, Marek, "Decision making system analysis for Safety and Security Certification Committee," unpublished report, University of Maryland, April 26, 2013.

Walton, Mary, *Car: A Drama of the American Workplace*, W.W. Norton & Company, New York, 1997.

Wertz, James R., and Wiley J. Larson, editors, *Space Mission Analysis and Design,* 3rd edition, Microcosm Press/Kluwer Academic Publishers, Torrance, California/Dordrecht, The Netherlands, 1999.

11

MODELING AND IMPROVING DECISION-MAKING SYSTEMS

Learning Objectives:

After studying this chapter, the reader will be able to do the following:

1. Describe characteristics of an organization that consistently makes good decisions (Chapter introduction).
2. Create a rich picture of an organization (Section 11.2).
3. Create a swimlane diagram of an organization (Section 11.3).
4. Create a root definition of an organization (Section 11.4).
5. Create a conceptual model of an organization (Section 11.5).
6. Identify models for representing a product development organization (Section 11.6).
7. List the steps in the Soft Systems Methodology (Section 11.7).
8. Describe an integrative strategy for improving decision-making systems (Section 11.8).

Organizations often perform poorly, unfortunately, due to problems with their decision making, which may take too long or be too contentious or generate

Engineering Decision Making and Risk Management, First Edition. Jeffrey W. Herrmann.
© 2015 John Wiley & Sons, Inc. Published 2015 by John Wiley & Sons, Inc.

bad ideas. For example, an engineering firm that does work for NASA, the Department of Defense, and other clients used a bid/no-bid process for determining whether to respond to requests for proposals (RFPs) that were issued by clients. The inputs are the RFPs. For each RFP, the firm's engineers did extensive research about the opportunity, gathered information, and evaluated, with respect to that particular RFP, the firm's resources, their experience, their competition, the expected time to generate a proposal, the potential revenue, and the strategic importance. This information was synthesized and summarized and then reviewed by the firm's executives, who decided whether to respond by generating a bid proposal.

The firm was unhappy with the time and resources spent to complete this process. After analyzing the process, they developed an improved system in which a "coarse" evaluation was used to screen RFPs, which would eliminate those to which the firm would clearly not respond (based on a low likelihood of winning the contract). A "fine" evaluation was used to evaluate the value of the contract and its strategic fit. Moreover, multiple opportunities would be compared simultaneously so that resources could be allocated to the most valuable RFPs.

The threshold for rejecting RFPs (based on the likelihood of winning) in the coarse evaluation was an important parameter of this system. If the threshold were too low, then too many RFPs would get past this step, which would lead to many proposals as well (which would be costly to develop). In contrast, if the threshold were too high, then too few RFPs would survive, which would lead to few contracts as well (which would reduce revenues). An intermediate value was best.

In general, decision-making systems that design and develop products and systems tend to become more complex over time (cf. the three stages discussed in Chapter 10). For example, software development organizations begin with some programmers writing code and shipping software, but eventually they add managers, designers, quality assurance personnel, and usability experts (Dubberly, 2013). These extra personnel are there to improve the development process by making sure that the software meets the customer requirements and works correctly, but they add time and money. The acquisition of weapon systems has also become more complex. The time required to obtain a weapon system has increased from 4 years (for the Polaris missile, which was developed in the late 1950s) to 22 years as the number of organizations involved has increased (Lehman, 2013).

Ideally, an organization would use appropriate decision-making processes and make good decisions. Matheson and Matheson (2007) listed nine "principles" of a "smart" organization, in which effective patterns of behavior lead to best practices in decision making and exert a positive influence on the organization's members. A "smart" organization understands its environment by adopting an outside-in strategic perspective, embracing uncertainty, and using systems thinking. A "smart" organization achieves its purpose by creating alternatives, establishing a culture of value creation, and continual learning. A "smart" organization mobilizes resources by aligning and empowering its members, using disciplined decision-making processes, and maintaining an open information flow.

Decision competency occurs when the organization satisfies the following conditions (Spetzler, 2007):

1. The organization routinely makes high-quality decisions using appropriate decision-making processes and avoiding decision failures.
2. The organization has appropriate decision-making tools, techniques, and processes and has personnel who know how to use them.
3. The organization's decision-makers understand their roles and have the appropriate knowledge and skills.
4. The organization has a shared understanding of quality decisions, values making quality decisions, and consistently operates that way.
5. The organization continually learns and improves its decision making.

This chapter discusses approaches for helping organizations improve their decision making so that they can be "smart" and "competent." Because understanding the system is a crucial step, this chapter presents various modeling techniques that can be used as part of the process. Decision-making systems, like other systems in which humans act, are difficult to model using engineering science or rigorous mathematical principles, however. Therefore, the models discussed herein include qualitative models that are effective for gaining insight into how an organization behaves and identifying opportunities to improve it.

Because decision-making systems (except those that have only extremely routine decisions to make) require creative human decision-makers, the process of modeling and improving decision-making systems can leverage the creativity of the persons in the system. Those who operate in the system can use knowledge about the system to change the system. The effort to improve a decision-making system should not be viewed as something that an "outsider" does "to" the system; instead, it can be viewed as something that those inside the system do for themselves. The models that are created and used in this process may be discarded, but the knowledge that is gained by the participants as they create the models is not.

Section 11.1 describes the need for modeling decision-making systems, and the next four sections highlight some specific techniques: rich pictures (Section 11.2), swimlanes (Section 11.3), root definitions (Section 11.4), and conceptual models (Section 11.5). Section 11.6 reviews some other models for product development organizations. Section 11.7 discusses approaches for improving decision-making systems, and Section 11.8 presents an integrative strategy that builds upon most of the material presented in this text. The example in Section 11.8 also shows the different models.

11.1 MODELING DECISION-MAKING SYSTEMS

The ideal model of an organization would "assemble the decision-making programs of all the participants, together with the connecting flow of communication, into a composite description of the organizational decision-making system" (Simon, 1997). Unfortunately, finding good representations of decision-making systems is a difficult task. Decision-making systems include humans, and modeling human behavior (and the flow of information) is a challenge. The available models range from simple descriptions such as organization charts and process flowcharts to sophisticated mathematical and computer simulation models. Different representations capture different aspects of a decision-making system. There is no single representation that can capture all of the relevant aspects. Section 11.6 discusses some models specific to product development organizations.

The most typical representation is an organization chart, which lists the employees of a firm, their positions, and the reporting relationships. However, this chart does not explicitly describe the decisions that these persons are making or the information that they are sharing. A flowchart can be used to describe the lifecycle of an entity by diagramming how some information (e.g., such as a customer order) is transformed via a sequence of activities into some other information or entity (such as a shipment of finished goods).

SIPOC diagrams are a simple way to represent the flow in a system (Driscoll, 2008). The acronym "SIPOC" represents Suppliers, Input, Process, Output, and Customers. A SIPOC diagram describes who supplies which inputs, what the process does with the input(s), the output(s) of the process, and who uses the output(s). Thus, it has some overlap with root definitions and the CATWOE elements discussed in Section 11.4.

Control systems theory provides another way to represent a decision-making system. For instance, See *et al.* (2004) modeled inventory management in a supply chain using proportional-integral-derivative (PID) control, a classic control systems approach. The viable system model (Beer, 1972) is a cybernetics model that decomposes an organization into predefined subsystems.

Mathematical and computer simulation models of decision-making systems are very difficult due to the enormous variability in the systems and the complexity of modeling human behavior. Herrmann (2010) did this for one particular product design situation, but the approach could be extended to other problems.

11.2   RICH PICTURES

A *rich picture* is a drawing of the system that identifies the elements of the system and their relationships in an informal way that describes the big picture (Checkland, 1999). Because a picture is more accessible than written or computational models, a rich picture is an effective and efficient way to describe one's current understanding about a system and invite others to comment. Checkland (1999) suggested building rich pictures to indicate the many components of a complex system and to encourage system-level thinking. An Internet search for images of "SSM rich pictures" will locate a variety of examples.

For example, Koski (2011) described and analyzed a reliability engineering program that the US Coast Guard Surface Forces Logistics Center implemented to improve the mission availability of its cutters. To express the problem situation, Koski developed a diagram of the organizational units that had roles in the reliability engineering program. After interviewing individuals throughout the engineering organization, which provided information about the reliability engineering program from many viewpoints, Koski developed a rich picture that shows the complex system and the many individuals, processes, and documents required for cutter maintenance.

11.3 SWIMLANES

Swimlanes are a special type of flowchart that adds more detail about who does which activities, a key component of a decision-making system. A swimlane diagram highlights the who, what, and when of a system in a straightforward, easy-to-understand format (Sharp and McDermott, 2001). Unlike other types of models, swimlane diagrams identify the actors in the system. Other names used to describe this type of diagram include process map, line of visibility chart, process responsibility diagram, and activity diagram.

A swimlane diagram is a structured model that describes the decision making and information flow and clearly shows the actions and decisions that each participant performs. One limitation is that the model does not show the structure of the organization. Also, representing a larger, more complex system would require swimlane diagrams at different levels of abstraction to avoid confusion.

A swimlane diagram includes the following components: *roles* identify the persons who participate in the process, *responsibilities* identify the individual tasks that each person performs, and *routes* connect the tasks through information flow.

Example 11.1   The NASA-led Center of Excellence for Collaborative Innovation (CoECI) published a swimlane diagram (Figure 11.1) that shows how a government agency would participate in the center (NASA, 2012). The figure has rows (swimlanes) for each participant and boxes for each activity in the process.

Sharp and McDermott (2001) presented techniques for modeling branching, optional steps, the role played by information systems, steps that iterate, steps that are triggered by the clock, and other details (see Figure 11.2). The following paragraphs summarize some key points.

A single diagram is the path of a single item (e.g., form or schedule) as it goes through a process. Each person gets a row (a swimlane) from left to right. (Vertical swimlanes are also used.) An organization, a team, an information system, or a machine can have a row. In the row go boxes, one box for each task that the person performs. Arrows show the flow of work from one task to another and also indicate precedence constraints.

If a task involves multiple actors, then its box should span the different actors' rows. Although there are multiple flowchart symbols available, Sharp and McDermott recommended a simple box with occasional icons to represent an inbox or a clock. Boxes should be labeled with verb–noun pairs (e.g., "create schedule" rather than "new schedule"). Transportation steps and other delays should be included.

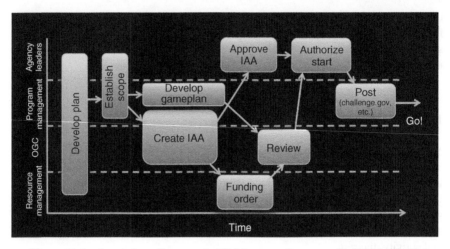

Figure 11.1   A swimlane diagram of a NASA center. (Image credit: NASA, 2012.)

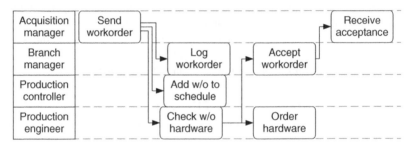

Figure 11.2   The details of a swimlane diagram.

Flow should go generally from left to right, with backward arrows for iteration. A conditional flow should have one line that leaves an activity and then splits into two lines. Flow from an activity to two parallel steps should have two lines. (These are shown in Figure 11.2.)

Managing detail requires multiple diagrams. The highest level shows one task per person per handoff. This clarifies the relationships and flow of information between persons. Another diagram can show the tasks that are key milestones that change the status of something, decisions, communication activities (passing and receiving information), and iteration. An even more detailed diagram can describe the specific ways in which the tasks are done (via fax or email, using specific tools or other special resources). As in other modeling efforts, the analyst should keep in mind and seek to achieve the purpose of the model (so that the model is good enough) without wasting time on unneeded details or scope.

11.4 ROOT DEFINITIONS

A *root definition* is "a clear definition of the purposeful activity to be modeled" (Checkland, 1999). In our context, the activity is the decision-making system, which may be a transformation system. In product development, for example, the transformation process is typically the transformation of information about the world (e.g., consumer preferences, regulations, and competitors) into a product design. The outputs of a transformation are generated from its inputs. A root definition specifies not only the transformation process but also various details about the customers, actors, owners, and environment. This requires the ability to see the system both as a whole and in its details. The root definition helps define the system boundary and answers the question of what is in the system and what is not. The system does not necessarily correspond to a single organization, however, if only some parts of the organization perform the activity or the participants are in multiple organizations.

A useful form for the root definition is, "do P by Q in order to contribute to achieving R." P is what the system does, Q is how the system does it, and R is why the system does it.

In many cases, it is possible to see multiple processes with means-end relationships between them. This is a useful insight, but it may make creating the root definition more difficult. That is, if the organization does Q in order to achieve P, which is done to achieve R, which is done to achieve S, and so forth, what is the root definition?

Selecting the appropriate level is key. The why, what, and how of one level are shifted from level to level. Example 11.2 shows this property.

Example 11.2 Consider the following possible root definitions for the US Navy's CAD/PAD design organization. (A CAD/PAD is a cartridge-actuated or propellant-actuated device that is used in ejection seats and other applications. Figure 11.3 shows some CAD/PADs in operation.) Each definition corresponds to the perspective of a different person in the organization.

Device delivery: A system that delivers devices to military services by identifying needs, acquiring and testing devices, and sending devices so that the military services can keep aircraft flying safely.

Better designs: A system that effectively and efficiently creates better designs by solving redesign problems quickly and correctly so that the CAD/PAD department can provide the military services with better devices.

Product improvement projects: A system that quickly and correctly solves redesign problems through design engineering and proper project management so that better designs are created effectively and efficiently.

Design engineering: A system that develops CAD/PAD designs using engineering knowledge and judgment, along with analysis and experimentation, to solve redesign problems quickly and correctly.

Figure 11.3   A U.S. Air Force pilot ejects from a F-16 Falcon. (Photo credit: Bennie J. Davis III, U.S. Air Force.)

Associated with a root definition are six elements that provide information about the system: the customer(s), the actors, the transformation, the worldview, the owner(s), and the environment. These are often called the CATWOE elements.

The *customers* are those who need and receive the outputs and benefits of the system. The *actors* are those who perform the transformation. The *transformation* converts the inputs of the system into its outputs; this should be what the system does (not why or how). The *worldview* (or "Weltanshauung") is the set of basic assumptions and values that the owner and the customer(s) share; this worldview gives meaning to the transformation. The *owners* are the ones who can shut down the system. The *environment* includes the constraints that influence the design and operation of the transformation process (thus, they limit the owner's ability to change the process).

Example 11.3   Emanuel (2012) generated the following root definition of the US Navy Fleet Replacement Squadron: "a system to qualify newly winged aircrew in combat aircraft tactics, techniques and procedures by providing classroom, simulator and flight instruction in order to achieve the aircrew manning requirements of the U.S. Navy." The customers are the combat-ready fleet squadrons that receive the new aircrew. The actors are the personnel in various departments who perform the training. The system transforms Navy personnel into trained aircrew. The worldview is that the Navy always needs new aircrew due to losses caused by retirement, resignation, career changes, medical disabilities, disqualifications, and other forms of attrition. The owners are the Wing Commodore, who can temporarily halt operations, the Chief of Naval Air Forces, and the Chief of Naval Operations. The environmental constraints include the combat procedures developed by the Navy's Weapons School.

11.5   CONCEPTUAL MODELS

The concepts expressed by a root definition (along with an understanding of the real-world system) can be used to create a *conceptual model* of the system (Checkland, 1999). A conceptual model uses a number of phrases (commands) to describe the activities that are necessary to perform the activity described by the root definition. That is, the conceptual model describes the activities that the system must do (not how they are currently done). Thus, this model, when compared with models of the existing system (such as a rich picture and a swimlane diagram), can help one see how the existing system fails to perform require tasks (or implements them poorly) and identify opportunities to improve the system.

A conceptual model does *not* represent the real-world system. It is a device to generate questions and debate that lead to identifying feasible, desirable changes. In particular, one can compare the conceptual model to the swimlane diagram to see where there may be problems, just as a pediatrician compares the list of what a 2-year-old should be able to do to the actual abilities of the 2-year-old who is being examined. Discrepancies between the list and the 2-year-old's abilities are signals that there may be a problem, an opportunity to help the child. In the same way, discrepancies between the conceptual model and the system's actual activities are opportunities to improve the system.

The following steps are a procedure for constructing a conceptual model (Checkland, 1999):

1. Write down a number of phrases (commands) that describe the activities that are necessary to perform the activity. The number of activities should be from five to nine.
2. Create a diagram of the activities and indicate the dependencies between them (similar to a graph).
3. Add monitoring and control activities.
4. Check that the activities are justified not by the real-world system but instead by the root definition (and common sense), and that all of the activities required by the root definition are in the diagram.

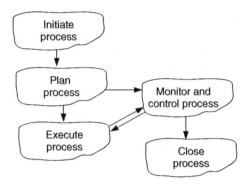

Figure 11.4   Conceptual model of project management.

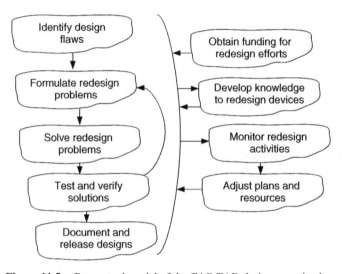

Figure 11.5   Conceptual model of the CAD/PAD design organization.

Example 11.4   A conceptual model of project management (based on the process groups of the Project Management Body of Knowledge [IEEE, 2011]) has five types of activities, as shown in Figure 11.4. This model is extremely generic but captures the key relationships between these types of activities. The freeform boxes were used to indicate that the model is not as formal and precise as a flowchart.

Figure 11.5 is a conceptual model of the CAD/PAD design organization. The curved vertical line in the center indicates an internal partition between the transformation activities and the activities that control them.

Koski (2011), after analyzing the reliability engineering program at US Coast Guard, developed a conceptual model that clearly shows that reactive maintenance and proactive maintenance are separate types of activities. Reactive maintenance includes the activities needed to repair failed machinery (which is clearly unexpected and unscheduled), whereas proactive maintenance includes both schedule-based and condition-based maintenance.

11.6   MODELS OF PRODUCT DEVELOPMENT ORGANIZATIONS

Some computational and quantitative models have been developed for representing various aspects of product development organizations. Some of these could be used for other types of decision-making systems.

The *design structure matrix* (DSM) is an information-based model of product development. A DSM represents the activities in a product development project, their duration, and the probabilities of repeating them (see, e.g., Smith and Eppinger, 2001; Carrascosa *et al.*, 1998; Yassine *et al.* 2000, for more information). Olson *et al.* (2009) created a simulation platform with 17 agents that represent the engineers on Team X, a design group at NASA's Jet Propulsion Laboratory, and their interactions and problem-solving strategies.

McGrath (1996) and Reinertsen (1997) discussed methods for managing a pipeline of product development projects. Adler *et al.* (1995) used capacity analysis and discrete event simulation to evaluate the performance of a product development organization. The organization is modeled as a queueing system (cf. Section 10.8). Jobs representing product development projects are processed by workstations representing groups within the organization. The models are used to evaluate resource utilization and project cycle times.

Ford and Sterman (1997) described a model that represents the dynamics of a product development project. The system dynamics model includes development processes, project resources, scope, and targets. Khurana *et al.* (2001) used a Markov decision process to determine optimal policies for managing a product development project.

11.7   IMPROVING DECISION-MAKING SYSTEMS

Improving any organization is a difficult challenge, and there are many different approaches. An important step is to assess the organization and the performance of its processes. A common approach is to assess *process maturity*. Tools for doing so include the quality management maturity grid (Crosby, 1979) and a design process maturity model (Moultrie *et al.*, 2007).

The suggestions for improving decision-making systems range from general to specific. Simon (1997) proposed the following general technique for designing an organization:

1. Examine the decisions that are actually made, including the goals, knowledge, skills, and information needed to make those decisions.

2. Create an organization pattern for the tasks that provide information for these decisions.
3. Establish (or change) the pattern of who talks to whom, how often, and about what (i.e., modify the flow of information).

Of course, this has to be repeated for the more specific decisions that form the more general decisions. One corollary of this approach is that comprehensive databases and management information systems are not solutions for improving decision making; the technology must be matched to the information and attention needs of the decision-makers (Simon, 1997).

This is not the only solution, of course. An organization can improve decision making by investing in appropriate decision processes and tools, by training its personnel how to use them and when to use which tools in their roles in the organization's decision-making processes, and by aligning all parts of the organization in a way that their actions work together to sustain better decision making (Spetzler, 2007). Regardless of the organization chart, specifying who will do what in the decision-making process (cf. Section 10.3) and establishing appropriate incentives, information flows, and culture can avoid decision-making delays and help the organization respond to opportunities promptly (Rogers and Blenko, 2006).

In the field of macroergonomics, a *work system* consists of multiple persons who interact in an organizational design (a structure and a set of processes) to perform a function (Hendrick and Kleiner, 2002). A work system includes a personnel subsystem (those who perform the work), a technical subsystem (the job design and the technology used to perform the work), and an internal environment (including physical, social, and cultural factors). A work system operates in and is influenced by an external environment. A decision-making organization is a type of work system, and one can use the techniques of macroergonomics to study decision-making systems as work systems. Macroergonomic studies of designers and design organizations include Ball *et al.* (1994, 1997) and Meredith (1997). Macroergonomics is closely related to the theory of sociotechnical systems, which has been used as a framework for describing the characteristics of a design organization (Hammond *et al.*, 2001).

To improve a product development organization, Reinertsen (1997) suggested using financial measures to make product development decisions, utilizing capacity intelligently, promoting prudent risk taking (and learning from the failures that do occur), establishing incentives that encourage thinking about the entire organization, designing the design process rigorously, and justifying control systems (similar to management reviews) using financial measures.

Improving a decision-making system requires addressing poorly defined (unstructured) problems in which multiple actors (stakeholders) have different perspectives, seek widely different and, perhaps, conflicting interests, and are facing uncertainty. Problem structuring methods (PSMs) are suited for these situations because the participants are not required to undergo specialized training; they can synthesize multiple perspectives into a common understanding; and they can identify feasible partial improvements, which avoid the problem of getting everyone to accept a single comprehensive solution (Mingers and Rosenhead, 2004).

The line around PSMs is not sharp, and "in fact it is common to combine together a number of PSMs, or PSMs together with more traditional methods, in a single intervention — a practice known as multimethodology. So the range of methodological choice is wider even than a simple listing of methods might suggest" (Mingers and Rosenhead, 2004). Despite the variety of methodologies, most PSMs work by finding a model or representation that describes the problem situation in a way that everyone understands and then identifying opportunities for feasible, desirable improvements that everyone supports.

The *Soft Systems Methodology* (SSM), a type of PSM, has four essential activities (Checkland, 1999): (1) finding out about a problem situation and the prevailing culture and politics, (2) formulating some relevant purposeful activity models, (3) debating the situation using the models in order to find feasible, desirable changes and the accommodations needed to implement them, and (4) taking action to improve the situation. These activities move from the real world (finding an unstructured problem situation and expressing it) to systems thinking about the real world (formulating the root definitions and conceptual models) and back again (comparing these models and the problem situation, identifying changes, and taking action).

The "finding out" activity includes drawing a rich picture (cf. Section 11.2), which can be useful in a discussion in which one asks participants to comment on whether the current understanding (expressed in the rich picture) is correct from their perspectives. The purposeful activity models include root definitions and conceptual models of the activity (cf. Sections 11.4 and 11.5). The conceptual model should describe the transformation system defined by the root definition, which requires real-world knowledge but is not focused on the real-world organization. The process of creating the models helps the participants generate and use a common language to describe the system and helps create a consensus about what the system is. The debate about the situation should include comparing the current organization (described by the rich picture) to the (idealized) system described by the root definition and the conceptual model.

11.8   AN INTEGRATIVE STRATEGY

This text has presented three different perspectives on decision making: the decision-making system perspective, the decision-making process perspective, and the problem-solving perspective. If we accept the validity of these perspectives, then we should exploit them in a coordinated way to improve a decision-making system.

The following integrative strategy for improving a decision-making system incorporates all three of these perspectives. It is important to note that, throughout this process, the input and feedback of all stakeholders must be included. This is a version of the approach that was originally presented by Herrmann (2006) for production scheduling systems. This version is relevant to improving any type of decision-making system. It incorporates the ideas of Simon (1997) and includes some techniques from SSM. It builds on many of the techniques discussed in earlier chapters of this text.

1. Study the decision-making system. Create swimlane diagrams to represent the persons in the decision-making system, their tasks and decisions, and the information flow between them. Create a rich picture to integrate multiple perspectives. Develop a root definition and conceptual model to identify the essential activities in the system. Scrutinize this model and determine whether changes to the information flow, task assignments, or decision-making responsibilities are desirable and feasible. If changes are needed, go to Step 4.

2. Given that the patterns of information flow are satisfactory, consider the decision-making processes that are being used. Is the decision-making process appropriate for the context (cf. Snowden and Boone, 2007)? Is there a consensus about the objective, and does sufficient technical information exist (cf. Daft, 2001)? Is more information needed (cf. Chapter 8)? Are pattern recognition and emotional tagging processes distorting decision making (cf. Campbell *et al.*, 2009)? Are risks being managed correctly (cf. Chapter 9)? Are there decision-making problems (cf. Section 9.8)? If changes to the decision-making processes are needed, go to Step 4.

3. If the decision-making process is adequate, then consider implementing appropriate decision-making techniques (perhaps implemented in a decision support system) that analyze relevant data, find nondominated solutions, search for optimal solutions, present the important uncertainties, and indicate the key tradeoffs (cf. Chapters 3–6).

4. Implement the changes that were selected.

5. Assess the impact of the implemented changes and repeat the above steps as necessary.

The structural validity of the approach can be justified by considering the validity of the constructs that it uses. An organization is a decision-making system (cf. Simon, 1997), and each decision-maker in that system uses a process of gathering and using information before ultimately making a selection. The approach used in Step 1 of the approach is a version of the SSM, which is appropriate for improving organizational situations. The questions asked in Step 2 come from the literature on decision-making processes. The possible solutions considered in Step 3 are all established techniques for improving decision making. The overall iterative structure is motivated by continuous improvement approaches such as the Plan-Do-Check-Act cycle and the iterative approach of the SSM.

The motivation for starting with the decision-making system perspective is that organizational changes can have the biggest impact on performance (cf. Hatamura, 2009). Starting with the problem-solving perspective runs the risk of wasting time and resources on solving the wrong problem. Going through the decision-making system and decision-making process perspectives first at least verifies that the problem is important.

An organization that wants to establish the performance validity of the approach in its domain should find examples of poor decision-making performance in its domain, apply the approach to the examples, measure the usefulness of the approach (the improvement in decision-making process quality or time, for instance), and establish that the usefulness was due to applying the approach (and not other factors). Then, along with the structural validity discussed above, the organization will have evidence to justify that the approach is generally useful for improving decision making in its domain (Pedersen *et al.*, 2000; Seepersad *et al.*, 2006).

Example 11.5   This example, which is based on but adapted from the situation at a real-world organization (cf. Herrmann, 2004), will be used to show the integrative strategy and some of the models discussed in this chapter. This example concerns the production scheduling system for a facility that assembles devices from components that are made in other shops at the same organization and components that are made by contractors.

The production scheduling system includes the following persons. The branch manager directs the operation of the facility. The production controller maintains the production schedules. (There are two other production controllers who help with ordering and preparing hardware.) The shop foreman directly supervises the operators in the shop. There are nine production engineers, who are each responsible for a range of products. The production engineers order components and other hardware, prepare everything needed for production, and solve any problems that occur.

Jobs are called workorders. Workorders arrive from the acquisition organization that is responsible for purchasing devices for the armed services. The branch manager logs the workorder. The production controller adds it to the long-range schedule. The production engineer determines whether the key hardware will be ready on time and informs the branch manager whether the required delivery date is feasible. The branch manager accepts the workorder and informs the acquisition organization.

The production system operates with two schedules: a long-range schedule (discussed later) and a weekly schedule. The weekly schedule is a list of about 24 operations (for 13 workorders) that are currently in process or ready to start. For each operation, it lists the product, the responsible production engineer, the number required, the operation, the workorder, the hours needed, the hours completed to date, the due date, and the hours completed in the previous week.

At the end of each week, the shop foreman tells the production controller how many hours were worked on which workorders. The production controller updates the weekly schedule (the one created at the beginning of the week) with this information and brings this interim schedule to the weekly meeting.

The primary communication mechanism in the production scheduling system is a weekly meeting (first thing Monday morning) of all the participants. The participants discuss the workorders scheduled for that week, the work performed the previous week, and any other updates. The primary objective of the meeting is to create an accurate picture of which workorders are ready for production and which have priority so that the shop foreman can determine what the shop will do.

Production engineers state whether any new workorders are ready for production. Any such workorders are added to the weekly schedule at this meeting. Production engineers provide information about how much work was done last week and how much time is left to complete the workorder. Production engineers provide information about any changes to the status of their workorders. For example, a workorder may be ready to be moved to the X-ray facility, hardware may have been moved from storage to the production building, or a piece of necessary equipment may be unavailable. The shop foreman adds similar information. The shop foreman is aware of the shop status, including any equipment problems, from direct observation or reports by operators and production engineers (for instance, the hogout facility may be down). Based on information from a monthly meeting with the acquisition organization, the branch manager identifies the workorders that have priority that week. After the meeting, the production controller updates the schedule accordingly, signs it, and distributes to all personnel that day.

The shop foreman makes decisions about which operators will work on which activities and when during the week tasks will be done. The shop foreman records the hours worked. When changes occur during the week (to the status of equipment, hardware, or workorders), the production engineers, production controller, and shop foreman react appropriately without changing the weekly schedule. These events are discussed at the next weekly meeting, and the schedule is updated accordingly then.

The long-range schedule lists approximately 80 workorders. For each workorder, it states the quantity, the customer due date, the responsible production engineer, the predicted labor hours, the workorder status, and has columns for each month in the next year. In each column is the number of production labor hours scheduled for that workorder in that month. This is based on the production engineer's estimate of when the necessary hardware and cartridges will be ready. The predicted labor hours on the schedule are rough estimates. Although the long-range schedule includes capacity estimates, satisfying the capacity constraints is not important because the requirements are not precise.

Once a month, the participants in the weekly meeting also discuss the long-range schedule. The group discusses each workorder on the long-range schedule and its status. The production controller updates the long-range schedule accordingly and distributes this to personnel in the branch and elsewhere. Any changes during the month are discussed at the monthly discussion.

Once a month, the branch manager meets with the acquisition manager and another production branch manager. At this meeting, the branch manager discusses the status of critical workorders and receives a list of priority workorders. (These are used to prioritize workorders at the weekly meeting.) The minutes of this meeting are distributed to personnel across the manufacturing organization.

The discussions at the weekly meeting include releasing orders that are ready for production and adding them to the weekly schedule, which functions more as a dispatch list than a schedule. In addition, this meeting serves as an information filter for the shop foreman, who makes the actual scheduling decisions based on the information discussed in the meeting.

Assume that the stakeholders and participants adopt the integrative strategy described in this section. Their first step is to consider the production scheduling process from the decision-making system perspective. Figures 11.6 and 11.7 are swimlane diagrams of the scheduling processes. Each horizontal bar corresponds to

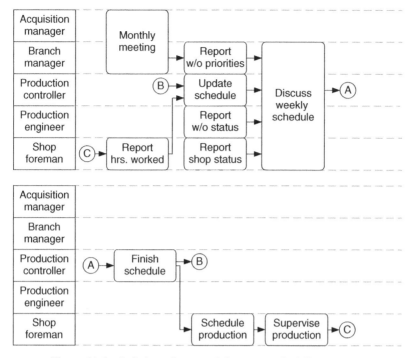

Figure 11.6 Swimlane diagram of short-term scheduling process.

a particular person and shows the activities in which that person participates. The links between the activities show the flow of information. Figure 11.8 is a rich picture that describes the situation. This emphasizes the connections between various actors and shows their relationships. The four actors in the middle are the primary ones in branch operations. The italic type indicates actors outside the branch, and the dashed lines indicate the fact that these relationships extend beyond the branch. The gray rectangle represents the shop itself. Although a more detailed (and more artistic) rich picture could be drawn, this one indicates the key components sufficiently.

The production scheduling process is a type of control system, for it continually monitors and influences the production operations. A reasonable root definition would be "the production scheduling process controls the assembly of CAD/PAD devices by receiving information about the status of workorders and production resources in order to meet customer requirements for devices." A conceptual model of the process (Figure 11.9) includes activities that gather information about the workorders that need to be completed, gather information about the resources in the production facility, generate a schedule (a plan for the future), compare to customer requirements, and communicate the schedule.

The analysis of this decision-making system shows that the acquisition manager, who represents the customer, has very little visibility about the status of the worko-rders. Monthly meetings with the branch manager are the only source of information,

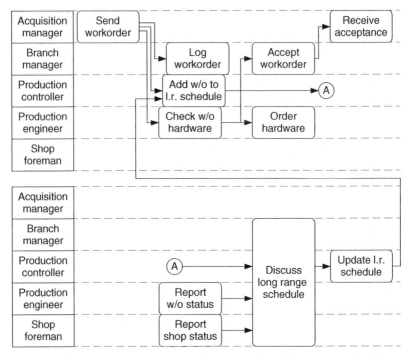

Figure 11.7   Swimlane diagram of workorder receipt and long-range scheduling.

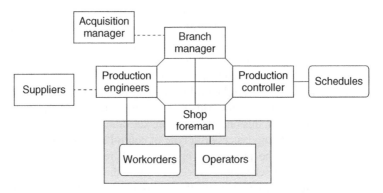

Figure 11.8   Rich picture of the scheduling system.

and the branch manager is only passing along second-hand and, perhaps, out-of-date information. This would suggest changes to the information flow so that changes to the status (and project completion date) of workorders are sent directly to the acquisition manager (via email, perhaps). A centralized schedule that everyone can view and update directly would also avoid indirect channels of information.

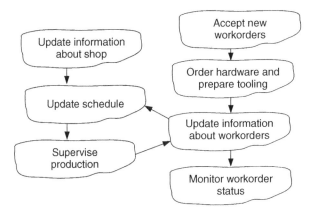

Figure 11.9 Conceptual model of the scheduling system.

If these changes are made and successful, then, in the next iteration, the stakeholders and participants consider the production scheduling process from the decision-making process perspective.

At this point, they realize that the production scheduling process is not managing risk. Because the weekly schedule is only a list of the workorders that are waiting to be done, it does not include any predictions of when these workorders will be completed. The long-range schedule does not include any time buffer for current workorders that may be delayed or capacity buffer for urgent orders that need to be done quickly after they are received. The weekly meetings focus on the current status and do not discuss what could happen. Better risk management would require information from the acquisition manager about potential future orders and information from the shop foreman about possible production problems.

From the problem-solving perspective, the production scheduling process is using a very simple, informal procedure for determining who should be doing what and when it should be done. The weekly schedule is simply a dispatch list that does not help the participants make a detailed schedule. By creating a detailed schedule, the scheduling process could avoid unnecessary setups and waste due to poor coordination, could make plans that work around other foreseeable interruptions (such as bad weather or VIP tours), and could keep everyone in the loop about what is happening. A first step toward this might be a weekly schedule that specifies the operations planned for each day.

EXERCISES

11.1. The British Institution of Structural Engineers defined structural engineering as follows: "Structural engineering is the science and art of designing and making, with economy and elegance, buildings, bridges, frameworks, and other similar structures so that they can safely resist the forces to which they may be subjected" (Petroski, 1992). Consider this statement as a root definition of structural

MODELING AND IMPROVING DECISION-MAKING SYSTEMS

engineering. What does structural engineering do? How does it do that? Why does it do that?

11.2. The Naval Air Warfare Center (NAVAIR) sponsored a research program at the A. James Clark School of Engineering at the University of Maryland. Every year, researchers at the university developed white papers that described proposals for research on topics related to the Navy's science and technology needs. The white papers were reviewed by the dean of the engineering school, who ranked them and sent these recommendations to the NAVAIR program manager, who, in turn, reviewed the white papers and the dean's recommendations. The program manager created a ranking and sent that to the NAVAIR program executive officer (PEO), who decided how many projects to fund and notified the program manager. The program manager then notified the researchers, who wrote formal proposals that were sent to the NAVAIR contract office, which awarded the contracts to the university. The researchers conducted the research, and these results were used to create ideas for the next year's white papers. Draw a swimlane diagram of this decision-making system. Draw a conceptual model of this decision-making system.

11.3. Select an organization with which you are quite familiar. (Note that the organization may be a relatively small group or unit within a much larger enterprise.) The organization should perform a transformation process that involves chiefly decision making. Clearly define the activity of the organization by providing a root definition. This should include a statement of what the organization does, how it does this, and why it does this. Also include information about the organization's customers, actors, owners, environment, worldview, and the transformation process.

11.4. Construct a swimlane model that identifies the key persons in the organization, the key decisions and activities, and the information that flows between them. (Note that this is a model of the organization's current processes.)

11.5. Construct a rich picture that identifies the elements of the system and their relationships in an informal way that describes the big picture.

11.6. Create a conceptual model. Identify the activities that the organization must do to achieve the root definition and draw a conceptual model. (Note that these are not necessarily how the organization currently operates.) The model does not describe the actual organization, but it must be reasonable. There should be five to nine verbs, connected in a logical manner. Include monitoring or supervisory activities as appropriate.

REFERENCES

Adler Paul S., Avi Mandelbaum, Vien Nguyen, and Elizabeth Schwerer, "From Project to Process Management: An Empirically-Based Framework for Analyzing Product Development time," *Management Science*, Volume 41, Number 3, pages 458–484, 1995.

Ball Linden J., Jonathan St.B.T. Evans, and I. Dennis, "Cognitive Processes in Engineering Design: A Longitudinal Study," *Ergonomics*, Volume 37 Number 11, Pages 1753–1786, 1994.

Ball Linden J., Jonathan St.B.T. Evans, Ian Dennis, and Thomas C. Ormerod, "Problem-Solving Strategies and Expertise in Engineering Design," *Thinking and Reasoning*, Volume 3, Number 4, pages 247–270, 1997.

Beer, S., *Brain of the Firm*, Allen Lane, London, 1972.

Campbell, Andrew, Jo Whitehead, and Sydney Finkelstein, "Why Good Leaders Make Bad Decisions," *Harvard Business Review*, Volume 87, Number 2, pages 60–66, 2009.

Carrascosa, Maria, Steven D. Eppinger, and E. Daniel Whitney, "Using the design structure matrix to estimate product development time," paper DETC98/DAC-6013, in Proceedings of DETC'98, 1998 ASME Design Engineering Technical Conferences, Atlanta, Georgia, September 13–16, 1998.

Checkland, Peter, *Systems Thinking, Systems Practice*, John Wiley & Sons, Ltd., West Sussex, 1999.

Crosby, Philip B., *Quality is Free*, McGraw-Hill Book Company, New York, 1979.

Daft, Richard L., *Organization Theory and Design*, 7th edition, South-Western College Publishing, Mason, Ohio, 2001.

Driscoll, Patrick J., "Systems thinking," in *Decision Making in Systems Engineering and Management*, G.S. Parnell, P.J. Driscoll, and D.L. Henderson, editors, John Wiley & Sons, Inc., Hoboken, New Jersey, 2008.

Dubberly, Hugh, "How do you design? A compendium of models," http://www.dubberly.com/articles/how-do-you-design.html, accessed on August 2014, 2013.

Emanuel, Roy, "US Navy Fleet Replacement Squadrons," unpublished report, University of Maryland, May 3, 2012.

Ford, David N., and John D. Sterman, "Dynamic modeling of product development processes," http://web.mit.edu/jsterman/www/SDG/ford_sterman.html accessed on August 2014, 1997.

Hammond, Janeen, Richard J. Koubek, and Craig M. Harvey, "Distributed Collaboration for Engineering Design: A Review and Reappraisal," *Human Factors and Ergonomics in Manufacturing*, Volume 11, Number 1, pages 35–52, 2001.

Hatamura, Y., editor, *Learning from Design Failures*, Springer, 2009.

Hendrick, Hal W., and Brian M. Kleiner, *Macroergonomics: Theory, Methods, and Applications*, Lawrence Erlbaum Associates, Mahwah, New Jersey, 2002.

Herrmann, Jeffrey W., "Information flow and decision-making in production scheduling," 2004 Industrial Engineering Research Conference, Houston, Texas, May 15–19, 2004.

Herrmann, Jeffrey W., "Improving production scheduling: integrating organizational, decision-making, and problem-solving perspectives," Proceedings of the 2006 Industrial Engineering Research Conference, Orlando, Florida, May 20–24, 2006.

Herrmann, Jeffrey W., "Progressive Design Processes and Bounded Rational Designers," *Journal of Mechanical Design*, Volume 132, Issue 8, 081005, 2010.

IEEE, *IEEE Guide–Adoption of the Project Management Institute Standard A Guide to the Project Management Body of Knowledge*, 4th edition, IEEE Standard 1490–2011, November 21, 2011.

Khurana, Anil, James R. Perkins, Pirooz Vakili, and Yanfeng Wang, "Managing the new product development portfolio and pipeline: an integrated approach," Proceedings of the 2001 NSF Design and Manufacturing Research Conference, Tampa, Florida, January 7–10, 2001.

Koski, Heidi Landry, "An Analysis of the Coast Guard's Surface Fleet Reliability Program for Medium Endurance Cutters," thesis, University of Maryland, College Park, 2011. http://hdl.handle.net/1903/11566, accessed August 2014.

Lehman, John, "More Bureaucrats, Fewer Jets and Ships," The Wall Street Journal, page A19, 2013.

Matheson, David, and James E. Matheson, "From decision analysis to the decision organization," in W. Edwards, R.F. Miles, Jr., and D. von Winterfeldt, eds., Advances in Decision Analysis: From Foundations to Applications, Cambridge University Press, Cambridge, 2007.

McGrath, Michael E., Setting the PACE in Product Development, Butterworth-Heinemann, Boston, 1996.

Meredith, Joe W., "Empirical Investigation of Sociotechnical Issues in Engineering Design," dissertation, Virginia Polytechnic Institute and State University, 1997. http://scholar.lib.vt.edu/theses/available/etd-576112239721111/, accessed August 2014.

Mingers, John, and Jonathan Rosenhead, "Problem Structuring Methods in Action," European Journal of Operational Research, Volume 152, pages 530–664, 2004.

Moultrie, James, Clarkson John P., and David Probert, "Development of a Design Audit Tool for SMEs," Journal of Product Innovation and Management, Volume 24, pages 335–368, 2007.

NASA, "Engagement Path: Agency Perspective," http://www.nasa.gov/pdf/654752main_engagement-path.pdf, accessed August 2014, 2012.

Olson, Jesse, Jonathan Cagan and Kenneth Kotovsky, "Unlocking Organizational Potential: A Computational Platform for Investigating Structural Interdependence in Design," Journal of Mechanical Design, Volume 131, Number 3, 031001, 2009.

Pedersen, Kjartan, Jan Emblemsvåg, Reid Bailey, Janet K. Allen, and Farrokh Mistree, "Validating design methods & research: the validation square," DETC2000/DTM-14579, Proceedings of DETC '00, 2000 ASME Design Engineering Technical Conferences, Baltimore, September 10–14, 2000.

Petroski, Henry, To Engineer is Human, Vintage Books, New York, 1992.

Reinertsen, Donald G., Managing the Design Factory: A Product Developer's Toolkit, The Free Press, New York, 1997.

Rogers, Paul, and Marcia Blenko, "Who Has the D? How Clear Decision Roles Enhance Organizational Performance," Harvard Business Review, Volume 84, Number 1, pages 53–61, 2006.

See, Tung-King, Edward M. Kasprzak, Tarunraj Singh, and Kemper E. Lewis, "Modeling of supply chain decision logic using PID controllers," DETC2004-57760, Proceedings of DETC'04, ASME 2004 Design Engineering Technical Conferences and Computers and Information in Engineering Conference, Salt Lake City, Utah, September 28-October 2, 2004.

Seepersad, Carolyn C., Kjartan Pedersen, Jan Emblemsvåg, Reid Bailey, Janet K. Allen, and Farrokh Mistree, "The validation square: how does one verify and validate a design method?" Chapter 25, in Decision Making in Engineering Design, K. Lewis, W. Chen, and L.C. Schmidt, editors, ASME Press, New York, 2006.

Sharp, Alec, and Patrick McDermott, *Workflow Modeling*, Artech House, Boston, 2001.

Simon, Herbert A., *Administrative Behavior*, 4th edition, The Free Press, New York, 1997.

Smith, Robert P., and Steven D. Eppinger, "A Predictive Model of Sequential Iteration in Engineering Design," *Management Science*, Volume 43, Number 8, pages 1104–1120, 2001.

Snowden, David J., and Mary E. Boone, "A Leader's Framework for Decision Making," *Harvard Business Review*, Volume 85, Issue 11, pages 69–76, 2007.

Spetzler, Carl S., "Building decision competency in organizations," in W. Edwards, R.F. Miles, Jr., and D. von Winterfeldt, eds., *Advances in Decision Analysis: From Foundations to Applications*, Cambridge University Press, Cambridge, 2007.

Yassine, Ali A., Daniel E. Whitney, Jerry Lavine, and Tony Zambito, "Do-it-right-first-time (DRFT) approach to design structure matrix (DSM) restructuring," paper DETC2000/DTM-14547, in Proceedings of DETC 00, ASME 2000 International Design Engineering Technical Conferences, Baltimore, Maryland, September 10–13, 2000.

INDEX

Engineering Decision Making and Risk Management, First Edition. Jeffrey W. Herrmann.
© 2015 John Wiley & Sons, Inc. Published 2015 by John Wiley & Sons, Inc.

Printed and bound by CPI Group (UK) Ltd, Croydon, CR0 4YY

23/04/2025

14660906-0004